SIR PHILIP SIDNEY

SIR PHILIP SIDNEY
COURTIER POET

Katherine Duncan-Jones

YALE UNIVERSITY PRESS
NEW HAVEN AND LONDON

First published 1991 in the United Kingdom
by Hamish Hamilton Ltd.

Published 1991 in the United States of America
by Yale University Press.

Copyright © 1991 by Katherine Duncan-Jones.
All rights reserved.
This book may not be reproduced, in whole or in part, including illustrations, in any form (beyond that copying permitted by Sections 107 and 108 of the U.S. Copyright Law and except by reviewers for the public press), without written permission from the publishers.

Typeset and printed in Great Britain by
Butler & Tanner Ltd, Frome and London

Library of Congress catalog card number: 91–65391
International standard book number: 0–300–05099–2

10 9 8 7 6 5 4 3 2 1

CONTENTS

LIST OF ILLUSTRATIONS

MAPS

PREFACE

Sidney is the earliest English writer of whom something approximating to a 'literary biography' can be written. Despite the shortness of his life – he died of an infected leg wound on 17 October 1586, a month before his thirty-second birthday – his literary remains are substantial. He left to posterity two versions of a romance, the second, though unfinished, as long as a Victorian novel; two sonnet sequences; a literary treatise; several other poems and entertainments; verse translations of the first forty-two Psalms; various other poems and entertainments; three political discourses; and well over a hundred letters. Many other documents and life records survive, and there are numerous early 'lives' or memoirs, including those of Edmund Molyneux, Thomas Lant, George Whetstone, Thomas Moffet and Fulke Greville. Though these are all in different ways eulogistic and idealized, all transmit details and impressions which are valuable from a biographical viewpoint.

In this respect, Sidney is enormously more accessible to us than Shakespeare. We do not have a single letter written by Shakespeare, nor even a single incontrovertibly genuine passage of his handwriting, and the Shakespeare biography-industry did not get going until nearly a century after his death. By the time of Nicholas Rowe's biographical essay in 1708 oral traditions had proliferated, but there was no one alive who remembered Shakespeare. In Sidney's case memoirs began to be written within weeks of his death. His father's secretary Edmund Molyneux, who contributed a memorial account to Holinshed's *Chronicle* in 1587, must have written this piece with journalistic speed. Books of elegies and commemorative verses were also produced extremely rapidly. The Cambridge volume of elegies, *Lachrymae*, was published to coincide with the day of Sidney's funeral, 16 February 1586/7.

It was not because of Sidney's importance as a writer that the early memoirs and elegies were written, but because of his unique rôle in the Elizabethan world. He was the rising sun in the Court of an ageing and childless Queen. When he died, it seemed to his contemporaries that 'the very hope of our age' was 'utterly extinguished'. He was a young man who knew his way round central Europe, and had visions of religious and political unity. Continental statesmen such as William of Orange assumed that he was destined for leadership. By the time of his death Sidney was heir to three leading courtiers of the previous generation: his uncles the Earls of Leicester and Warwick, and his father-in-law Sir Francis Walsingham. Both materially and politically, he enjoyed great expectations. His own military heir, the young Earl of Essex, who inherited Sidney's 'best sword' and proceeded to marry his widow, may have felt of him, as Fortinbras says of young Prince Hamlet, that

> he was likely, had he been put on,
> To have proved most royal.[1]

Unlike Hamlet, Sidney was not a prince. He was not even a knight until 1583, by which time the bulk of his poetry had been written. Yet his position as son of the Lord Deputy Governor of Ireland, Sir Henry Sidney, and heir to the Queen's favourite Leicester, together with his personal talents and achievements, gave him a unique status and prestige which was perceived by many admirers, especially abroad, as virtually royal. He was also one of a very small number of Elizabethan noblemen to die as a result of war.

Though Sidney is so well documented, there is, unfortunately, a wide gap between the letters, records and early memoirs, which are overwhelmingly concerned with his life as a courtier and soldier, and his imaginative, literary works, which reflect many other preoccupations, emotional, aesthetic, erotic, religious. Complete integration of the outward and inward lives is impossible, for Sidney's public career is reflected only indirectly in his literary works. Previous biographers have dealt with the problem by discussing the poetry separately from the documented, external events. For instance, Malcolm Wallace, in his still unsurpassed historical *Life* published in 1915, dealt with 'Sidney as a man of letters' and '*Astrophel and Stella*' in two central chapters, making little reference to Sidney's poetry in the other nineteen. J. M. Osborn's useful collection of records and correspondence relating to Sidney's travels, *Young Philip Sidney* (1972), stops just short of the period when Sidney is thought to have begun to write the *Arcadia*. On the other hand, John Buxton's admirable study of Sidney's literary patronage, *Sir Philip Sidney and the English Renaissance* (1964), illuminates the rich cultural penumbra of Sidney and his sister, but does not tell the story of his life. Recent attempts to forge links between Sidney's active life and his imaginative writing have focused almost exclusively on political ideas, discovering political implications in many apparently lightweight writings. This will not be my approach. I hope rather, by moving continually to and fro between Sidney's outward and inward lives, to suggest many connexions which have not hitherto been noticed.

While Sidney's rôle in public life, and his minor, yet potentially important, place in English and European history must never be overlooked, my chief concern will be to explore his development as a writer. Political events are not the only ones that matter. For Sidney, as a born poet, one to whom verses came, in Keats's phrase, 'like leaves to the tree', many experiences, trivial as well as weighty, had a bearing on the way he wrote and the things he wrote about. The books he read, the people he knew, and the many places he saw (he was certainly the most widely travelled of the major Elizabethan writers) all contributed to his imaginative life. The precise way in which these influences operated must necessarily be a matter of speculation, as must the exact chronology and genesis of many of the works themselves. Rather than clutter every page with incessant 'perhapses' and 'possiblies', I shall often write without such modifiers. I avail myself of the freedom Sidney would call 'poetical', identifying causes and connexions which make the narrative coherent, even if they cannot always be documented or clinchingly proved. I shall feel free also to be 'poetical' in another sense. Since Sidney is still the least-read of the major Elizabethans, I quote liberally from his writings, hoping to lead readers unfamiliar with his work into some local acquaintance with it.

The early elegists and biographers sought to accommodate Sidney to an exemplary ideal, moral, political, religious, or all three. It also suited the purposes of most early biographers to present Sidney as being, throughout his life, a convinced and dedicated Protestant. This is open to challenge. So is the notion that Sidney was an ideal courtier. Actually, Sidney was ill at ease at the Court of Elizabeth I, and grasped at every opportunity of absenting himself. Many of the nineteenth- and early twentieth-century biographers also wrote of him as a 'public-school hero', a model of sexual fidelity, courage, patriotism and Protestant piety. In all such accounts, the most important event in Sidney's life is his soldier's death, which is allowed to cast idealizing beams of light back over what went before, as in Shelley's image of

Sidney, as he fought
And as he fell, and as he lived and loved
Sublimely mild, a spirit without spot ...[2]

My aim will be to avoid this rather faceless image of Sidney as 'sublimely mild'. No more space will be given to Sidney's death than to any other well-documented episode in his life. As far as his life as a writer is concerned, his boyhood is far more important. I shall fasten wherever possible on particularizing detail, and on incidents that seem individual rather than typical.

Many features of the world in which Sidney lived – its buildings, the clothes and jewels people wore, the food they ate, the shape of family life, methods of communication – could be taken for granted by early biographers, whose own world was not so very different. Nor would they have considered such details important unless, like the probably spurious story told by Fulke Greville of the wounded Sidney offering his water-bottle to a common soldier, they could be used for exemplary purposes. But for a late twentieth-century reader, curious about 'the history of private life', the physical characteristics of Sidney's world may be quite as interesting as its moral ones.

Far from being 'sublimely mild', Sidney was a hot-tempered, arrogant, and in many ways 'difficult' young man, who was not liked by all his contemporaries. Nor was Shelley's 'spirit without spot' a perfect physical specimen. Yet I believe that Sidney's talents as a writer are so abundant and manifest that they can survive the discovery that he was pockmarked from a childhood illness, and may even have been, as Ben Jonson claimed in his cups, 'no pleasant man in countenance, his face being spoiled with pimples and of high blood and long'.[3]

Neither physically nor morally was the living Sidney spotless. Nor did he claim to be so. Indeed one of the tournament devices closely associated with him is 'a sheep marked with pitch, with this word: "Spotted to be known"'.[4]

My aim is not to 'debunk' Sidney. I hope rather to summon him to life, spots and all, by tracing some of the complex processes which shaped his development as a commanding and innovative writer.

ACKNOWLEDGEMENTS

My first thanks are due to Anne Elliott, with whom I first studied Sidney. I have incurred many other debts during the preparation of this book. Dr H. R. Woudhuysen has read every chapter, generously providing me with numerous references which I would otherwise have missed. His own work on Sidney's texts, when it is complete, may disprove some of my guesses about the chronology of Sidney's works. Dr Simon Adams has also read some sections and made enormously useful comments. Mr A. N. Wilson kindly tested the first half of the book for readability. Corinne Richards devoted a snowy morning to photographing the effigy of Sidney's little cousin, Baron Denbigh, at the Beauchamp Chapel, Warwick. My mother, Mrs E. E. Duncan-Jones, has shown confidence in my ability to complete this project even when I had none. For this, and for her astute comments on many points of detail, I am deeply grateful. My brother, Dr R. P. Duncan-Jones, has patiently and generously taught me how to process words.

The staff of the Bodleian Library, in particular William Hodges, Jean-Pierre Mialon, Judith Priestman and Julian Roberts, have been unfailingly helpful. I have also been treated well at the Public Record Office, the Manuscripts Room of the British Library, the Cambridge University Library and the library of Trinity College, Cambridge, and the archives of the Teyler Museum, Haarlem. The late Viscount De L'Isle kindly gave me permission to consult his papers in the Kent County Archives Office. Dr Kate Harris was particularly generous with her time and expertise in the archives at Longleat.

Some particular debts are recorded in the notes. Among the numerous individuals who have helped me are Dr Helen Hackett, Dr Helena Hamerow, Mr W. H. Kelliher, Dr Andrea McDowell, Professor S. W. May, Mr Julian Munby, Dr Claire Preston, Dr Richard Sharp, Mr Daniel Waissbein, Professor

A. G. Watson, Dr Hanneke Wirtjes, Miss Jane Wiseley. Finally, I would like to thank my editors, Keith Taylor and Judith Wardman.

Three eminent Sidney scholars died while this book was being completed: John Buxton, Jean Robertson and Dr Alois Bejblik. It is dedicated to their memory.

A NOTE ON THE TEXT

Two systems of dating were used in England during this period. New Year's Gifts to the monarch, and some other ceremonies, were associated with 1 January; but for most purposes New Year was reckoned to begin at the Feast of the Annunciation, 25 March. Accordingly, for events occurring between 1 January and 25 March, two years are cited, with a solidus (e.g., 1585/6).

All quotations have been modernized, whether or not they derive from modernized texts. Book titles, however, are given in their original form. No place of publication is given for books published in London.

The Duke of Alençon is referred to as such throughout, even though he became Duke of Anjou on the accession of Henri III. However, Sir William Cecil is referred to by his new title after he became Lord Burghley, since this promotion was significant for the Sidney family.

The following short titles and forms of abbreviated reference are used:

A Letter	R. J. P. Kuin ed., *Robert Langham: A Letter* (Leiden 1983)
AS	Sidney, *Astrophil and Stella*
Berry, *Stubbs*	Lloyd E. Berry ed., *John Stubbs's Gaping Gulf with Letters and other relevant documents* (Charlottesville 1968)
Brennan	Michael G. Brennan, *Literary Patronage in the English Renaissance* (London and New York 1988)
Bryskett, *Works*	J. H. P. Pafford ed., *Lodowick Bryskett: Literary Works* (1972)
Buxton	John Buxton, *Sir Philip Sidney and the English Renaissance* (2nd edition 1964)

Collins	Arthur Collins ed., *Letters and Memorials of State [of the Sidney family]* (2 vols., 1746)
Complete Peerage	G. E. C. and Vicary Gibbs eds., *The Complete Peerage of England, Scotland, Ireland, Great Britain and the United Kingdom* (1910–40) 3 vols.
CS	Sidney, *Certain Sonnets*
CSP	*Calendars of State Papers*
DNB	*Dictionary of National Biography*
ELR	*English Literary Renaissance*
Feuillerat	Albert Feuillerat ed., *The Prose Works of Sir Philip Sidney* (4 vols., Cambridge (reprint) 1962)
FQ	Edmund Spenser, *The Faerie Queene*
Greville, *Prose Works*	John Gouws ed., *The Prose Works of Fulke Greville, Lord Brooke* (Oxford 1986)
Hannay	Margaret P. Hannay, *Philip's Phoenix: Mary Sidney, Countess of Pembroke* (New York and Oxford 1990)
HMC	*Historical Manuscripts Commission*
Kay	Dennis Kay ed., *Sir Philip Sidney: An Anthology of Modern Criticism* (1987)
'Lady Rich'	Katherine Duncan-Jones, 'Sidney, Stella, and Lady Rich', in J. van Dorsten, D. Baker-Smith and A. F. Kinney eds., *Sir Philip Sidney: 1586 and the Creation of a Legend* (Leiden 1986) 170–92
Lant, *Roll*	Thomas Lant, *Sequitur celebritas et pompa funebris . . .* (1587), reproduced in A. M. Hind, *Engraving in England in the Sixteenth and Seventeenth Centuries* (1952) i
Leicester's Triumph	R. C. Strong and J. A. van Dorsten, *Leicester's Triumph* (Leiden and Oxford 1964)
Leycester Correspondence	John Bruce ed., *Correspondence of Robert Dudley, Earl of Leycester, in the years 1585 and 1586* (Camden Society xxvii, 1844)
May, 'Oxford and Essex'	S. W. May, 'The Poems of Edward de Vere, Seventeenth Earl of Oxford, and of Robert Devereux, Second Earl of Essex', *Studies in Philology* LXXVII (1980) 1–132
Misc. Prose	K. Duncan-Jones and J. van Dorsten eds., *Miscellaneous Prose of Sir Philip Sidney* (Oxford 1973)
MLR	*The Modern Language Review*

NA	Victor Skretkowicz ed., *The Countess of Pembroke's Arcadia (The New Arcadia)* (Oxford 1987)
Nashe	R. B. McKerrow ed., *The Works of Thomas Nashe* (Oxford 1966)
Nichols	J. G. Nichols ed., *Progresses of Queen Elizabeth* (3 vols., 1823)
Nobilis	V. B. Heltzel and H. H. Hudson eds., *Nobilis, or A View of the Life and Death of a Sidney . . . by Thomas Moffet* (San Marino, California 1940)
OA	Jean Robertson ed., *The Countess of Pembroke's Arcadia (The Old Arcadia)* (Oxford 1973)
OP	Sidney's 'Other Poems', as identified by Ringler
Osborn	J. M. Osborn, *Young Philip Sidney 1572–1577* (Yale 1972)
Ottley	Peter Beal, 'Poems by Sir Philip Sidney: The Ottley Manuscript', *The Library*, 5th series, xxxiii (1978) 284–95
Pears	Steuart A. Pears ed., *The Correspondence of Sir Philip Sidney and Hubert Languet* (1845)
Peck, *LC*	D. C. Peck ed., *Leicester's Commonwealth and Related Documents* (Ohio 1985)
Poort, 'Successor'	Marjon Poort, 'The Desired and Destined Successor', in van Dorsten, Baker-Smith and Kinney eds., *Sir Philip Sidney: 1586 and the Creation of a Legend* (Leiden 1986) 25–37
Rebholz	R. A. Rebholz, *The Life of Fulke Greville* (Oxford 1971)
RES	*Review of English Studies*
Ringler	W. A. Ringler ed., *The Poems of Sir Philip Sidney* (Oxford 1962)
Robert Sidney	Sir Robert Sidney, *Poems*, ed. P. J. Croft (1984)
Rosenberg	Eleanor Rosenberg, *Leicester, Patron of Letters* (New York 1955)
Sargent	R. M. Sargent, *The Life and Lyrics of Sir Edward Dyer* (Oxford 1968)
STC	A. W. Pollard and G. R. Redgrave, *A Short-Title Catalogue of . . . English Books 1475–1640* (1926)
Sidney	K. Duncan-Jones ed., *The Oxford Authors: Sir Philip Sidney* (1989)
Simpson	R. Simpson, *Edmund Campion: A Biography* (1867)
Stern	Virginia F. Stern, *Gabriel Harvey: A Study of his Life, Marginalia and Library* (Oxford 1979)

Three Letters	Gabriel Harvey, *Three proper and wittie, familiar Letters: lately passed betwene two Universitie men: touching the Earthquake in Aprill last, and our English refourmed Versifying* (1580)
Wallace	M. W. Wallace, *The Life of Sir Philip Sidney* (Cambridge 1915)
Woudhuysen	H. R. Woudhuysen, *Leicester's Literary Patronage: A Study of the English Court 1578–1582*, unpublished D.Phil. thesis, University of Oxford (1980)
Young	Alan Young, *Tudor and Jacobean Tournaments* (1987)

1

1554–63

HIS SISTERS AND HIS COUSINS AND HIS AUNTS

I am not yet come to that degree of wisdom to think light of the sex of whom I have my life: since if I be anything ... I was come to it born of a woman and nursed of a woman ... And truly, we men and praisers of men should remember, that if we have such excellencies, it is reason to think them excellent creatures of whom we are, since a kite never brought forth a good flying hawk.[1]

> ... thou shalt find in women virtues lie,
> Sweet supple minds which soon to wisdom bow,
> Where they by wisdom's rules directed are,
> And are not forced fond thraldom to allow.[2]

> His sisters and his cousins
> Whom he reckons up by dozens
> And his aunts.[3]

In most Elizabethan writers the modern reader will find passages of appalling misogyny. Shakespeare's heroes, for instance, are quick to generalize from individual experience or misapprehension about the viciousness of women in general. Hamlet, after his mother's 'o'er-hasty marriage', bids Ophelia go to a 'nunnery' which may be a brothel. Othello convinces himself that Desdemona must die, 'lest she betray more men'; and Lear, embittered by the unkindness of his elder daughters, unleashes revolting diatribes against all womankind. Nor is this untypical; attacks on women in the works of Shakespeare's contemporaries are widespread. Even Spenser, whose *Faerie Queene* was the most complex literary celebration of the Virgin Queen, portrayed with surprising tolerance the Don Juan-like Squire of Dames who, travelling up and down the length and breadth of Faerie Land, or England, finds only three women resistant to his charms. Yet this is not so in the writings of Sidney. When he describes

Woodcut of Elizabethan schoolboy from Alexander Nowell's *Catechismus*, 1584 (Bodleian Library)

a Don Juan-like figure, Pamphilus, in the 'New' *Arcadia*, he pays most attention to the woman's point of view, giving a surprisingly profound insight into the psychology of seduction in the recollections of one disillusioned cast-off mistress:

> I must confess, even in the greatest tempest of my judgement was I never driven to think him excellent, and yet could so set my mind, both to get and keep him, as though therein had lain my felicity: like them I have seen play at the ball, grow extremely earnest, who should have the ball, and yet everyone knew it was but a ball.[4]

In Sidney's work, misogyny is never allowed to stand uncorrected. Marriage is frequently recommended, and husbands are advised to be faithful and kind to their wives. In the 'New' *Arcadia* the overbearing and vain Anaxius ('Lordly') confirms the poor opinion the reader is invited to have of him when he declares that he scorns all women, 'as a peevish, paltry sex, not worthy to communicate with my virtues'.[5] In both its versions, one of the most original features of the *Arcadia* is the portrayal of the heroines, of whom C. S. Lewis rightly said:

> English literature had seen no women to compare with them since Chaucer's Criseide; and, apart from Shakespeare, was to wait centuries for their equals.[6]

In the 'New' version the heroines increasingly upstage the heroes, both in narrative interest and in moral stature. There are also detailed studies of many other female characters, such as Gynecia, Cecropia and Parthenia.

The reasons for Sidney's unusually sympathetic and attentive literary treatment of women lie in his own beginnings. No doubt it was from women – nurses, mothers, aunts, sisters – that most Elizabethan little boys received their earliest care. But Sidney had the unusual advantage of being surrounded from birth by sophisticated women who had enjoyed the benefit, all too rare for girls, of a humanist education. A highly educated Queen, Mary Tudor, was on the throne when Sidney was born, on 30 November 1554. Her new husband, Philip II of Spain, was the baby's godfather and namesake. According to Dr Thomas Moffet, one of Sidney's earliest biographers, that severe Hapsburg monarch, whose own attempts to establish a dynasty in England were to come to nothing, enjoyed dandling and playing with the infant. Little Philip was the first-born child of a Kentish gentleman, Sir Henry Sidney, who had been 'henchman' to King Edward VI, and in whose arms the boy King is said to have died. We may assume that Queen Mary, who is known to have loved children, and who desperately persuaded herself that she was to become a mother, also fondled her husband's new godson with wistful pleasure.[7] Mary Tudor was not the only staunchly Catholic woman closely connected with Sidney in his infancy. One of his first cousins was Jane Dormer, who met and married a member of Philip II's retinue, the Count of Feria, and in subsequent decades became a powerful focus for English Catholic exiles in Spain. Sidney's relations with Catholics will be considered in more detail later, but at this point it is worth noting that the only surviving letter from him to a woman other than the Queen is a kindly communication to the recusant Lady Kytson about the likely mitigation of fines imposed on Catholics.[8]

Nearer to home, Sidney's mother, who was one of thirteen children of the ambitious John Dudley, Duke of Northumberland, was no Catholic. How she, or for that matter any of her generation, dealt in her heart with the religious changes which swept through England in the middle years of the sixteenth century, it is hard to guess. Perhaps the Dudleys followed the survival formula defined by Amyas Paulett, Marquis of Winchester, who sustained positions of favour in four successive reigns by 'patience, silence, mild speech, and refusal to nurse injuries'.[9] Like the Pauletts, the Sidneys and the Dudleys must have been highly adaptable, externally at least, to fast-changing conditions. Many were no doubt expert in 'Marranism', or pretended conformity in religious practice. There can be no doubt of Mary Sidney's piety. Some early jottings show her to have regarded herself, when newly married, as 'a happy woman'. They also reveal that she could versify, albeit at a fairly basic level:

> To wish the best and fear the worst
> are two points of the wise:
> to suffer then what happen shall
> that man is happy thrice. 1551.
>
> Mary Sidney.
> Fear God.[10]

Another jotting is:

> Will not the thing that thou may'st not attain,
> For thou and none other art cause of thy let
> If that which thou may'st not thou travail to get.
> scriptum manu felix. M.S.

Though undistinguished as a poet, Mary Sidney was a highly articulate writer and speaker and a fierce defender of her position, which, in the later years of Elizabeth's reign, seems never to have been very secure or comfortable. It is doubtful whether in the 1560s and 70s she would still have called herself '*une femme heureuse*', as she did in 1551. Numerous letters in her small, neat, italic hand show her begging pathetically for a better lodging at Court, or for the loan of hangings from the Queen's Wardrobe to make her rooms warmer. The patient endurance recommended in her early verses was not something that came easily to her. Lady Sidney ought to have been able to stir uncomfortable feelings of guilt in the Queen's breast, for in 1562 she helped to nurse Elizabeth through an attack of smallpox which left the Queen unscathed but Mary Sidney terribly scarred. As Sir Henry Sidney later put it:

> When I went to Newhaven [Le Havre] I left her a full fair lady, in mine eyes at least the fairest, and when I returned I found her as foul a lady as the small-pox could make her, which she did take by continual attendance of her Majesty's most precious person ... so as she lives solitarily *sicut nicticorax in domicilio suo.*

The quotation is from Psalm CII. 6: 'I am like the pelican of the wilderness; I am like an owl of the desert'. The kind of owl called a 'nicticorax' is unusual in having favourable symbolic connotations, being linked with the humility of Christ.[11] Just as the nicticorax would hide until it was dark, Lady Sidney was loath to show her face in public, and it was said that she wore a mask when she resided at Court. Witnessing his father's continued devotion to his facially scarred mother must have contributed to Sidney's sense that the only true love is that which does not 'alter when it alteration finds'. The odious Pamphilus, the Don Juan figure already mentioned, pours scorn on

> these constant fools [who] though their mistress grow by sickness foul, or by fortune miserable, yet still will love her.[12]

The episode in the *Arcadia* with the longest continued popularity is the touching tale of the constant Argalus, who still loves his fiancée Parthenia when her face has been hideously scarred with acid. Using fiction's power to fashion a better nature, Sidney has his heroine Parthenia's beauty miraculously restored. No such cosmetic miracle was possible for his own mother, and the bitter and obsessive tone of her many letters of complaint and supplication may have something to do with her maimed appearance. It certainly aggravated the financial problems of the Sidney family, for after her illness Lady Mary and Sir Henry Sidney kept separate households and retinues, with consequent doubling of expenses. Besides her scarring and her impoverishment, Mary Sidney had some less mentionable causes for bitterness and disappointment, which must have played a part in provoking Queen Elizabeth's cautious and ungenerous attitude to the Sidney family. One of Mary Sidney's brothers, Lord Guilford Dudley, had been married to the unfortunate Lady Jane Grey, as part of his father Northumberland's strategy to gain control of the throne and secure a Protestant succession. Though Jane Grey, as is well known, was to be 'Queen' for no more than nine days, it should be remembered that she had been publicly nominated as his successor by Edward VI, whose henchman Henry Sidney had been, in his second 'Device of Succession'. It may not have seemed anything like so obvious to the Dudleys and their immediate circle as it did to other courtiers that Jane Grey's claim was void. For a couple of heady days, Sidney's uncle Guilford had even been referred to as King.

Mary Sidney, Jane Grey's sister-in-law, must have remembered those few days very vividly. In his *Defence of Leicester* Sidney is fiercely protective of his grandfather Northumberland, referring to his execution and that of his son Guilford merely as 'calamities', and affirming finally 'let the last fault of the Duke be buried'.[13] Whether by his 'last fault' Sidney means his elevation of Jane Grey to the throne or his last-minute attempt to avoid execution by converting to Catholicism is not clear. What is clear is that, despite their remarkable history of attainders and executions in three generations, Sidney had been brought up to be passionately proud of his Dudley forebears. His father stressed this in the first letter he wrote to him, while Philip was at Shrewsbury School: 'Remember, my son, the noble blood you are descended of by your mother's side ...' No doubt his Dudley mother stressed this even more strongly. She may also have instilled into him a staunch family loyalty to the memory of Jane Grey. A romanticizing poem about Sidney written a couple of decades after his death suggests this when he is made to boast rather crudely to Lady Rich:

> I might have had a Queen unto my aunt.[14]

There were at least four ways in which Sidney 'might have had a Queen' for his aunt. At different moments his uncle, the Earl of Leicester, came close to marrying either Elizabeth I or Mary Queen of Scots. An uncle by marriage, the Earl of Huntingdon, was regarded by a substantial faction as having a strong claim on the throne. However, the poem's accompanying notes link the boast with Lady Jane Grey. Though the connexion is clumsily made, it draws attention to something which was probably important to Sidney. He really did have a nine days' Queen for his aunt, and Jane Grey's high intelligence, her piety, her love of reading, and her awkward habit of telling obstinate Papists that they were going to hell, were all vividly remembered by Sidney's parents. His mother, in particular, must have seen to it that her son knew at a very early age about his aunt Jane, who so nearly became England's first Protestant Queen. She was executed just about the time Sidney was conceived, in February 1553/4. Recollections of Lady Jane Grey's dignity and composure while she was manipulated, and finally destroyed, as a political pawn whose personal feelings mattered little to the older people around her, may have contributed to some of the most powerful and original passages in the 'New' *Arcadia*, when Sidney describes the courage and eloquence of the imprisoned Pamela. From 1563 onwards he could read documents in John Foxe's *Actes and Monuments* which testified to Jane Grey's eloquence both in speech and writing, her tenderness to her younger sister, her stoical piety in prison, and even her skill in versifying, comparable with that of her sister-in-law Mary Sidney, expressed in 'Certain pretty verses written ... with a pin'. These were presumably scratched on a glass window in the Tower:

> Do never think it strange,
> Though now I have misfortune;
> For if that fortune change,
> The same to thee may happen.
> Jane Dudley.

A long letter of spiritual counsel to a friend of her father's ended in a verse precept:

> Be constant, be constant, fear not for pain;
> Christ hath redeemed thee, and heaven is thy gain.

Reinforced by his parents' personal memories of Jane Grey, these records contributed substantially, I believe, to Sidney's account of the sufferings of Pamela.

Like her sister-in-law Jane Grey, Sidney's mother was a woman of outstanding intelligence, learning and piety. Geffrey Fenton, a gentleman who had fallen on hard times and lived for a while in Paris, dedicated a collection of powerful translations from Bandello's *novelle*, as *Certain Tragicall Discourses*, to Lady Sidney in 1567. He paid handsome compliments to her 'sincere and devout order of living', admired both in England and abroad.[15] Her subsequent support of him probably helped him to the successful career in Ireland, initially under Sir Henry Sidney, which followed. Like other women of the period whose husband's posts kept them away from London, Mary Sidney had to fight many of her husband's political battles for him, and, despite her scarred appearance, needed to maintain a frequent presence at Court. In a letter to his father in 1578 Sidney paid tribute to the thoroughness and wisdom with which his mother was promoting the absent Sir Henry's interests, adding that 'For mine own part, I have had only light from her.'[16]

We do not know whether Mary Sidney also found strength to give suck to her own children, as a seventeenth-century Countess was to advise.[17] Most probably she did not. That same Countess confessed that she had given all her own eighteen children out to wet nurses, but later bitterly regretted having failed to nourish them herself. Even fifty years or so after Sidney's birth, when Webster wrote *The White Devil*, it was unusual for well-born women to feed their own children, though many educational theorists advised it. In Webster's play the boy prince Giovanni, remembering his murdered mother Isabella, says:

> I have often heard her say she gave me suck,
> And it should seem by that she dearly loved me,
> Since princes seldom do it.[18]

Mary Sidney certainly loved her son dearly, but may not have expressed her love in such a physical manner. Dr Moffet refers to the *matres* – both mother and foster-mother – who gave the baby Sidney 'life and the breast'. Possibly the comfortingly named Anne Mantell began her long career with the Sidney family as Philip's wet nurse. She and her husband Robert were certainly in charge of the nursery, and she may, like Juliet's Nurse, have graduated from wet nurse to 'nanny' and staunch ally. In 1560, when Philip was six, Sir Henry Sidney paid her £18 6s. 3d., £12 of which was for young Philip's 'board'. £3 16s. paid to the 'poticary' (apothecary) in the same year[19] may relate to the attack of 'measles and smallpox' which, Moffet says, laid waste the boy's pretty features 'as with little mines'.[20] But it is more likely that the scarring illness occurred a couple of years later, and that the child shared his mother's affliction in 1562, as the 'Sidney horoscope' seems to indicate. Thomas Moffet did not enter Sidney's sister's household until the early 1590s, which explains his often shaky grasp of the order of events in Sidney's early life. But Moffet tells one anecdote of Sidney's infancy, not recorded elsewhere, which he may have learned from old Mrs Mantell. Certainly Mrs Mantell accompanied Sidney's sister Mary in her marriage journey to Wilton, and may have been one of few people still alive in the 1590s who could recall Sidney's infancy. The incident records the kind of behaviour that would make a strong impression on an affectionate 'nanny', privileged with the custody of a child destined for high things:

> When as a three-year-old he beheld the moon, with clean hands and head covered he used to pray to it and devoutly to worship – as if in his earliest years he had compassed the heavens with his mind, and wondered at the works of his Creator.[21]

Those 'clean hands' would make a great impression on a nursery governess. The moralizing comment is evidently that of Moffet, writing an 'exemplary biography' thirty years later; but there may be some truth in his picture of Sidney's awestruck response to the beauty of creation, for such a response is mentioned also in an account of his death. As he struggled to reconcile himself to the God who had allowed him to be wounded he reflected:

> He is a most good spirit; for otherwise how should the world continue in the beauty it hath?[22]

Sidney's keen response to the beauty of the 'too much loved earth' may have become apparent at a very early age, exciting the notice of the women who cared for him.

No doubt the infant Sidney made a strong impression on his nurses. What is more remarkable, perhaps, is that they seem to have made a strong impression on him. For instance, in February 1576/7, while he was deep in preparations for his embassy to the Holy Roman Emperor, Sidney found time to write to his father's steward, Robert Walker, to remind him that Mrs Mantell's salary of £20 (quite a handsome rate for an upper servant) was due.[23] His emphatic tone suggests that this was a matter that concerned him greatly: 'If you possibly may I pray you do this, and you shall do me a great pleasure.' As a poet, Sidney often recollected infancy. A cluster of images of lovers as suckling children runs through his poetry like a minor obsession. It is the subject of the only lyric that survives in his own hand, 'Sleep, baby mine, Desire', where the troublesome child 'Desire' stays awake and cries out for the 'pap' – baby food – of fulfilment. He used the image at least twice more: in 'Lamon's Tale' 201–3:

> But glad Desire, his late embosomed guest,
> Yet but a babe, with milk of sight he nursed;
> Desire, the more he sucked, more sought the breast ...

and in *Astrophil and Stella* 71. 14, where the image of love as an importunate baby sums up the central problem of the relationship:

> 'But ah!' Desire still cries, 'give me some food!'

This crucial line comes at the exact mid-point of the sequence, if all the lines of both songs and sonnets are counted.[24] On one level the love of Astrophil for Stella may be sterile, yet the sequence has a baby at its centre. Sidney's most public use of the image of lovers as hungry, dependent babies came in the elaborate *Triumph*, devised chiefly by him, which was performed before the Queen and a very large French delegation in May 1581. Sidney and three fellow courtiers called themselves 'fostered children of Desire', who had been 'a great while nourished up with that infective milk ... (though full oft that dry nurse, Despair, endeavoured to wean them from it) ...' Here 'Desire' was as much political as amorous, figuring the eager dependency of courtiers on the Queen's favour. The show was an elaborate allegorical display of the passionate devotion of these four young courtiers to the Queen, whom they did not want to see alienated from them by marriage to a foreigner. The French delegation had come to further the courtship of the Duke of Alençon. Sidney's use of frankly physical imagery, with aspiring courtiers as thirsty babies, is characteristic of his readiness to use homely metaphors even in the grandest situations. The real-life analogue to this was his ability to remember Mrs Mantell's wages amid the hectic preparations for his embassy to the Imperial Court. Given, also, Sidney's perpetual awareness of names, words and double meanings, another recollection of Anne Mantell may be buried in a line from the first stanza of his political beast fable:

> Each thing with mantle black the night doth soothe ...[25]

Because of the name of his nurse, Sidney had special reason to associate a 'mantle' with bed-time and security.

The complex ways in which Elizabethan noble families interconnect make the detailed study of their family history extremely confusing. When we turn to the subject of Sidney's aunts, the problem arises in acute form. In all, Sidney had at least fourteen aunts: seven 'blood' aunts and seven or eight aunts by marriage. The second total varies according to whether we include Leicester's union with Douglass Sheffield, which he later repudiated. Of the seven 'blood' aunts, six were on the Sidney side. Little Philip may have had hazy recollections of two unmarried aunts, Mabell and Elizabeth, who were loyal members of the household of Mary I, and devout Catholics. They apparently died in her service. Certainly nothing is known of them after Mary's death in 1558, when their nephew was almost four; but it is possible that they lived on obscurely in one of the remoter Sidney residences, practising their religion in secret. The four other Sidney aunts made good marriages. Mary was the wife of Sir William Dormer. Her daughter Jane, the Countess of Feria, has already been mentioned. Lady Dormer died young, twelve years before Sidney's birth. Lucy Sidney married James Harington of Exton, first cousin of the translator of Ariosto, and was the grandmother and namesake of Donne's patroness, Lucy Harington, Countess of Bedford. Anne Sidney married Sir William Fitzwilliam, who served the Queen thanklessly in various senior posts in Ireland. The best marriage on this side of the family was made by Frances, who married Thomas Ratcliffe, Earl of Sussex, in 1555 and was posthumously the founder of Sidney Sussex College, Cambridge, through her bequest of £5,000. Like most of Sidney's grander relations, she was childless.

Relations between Sidney's most prominent Dudley uncle, the Earl of Leicester, and his most eminent uncle by marriage, the Earl of Sussex, were about as bad as they could be. They were openly opposed on most matters of policy, and especially on the question of the Queen's possible marriage to a foreigner. Sussex gave Leicester the nickname 'The Gypsy', and at his death in 1583 is said to have warned against Leicester's malign influence: 'Beware the Gypsy, for he will be too hard for you all: you know not the beast so well as I do.'[26] As Lord Chamberlain of the Royal Household from 1572, Sussex was able to exercise considerable power over his Dudley in-laws. Mary Sidney's recurrent bitterness about her poor accommodation at Court should be seen in this context: Sussex may have used his position to cut his relations down to size. Mary Sidney's bitterness may also have been compounded by envy of her more prosperous sister-in-law, comfortably ensconced in palatial apartments either at Court or her new mansion, New Hall, Boreham, Essex, while she herself had to move between such remote places as Wales and Ireland, also finding herself in cold and cramped quarters in royal residences such as Hampton Court or Greenwich, where Sussex was in charge of the allocation of rooms to courtiers.

It was on the Dudley side of the family that Sidney's most powerful aunts were to be found. The ambitious John Dudley had given an excellent humanist education to his two surviving daughters, Mary, Sidney's mother, and Catherine. Mary presumably used hers to instil the rudiments of learning into her own children. Her younger sister Catherine, who married Henry Hastings, Earl of Huntingdon, in 1553, had no children of her own, but seems in effect to have run a kind of boarding school for well-born orphans, especially girls. She boasted in old age that 'I think there will none question but I know how to breed and govern young gentlewomen.'[27] The Huntingdons turned the profitable business of gaining 'wardships' of young orphans to useful ends. They shared a passionate interest in 'Puritan' education, which they fostered both in their own household and in local grammar schools. One of the Countess's pupils, Margaret Hoby (née Dakins), left a diary recording her practice of the ideals and way of life she had learned from the Huntingdons at Ashby de la Zouch. Her day began and ended with prayer; she tended the sick on her estate, dressing their wounds and broken limbs and presiding at childbeds; she read and heard sermons and devotional books. Apart from some conversations with her husband, which may occasionally have touched on secular matters, that seems to be about all, at least as far as her diary is concerned.[28] However, another alumna of the Huntingdon household, Penelope Devereux, graduated to a much more varied and exciting life at Court, despite her marriage to a Puritan husband carefully chosen for her by the Earl of Huntingdon. As I shall explain in a moment, Penelope Devereux, model for

Sidney's 'Stella', can in a sense be included among the ranks of his talented female relations, if we count connexions by marriage. The Huntingdons played an important part in the lives of the Sidney family. The Countess, in particular, took a close interest in her Sidney nephews and nieces, whose parents were often far away. The child to whom she was closest was Philip's youngest brother, Thomas, who accompanied his aunt to Court as a page in 1574, when he was only five, being rewarded by the Queen herself with 'a cap embellished with hearts and roses in gold and enamel'.[29] After the deaths in 1586 of both his parents and his eldest brother, Thomas was taken entirely into the care of the Huntingdons, who arranged his marriage to the diarist Margaret Dakins, already, aged twenty, the widow of yet another of their charges, Penelope Devereux's younger brother Walter. In 1578/9 Sir Henry Sidney is recorded as having made the Countess of Huntingdon a lavish New Year's gift of '23 yards of cloth of gold'.[30] This is doubtless typical of the warm relations that prevailed between the Sidneys and the Huntingdons. In Sidney's will she comes first in a list of three aunts to whom he bequeathed 'a jewel, the best I have'.[31] Though the order is that of seniority, it may also reflect their rank in his esteem.

Aunts Two and Three in the will were strongly contrasted, both with the Countess of Huntingdon and with each other. Aunt Number Two was the Countess of Warwick, who, as Anne Russell, was eldest daughter of Francis Russell, 'commonly called the good Earl of Bedford'.[32] As her niece Anne Clifford later recorded, Anne Russell came into Elizabeth's service very young, and served her constantly, as maid, wife and widow, 'being more beloved and in greater favour with the said Queen than any other woman in the kingdom, and no less generally esteemed and honoured throughout the whole court'.[33] It was a mark of royal favour to the twice-widowed old soldier Ambrose Dudley, Earl of Warwick, that this marriage was arranged. It was conducted 'with great state' at the Royal Chapel at Whitehall on 11 November 1565. Lady Warwick continued to spend most of her time attending the Queen, rather than on her husband's estates in the Midlands and elsewhere. There are many contemporary portraits of her, showing her as an elegantly dressed lady with a lively, amused-looking face. Her relations probably saw her most often at great court occasions. Like the Huntingdons, the Warwicks were childless and, also like the Huntingdons, they participated with their Sidney nephews in ceremonials at Court. For instance, in 1575 Philip, who had returned from his three years of travel in the previous June, assisted at the christening of a Russell niece of the Countess of Warwick.[34] It took place in Westminster Abbey, which was splendidly decked for the occasion with hangings of crimson taffeta, and the baptismal basin was surrounded with flowers. The Countess deputized for the Queen, and herself named the child with the Queen's name.

Sidney then emerged from St Edward's Shrine with a towel on his left shoulder, and knelt while his aunt dried her hands on it. A banquet followed.[35] For the Elizabethans, a 'banquet' was something like what now survives as 'dessert' in Oxford and Cambridge colleges, with sweet wine, fruit, nuts, spiced 'comfits' (sweets), and perhaps marchpane tarts decorated with gold leaf. It was at such festive occasions that Sidney most often encountered his aunt Anne Warwick. Her youngest brother William Russell was to become a close friend and comrade in the last year of Sidney's life.

Perhaps because of her closeness to the Queen, the Countess of Warwick attracted a substantial number of dedications. At least twenty printed books were dedicated to her, on a wide range of devotional and secular subjects. One which probably attracted Sidney's attention was George Turberville's *Epitaphes, Epigrams, Songs and Sonets, with a Discourse of the Friendly affections of Tymetes to Pyndara*. Surviving copies are of the second edition, printed in 1567; a previous edition, of which this is a revision, was probably read to pieces, for no copy survives. Lady Warwick is addressed both in a prefatory letter, an opening verse eulogy, and a concluding poem, where she is implored to

take with hand
This ragged rime, and with courteous look
And countess' eye, peruse this trifling book.

As he disarmingly confesses, Turberville is a far from distinguished poet. Yet the volume is an attractively readable collection of over 150 lyrics, many in ballad metre, with an unusually wide variety of themes, frivolous, occasional and satiric. Some motifs were later developed by Sidney. For instance, though there is a common source in Catullus, Turberville's lyric addressed apologetically to his lady 'when he kissed her and made her lip bleed' may lie somewhere behind Astrophil's assurance to Stella:

I will but kiss, I never more will bite.[36]

Turberville's lover, rather more crudely, invited his lady to exact revenge by biting him back. Like Astrophil, Turberville's lover begs the Thames to stay calm while his mistress is travelling on it; and like Astrophil, he addresses his sleepless bed (pp. 18, 35). His dismissal of life at Court as nothing but 'daily diligence' (p. 41) may be picked up in the unfinished fairy tale told by the simple-minded Mopsa in the 'New' *Arcadia*, in which a knight woos his lady with 'Daily Diligence and Grisly Groans'.[37] The only scholar who has hitherto studied Sidney's reading of Turberville concludes that 'he had read "Pyndara and Tymetes" with active disdain'.[38] But he may in fact have felt some affection for this old-fashioned but entertaining collection dedicated to his aunt, which he probably read when he was in his early teens.

Another amusing and fanciful work dedicated to the Countess of Warwick was Hugh Plat's *The flowres of philosophie, with the pleasures of poetrie annexed thereunto* (1572). Its young author later wrote many books on cookery and household management; he seems to have enjoyed entering these 'female' spheres of knowledge. This book, too, had things in it which may have pleased Lady Warwick's nephew, and it confirms the evidence given in her portraits that she had a strong sense of humour. Plat's interest in food is reflected in some of his poems, such as his 'merry tale of Master Mendax and his friend Credulus', a tall story in which a house made of pastry is described:

> The posts be all of cinnamon,
> and ginger jointly joined ...
> The table made of biscuit bread
> on comfits four doth stand.
> Each corner hath an antic boy
> that holdeth out his hand
> To deal about some caraways
> to all the passers by ...

The fantasy develops to include custard walls mended with egg yolk, paper fly-traps baited with marmalade, and pigs with knives hanging by their waists shrieking out to be killed and eaten. Ridiculous though all this is, Plat's final comment has serious implications:

> All things are to poets' pens
> and painters' pencils free.

For Sidney, who was to celebrate poetic freedom in the *Defence of Poesy*, Plat's free play of fancy may have had its attractions. Of all his aunts, Lady Warwick probably came closest to sharing his literary interests.

Aunt Number Three, in the list in Sidney's will, was the Countess of Leicester. While the Countess of Warwick enjoyed an unusually long and secure relationship with the Queen, the Countess of Leicester, initially in a position of some favour, later became her *bête noire*. Her mother, Catherine Carey, was daughter to Anne Boleyn's sister, and so a first cousin to the Queen. Catherine Carey married Sir Francis Knollys, and remained a high favourite with her cousin Elizabeth until her death at Hampton Court in 1568/9. But her daughter Lettice was a different proposition. Her first husband, Walter Devereux, Earl of Essex, died in Ireland in 1576 in circumstances felt by Leicester's enemies to be suspicious. She may have embarked on an affair with Leicester during her husband's lifetime. Certainly she was a frequent visitor to Kenilworth, and was among Leicester's guests there, without her husband, in 1575. When, in September 1578, she married Leicester, it was noted by the clergyman who conducted the private ceremony that she was wearing a 'loose bodied gown'. Leicester's previous marital history was, to say the least, unpromising. His first wife, Amy Robsart, died from a fall downstairs at Cumnor Place, near Oxford, in 1560. Though modern analysis of the evidence suggests that she may have broken her neck accidentally as a secondary result of the breast cancer from which she had been suffering for some time, many contemporaries believed that Leicester had caused her to be murdered, a suspicion from which he could never wholly clear himself. In 1573 Leicester contracted some kind of union with a widow called Douglass Sheffield, which produced a son, Roberto. But he later denied that this had been a marriage, and would not accept Roberto as his heir. The spurned lady married Sir Edward Stafford in 1579, and thereafter the Staffords became a powerful focus of anti-Leicester propaganda. Leicester himself had married Lettice Knollys in the summer of 1578, and probably some time in the winter of 1580–81 Lettice gave birth to the only child Leicester acknowledged, Robert, Baron Denbigh, during whose short lifetime Sidney was displaced from his position as Leicester's chief heir. The little boy died on 19 July 1584, being, according to Stow, 'of the age of three years and somewhat more'.[39] A touchingly tiny suit of armour made for the little boy who stood to inherit so much is still to be seen at Warwick Castle, and the pictures kept by his father at Leicester House in London included one of 'the Baron of Denbigh, naked'. If this survives anywhere, it is probably unique as an Elizabethan portrait of a naked baby.

In her own way, Leicester's wife was quite as remarkable as Sidney's other aunts by marriage, though perhaps her greatest gift was that of sheer survival. Her bad relationship with the Queen must have made her unattractive as a patroness, for in the course of a very long life she received only about half a dozen dedications and commendations in printed books. After her marriage to Leicester she had to put up with implacable royal disfavour. The Queen learned about the marriage with great indignation from the French envoy Simier in the summer of 1579. Though Leicester was eventually received back into intimacy, Lettice was never allowed back to Court, despite her husband's persistent efforts. However, she kept up semi-royal state at Wanstead, Kenilworth and elsewhere, and George Gower's portrait of her, now at Longleat, shows her as a resplendently beautiful and opulently dressed Queen Elizabeth look-alike in the early 1580s. There may actually have been some facial resemblance between Lettice and Elizabeth, for they were first cousins once removed. This may have contributed to Elizabeth's hatred of her, while also making her especially attractive to Leicester as a younger version of Elizabeth who, unlike the Queen herself, was sexually available. After Leicester's death in 1588 Lettice married a third, much younger, husband, Christopher Blount, who, along with her son Essex, was executed in 1600/1. She weathered this storm, too, living to the age of ninety-six, still able to 'walk a mile in the morning' until shortly before her death in 1634.[40] It is a pity that she wrote no memoirs. In a period when few lived much beyond sixty, her longevity is extraordinary.

What sort of rapport, if any, existed between Sidney and his aunt Lettice is hard to conjecture. As the mother of 'Stella', she can be seen making a cameo appearance in the Fourth Song of *Astrophil and Stella*:

> Your fair mother is abed,
> Candles out and curtains spread;
> She thinks you do letters write,
> Write, but first let me endite . . .

Lettice seems to have enjoyed good relationships with her children, sharing some of Penelope Devereux's circle of friends and protégés in the 1590s, and it is possible that, as Stella's 'fair mother', she was among the very earliest readers of *Astrophil and Stella*. But we know little for certain of her relations with her nephew Philip. He may have felt embarrassed by her flamboyantly extravagant way of life, as well as threatened by her ability to displace him in his uncle's favour. His most extensive reference to her comes in a letter written from Utrecht on 24 March 1586, and suggests that he regarded her as a considerable liability. He was desperately anxious that she and her large retinue should not come over to join Leicester in the Netherlands.[41]

Moving down to the next generation, younger female relations also abounded in Sidney's world. After his own birth in 1554 there were four younger sisters: Margaret, born 1556, died 1558; Elizabeth, born about 1560, died 1567;[42] Ambrosia, born about 1564, died 1575, who may have been the well-born girl whose death was commemorated in Spenser's 'November' Eclogue; and Mary, born 1561, who was summoned to Court to escape the bad air of Ludlow, which, the Queen thought, might have caused Ambrosia's death. Within two years of her arrival at Court, in 1577, Mary married the Earl of Pembroke. Because of the peripatetic life of the Sidney family it is hard to know how much Sidney saw of his little sisters in their infancy. If he saw much of any younger siblings, it would have been his sisters, for by the time Robert and Thomas were born (in 1563 and 1569) he was away at school and university. In his earliest years at Penshurst he probably did see something of them. A recollection of their attempts to peruse such handsome medieval manuscripts as the fifteenth-century 'Sidney Psalter', now at Trinity College. Cambridge, may lie behind an image he uses several times of children trying to play with illuminated books:

like a child, that some fair book doth find,
With gilded leaves or coloured vellum plays,
Or at the most on some fair picture stays,
But never heeds the fruit of writer's mind ...[43]

Since the 'Sidney Psalter' was used to keep family records of births, deaths, christenings and marriages, it may regularly have been taken out in the presence of the children.

The only one of Sidney's sisters who survived to adulthood, Mary, was of incalculable importance to him as a writer, for she and her entourage of 'fair ladies' at Wilton were the audience for whom he originally wrote the *Arcadia*. She is also the most plausible candidate for 'Mira', the first named object of devotion in Sidney's poetry. Given their relative ages, Sidney saw little of her as an infant at Penshurst, but had the excitement of discovering her as a young married woman, aged sixteen, in the autumn of 1577. Mary Herbert's work as self-appointed literary executrix and editor largely determined the form in which Sidney's literary remains were published after his death.

Of all the women who shaped Sidney's responses to the female sex the most crucial, but also the most enigmatic, is the Queen. He expressed his sense of her centrality to the life of the whole realm in his public image of her as the unassailable 'Fortress of Perfect Beauty', showing her also as a mother to her people who is threatening to deny sustenance to her suckling courtiers, in the 'Four Foster Children of Desire' entertainment in 1581. A letter written to a German friend soon after his return to England from the Grand Tour in 1575 suggests some of the paradoxical emotions that Elizabeth provoked in him. On the one hand he describes her as 'somewhat advanced in years' – a callow twenty-year-old's view of a woman of forty-one. On the other, he compares her to 'Meleager's brand' – the torch which, in Greek mythology, had to stay alight to keep the hero Meleager alive. When she perishes, says Sidney, 'Farewell all our quietness'.[44] Though this may sound as if he was alarmed at the prospect of the Queen's imminent death, other letters of the period suggest that Sidney did not regard England's 'quietness' under Elizabeth as an unmixed blessing, and may have looked forward to the future with a certain excitement. Some young courtiers succeeded in charming Elizabeth, but Sidney was never one of her 'minions', and may have viewed his uncomfortable relationship with her as one that must soon be terminated by her demise. It probably never crossed young Sidney's mind that Elizabeth would outlive him by seventeen years. Six months before his own death, he made a rather desperate allusion to the Queen, reflecting acute anxiety about her half-hearted and ungenerous support of the English forces in the Netherlands:

If Her Majesty were the fountain I would fear, considering what I daily find, that we should wax dry; but she is but a means whom God useth, and I know not whether I am deceived, but I am faithfully persuaded that if she should withdraw herself other springs would rise to help this action ... If the Queen pay not her soldiers she must lose her garrisons, there is no doubt thereof.[45]

The Queen as a mother, offering the milk of favour to her suppliant, infantile courtiers, has here been transformed into a financial well-head. As the golden stream of the English Treasury looked like being dammed, Sidney hinted that he would try to drink elsewhere. His ready familiarity with 'other springs' – other sources of power, money and influence in Protestant Europe – did not commend itself to the Queen, nervous of European initiatives that might move beyond her control. However, neither this letter nor the majority of Sidney's literary works were intended for Elizabeth's perusal.

This marks a fundamental difference between Spenser's *Faerie Queene*, written for publication as a celebration of Elizabeth and her England, and Sidney's *Arcadia*, circulated in manuscript in a way that was at first carefully controlled. If Spenser wanted to criticize some aspects of Elizabeth's policy – and he clearly did – he had to adopt ingeniously covert or ambiguous strategies for doing so. Sidney, writing primarily for his sister Mary and her circle, was able to let off steam in numerous saucy asides. One such, in the revised *Arcadia*, is his comment on the appearance of Andromana, Queen of Iberia, a well-preserved 'older woman' whose looks remind the reader of someone else:

but an exceeding red hair with small eyes did (like ill companions) disgrace the other assembly of most commendable beauties.[46]

There are other indications that Andromana, whose name means 'man-mad', is one of the refracted images of Queen Elizabeth in the revised romance. For instance, the account of the 'Iberian jousts' held on her wedding anniversary every year is a thinly veiled description of the annual tilts held on Elizabeth's Accession Day, 17 November, often referred to as the day when she married England. Sidney probably never reckoned on his snide comment on Andromana's red hair and small eyes being read by Elizabeth herself. Another little aside which surely reflects the impatience of the young courtier, compelled publicly to elaborate the fiction of the ageing Elizabeth's 'Perfect Beauty', but finding release in mischievous remarks to his sister, is his comment on the only moderately good-looking Queen of Laconia:

one that seemed born in the confines of beauty's kingdom; for all her lineaments were neither perfect possessions thereof, nor absolute strangers thereto; but she was a queen, and therefore beautiful.[47]

Though Elizabeth exercised enormous power over Sidney, she was not all-powerful. He was unusually bold in his dealings with her, as his letter of advice about the proposed French marriage shows;[48] and in his early twenties he chose to absent himself from Court for longish periods, even when under pressure to attend. He stayed instead at the younger, more predominantly feminine court or 'little college', as Aubrey calls it, presided over by his sister at Wilton House, and it was during these periods that his life as a writer was most vigorously sustained. In the *Defence* he celebrated with particular enthusiasm the freedom of the poet, 'ranging only within the zodiac of his own wit'. Writing poetry was associated for him with personal freedom and relaxation, and with areas of his life over which the Queen had relatively little control. Some of Sidney's allusions to tiresome or physically unappealing monarchs may have provoked releasing laughter in Mary Herbert and her companions, rather like schoolgirls tittering behind the headmistress's back. Writing for lively young women, often away from Court, liberated Sidney from all sorts of constraints which would have operated had he chosen to write fiction for the Queen, or Cecil, or Walsingham. Yet, though Elizabeth may not have been Sidney's chosen audience, she cannot have failed to contribute to his awareness of the talents and capacities of women.

Probably all the women I have described in detail played a part in Sidney's early imaginative development. Many, from the Queen downwards, were literary patronesses, and were well able both to speak up for themselves and to pen cogent letters, neat verses, and learned translations. Professor Ringler has pointed out that Sidney never discusses vernacular poetry in his correspondence.[49] Though this is true, the reason may lie in the nature of the correspondence which survives, which is overwhelmingly concerned with politics and public affairs, and with only two exceptions is addressed to men. We have none of Sidney's personal letters to his sister, to Lady Rich, to his mother, his wife, or even to his most intimate male friends, Fulke Greville or Edward Dyer, though we can be sure that he must have written on occasion to all of them. Thomas Moffet, whom we can trust in this matter since he was living at Wilton, singles out for special praise Sidney's many letters, both in prose and verse, to the Queen, to his friends, and above all to his sister Mary.[50] Presumably these last perished in one of the fires which devastated Wilton House in the mid-seventeenth century. On the still controversial question of what should be done with the personal letters of dead poets, Mary Herbert would surely have had definite views. Her brother's private letters would have been locked up in a cabinet, not offered to a publisher. In trying to imagine what Sidney's letters to his sister may have been like, all we have to go on is the enchanting letter prefixed to the 'Old' *Arcadia*, in which he presents his sister with the romance written at her request:

> you desired me to do it, and your desire to my heart is an absolute commandment ... Read it then at your idle times, and the follies your good judgement will find in it, blame not, but laugh at.[51]

If we could read some of Sidney's other letters to women, especially more of those he wrote to his sister, we might have some immediate, unstudied insight into his motives for writing and his thoughts on his literary work-in-progress. We might also get more of the flavour of his relationship with the predominantly feminine coteries with which both the 'Old' *Arcadia* and *Astrophil and Stella* were associated.

As it is, we must make what we can of the literary works themselves. Despite frequent appeals to 'you, fair ladies', these works all too rarely link up in a direct and explicit way with surviving correspondence and biographical documents. Yet now and then they seem to offer glimpses of the environment in which they were created. For instance, one short passage suggests that, like W. S. Gilbert, Sidney regarded the possession of a multiplicity of aunts as rather comic. The rustic Mopsa, in a crude rendition of a medieval romance, describes the painful journey of her heroine

> over many a high hill, and many a deep river; till she came to an Aunt's house of hers, and came, and cried to her for help: and she for pity gave her a Nut; and bade her never open her Nut, till she was come to the extremest misery that ever tongue could speak of. And so she went, and she went, and she went, and never rested the evening where she went in the morning; till she came to a second Aunt; and she gave her another Nut . . .[52]

At the mention of the second benevolent aunt the hearers decide they have had enough. It may be that their own very plentiful supply of aunts was something of a joke for the Sidney children.

It is noticeable also that Sidney, writing for a female audience, presents many scenes in which women are entertaining each other. Pamela tactfully asks Mopsa to save up the rest of her tale to tell to the women assembled on her wedding day, and at Kala's wedding in the Third Eclogues, we are told that 'the women (for such was the manner of that country) kept together to make good cheer among themselves'.[53] Disguised as a woman, Sidney's hero Pyrocles is able to enter the Arcadian world of fictional 'fair ladies' on apparently equal terms. Though Sidney may never seriously have wished himself to be a horse, as he jokingly pretended at the beginning of the *Defence*, he may really have had moments of wishing himself to be a woman. Using the freedom of the poet's pen he could imaginatively enter an all-female world, even as Pyrocles does in his Amazon dress.

As inspiration, audience, and subject-matter, women occupied a central place in Sidney's birth as a writer. The knowledge that his fictions were to be read by women was one factor inhibiting him from the outbursts of misogyny indulged in by his contemporaries. But he may not even have felt the temptation to write misogynistically. After all, it was open to him to write for male audiences if he so wished. It seems likely that he genuinely enjoyed the company of women, and had a high view of their moral and intellectual capacities – what Richard Mulcaster called the 'natural towardness' of girls. [54] His presentation of the Arcadian heroines as figures of moral authority suggests as much. In the 'Old' *Arcadia* Philoclea argues movingly and profoundly against self-slaughter, her instinctive eloquence and thoughtfulness showing the moral and emotional collapse of Pyrocles in a very poor light.[55] In the 'New' *Arcadia* Pamela sets out sophisticated arguments for the existence of Divine Providence.[56] Perhaps these are images of 'what may be and should be', rather than direct notations of female speech. Yet the links between Pamela and Lady Jane Grey root the fictional heroine's fortitude and eloquence in a real-life martyrdom in Sidney's family. Pamela's intellectual maturity is not achieved at the price of conventional feminine virtues, for she beguiles the time in prison with skilful embroidery. This, too, may have links with real life, for several female rulers in Europe, such as Margaret of Parma, Regent of the Netherlands, are known to have worked at embroidery while presiding over council meetings, and Mary Queen of Scots produced many embroideries during her long imprisonment. Though his surviving letters give little hint of this, Sidney was a close observer of women and their worlds.

Sidney's lover-persona Astrophil admits to enjoying feminine society in general, not just the proximity of 'Stella':

> ... here I do store of fair ladies meet,
> Who may with charm of conversation sweet
> Make in my heavy mould new thoughts to grow ...[57]

'Charm' here probably means, besides 'fascination', 'the blended singing or noise [as] of many birds';[58] and Sidney is the earliest English writer to use the word 'conversation' in *OED*'s sense 7, 'interchange of thoughts or words; familiar speech'. Whether it was the musicality of their voices or the interest of what they said that most fascinated Astrophil, it is likely that Sidney enjoyed it, too. From the moment of his birth he was frequently in the company of women who, thanks to their access to education, could charm by means of 'conversation', rather than simply by youth, good looks or fine clothes.

2

1564–7

DUTCH UNCLES

To talk to a person like a Dutch uncle: to give him advice in a kindly, heavy manner.

(*Shorter Oxford Dictionary*)

Think upon every word that you will speak, before you utter it, and remember how nature hath rampiered up (as it were) the tongue, with teeth, lips, yea, and hair without the lips, and all betokening reins, or bridles, for the loose use of this member.

(From Sir Henry Sidney's letter of advice to his son, then aged eleven)

PHILISIDES: Hath any heard what this old man hath said?
Truly, not I . . .[1]

Sidney's behaviour as a child and a young man was evidently not faultless. Even the idealizing Dr Moffet describes him as lamenting 'the lubricity of his youth'. But rage, not lust, seems to have been Sidney's besetting vice. Moffet gives an account of the astonishment felt by friends and servants when Sidney's pent-up wrath suddenly descended on them like a thunderbolt.[2] There are numerous documented instances of his extreme and incautious irascibility. He had what would now be called 'a short fuse', and it was probably not without self-knowledge that Sidney chose for the 'younger, but chiefer' hero of the *Arcadia*, Pyrocles, a name suggesting 'fieriness', or excess of passion. Both the name and its meaning were developed further by Spenser in Book II of *The Faerie Queene*, in which the angry passion of the choleric 'Pyrochles' leads at one point to his spontaneous combustion:

'I burn, I burn, I burn,' then loud he cried,
'O how I burn with implacable fire!
Yet nought can quench mine inly flaming side,
No sea of liquor cold, nor lake of mire,
Nothing but death can do me to respire . . .'[3]

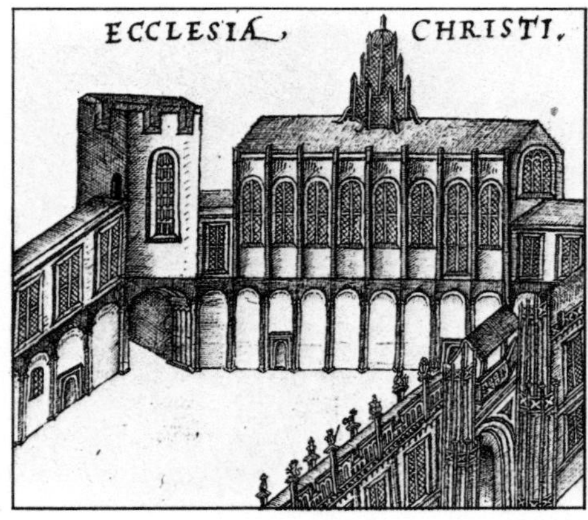

Pen drawing of Christ Church, Oxford, in 1566, by John Bereblock (Bodleian Library)

Like the unknown subject of a famous miniature by Nicholas Hilliard (now in the Victoria and Albert Museum), Sidney's hero seems to inhabit the element of fire. Near the end of his unfinished 'New' *Arcadia* Sidney refers approvingly to 'the Pyroclean nature, fuller of gay bravery in the midst than in the beginning of danger',[4] suggesting that in combat this energetic inflammability was a source of strength. However, in everyday life Sidney's own 'Pyroclean', or fiery, nature could lead him to impetuous behaviour which was not always appropriate. Hubert Languet, his chief 'Dutch uncle' during the Grand Tour, was aware of his tendency to become uncontrollably angry with his friends for little cause, and warned him of it:

I see ... by your last letter that you have digested your wrath, and suffered yourself to be talked over ... you will have to adopt this plan many times before you reach my age, unless you wish to pass your whole life in quarrelling.[5]

Wallace chronicles a disagreeable tendency to accuse his friends of stealing money from him, often on slender evidence.[6] One famous letter of Sidney's to his father's secretary, Edmund Molyneux, speaks for itself. It is perhaps the Elizabethan letter one would least like to have received:

Mr Molyneux: Few words are best. My letters to my father have come to the eyes of some; neither can I condemn any but you for it. If it be so, you have played the very knave with me, and so I will make you know if I have good proof of it. But that for so much as is past. For that is to come, I assure you before God that if ever I know you do so much as read any letter I write to my father, without his commandment, or my consent, I will thrust my dagger into you. And trust to it, for I speak it in earnest. In the mean time, farewell. From Court this last of May 1578.

By me
Philip
Sidney[7]

Here, again, the accusation was false, but though Sidney changed his tone to the unfortunate Molyneux in subsequent letters, there is no record of his having apologized to him.

Nor did the choleric young Sidney always cut an impressive figure. He often comes across as petulant and unreasonable. Even as reported many years later by his devoted friend Fulke Greville, his riposte to the Earl of Oxford on the royal tennis-court at Whitehall sounds pompous and feeble. On being twice called a 'Puppy' by Oxford, who wanted to play and found Sidney and a partner (Greville?) installed, Sidney angrily responded that this was a 'lie impossible', 'in respect all the world know puppies are gotten by dogs and children by men'. Since an insult to his family was exactly what Oxford intended, Sidney's spelling out of his imputed canine heritage scarcely strengthened his position. If Greville's account accurately represents Sidney's answer, we must, even at this distance, feel embarrassed at how silly he must have seemed to the large audience of visiting French noblemen drawn to the tennis-court by the sound of raised voices.[8] Perhaps, as Molyneux hinted in his obituary, Sidney was more fluent with the pen than with the tongue. His father's advice, quoted at the head of this chapter, may have been excessively inhibitory. On the other hand, if the child was father to the man, it may have been precisely because young Philip was subject to vehement outbursts of rage that Sir Henry impressed on him the need to think and pause before speaking.

Advice was something the young Sidney was not short of. Even by the standards of an age in which 'advice to a son' was a highly popular genre – one that Shakespeare brilliantly parodied in Polonius's advice to Laertes – he was at the receiving end of an exceptional amount of counsel and guidance from older men all eager to play the Polonius rôle. This abundance of advice may in turn have contributed to a build-up of rage and frustration in a child who was unusually passionate and sensitive. The classical model for the genre was a text much studied by Elizabethan schoolboys, Cicero's *De Officiis*, which comprises Cicero's advice to his son Marcus. Foremost among the Cicero/Poloniuses in Sidney's boyhood was, of course, his own father. Sir Henry Sidney's first letter, written while Philip was at Shrewsbury School, combines commonplace advice about obeying schoolmasters, working hard, and taking exercise, with some sensible and humane suggestions based on his own experience:

Seldom drink wine, and yet sometimes do, lest being enforced to drink upon the sudden you should find yourself inflamed ... Give yourself to be merry, for you degenerate from your father if you find not yourself most able in wit and body to do anything, when you be most merry, but let your mirth be ever void of all scurrility and biting words to any man.[9]

Many other avuncular figures took a close interest in Sidney's development. They included his potential fathers-in-law, Sir William Cecil, the first Earl of Essex, and William of Orange; his actual father-in-law, Sir Francis Walsingham; his uncles, chief among them the Earls of Leicester and Warwick; and the Protestant statesman Hubert Languet. Though not all of them wrote formal letters of advice and counsel, as Languet did, they all stood to him in semi-tutelary rôles, as older men whose position and authority commanded respect. This large body of 'Dutch uncles' presided over Sidney's education at a higher level than the nurses, schoolmasters and tutors who nurtured and instructed him on a day-to-day basis. From his earliest years, it was on the approval of such figures that Sidney's prospects depended.

We do not know much about Sidney's pre-school education. A passage in the 'New' *Arcadia* about the early education of Pyrocles and Musidorus suggests that maps, military games, and nursery tales of heroism may have been used to stimulate an interest in warfare:

Almost before they could perfectly speak they began to receive conceits not unworthy of the best speakers; excellent devices being used to make even their sports profitable, images of battles and fortifications being then delivered to their memory, which, after, their stronger judgements might dispense; the delight of tales being converted to the knowledge of all the stories of worthy princes.[10]

If this passage is autobiographical, we may be struck by a remark a little further on that 'no servile fear' or 'violent restraint' was used towards these young boys. If he was taught without use of the rod, Sidney was much luckier than most of his contemporaries. However, the passage may offer Sidney's own ideal programme for the early training of princes and noblemen, rather than a recollection of what happened in the nursery at Penshurst.

We may assume that Sidney learned to read very young. Moffet implies this when he says, immediately after his anecdote about the three-year-old child worshipping the moon, that 'he would scarcely ever sleep, still less go forth, without a book'.[11] If he was indeed taught with respect and kindness, rather than fear, perhaps he was helped through his ABC and catechism by the pleasant teaching aid used with the four-year-old Francis Willoughby in 1550, for whom 'a pound of sugar plate and great comfits' were purchased 'to make him learn his book'.[12] 'Sugar plate' was a kind of sugar brittle, often prettily coloured in contrasting stripes, such as cowslip yellow and violet blue;

'great comfits' were large sweets made by candying seeds and spices in sugar. But Sidney must quickly have outgrown the need for such inducements, becoming a fluent and enthusiastic reader. In later life he was not always realistic about the more laborious reading of others. He made a display of his own speedy and voracious reading, perhaps calculatedly, when advising an older friend, Edward Denny, whose Latin was shaky, about a course of study. After citing over twenty ancient historians, untranslated, he observed that 'this might seem too long, though indeed not so long as a man would think'.[13]

After mastering basic reading skills in English, Sidney probably started very early with French, a language in which he evidently felt at ease in later life. Lodowick Bryskett, his companion during three years of European travel, recorded the astonishment of French courtiers that the eighteen-year-old Sidney could 'speak the French language so well and aptly, having been so short a while in the country'.[14] Sidney's ease can probably be attributed to his having studied with a native French speaker from a very early age. Bryskett himself – an Italian, born about 1545, called originally Lodovico Bruschetto – may have helped Sidney with languages. He did not enter Sir Henry Sidney's service until 1564, the year Sidney entered Shrewsbury School. Confusingly, the Sidney family also employed another Italian called 'Lodowick', who was tutor to Sidney's sister Ambrosia. This Lodowick was rewarded on at least one occasion with a two-pound box of marmalade.[15] However, Philip's language tutor in his pre-school years seems to have been a French speaker, one Johan or Jean Tassel. In 1569 Sir Henry sent Tassel to Sir William Cecil to teach French to his daughter Anne, at that time the intended bride of Philip, with a warm recommendation: 'he can do it well and doubtless is very honest, he hath served me a long time'.[16] Probably Tassel was a Huguenot refugee. The Sidney family was well placed for getting to know talented refugees, for their main London residence, St Antony's, also known as 'Lady Tate's house', adjoined the church and former chantry school of St Antony's. The site was owned by the Dean and Canons of Windsor, the house being leased first to Sidney's grandfather Sir William Sidney, and then, from 1563 onwards, to his father, at an unchanged and modest-sounding rent of £6 13s. 4d.[17] The school was traditionally a rival to nearby St Paul's, the 'pigs' of St Antony's having many a street battle with the 'pigeons' of St Paul's. According to Stow, St Antony's fell into some decay in the Elizabethan period, though still functioning as a 'free school'.[18] The indenture shows that rooms formerly occupied by the resident schoolmaster were included in the property rented by Sir Henry Sidney. Most to our present purpose, the former St Antony's Church, adjoining the house and school, was leased to the French Protestant congregation of London, whose numbers were augmented by many fresh contingents of refugees during the 1560s and 70s. There was also a large French community in Canterbury, within easy reach of Penshurst. When resident in London, the Sidney family must have heard the sound of the French Protestant services through the walls of their house.

We know little of John Tassel, Sidney's first tutor. He is not even named by previous biographers. There seems to be no record of him in the registers of the French Church in London, or in surviving lists of 'denizened', or naturalized, foreigners. Yet there is no doubt of his place in the Sidney household. In 1566 Sir Henry Sidney cleared 'his debt' – presumably back wages owed to him – and gave him in addition a reward of £10, perhaps marking the conclusion of his major responsibility for Philip's tuition.[19] Even while Sidney was in his second year at Shrewsbury School Tassel seems to have played some part in his tutelage, for he is recorded as collecting 'shoes and boots' for his charge in the winter of 1565/6.[20] He may have continued to act as French tutor to Sidney during his years at Shrewsbury, supplementing the grounding in Latin and Greek provided by the school.

Geographical factors played an important part in the choice of Shrewsbury. Sidney and his friend and future biographer Fulke Greville were enrolled on 17 October 1564, both being immediately assigned to an advanced form.[21] The school was only twenty miles from Ludlow, Sir Henry Sidney's residence as Lord President of the Marches of Wales, a post he had held since the summer of 1559. The city of Shrewsbury fell within his jurisdiction, and he frequently visited it, staying in the Council House opposite the school.[22] An imaginative and innovatory 'Puritan' headmaster, Thomas Ashton, a Fellow of Trinity College, Cambridge, had been appointed in 1561, and at this date the school had about four hundred scholars. The 'Ordinances' which he drew up for the school after his retirement in 1577 probably consolidate practices already brought into effect during his headmastership. The school flourished despite an appalling lack of physical amenities. Boys were boarded out with families in the town, and the single timber-framed school building, on the outskirts, adjoined the town gaol, being approached by the inauspiciously named Ratonyslane (Rats' or Rotten Lane). The building lacked privies, boys being compelled to use a nearby field as a 'place of easement'.[23] Sidney was boarded with Mr and Mrs George Legh, and in his third year at the school stood godfather to a baby son of theirs.[24]

It is difficult to estimate how far the Lord President's son was treated as 'special', or how far he was required to fall in regularly with the exacting school routine. He may not have had to use the outdoor latrines, for the Sidney accounts refer to the purchase of a close stool specifically for his use.[25] But the detailed accounts of Thomas Marshall covering the period from December 1565 until September 1566 suggest that, with some glittering intermissions, Sidney did have to fit in to the term-time regimen. His father advised him to 'apply your study such hours as your discreet master doth assign you'. According to Ashton's timetable, this meant beginning school at six in summer, seven in winter. Presumably Sidney went back to the Leghs' house for dinner, from eleven to 12.45. Most of the authors studied were Latin; they included Cicero, Virgil, Sallust and Cato. Sidney may also have studied some Greek, such as the New Testament, and a work he responded to warmly, Xenophon's *Cyropaedia*, a fictionalized account of the youth and education of an exemplary ruler. Calvin's *Catechism* was used. The afternoon session ended at 5.30 in summer, 4.30 in winter. There may have been homework, for scholars were required on Monday mornings to 'give up their themes or epistles'.

We do not know how well the Leghs looked after Sidney, or where their house was. If we did, we would know where Sidney went to church, for scholars were required to attend church with their hosts. George Legh was a wool merchant, a bailiff of Shrewsbury and a former Member of Parliament, who owned a certain amount of land in Shropshire.[26] No doubt he lived in good bourgeois style. Sir Henry Sidney's advice to his son to drink wine now and then implies that he expected it to be available. Hollyband's *Campo di Fior* (1583) gives a vivid account of the domestic routine of a privileged schoolboy in this period, which may be similar to Sidney's. The day began with the boy's imperious commands to the maid to fetch his clothes, inkhorn, satchel, penknife and books. Some of his clothes were liable to be dirty or torn from playground activities the day before, and some of his 'points' (laces or tags used for fastenings) were either snapped or lost in wagers with other boys. At the high-grade French school in London described by Hollyband, meals were provided on the premises. There was brown bread and butter and fruit for breakfast; stewed cabbage, porridge, or bread and milk were provided for dinner (the mid-day meal), accompanied by beer or wine and water; and an excellent-sounding supper was served, starting with a 'salad cut small with salt upon it, and moistened with oil of olives ... and with vinegar', followed by stewed mutton with prunes and vegetables, or 'sometimes a very good gallimaufrey [stew], now and then a minced meat of marvellous savour'. On fasting days each boy had, instead of meat, two eggs cooked to taste, baked, fried, poached, or in the form of a 'pancake' (omelette). Unlimited bread was provided, and cheese and nuts rounded off the evening meal. These, however, were strictly rationed, as a senior pupil explains to a visiting Flemish boy (the Dutch were held to be very greedy):

> Thinkest thou that we are hogs or men? Know that this is a school, and not a place to feed cattle.[27]

While they enjoyed the school fare, the young gentlemen were also trained in manners, both at a fairly basic level – enjoined not to let their ample shirt sleeves fall in the fat, and to pick their teeth 'discreetly' with a quill, not crudely with a fork – and also at a more sophisticated level, as they practised 'pledging' each other in draughts of wine and water. For a boy who was to inherit his father's post of 'Royal Cupbearer', mastering these social rituals was particularly important. Legend has him still practising the ritual of 'pledging' on the battlefield when gravely wounded.

Sidney probably practised his table-manners at the Leghs' house in the company of his own small retinue before putting them into use during holiday visits to county families. In addition to the adults Thomas Marshall and perhaps the French tutor John Tassel, there was another little boy, Randall Calcott, who was his personal attendant and schoolfellow. (Fulke Greville lodged elsewhere.) We know more about this boy's footwear than anything else. As Wallace points out, young Randall 'seems to have been hard on shoes', getting through seven pairs in nine months.[28] Playground activities – shooting the longbow, running, wrestling, and leaping were among the games allowed by Ashton – or running errands for his young master may account for this wear and tear. But Sidney too had chronic problems with his shoes and clothes, needing, for instance, a new black cloak for his second Christmas holidays, 'not having any fit garment to go in'.[29] He also regularly required 'silk points', and radical repairs and adjustments to already patched-up-sounding shirts, coats and breeches. One example may suffice: in July 1566 Marshall paid 6s. for lining 'a pair of velvet overstocks that I made him of his old short black velvet gown'.

From documents and early lives some picture can be formed of the wearer of these patched garments. According to Moffet, he liked to read at meals, or even instead of meals:

> Scarcely was he unoccupied at breakfast, still more rarely at dinner. Indeed, in place of dinner and supper he used often to imbibe sciences, liberal arts, and every kind of discipline.[30]

So, unlike most little boys, he may have been indifferent to the attractions of gallimaufrey and savoury mince. Perhaps he also found the company of Randall Calcott and the others uninteresting. Some antipathy to his playfellows seems to be hinted at in Moffet's account of the boy Philip being often called by servants or friends to take part in games, but participating only 'negligently', for 'among those whom he could have excelled, he desired only to be an equal'. Arrogance, rather than humility, may explain the boy's reluctance to throw himself into sports with Randall and the others. Probably also, in the manner of 'gifted children', he was deeply absorbed in his own reading and train of thought, and annoyed by interruptions. His writings show his span of concentration to have been unusually long, and he may have found the shorter attention-span of his coevals tiresome. Writing as a doctor, Moffet conveys disapproval of Sidney's lack of interest in sport, even while admiring his extraordinary bookishness:

> His bedroom overflowed with elegant epistles; the master commanded his delight and joy, so far as he assigned passages for recitation to be drawn from ancient writers, or modern lore to be devoured. Nights and days in ceaseless and related studies he worked upon the anvil of wit, reason and memory, at some harm to his welfare; yet he did not wish on this account to give over literary studies, which lie in wait against health.[31]

Perhaps, like Lady Anne Clifford, young Philip Sidney pinned up favourite passages from literature on the curtains of his bed. Marshall's accounts confirm the suggestion that Sidney's health was often threatened. For instance, there was an outbreak of sickness at the school in the spring of 1566, and Philip had recurring leg troubles. These were attributable, however, to riding rather than reading. In January 1565/6 oil of roses and camomile was purchased 'to supple his knee, that he could not ply or bend',[32] and in the following summer heat and horse-riding gave him recurrent 'merry-galls', or sores caused by chafing. Reading too much and being over-serious seem also to have been perceived as problems by Sir Henry Sidney, whose letter of advice stressed the importance of merriment, and of working as much as his schoolmaster required, but not more. In October 1569, when Philip was at Oxford, Sir Henry expressed anxiety to Lady Cecil, which may have been partly an excuse for boasting:

> I fear he will be too much given to his book, and yet I have heard of few wise fathers doubt that in their children.[33]

Fulke Greville's account of Sidney's solemnity tallies with the other evidence:

> Of whose youth I will report no other wonder but this, that though I lived with him and knew him from a child, yet I never knew him other than a man, with such staidness of mind, lovely and familiar gravity, as carried grace and reverence above his years; his talk ever of knowledge, and his very play tending to enrich his mind, so as even his teachers found something in him to observe and learn above that which they had usually read or taught.[34]

The Elizabethans did not cherish childishness as such; educationalists sought to put old heads on young shoulders with all possible speed. Nor would it have suited Moffet's or Greville's larger purposes to have shown Sidney as a 'normal' boisterous schoolboy. Yet it may be that he did indeed often conform to this grave ideal, being unusually bookish and solemn. A single surviving relic of his schooldays suggests as much. Among very few books known to have belonged to Sidney there is one, now in the Walpole Collection at the King's School, Canterbury, which is probably to be associated with his first year at Shrewsbury, when he was ten. It is a copy of the French version of Bandello's romances, *Histoires Tragiques* (1561), the same collection from which Lady Mary Sidney's friend Geffrey Fenton derived his *Tragicall Discourses* (1567). The book may have been used, on Tassel's advice, to maintain Sidney's fluency in French,[35] and it is in French that he inscribed it:

Je suis apartenant a monsieur Philipe Sidnaie qui me trouve cy me rende a qui je suis [I belong to Master Philip Sidney; let anyone who finds me return me to my owner].

In a school with four hundred boys milling in and out of too small a building, books must often have gone missing. Marshall's accounts confirm this, referring to a payment of 12d. 'for a Cato, his former being lost', and an inserted note adds 'and a French grammar', presumably also a replacement.[36] Even at the Leghs' house the Lord President's son had difficulties in keeping his possessions safe, for Marshall records payments 'for mending of the lock of Master Philip's coffer and for an iron bolt to his chamber door'.[37] The page of Bandello which Sidney inscribed vividly reflects the crowded jostling of the school room, for it contains also, in a smaller, neater, hand, 'foulke grivell', and, sideways on, 'foulke grivell is a good boy witness [illegible name]'.[38] One can imagine the ten-year-old Sidney – for it is hard to believe that he was much more – rapidly writing his note of ownership in the book to secure the precious new acquisition, only to have young Greville on his left, together with another boy, annoyingly add their own notes, sideways on, in the way that schoolchildren have always done. Sidney, already a serious bibliophile, may have felt some contempt for the boys who were being so puerile around him. In turn, his preternatural solemnity may have provoked others to tease him, making his reluctance to join in games still greater. After his death Sidney's precocity was praised:

In childish years he was esteemed a man,
And half a man, more half a magistrate ...[39]

But other children, even his 'best friends', could not be expected to treat this rather self-important child with consistent deference, and they may have enjoyed getting a rise out of him, especially if, as I have suggested, he was peculiarly irascible. It must also have been extremely galling for the many less distinguished boys around him if, as Moffet and Greville both claim, Sidney was treated by his schoolmasters as having more to teach than to learn.

Yet Sidney is unlikely to have escaped all group activities at Shrewsbury School. In the passage quoted above, Moffet refers to his concentration on 'passages for recitation', which were doubtless a frequent assignment. One of

Ashton's most distinctive innovations at Shrewsbury was his encouragement of drama. Every Thursday, a half-day, the boys in the top class were required to 'declaim and play one act of a comedy' before breaking up for the afternoon. This practice may explain Sidney's ready familiarity with the plays of Terence, manifested in letters to Languet and in the *Defence of Poesy*; he also adopted a number of proper names from Terence for use in the *Arcadia*. At Easter and Whitsun 'Master Ashton's scholars' performed full-length plays in a large outdoor theatre, the Quarry, near the River Severn. According to Thomas Churchyard, a prolific poet who was a native of Shrewsbury, this arena held enormous audiences:

> Where well might sit ten thousand men at ease,
> And yet the one the other not displease.

When he comes to describe the annual performance by the schoolboys, his estimate doubles:

> At Ashton's play who had beheld this then
> Might well have seen there twenty thousand men.[40]

Churchyard's number is probably exaggerated, but there is no doubt of the fame and popularity of Ashton's productions. In 1566 the Queen herself, on Progress at Coventry, hoped to travel to Shrewsbury to see that year's play, *Julian the Apostate*, but the performances were finished, perhaps because of a plague outbreak.[41] She may have missed a chance of seeing young Sidney in a leading rôle. He must surely have played major parts in the weekly schoolroom plays, for the ability to speak well before an audience was one that he needed to master for his future career. Whether it would have been thought appropriate also for the Lord President's son to speak before the large, socially mixed audiences which flocked to the Whitsuntide plays may be open to question; but it is a possibility. The purchase in March 1565 of Radulphus Gualterius Tigurinus's book on syllables and quantities in Latin verse may be relevant here, for Ashton's plays were normally in Latin, and it seems safe to assume that rehearsals for the major play would begin some weeks before performance. Sidney's interest in metrics and verse speaking may have been first stimulated by Ashton's requirement for his top scholars both to speak and to compose Latin verse.

Sidney's later attitude to acting is paradoxical. In the *Arcadia*s he shows his young heroes as exceptionally gifted in arts of language which at times come close to acting, as when Pyrocles, dressed as an Amazon, pacifies a drunken and violent mob with a beautifully delivered speech.[42] However, in the 'New' *Arcadia* he depicts a specious villain – whose name, appropriately enough, derives from the plays of Terence – as an ex-actor:

This Clinias in his youth had been a scholar (so far as to learn rather words than manners, and of words rather plenty than order) and oft had used to be an actor in tragedies, where he had learned, besides a slidingness of language, acquaintance with many passions, and to frame his face to bear the figure of them.[43]

Probably Sidney would have seen a clear distinction between 'acting' of the kind Clinias had engaged in, and declamation or public speaking, even in disguise or fancy dress, which fulfilled serious social, moral or intellectual functions.

Whether or not he starred in *Julian the Apostate*, Sidney certainly began to play an increasingly public rôle in the summer of 1566. Fortunately this is the period covered by Marshall's accounts, so an unusual amount of detail survives. The year saw the physical withdrawal of Sir Henry Sidney, who was appointed Lord Deputy Governor of Ireland in the autumn of 1565. After saying goodbye to their son at Chester on 2 December, Sidney's parents had a wretched winter, waiting in great discomfort at Holyhead, described by Camden as 'a little poor town',[44] for favourable winds to take them across the Irish Sea. When they eventually reached Dublin, in mid-January, the storms had sunk a ship containing clothes, jewels and household stuff to the value of £500.[45] Marshall's valiant attempts to refashion his young charge's clothes should be considered against this background. Sir Henry Sidney's promotion to the Irish post, which he was to hold three times, was very costly. By 1583 he was £5,000 in debt, and had not 'so much land as would graze a mutton'.

Meanwhile, in 1566, the eleven-year-old Sidney lacked his father's presence and guidance. It was doubtless Sir Henry's departure for Ireland that occasioned the letter of advice already quoted. His attendants had to keep up the young scholar's state on slender resources. The black coat purchased by Marshall for Christmas 1565/6 may have been worn first at the civic celebrations of Christmas at Shrewsbury, which Churchyard mentions as second only to those of London in magnificence. It would certainly have been worn at Eton, near Wroxeter, where Sidney spent the New Year with Sir Richard and Lady Newport. Their daughter Magdalen was to be the mother of one great English poet, George Herbert, and patroness of another, John Donne, who in his funeral sermon for her in 1627 praised the Newport family's 'love of hospitality'. We may conjecture that the Newport household was both pious and intellectual, well suited to the serious little boy. However, Marshall's accounts record only the more mundane features of the Christmas holidays. Sidney and Randall Calcott had been prepared for the festivities by having their hair cut, and by being provided with 'certain bird bolts to shoot at birds'.[46] After the holiday, work went on at school from mid-January until Easter, on 13 April, for which Sidney was equipped by Marshall with 'a girdle of silk', a 'pair of knit hose', and a new pair of shoes. In May came the outbreak of sickness which seems to have cut short the run of *Julian the Apostate*, and Sidney and Randall spent three weeks away from school, partly with the Newports and partly with the family of Sir Andrew Corbet of Moreton Corbett, a distant relation of the Sidneys and a leading burgess of Shrewsbury. Sir Andrew's eldest son, Robert, was to accompany Sidney on his European tour, and Sidney described him to Languet as 'my greatest friend'.[47]

In the absence of his father, Sidney's other 'Dutch uncles' increasingly assumed responsibility for his care. He must surely have been beguiled by the lavishness of what they had to offer, as compared with the meagre and fast-diminishing resources of his immediate family. In June and July Marshall's accounts indicate elaborate preparations to equip Sidney for a journey to Kenilworth and Oxford, the latter to be visited by the Queen. Walter Devereux, Viscount Hereford, who was to be created Earl of Essex in 1572, gave the little boy a splendid 'red horse', perhaps bred on his estate at Chartley in Staffordshire. Whether Sidney visited Chartley at some point in his school years we do not know. Since Marshall's accounts cover only ten months out of the three or four years Sidney spent at Shrewsbury, the absence of a reference to such a visit does not preclude the possibility. If Sidney did visit Chartley during one holiday, he would have seen there a little girl called Penelope Devereux, aged no more than two or three –

> And yet could not by rising morn foresee
> How fair a day was near . . .[48]

Whether or not Sidney saw little Penelope at this stage, it was probably with the hope of eventually having him as his son-in-law that Walter Devereux cultivated his friendship and gave him the horse. As the likely heir of the two great Earls of Warwick and Leicester, Sidney already had special attractions for the impoverished fathers of daughters. Devereux's eldest son Robert, who was to become Sidney's friend, companion and military heir, was born in November 1565,[49] so Sidney's schoolboy acquaintance with him cannot have amounted to much.

Riding the red horse, for which a black-silk-fringed saddle had been made, Sidney set off for the Midlands in late July 1566. He was accompanied by his headmaster Thomas Ashton, his servants Thomas Marshall and Randall Calcott, a school friend, Edward Onslow, and his host George Legh. Large quantities of books and of shoes were carried in 'two canvas alum bags', presumably on a packhorse. After a false start and a return to Shrewsbury,[50] a diminished party – minus young Onslow and George Legh – set out again on 14 August, spending their first night at Sir Richard Newport's house at High Ercall. Marshall's accounts identify the next three overnight stops as Wolverhampton, 'Brummagem', and Hampton on the Hill. At Coventry they met the Earl of Leicester, before travelling, next morning, 18 August, to his magnificent Kenilworth Castle. This was probably not Sidney's first visit to Kenilworth, for in August 1565 the Queen had visited Leicester there, and the ten-year-old Sidney may well have been present. The 'Sidney horoscope', cast when he was sixteen, records him as having spoken before the Queen in his eleventh year, and this was probably at Kenilworth in 1565, rather than, as Osborn suggests, at Oxford in 1566. Since Sidney himself must have given the astrologer the retrospective information included in the horoscope, the reference to his age is probably correct. Unfortunately little is known of the Queen's 1565 visit to Kenilworth, except that it was apparently not a great success in terms of her relationship with Leicester. Sidney may, alternatively, have spoken before the Queen at the marriage of his uncle Ambrose Dudley to Anne Russell in November 1565, a fortnight before his eleventh birthday.

In 1566, though it lacked a royal retinue, Kenilworth seems to have been bustling and crowded, and Sidney's little party were swamped by the throngs of servants and guests in the castle.[51] However, one major benefit marked this stage of Sidney's journey. After a conference with Marshall, Leicester, himself a notoriously expensive and fashionable dresser, agreed to provide his nephew with a complete new wardrobe. This abundant collection of splendid garments put his old patched doublets and linen hose in the shade. Perhaps he passed the cast-offs to Randall. Among other things, there was a damask gown trimmed with lace, a crimson satin doublet, a green taffeta doublet, crimson velvet hose, and three leather jerkins, one, a white one, edged with 'parchment gold lace'. Perhaps this was the one to be worn in the Queen's presence. Six pairs of 'double soled shoes', white, black and blue, ensured that he would not need shoeing again for some months, though these, like the rest of the finery, may have been too good to wear in the school yard. A new pedagogue joined Sidney's party at Kenilworth, Dr Thomas Wilson, author of the amusing and classic *Arte of Rhetorique* (1553). Wilson, born *circa* 1525, had long-standing connexions with the Dudley family, and as a humanist scholar who also achieved success as a politician and diplomat he was a good 'rôle model' for the young Sidney.

After one more overnight stop the Sidney party reached Oxford, where they stayed first at an inn and then at Lincoln College. One of Leicester's chaplains, John Bridgwater, who was Rector of Lincoln, acted as host and guide throughout the fortnight of their stay. Despite the crowds assembling in anticipation of the Queen's arrival, Oxford with its sixteen colleges seemed spacious and opulent compared with the single building of Shrewsbury School. As so often in Oxford in late summer, it was pouring with rain. Two days before the Queen was expected, the Earl of Leicester, as Chancellor of the University, arrived with Sir William Cecil, the Marquis of Northampton and other noblemen. Scholars were lined up to greet them in 'Tom Quad', the great front quadrangle of Christ Church, but 'it rained so vehemently that they entered straightway into Dr Kennall's lodging'. Dr Kennall was the Vice-Chancellor. Leicester and Cecil were each treated to orations, presumably indoors, and after dinner and a disputation on the still controversial question of whether riches or poverty were more conducive to learning, they went to Woodstock to join the Queen's party. This was the Queen's first visit to Woodstock Palace since she had been there as a prisoner during the reign of her sister Mary.

On the evening of 31 August the whole royal party arrived in Oxford, travelling down the Woodstock Road. They were met on the very edge of the city boundary, near what is now the Northern Bypass, by the University dignitaries, all in formal dress, and the Mayor and aldermen. In addition to many English noblemen, the Queen's company included the Spanish ambassador, Don Guzman de Silva, who would be able to report back on the enthusiastic loyalty with which the Queen was received. We do not know where Sidney and his little retinue were, but they were probably waiting at one of the further stages of her stately journey, either at the 'Bocardo', or north, gate of the city or at her ultimate destination, Christ Church. The vision was worth waiting for. After the heralds, the Chancellor, the Mayor and the noblemen, the final and most splendid contingent followed, described here by Wallace:

> Next in order rode the royal lictors bearing huge sceptres, and then the Earl of Sussex, who carried a sword, the hilt of which was richly decorated with gold work and gems, in an elaborately chased scabbard. A short distance behind came the chariot of the Queen, slowly drawn by beautiful horses decorated with scarlet trappings. The chariot was open on all sides, and on a gilded seat in the height of regal magnificence reposed the Queen. Her head-dress was a marvel of woven gold, and glittered with pearls and other wonderful gems; her gown was of the most brilliant scarlet silk woven with gold, partly concealed by a purple cloak lined with ermine after the manner of a triumphal robe. Beside the chariot rode the royal cursitors, resplendent in coats of cloth of gold, and the marshals, who were kept busy preventing the crowds from pressing too near to the person of the Queen. Immediately behind the chariot came the royal attendants and women-in-waiting ... Then followed a number of high-bred Spanish jennets decorated with silk and gold trappings; these were led and had no riders ... The royal guard, magnificent in gold and scarlet, brought up the rear. Of these there were about two hundred ... and on their shoulders they bore huge bows and iron clubs like battle-axes.[52]

This vision of his monarch in all her power and glory cannot have failed to impress the eleven-year-old Sidney, who later showed himself acutely aware of the close connexion between visual display and effective government. In the 'Old' *Arcadia*, for instance, Euarchus ('Good ruler') did wisely consider the people to be naturally taken with exterior shows far more than with inward consideration of the material points ... in these pompous ceremonies he well knew a secret of government much to consist.[53]

But in Oxford in 1566 Sidney may also have felt painfully aware of the contrast between the splendour of the ceremonials presided over by his uncles, Sussex, Leicester and Warwick, and the discomforts and dangers probably endured by his parents at that very moment as his father struggled to establish the Queen's peace in the 'wild' parts of faraway Ireland. However, if he felt momentary anxiety or loneliness, there were many distractions. The Queen's social and verbal skills were almost as impressive as her clothes. As she passed along North Gate Street (now the Cornmarket) rows of scholars sank to their knees crying 'Vivat Regina Elizabetha!' and crowds of townsfolk took up the cry, to which she replied repeatedly, 'Gratias ago, gratias ago!' At Carfax, the crossroad which marks the intersection of Oxford's four main roads, the Regius Professor of Greek made her a Greek oration, and she replied in the same language, praising his speech as the best she had ever heard. At the door of Christ Church Hall she heard an oration by Dr Kingsmill, 'whom she thanked and assured that he would have done well had he had good matter'. She entered the cathedral under a canopy, and prayed for a while in the choir before hearing the *Te Deum* sung to the accompaniment of cornets.

For the next five days sermons, orations and disputations filled the days, and in the evenings plays were performed in Christ Church Hall. On the evening of the first full day, Sunday, there was a Latin play, *Marcus Geminus*, which illustrated, no doubt with an implied analogy to Elizabeth, the wise judgement of the Emperor Alexander Severus. The story of the calumniated senator Marcus Geminus is told in Sir Thomas Elyot's *The Image of Governance* (1550), which may have been the play's source. Its author, aged only twenty-two, is now known to have been Tobie Matthew, who later became Dean of Christ Church, then Archbishop of York, and a friend of Sidney's sister.[54] The Queen, who spent the day resting, missed it, but heard such enthusiastic reports that she resolved that she would 'lose no more sport hereafter'. The hall had been decked out with gold panelling, there was a raised stage lit with wax candles, and tiered seating had been installed. The Queen's seat, directly opposite the stage, was 'a veritable bower covered with golden hangings and furnished with tapestries and cushions'.[55]

On Monday and Wednesday *Palamon and Arcite*, a two-part drama by Richard Edwards, Master of the Children of the Chapel Royal, was performed, in English. Unfortunately the crowd was so dense at the Monday performance that a stone wall collapsed, killing three people and injuring five others, to whom royal surgeons were promptly dispatched. Despite this accident, the Queen 'laughed heartily' at the play, which was closely based on Chaucer's

Knight's Tale, and praised both actors and author.[56] *Palamon and Arcite* seems to have been performed with lively verisimilitude. A 'special effect', of a fox-hunt in the quadrangle below the hall, was so convincing that scholars looking out of the windows thought there really was a fox loose, shouting in excitement, 'Now, now! – there, there! – he's caught, he's caught!' The Queen 'merrily' remarked, 'O excellent! Those boys, in very troth, are ready to leap out of the windows to follow the hounds!' Sadly, the text of *Palamon and Arcite* does not survive, but a good deal is known about its casting. The young actors included Tobie Matthew, Sidney's future tutors Thomas Thornton and Robert Dorset, and John Rainolds, later President of Corpus, distinguished Greek scholar and author of a virulent attack on the theatre. He himself revealed that he had played the part of Hippolyta, but had subsequently come bitterly to disapprove of cross-dressing.[57] This may indicate the pressure that talented boys were under to enact female rôles. On Thursday evening a less enjoyable play was performed: *Progne*, a Latin tragedy by James Calfhill. Calfhill's Calvinism and his printed attack on a theologian (John Martiall) who had defended the Queen's use of a crucifix in her private chapel cannot have commended him to her.[58] Earlier in the day there had been a performance by the Queen herself, who made a Latin oration in the University church, St Mary's.

We do not know whether Sidney made any public oration during the Queen's visit. One young boy, Peter Carew, certainly did. His father was Dean of Windsor, and a former Dean of Christ Church. Young Carew's speech pleased the Queen so much that she summoned Cecil to hear a repeat performance, saying, 'I pray God, my fine boy, thou may'st say it so well as thou didst to me just before', which must have been extremely nerve-racking. Carew appears to have been a young boy whose voice had not yet broken, and it may have been he who played the part of Lady Amelia (Emily) in *Palamon and Arcite*, being rewarded by the Queen with eight angels for his sweet singing.[59] Young John Rainolds was given the same sum for his performance as Hippolyta. Given Sidney's special position, as nephew and heir to the Chancellor of the University, we might expect him, too, to have been put forward at some point during the Oxford junketings, but there is no evidence that he was. If he played a part in any of the plays, it would, given his age, have been that of a page or a woman, and he might, like Rainolds, have been compelled to take such a rôle whether he liked it or not. The fact that Pyrocles in the *Arcadia*, who, I have suggested, has a certain amount in common with Sidney himself, is disguised as a woman almost throughout the action of the romance, in both its versions, may reflect early experience of the paradoxical freedoms given to a youth by feminine dress. There are plenty of literary precedents for Pyrocles' transvestism, such as the story of the youth of Achilles in Statius's *Achilleid*, and episodes in the romance *Amadis de Gaul*. But one slightly odd remark made soon after Sidney's death suggests that a suspicion that he at some time wore women's clothes required to be quashed. In his completion (or reworking) of Sidney's translation of Du Plessis Mornay's treatise on the truth of the Christian religion, Arthur Golding praises Sidney for going to war in manly fashion, not 'being disguised in Ladies' attire after the manner of Achilles'.[60] More probably, though, Golding was anxious to distinguish the martial and manly real-life Sidney from the Amazonian Pyrocles.

Sidney's return to Shrewsbury, two days after the Queen's departure from Oxford, on 8 September, must have seemed something of an anti-climax. But it may also have been a relief, after the crowds, noise and high excitement. He still had the splendid clothes given him by his uncle. Marshall commissioned a special saddle and trunk embossed with the 'Warwick staff' – that is, the bear and ragged staff which was the crest of the Dudleys – to hold all the new clothes, and an extra horse, borrowed from 'Mr Yates of Gloucestershire', was used to carry this luggage. The party was augmented on the return journey by 'one Oliver, a Frenchman', from the service of the Earl of Warwick. By this stage little Sidney was bestowing as well as receiving favours. An entry in Marshall's accounts provides the earliest record of Sidney's patronage of the arts:

> Item, given by Mr Philip's commandment to a blind harper who is Sir William Holles' man of Nottinghamshire 12d.

It is not clear where the blind harper entertained the party. It may have been at Chipping Norton, or at Stratford-on-Avon, or at some inn or 'baiting place' between the two. No doubt Sidney heard and admired numerous blind musicians during his adolescence, yet it may have been this very man whose ballad singing inspired his account of popular poetry in the *Defence*:

> Certainly, I must confess mine own barbarousness, I never heard the old song of Percy and Douglas that I found not my heart moved more than with a trumpet; and yet is it sung but by some blind crowder [fiddler] with no rougher voice than rude style.[61]

Heart-stirring sounds, including trumpets, had been heard by Sidney in Oxford, and after the elaboration of those plays, debates and orations the rude eloquence of the ballad sung by Sir William Holles's man surely came as a relief. Harry Percy, whose defeat and capture are described in the 'old song' – at least, in the *Battle of Otterburn* version – had local interest for a schoolboy from Shrewsbury, for it was there that he was killed, in 1403, fifteen years after the events described in the ballad. *The Battle of Otterburn* is one of those characteristically English works which celebrate heroic defeat rather than victory. The Scots led by Douglas are shown as no less admirable than the

English led by Percy, and both leaders are true gentlemen, who pledge each other in wine over the walls of Newcastle to seal their agreement to meet and fight at Otterburn. If the same 'blind harper' regularly sang the ballad in the environs of Stratford, he may have been heard a few years later by the boy Shakespeare, whose dramatization of Percy's life and his death at Shrewsbury in *1 Henry IV* was to displace the ballad in the English imagination.

Marshall's accounts end at Michaelmas 1566, and suggest that life returned to normal at school that autumn. Lost books needed to be replaced, ink and 'points' to be bought, and a silk ribbon 'to hang his tablet [notebook] at' – perhaps one of those books without which, according to Moffet, the young Sidney would not stir. An unusually large laundry bill of 7s. 6d. reflects the unglamorous consequence of the summer's travels. This was probably Sidney's last term at Shrewsbury. On 2 February 1566/7 he was enrolled as a member of Gray's Inn, and this, combined with a record of £49 spent for his journey from Shrewsbury to London,[62] suggests that some of the year was spent there, partly at Cecil House, partly with his parents. Sir Henry Sidney enjoyed a welcome spell of leave from the Irish post in the late autumn.[63]

A reference in Sir Henry's accounts to a payment of £48 to Dr Cooper (Dean of Christ Church) for seventy-two weeks' 'diets', ending at Midsummer Day 1569, indicates that Sidney's time as an undergraduate at Oxford began in February 1567/8, when he was thirteen. Of his three years or so at Christ Church remarkably little is known. There is no equivalent of Marshall's accounts to flesh out details of day-to-day life. No record survives either of his matriculation or graduation, and what Moffet refers to in saying that Sidney 'was crowned with the first and second laurels of the literati' is unknown. Somewhere in the picture of Sidney's higher education must also be accommodated an allusion by George Whetstone, in what he claimed was a carefully 'researched' memorial poem, to Sidney as an outstanding scholar at Cambridge.[64] Cambridge University was quick off the mark in producing a learned volume of elegies for Sidney in 1586/7, and it may be that he did indeed spend some time there, but it is impossible to say when this was, or which was his college.

Sidney's only direct reference to the Oxford curriculum is somewhat disparaging. It comes in a letter of advice to his younger brother Robert, written in October 1580:

> So you can speak and write Latin not barbarously, I never require great study in Ciceronianism, the chief abuse of Oxford, *qui dum verba sectantur, res ipsas negligunt* [who while they chop up words neglect essential matters].[65]

A detailed account of a day's study by a Swiss student, Conrad ab Ulmis, at Broadgates Hall (an annexe of Christ Church) in 1552 confirms the emphasis on Ciceronianism. Cicero seems to have dominated the middle hours of the day:

> Immediately after dinner I read Cicero's *Offices*, a truly golden book, from which I derive no less than a twofold enjoyment, both from the purity of the language and the knowledge of philosophy. From one to three I exercise my pen, chiefly in writing letters, wherein as far as possible I imitate Cicero, who is considered to have abundantly supplied us with all instructions relating to purity of style.[66]

As mentioned above, Cicero's *Offices* was the archetypal 'advice to a son', and though doubtless Sidney got to know this work, and its second-hand account of Greek philosophy, extremely well, we may well believe that he found the exercise irksome, and felt in retrospect that he had learned little from it, especially as a writer. A purchase for Robert Sidney at Oxford in 1575 of 'a great paper book and Tully's Offices'[67] indicates that the Ciceronian grind continued for the younger Sidney some years after Philip had left.

Sidney lodged with the Dean of Christ Church, Dr Thomas Cooper, author of a famous Latin–English dictionary which was dedicated to Leicester.[68] If Aubrey is to be believed, there was considerable domestic tension in the Deanery. It was said that Cooper's wife was 'a shrew', who was so annoyed at her husband's staying up late night after night to work on the dictionary that she threw it, half completed, into the fire. However, 'that good man had so great a zeal ... that he began it again, and went through with it to that perfection that he hath left it to us'.[69] Sidney's first tutor seems to have been Thomas Thornton. On his young pupil's recommendation, Thornton was appointed to a canonry early in 1570, and thereafter Cooper himself seems to have acted as Sidney's tutor or director of studies.[70] Thornton, who ended his days as Master of Ledbury Hospital, in Herefordshire, was proud of his connexion with Sidney, which was mentioned on his tombstone after his death in 1629.[71] Another of Thornton's and Cooper's pupils, the future historian William Camden, may have been one of Sidney's closest friends at Oxford. Camden appears to have presented him with a copy of Horace,[72] and Sidney's undistinguished rendering of *Carmina* ii. x (*CS* 12) may belong to this time. A third tutor, Nathaniel Baxter, a Calvinist possibly attached to Magdalen, also invoked his connexion with Sidney many years later. In a strange and embarrassing poem called *Ourània* (1606), which purported to contain 'all philosophy', Baxter made a visionary armed figure of 'Astrophill' appeal to his sister, the Countess of Pembroke, for favour to his old 'reader':

> My dearest sister, keep my Tutor well,
> For in his element he doth excel.[73]

No evidence external to the poem links Baxter with Sidney, yet his reported nickname, 'Tergaster' ('Back-ster', or, alternatively, 'Three-stomached'), does sound like the kind of soubriquet Sidney, ever a player with names, might have invented, especially if Greek was what Baxter was supposed to be teaching him. Earlier published work shows Baxter to have been interested in Calvinism and in Ramist logic, both of which might have appealed to Sidney. But a translation of some of Calvin's sermons dedicated to Sir Francis Walsingham in 1578 was prefaced by a savage attack on secular fiction and poetry which can scarcely have pleased his former pupil, who by then was embarking on his *Arcadia*. Baxter refers to 'that infamous legend of K. Arthur' and 'the vile and stinking story of the Sangreal'. Judging by the quality of Baxter's own English verse, Sidney as a writer had little to learn from him.

At Oxford, as at Shrewsbury, Sidney was rather standoffish, preferring the company of his elders to that of his peer group. Moffet reports:

> He did not very willingly join in conversation, whether in light or serious vein, with the reprobate. Not upon pleasures did he spend the funds provided by the kindness of his uncles and the affection of his parents, but he distributed them either frugally for his own uses or more generously for the alleviation of learned men.[74]

Though Moffet praises Sidney's 'affability of speech' in chance encounters with learned men in the streets of Oxford – 'not by hands alone were they joined, but even by heart's desire' – it is in this same passage that he describes his treatment of his servants:

> He very seldom rebuked his servants openly or severely, when they deviated from their duty; but, speaking by a kind of circumlocution, and, as it were, distantly, he admonished them. If they lapsed too often, he punished them with words; and those continually repeating an old offence he so frightened by masculine speech that, as if leaping from a rock or struck by the final bolt of Jove, they could not lift their eyes again.[75]

Sidney's dagger-flashing letter to Molyneux, quoted above, must be a specimen of the 'masculine speech' to which Moffet refers, and it is noteworthy that it relates, not to a manifest and repeated offence, but to an imagined one. Even while praising Sidney Moffet betrays an awareness of the young man's fiery temper and readiness to feel injured.

A frequent allegation of Sidney's enemies was that he was 'proud', and this, too, Moffet unconsciously confirms in describing his demeanour at Oxford:

> He was never seen going to church, to the exercise ground, or to the public assembly hall (where he frequently employed himself) except as distinguished among the company of all the learned men. In their presence he maintained such a gravity, joined with modesty, that one did not know whether the spirit he had was rather elevated, sublime, and looking away from the world, or courteous, retiring and humble.[76]

This being interpreted suggests that Sidney, in his mid-teens, partook of the solemnity and aloofness of bearing of the much older men who were his preferred companions. Oxford in the late 1560s was full of young men who were to achieve great distinction, such as George Peele, Richard Hakluyt, Walter Ralegh, Thomas Bodley, Richard Hooker and perhaps John Lyly. But at least one of these, Ralegh, acknowledges that he envied Sidney and refused to join in the chorus of praise for him:

> I, that in thy time and living state,
> Did only praise thy virtues in my thought,
> As one that seld the rising sun hath sought ...

In asserting at the end of this elegy that after Sidney's death

> Envy her sting, and spite hath left her gall,
> Malice herself a mourning garment wears ...[77]

Ralegh seems to acknowledge that he himself disliked Sidney while he was alive – an unusual confession to make in an elegy. Another Oxford contemporary, the Cornish translator and topographer Richard Carew, elder brother of the boy whose oration had so pleased the Queen in 1566, recalled the frightening experience of being required to engage in a public disputation with Sidney:

> Being a scholar in Oxford of fourteen years' age, and three years' standing, upon a wrong-conceived opinion touching my sufficiency, I was there called to dispute *ex tempore* (*impar congressus Achilli*) with the matchless Sir Ph. Sidney, in presence of the Earls of Leicester, Warwick, and other great personages.[78]

These distinguished Earls were, of course, Sidney's uncles, but not Carew's. The occasion may have been a visit to Oxford by Leicester in June 1569.[79] If Sidney got the better of the disputation, as presumably he did, this was doubtless part of the plan for the occasion. It was increasingly Sidney's rôle to gratify older men with displays of wit, eloquence and good judgement, as can be seen from his three earliest letters, two in Latin, one in English, written from Oxford to Sir William Cecil. The Latin ones, written in March and June 1569, are little more than exercises in polite deference dressed up in elaborate language. They may have been composed as afternoon-exercises in Ciceronianism of the kind Ulmis described. However, most undergraduates did not have such grand persons to whom to send their epistles. His special position, as the darling of so many older men, must inevitably have provoked some envy and unease among talented but less well-connected contemporaries.

But his odd position must also have generated considerable frustration in Sidney himself. He cannot always have enjoyed being required to 'perform' publicly and to behave with precocious maturity. His self-projection in the figure of Philisides in the 'Old' *Arcadia* gave him an opportunity to release some of this tension. Like the young Sidney, Philisides is somewhat aloof from company, being described first as

> another young shepherd ... who neither had danced nor sung with them.[80]

When the sententious Geron ('Old man'), a composite figure, perhaps, of Sidney's many 'Dutch uncles', attempts to persuade Philisides to join in the Arcadian pastorals, he provokes the young man to a bitter attack on such Polonius-figures:

> ... herein most their folly vain appears,
> That since they still allege, 'when they were young',
> It shows they fetch their wit from younger years ...
> Old houses are thrown down for new, we see;
> The oldest rams are culled from the flock;
> No man doth wish his horse should aged be;
> The ancient oak well makes a fired block ...

Geron's sage advice to Philisides to keep himself active and well occupied with hunting, shooting and fishing falls on deaf ears:

> Hath any heard what this old man [hath] said?
> Truly, not I ...

As he grew older, this may have been how Sidney dealt with those parts of his education that did not interest him. In his literary works, he seems to take it for granted that the older generation are often tiresome. Pyrocles, for instance, asks the Arcadian rebels:

> Have any of you fathers that be not sometime wearish [peevish]?[81]

Even the exemplary Pamela concedes that her father is 'peevish', though she is bound to obey him.[82] Sidney, likewise, though frequently irked by the demands and advice of his own 'Dutch uncles', could not afford seriously to antagonize them. Too much depended on their favour.

3

1568–72

GREAT EXPECTATIONS

... To my birth I owe
Nobler desires, lest else that friendly foe,
Great expectation, wear a train of shame.[1]

For my boy, I confess if I might have every week a boy, I should never love none like him.

(Sir Henry Sidney to Sir William Cecil, 9 April 1569)[2]

I was brought up from my cradle age with such care as parents are wont to bestow upon their children whom they mean to make the maintainers of their name ... perchance by a sooner privilege than years commonly grant ... I was suffered to spend some time in travel, that by comparison of many things I might ripen my judgement.[3]

Much was expected of Sidney, and he expected much. Some of the earliest and keenest expectations focused on him were dynastic. As the only legitimate male descendant of John Dudley, Duke of Northumberland, Sidney was trained from boyhood to consider 'that my chiefest honour is to be a Dudley'.[4] He must have realized that it fell to him to rebuild the fortunes of that ambitious family. Though John Dudley's bid for control of the throne had foundered disastrously with the failure of his attempt to set up Jane Grey as Queen in 1553, it seems to have been felt by surviving Dudleys that this episode was an unlucky near-miss, not a cause for shame. Some may have felt that the desired end, of preventing a Catholic succession, fully justified the means. Sidney himself in 1584 referred to the episode merely as 'the calamities fallen to that house',[5] rebutting the charge that the Dudley line was stained by it.

Of the eight children of John Dudley who survived to adulthood, four died young. Guilford, the husband of Lady Jane Grey, was executed, along with

Paris, *circa* 1572 (Mansell Collection)

his father and Lady Jane, in February 1553/4, aged about eighteen. His eldest brother, John, was eventually pardoned for his part in the affair, but died a few days after release from the Tower of London – a residence which often undermined the health of its inmates. Two sons called Henry were killed in French wars, one at Boulogne in 1544, the other at the battle of St Quentin on 10 August 1557, an action in which his brother Ambrose received a severe leg wound.[6] As already mentioned, Ambrose Dudley, though three times married, was childless; his only son had died in infancy two years before Sidney's birth. Catherine, née Dudley, the Countess of Huntingdon, was also childless, and so, until about 1580, was Robert, Earl of Leicester. Of the four Dudleys surviving into Elizabeth's reign, then, only Sidney's mother Mary appeared to be capable of producing issue to continue the family line, together with the family tradition of service to the monarch. Even within his immediate family, expectations rested especially heavily on Philip Sidney, for until 1563 all his siblings were girls (see p. 15).

Perhaps it was a genetic advantage to her children that the Dudley heritage was tempered, in Mary's case, by that of the Sidneys. Her marriage was distinctly less grand than those of her sister and brothers. Despite his closeness to the boy-king Edward VI, Sir Henry Sidney had not reached the ranks of the hereditary nobility, though he was made a Knight of the Garter on 14

May 1564. He seems always to have been aware that his wife, as daughter to a Duke, albeit an attainted Duke, was his social superior. In Ireland he used the Dudley badge to enforce his own status. Philip openly acknowledged the relatively modest standing of the Sidneys:

> I am by my father's side of ancient and always well-esteemed and well-matched gentry[7]

– gentry, that is, not nobility. The Sidneys were highly respected and 'well-esteemed', especially in Kent, but they were not rich or famous. It was as a Dudley, and heir apparent to the two great Earls of Warwick and Leicester, that Sidney was to shine out in the courts and universities of Europe. Yet it was, meanwhile, his gentleman-father who was chiefly responsible for his education and financial support. From this many difficulties followed.

As Sidney grew towards physical and intellectual maturity a conflict appeared between two kinds of 'expectation'. On the one hand, there was the dynastic expectation just mentioned. It was rather urgent that he should marry, both to strengthen his family's political power base and to ensure continuance of the Dudley line. On the other hand, as a youth of manifest talent, who looked likely to command major diplomatic and political posts through his own abilities, he needed to complete his education at the highest level by travelling and studying on the Continent. The normal way in which these conflicting interests were reconciled was by securing either a marriage or a binding betrothal before a young aristocrat's departure, which would be completed and consummated on his return:

> By this means lengthy cohabitation was effectively postponed, and the young man prevented from getting trapped into an unsuitable marriage abroad.[8]

This seems to have been the scenario Sir Henry Sidney planned for his firstborn. Unfortunately it went wrong.

The three earliest surviving letters written by Sidney are all addressed to Sir William Cecil, from Oxford, during the years 1568–9. It was during this period that Sidney became engaged to Cecil's elder daughter Anne, then aged thirteen. A formal marriage settlement was drawn up on 6 August 1569.[9] Sir Henry Sidney approached the project with an air of naivety which he may have assumed in the hope of disarming the wily Cecil, writing to him from Ireland in April 1569:

> These things once known to you, let me know what you would have me do, and you shall find me ready. For before God, in those matters I am utterly ignorant, as one that never made a marriage in his life. But I mean truly and sincerely, loving your daughter as one of my own.[10]

As Master of the Court of Wards and Liveries since 1561, Cecil had indeed much experience in 'those matters', and brought a keenly practical eye to the negotiations. Though Sir Henry stressed his determination to give his eldest son all possible financial provision – 'I do not know above a hundred a year that I have not already assured him' – Cecil was not convinced that this would really amount to much compared with his own contribution, and perhaps he was right. Since 1564 Sidney had enjoyed the income from a church benefice in Wales, which at this time brought in eighty pounds a year; he also received the emoluments of another Welsh benefice from 1565.[11] By the terms of the marriage settlement, he was to have four hundred marks in income from land – bits and pieces in Lincolnshire, Rutland, Hampshire, Kent and Sussex – immediately on marriage, with the promise of about £150 a year more after his father's death. A 'mark' was only about two-thirds of a pound, and the total income promised, even after Sir Henry's death, came to less than £500. Cecil's doubts about what all this would add up to can be seen in a note in which he made his own detailed reckoning of 'Sir Henry Sidney's living'.[12] The truth was, as Cecil realized, that Sir Henry Sidney's government service in the Welsh borders and in Ireland was desperately costly to him, and though he did his best to see that his estates were carefully managed by reliable stewards during his absences, he was a relatively small-scale landowner. By the time Sir Henry died, Cecil may well have calculated, debts and entails could easily swallow up the modest income promised in the settlement. Philip's best chances of substantial inheritance lay with his Dudley uncles and aunt, yet this could not be absolutely assured: the birth of a son to any of them could displace him.

In the short term Anne would bring far more to the marriage than Philip. Her dowry of £1,000 was to be paid in two instalments within the first year of marriage, lands with an income of £200 were to revert to her, 'and also a dwelling house within 13 miles of London, meet for a gentleman, of £500 lands'. This was probably Theobalds, in Hertfordshire, a house enlarged and extended by Cecil until by 1585 it was a palatial residence second in magnificence only to Longleat and Wollaton.[13] For the first two years of their marriage the young couple were to enjoy 'diet and lodging' at Cecil House, so Sir Henry Sidney would be immediately relieved of day-to-day financial responsibility for Sidney and his servants. Cecil reckoned this expense as £6 12s. 3d. out of term, £6 in term, apparently per week.

Residence at Cecil House would not have been a new experience. Sidney seems often to have stayed there while in London in the absence of his parents, both before and during his years as an Oxford undergraduate. It may have been from there that he was enrolled at Gray's Inn – which was Cecil's Inn – at Candlemas 1566/7. Cecil House contained what was in effect a school for young aristocrats. During this period these included two personal wards of Cecil's who were both also possible husbands for Anne, the young Earls of Rutland and Oxford. Together, Gray's Inn and Cecil House formed a complementary pair of finishing schools for young courtiers. Cecil's curriculum for the young Earl of Oxford included, in addition to Latin and French, dancing, drawing and calligraphy.[14] At Gray's Inn participation in mock disputations and in revels and plays was obligatory, for these festivities served an educational purpose:

> Dancing, music, declamation, acting, the etiquette of a formal procession on foot or on horseback, the proper ordering of a banquet, the exchange of courtesies in speech or in writing, all these are essential parts of the elaborate make-believe. And they are there because this kind of behaviour was expected of the public figures of the age, among whom, in due course, these young men would take their place.[15]

Sidney's admission to Gray's Inn probably formed part of a Candlemas revel in 1567. His rival the Earl of Oxford had been admitted at Candlemas the previous year, which suggests a regular event presided over by Cecil, who undoubtedly sponsored the well-documented Gray's Inn revels of 1594.[16] Two plays by Oxford's kinsman George Gascoigne, the comedy *Supposes* and the tragedy *Jocasta*, were performed at Gray's Inn some time in 1566. They may belong either to the New-Year-to-Shrovetide festivities in 1565–6, or those of 1566–7; Gascoigne seems to have spent time at Gray's Inn in both years.[17] Sidney's presence at their performance is highly probable.

By the end of 1569, the year of his betrothal to Anne Cecil, Sidney was becoming a polished, precociously learned, perhaps rather stuck-up fifteen-year-old. He may still have looked very much a child, since those who met him during his travels even three or four years later were struck by his youthful appearance. His flushed, pock-marked face, his bookishness, and his edgy awareness of his expected position in the world may not have made him particularly attractive to little 'Tannikin', as Anne Cecil was affectionately called in babyhood.[18] We may notice that in writing to her father, Sir Henry Sidney mentioned his own love for Anne, but said nothing of Philip's. Anne was a much-loved daughter. At New Year 1565/6, for instance, Cecil gave Anne, then just ten, a present of a spinning wheel, accompanied by verses written by himself:

As years do grow, so cares increase,
And time will move to look to thrift;
Though years in me work nothing less,
Yet for your years and New Year's gift,
This housewife's toy is now my shift:
  To set you on work some thrift to feel
  I send you now a spinning wheel.

But one thing first I wish and pray,
Lest thirst of thrift might soon you tire:
Only to spin one pound a day,
And play the rest, as kin require:
Sweat not (O fie!); fling rock in fire;
  God send, who send'th all thrift and wealth,
  You long years, and your father health.[19]

The 'rock' was the distaff or spindle; Cecil seems to be telling his daughter to spend a little time in spinning as an instructive amusement, but not to exhaust herself with prolonged toil. The wheel was probably a miniature one, comparable with knitting and sewing kits given to small girls today, designed more as playthings than instruments of manufacture. The extent to which Cecil's own happiness was bound up with Anne's welfare is touchingly suggested in the final line.

Clearly Cecil wanted the best possible husband for his daughter. But his uncertainty about whether Sir Henry Sidney was really what Shylock calls 'a good man' – that is, financially prosperous, credit-worthy – was not the only thing which put Philip's engagement to her in jeopardy. While the young people saw each other at fairly regular intervals, and may not have been much taken with each other, Sir Henry Sidney was far away, and fast lost control of the situation. Soon after the marriage contract was signed, in September 1569, he began his second spell in Ireland, which was even more taxing and distressing than the first. Ulster he found in relatively good order, and the district round its capital, Carrickfergus, was positively flourishing, with cheap provisions, good trade relations with the west of Scotland, and abundant supplies of French wine. But Munster, the large southern province, was in a state of near-anarchy. Supporters of the imprisoned Fitzgeralds, led by the Butlers and James Fitzmaurice, brother of the Earl of Desmond, conducted a large-scale rebellion against English rule, which Sir Henry tried to quell with a succession of tribunals and executions in the course of his progress through the country. Understandably, these did not enhance his popularity. In February 1569/70 he wrote to Cecil in great anguish about the intense sufferings both of the native Irish and of his own troops, many of whom were starving. All classes of Irish society resented his policies, and he found little support or comfort in the members of the Irish Council, the body which administered English rule; several of them were too old or infirm to be of any use. Finally, 'to knit up this sack of sorrows', he felt that his own health was failing, yet not so much that he could resign from his post or die. The last sorrow of all was that Cecil had accused him of 'coldness' about the betrothal of Anne and Philip, which he vehemently denied:

For my part, if I might have the greatest Prince's daughter in Christendom for him, the match spoken of between us on my part should not be broken.

However, he had to make the embarrassing admission that his own copy of the marriage contract had somehow got lost, and acknowledged also that while immersed in the troubles of Ireland he was quite unable to turn his mind to questions of 'how and which way' the marriage was to be accomplished.[20] During this period Sir Henry Sidney seems to have had altogether a shaky control over his own family affairs, even in the most intimate matters. When his third son and last child was born, on 25 March 1569, he was given the name 'Thomas', after his uncle by marriage, the Earl of Sussex. This was contrary to Sir Henry's explicit instructions 'that if it were a boy it should have been a William, if a wench, Cecil'.[21] Cecil may not have minded too much about not being godfather to this little boy, but the mislaying of the marriage contract was extremely unfortunate for the Sidneys, giving Cecil an easy opportunity to slide out of the agreement.

Meanwhile the younger Sidney was continuing his studies at Oxford. Probably some time in 1571 a learned Oxford mathematician, who may have been Dr Thomas Allen, cast his horoscope. The document seems never to have left Oxford, and is now in the Bodleian Library.[22] There is much about it that is perplexing, and it has never been translated (from Latin) in its entirety. One major problem is how to reconcile its existence with evidence that Sidney was vehemently opposed to judicial astrology, and that this attitude was already formed at Oxford. Moffet, in describing Sidney's wide-ranging study of letters and sciences at university, is most emphatic:

Astrology alone ... he could never be so far misled as to taste, even with the tip of his tongue. Nay, he seemed purposely to slight it, among all accepted sciences, even with a certain innate loathing.[23]

The whole plot and didactic framework of the 'Old' *Arcadia* rests on Basilius's ill-judged attempt to discover his future destiny by consulting the Delphic Oracle. In so doing, says Sidney, the Duke manifests

the vanity which possesseth many who, making a perpetual mansion of this poor baiting place of man's life, are desirous to know the certainty of things to come, wherein there is nothing so certain as our continual uncertainty.[24]

In the light of this, it is exceedingly odd that the 'Sidney horoscope', which required its subject's co-operation in providing biographical details, should ever have been drawn up. But in the ferment of concern and uncertainty that built up during 1570 about whether Philip's marriage to Anne would take place, one of his 'Dutch uncles' may have insisted on a session with the astrologer, rather as a modern parent might insist on a visit to a careers counsellor. Dr Thomas Allen, if it was he who cast the horoscope, was a protégé of the Earl of Leicester.[25] Leicester seems not to have shared his nephew's dislike of astrology, but to have accepted it as an art closely allied to medicine.[26] As Chancellor of the University of Oxford he was well placed to arrange Sidney's interview with the learned astrologer. The horoscope is a sixty-two-page document, much of it highly technical. Many matters concerning Sidney's past life and future prospects are touched on. From a biographical viewpoint, the most telling passages are the consecutive ones headed *De Coniugio* ('Concerning Marriage') and *De Itineribus* ('Concerning Journeys'). The astrologer pronounces emphatically that the time which is most propitious for marriage is now, immediately after Sidney's sixteenth year. Unless this time is seized, there will not be another suitable moment for marriage for another decade. The dates here are not easy to pin down precisely. The reference may be either to the year during which Sidney was aged fifteen (November 1570–November 1571), or to the year after (November 1571–November 1572). But in either year, the ultimate purpose of the horoscope may be the same: to accelerate the pace of the match with Anne Cecil by suggesting that time is running out. Since there are no contemporary allusions to the horoscope, however, it is hard to be sure of its function and status. Perhaps its contents were communicated to Cecil, in the hope of introducing some urgency into the marriage plans. More probably, though, it may have been used to put pressure on Sidney himself, thus indicating some reluctance for marriage on his part. This would not be at all surprising, given many later instances of his reluctance to commit himself to marriage. Though the Cecil connexion was attractive to Sidney, little Anne herself may have been of relatively little interest. It is noticeable that in his three early letters to Cecil he fails to mention her, although the first two (March and July 1569) were written during the height of the marriage negotiations.

Even if Sidney was not particularly attracted to Anne, he cannot have failed to be angered and distressed at what happened next. By the summer of 1571 the Cecil–Sidney contract must be deemed to have lapsed, for Cecil (now Lord Burghley) embarked on a new project. He wrote to the young Earl of Rutland, who was in Paris, breaking the disappointing news – for Rutland, too, had had hopes of becoming his son-in-law – that Anne was betrothed to the Earl of Oxford. Cecil explained that his plan had been to wait until Anne was sixteen, which would not be until December 1572. However, to his surprise, the Earl of Oxford had asked to marry her, and Cecil had agreed, persuading himself that 'there is much more in him of understanding than any stranger to him would think'.[27] This was a generous but mistaken judgement. Cecil had already allowed his normal caution and integrity to be overruled by admiration for his ward's high rank on a previous occasion, when Oxford killed an undercook at Cecil House, Thomas Brincknell, in 1567. Cecil covered up the murder by claiming that Oxford had killed the servant in self-defence, though he later admitted that this had been a mistake.[28] It was extremely foolish of him to think this violent young man a fit husband for his beloved daughter. But in the summer of 1571 it seems that the fifteen-year-old Anne was irresistibly beguiled by the glittering prospect of becoming a Countess, and her doting father was persuaded to let her have what she wanted. Oxford was rich, worldly and showy, and many young women were 'after' him. From an early age he was a conspicuous consumer. On his father's death in 1562, for instance, the newly acceded Earl, aged twelve, rode from Castle Hedingham in Essex to London to join his guardian, Cecil, accompanied by 'seven score horsemen' in black liveries. The spendthrift ways which were eventually to drive him to make over Castle Hedingham to Cecil and to beg him for money may at this early stage have seemed fitting and attractive for a young man whose Earldom, along with the hereditary post of Master Chamberlain, went back to the twelfth century. Contemporary comments on Anne Cecil's marriage suggest that she took some initiative. A more candid account than Cecil's is given in another letter to the young Earl of Rutland, from Lord St John:

> The Earl of Oxenford hath gotten him a wife – or at least a wife hath caught him – that is, Mistress Anne Cecil, whereunto the Queen hath given her consent, the which hath caused weeping, wailing and sorrowful cheer of those that hoped to have had that golden day. Thus you may see whilst that some triumph with olive branches, others follow the chariot with willow garlands.[29]

In addition to the willow-wearing court ladies, there was at least one willow-wearing young man, Anne's previous fiancé. However lukewarm he may have been over the match, it was intensely galling to see Oxford's wealth and rank preferred to his own talent and promise. The animosity between Sidney and Oxford that exploded into murderous hatred in 1579–80 probably began in 1571. Both young men were choleric, Oxford to an almost psychopathic extent, and both were intensely proud, Oxford matching Sidney's neurotic loyalty to his Dudley lineage with a fiercely arrogant awareness of being the seventeenth Earl of Oxford.

It is difficult to know what deeper impressions the collapse of his first attempt at marriage made on Sidney. Possibly it induced extreme, self-protective caution in this area, for he did not finally marry until he was nearly thirty, an advanced age for an Elizabethan aristocrat whose dynastic responsibility was heavy. No doubt he realized smugly that he would have been a better husband to Anne than Oxford. That would not have been difficult. In 1576, for instance, Oxford was to deny paternity of their first daughter, refusing for some months to speak to any member of the Cecil family. Apart from his appalling marital behaviour, his close involvement with his Catholic cousins the Howards, including, in the first year of his marriage, some complicity in the 'Ridolfi plot' which led to the execution of the Duke of Norfolk on 2 June 1572, must have been deeply distressing to the Protestant Cecils. Lady Cecil seems never to have liked Oxford, and it was a pity that her counsels did not prevail. She seems, on the other hand, to have been extremely fond of Sidney. As his mother-in-law, she could happily have joined the ranks of well-educated older women who presided over his career, for she was born Mildred Cooke, most learned of the five learned daughters of Edward VI's tutor Sir Antony Cooke. She took a particular interest in the Eastern Church Fathers, translating part of St John Chrysostom from Greek into English. Her daughter Anne's aptitude was less markedly impressive. Yet she too seems to have been able to write, at least in English, and perhaps used writing to reflect on her wretched life. Concealed in the middle of a mediocre collection of poems obsequiously addressed to Oxford, John Soowtherne's *Pandora* (1584), are four epitaphs by her on the only boy to whom she gave birth, the short-lived fruit of conjugal relations with Oxford resumed in 1582. The metre of the poems is so uncertain that I suspect them to be authentic; someone, such as her father, helping with them would surely have regularized them. It should be said, however, that there is some resemblance to Soowtherne's own faltering lyrics, and it is possible that he is their author.[30] This specimen is characteristic:

> With my son, my gold, my nightingale and rose,
> Is gone: for 'twas in him and no other where:
> And well though mine eyes run down like fountains here,
> The stone will not speak yet, that doth it enclose.
> And destin's, and gods, you might rather have ta'en here
> My twenty years, than the two days of my son.

Whether Anne herself wrote them, or the possibly pseudonymous 'Soowtherne' wrote in her person, the artlessness of the poems is extremely touching. The anguish of Anne's plight, with production of a living male child her only available route to favour in her husband's eyes, was probably not lost on her childhood fiancé. Sidney must have followed the course of Anne's unhappy marriage with intense interest, and it may have had some impact on his fiction. The 'New' *Arcadia* includes several images of wretchedly unhappy marriages, most notably the tragic story of Erona, briefly married to the insolent Antiphilus. Antiphilus is base-born, which was not one of Oxford's handicaps. But Erona, a carefully brought-up girl who falls disastrously in love with someone quite unsuitable living in her father's house, does seem rather like Anne Cecil. The suggestion that the two princes ought to be rescuing the imprisoned Erona instead of pursuing their own amours could have some applicability to Sidney's own impotent misery about Anne in the later 1570s. In real life, the end of Sidney's betrothal to Anne was in some ways disappointing but in others liberating. While he missed the opportunity of close alliance to the Queen's longest-standing, most trusted and most influential counsellor, he gained a certain freedom to forge other links, both in England and on the Continent. This was the next stage of his expectations.

Sidney's first trip abroad happened at an exciting time. In the spring of 1572 hopes were high in England that the position of the French Protestants, who included many leading noblemen and intellectuals, was on the point of being officially secured, with the blessing of the almost all-powerful Queen Mother, Catherine de' Medici. Three months of negotiation by an Anglo-French committee produced the mutually supportive Treaty of Blois, signed in draft on 19 April 1572, before the official simultaneous signing in France and England planned for the summer. By the terms of the treaty, the French agreed not to help Catholic Spain in any attack on England. The imminent marriage of Catherine de' Medici's youngest daughter, Marguerite de Valois, to the Protestant Prince of Navarre, Henri de Bourbon, appeared to be a most promising indication of a future in which Catholics and Protestants might at last co-exist peacefully in French territories, after years of conflict and persecution and the flight of many Huguenot refugees. Perhaps the Anglo-French alliance would even serve to challenge Spanish rule over most of the Netherlands. Some dreamed of expelling the Spaniards and dividing up the Dutch provinces three ways between the House of Orange, already leading effective rebellion against Spanish rule, the French and the English. The most exciting possibility of all was that Queen Elizabeth might marry one of Catherine de' Medici's younger sons, Henri, Duke of Anjou, or François, Duke of Alençon.[31] By this time the likelier spouse was the younger and less physically appealing François, who had, however, the advantage of appearing flexible in matters of religion. A climate of religious tolerance might make the match acceptable to at least a proportion of Elizabeth's courtiers, though Sidney's uncle Leicester was not of their number. For the time being this marriage scheme was in abeyance, but if all went well after the official signing of the treaty, much might be accomplished.

The Treaty of Blois provided the occasion for the first stage of Sidney's Grand Tour. An old family friend, Edward Fiennes de Clinton, was appointed head of the English delegation, and Sir Henry Sidney arranged for the seventeen-year-old Philip to be attached to his large party of English noblemen and gentlemen. Clinton was a long-standing associate of the Dudleys, and as Governor of the Tower in 1553 he seems to have had some complicity in their attempt to put Lady Jane Grey on the throne. He weathered the Jane Grey storm better than they did, becoming a successful military commander under both Mary and Elizabeth. For young Sidney, Clinton had an additional element of glamour unrelated to his military achievements. His third wife was Elizabeth, née Fitzgerald, who had been celebrated in a sonnet by the Earl of Surrey as 'Geraldine'. Though Clinton was a man of action rather than of letters, attracting no literary dedications, his marriage to 'Geraldine' linked him with an English poet uniquely praised by Sidney in the *Defence of Poesy* as having written 'many things tasting of a noble birth, and worthy of a noble mind'.[32] Surrey's poetic celebration of 'Geraldine' moved from actuality to legend in a manner comparable to Sidney's of Penelope Devereux, and Sidney himself was later seen as Surrey's poetic heir.[33] His journey to France with 'Geraldine''s husband may have started him thinking about the rôle of the Tudor court poet; and for special reasons the Earl of Surrey may have been in many minds, for even as Sidney and the rest were en route from London to Paris, on 2 June 1572, Surrey's son, the Duke of Norfolk, was beheaded for his plot to marry the Queen of Scots.

For 'Geraldine''s husband, Edward Clinton, the journey to Paris was the high point of his career. He was fifty, an advanced age in Elizabethan terms, and in order to give him a status befitting his mission, the Queen, notoriously stingy with honours, created him Earl of Lincoln. One of many embittering experiences for the Sidney family was that at the same moment the Queen also offered Sir Henry Sidney a barony, but in default of any accompanying gift of money or land he felt obliged to refuse it, and his wife asked the Queen not to raise the matter again.[34] However, hope and distraction were surely provided by the pressing need to equip young Philip for his adventure. His passport, which survives in the archives of New College, Oxford, was signed by the Queen on 25 May 1572, probably a day or two before the expedition began.[35] It gave him permission to travel overseas for two years, 'for his attaining to the knowledge of foreign languages', with three servants, four horses, and no more than £100, together with 'bags, baggages and necessaries'. A hundred pounds, for what was to turn out to be three years on the Continent, was manifestly inadequate, and further instalments of £120 or so dispatched by his father at regular intervals left him still in need of credit. Nor was the requirement in the passport that Sidney was not to 'haunt or keep company with' any unlicensed English exile to be strictly observed: he consorted with several Catholic exiles in Venice, such as Sir Richard Shelley and Edward, Lord Windsor. Sidney's gentleman companion was a man who has already been mentioned, Lodowick Bryskett, later to become a close friend and colleague of Edmund Spenser in Ireland. He was presumably licensed in a separate passport, and may have had his own servants and horses. Sidney's three servants were a retainer from Penshurst, Harry White; a Welshman, Griffin Maddox, who acted as secretary and personal attendant; and one John Fisher.

We do not know the names of the horses, nor whether any of the four survived the three-year peregrination. Nor do accounts survive to tell us what clothes, books and other necessaries were taken, but some splendid outfits would have been needed for Sidney's attendance at the French Court. Since this was an educational tour, a substantial nucleus of books and writing materials must have been carried; and a case of medicines and cordials would have gone in, perhaps including marmalade, the specific against sea-sickness. Sidney was vulnerable to infection and stress. He had spent what may have been his last Oxford term – either summer or autumn 1571 – at Reading, where students were taken to avoid a long-drawn-out plague outbreak in Oxford.[36] Though he appears to have escaped infection on this occasion, Moffet, Marshall's accounts, and the 'Sidney horoscope' all concur in indicating that Sidney was often laid low in various ways – sore legs, infected eyes, fever and general weakness.[37]

It must have been with considerable anxiety that his family saw young Philip off for his journey to one of the most congested and filthy cities in Europe. Elizabethan travellers such as Thomas Coryat were eager to associate the Roman name of Paris, Lutetia, with *lutum*, 'which signifieth dirt, because many of the streets are the dirtiest, and so consequently the most stinking, of all that I saw in any city in my life'.[38] In appearance, the city Sidney saw was quite unlike the Paris of today. It was strongly fortified, surrounded with thirty-foot-high walls with an earth dyke outside, and visually it was dominated, in a manner now hard to imagine, by its medieval churches, colleges and religious houses, mostly of grey stone. Then as now, many English visitors felt its cathedral, Notre Dame, to be less impressive than the great cathedral of Amiens, often viewed en route. It was on 8 June that the large English mission arrived in Paris, or rather at the abbey of St Denis, two miles outside the walls, where the Marshal de Cossé, deputizing for the King, gave them an excellent dinner. No letters from Sidney himself survive from the first year of his travels, so his impressions can only be conjectured. A letter from Leicester to Walsingham, resident as English ambassador in Paris at this time, suggests some nervousness among Sidney's older relations about how well the boy would cope with his new experiences:

Mr Walsingham: For as much as my nephew, Philip Sidney, is licensed to travel, and doth presently repair to those parts with my Lord Admiral, I have thought it good to commend him by these my letters friendly unto you as to one I am well assured will have a special care of him during his abode there. He is young and raw, and no doubt shall find those countries and the demeanours of the people somewhat strange unto him; and therefore your good advice shall greatly behove him for his better direction, which I do most heartily pray you to vouchsafe him ... His father and I do intend his further travel if the world be quiet and you shall think it convenient for him.[39]

This letter, dated on the same day as the passport, ensured that Sidney would not lack 'Dutch uncles' on the other side of the Channel. Though he cannot have known it, he was leaving behind a father-in-law manqué, Cecil, for a father-in-law to be, Francis Walsingham. But this relationship was more than ten years off, and his future bride, Frances, whom he probably saw first in Paris, was at this time only five. For some, at least, of his three months in Paris, Sidney stayed in Walsingham's house, on the Quai des Bernardins. But he may not have taken up residence there until the bloody deeds of St Bartholomew's Day began. In the first three weeks he can be assumed to have lodged and dined in some splendour with the English mission, attending the many merrymakings which followed the signing of the Treaty of Blois on 15 June. These included feasting, music, the performance of an Italian comedy, wrestling, and acrobatics. The weather was hot, and an outdoor supper given by the Duke of Nevers, Louis de Gonzaga, in his park was agreeable after several days of crowded indoor ceremonies in the Louvre and the Château de Madrid.

Lord Lincoln's delegation left Paris on 23 June, and from then on Sidney's little party was probably under the guidance and protection of Walsingham. There was no let-up in the succession of junketings. The King, Charles IX, had a particular, even perverted, obsession with slaughtering animals, which went well beyond the pleasure in hunting and animal-baiting common to most aristocrats at this period. He was quite capable of alleviating boredom by putting penned-up deer to the sword, or of baiting such exotic animals as lions or leopards. St John's Eve, 23 June, was observed as a great midsummer feast all over France, and was marked in Paris this year with an exceptionally vile *pièce de résistance* in which a bag full of live cats and a fox was suspended thirty feet up over a huge bonfire, until the flames pulled the screaming mass down.[40] There seems little doubt that Sidney would have witnessed this spectacle in the Place de Grève. There is reason to think that in later life he had a distaste even for the ordinary English field sports. According to Sir John Harington, 'the noble Sir Philip Sidney was wont to say; that next hunting, he liked hawking worst'.[41] Exposure to such large-scale and pointless cruelty to animals as Paris gave him in 1572 may have stimulated him to align himself with the humanists Erasmus, More and Calvin, and against the vast majority of his less reflective contemporaries, as one who viewed the killing of animals except for food as a degrading and disgusting activity.[42] A poem explicitly rooted in his continental travels suggests as much. The beast fable against tyranny beginning 'As I my little flock on Ister bank' concludes with an appeal for tenderness towards the lower orders of creation. Its political application functions fully only if it is accepted also on a literal level:

But yet, O man, rage not beyond thy need;
Deem it no gloire to swell in tyranny.
Thou art of blood; joy not to make things bleed;
Thou fearest death; think they are loath to die,
A plaint of guiltless hurt doth pierce the sky ...[43]

More 'plaints of guiltless hurt' besides those of the wretched cats were soon to be heard in Paris. There was a succession of troubling events, and storm clouds were gathering. The Prince of Navarre's mother, the Protestant Jeanne d'Albret, died very suddenly on 9 June, and Protestants suspected that she had been murdered. Charles IX somewhat provocatively wore mourning for only seven days, because of the Treaty of Blois. The Protestant Admiral Coligny had persuaded Charles to give active support to the rebellion against Spanish rule in the Netherlands, but this was not going well. On 17 July the Duke of Alva routed a large combined French, Dutch and English force at Mons, which had been taken some weeks earlier by troops led by Lewis of Nassau. The Catholic majority in Paris rejoiced at this event, and were becoming dangerously excited and over-heated. Sidney was in process of making many new friends among the Protestant intelligentsia, but at least one of them, the innovatory logician Pierre de la Ramée (Ramus), was not to outlive August.

Before the storm broke, there was one happy interlude for Sidney. On 9 August the French King created him a 'gentleman of the bedchamber' and a baron. The reasons for this were doubtless political and diplomatic, and honour was being done, via Sidney, to his father and his Dudley uncles, as well as to the English Crown. The title was of no value back home: Elizabeth I liked to say 'My dogs wear my collars', and Sidney had to maintain a tactful silence about this foreign honour in later years. He may in any case have soon come to feel disgusted by it. Nevertheless, to the ambitious seventeen-year-old so recently disappointed by his father's refusal of an English barony, the French title probably gave keen, though momentary, pleasure. Lodowick Bryskett was particularly remembering the occasion of Sidney's investiture when he recorded the good impression made by Sidney's fluency in French:

He was so admired among the graver sort of courtiers that when they could at any time have him in their company and conversation they would be very joyful, and no less delighted with his ready and witty answers than astonished to hear him speak the French language so well and aptly, having been so short a while in the country.[44]

Sidney's early lessons with Mr Tassel stood him in good stead. But Bryskett too was a fluent linguist, and his pride in Sidney's skill reflects his own success as Sidney's later instructor.

Yet another round of festivities preceded disaster. On 18 August the long-expected marriage between Marguerite de Valois and Henri de Bourbon, now King, rather than Prince, of Navarre, was solemnized. The ceremony took place on a specially constructed stage outside Notre Dame, and was followed by a nuptial Mass inside the cathedral in which the bride alone participated. The bridegroom's Huguenot followers were soberly dressed, in contrast with the flashing yellow silks and jewels worn by the Valois brothers and their supporters. Ominously, the bride, who had been pre-contracted to the Duke of Guise, refused to voice her assent to the marriage, but the King pushed her head forwards to signal assent, and the service continued. Sidney presumably watched the outdoor ceremony, and participated in the subsequent feasting and entertainment. This included yet more disgusting animal shows. One consisted of a three-cornered fight between a lion, an ox and a white bear, which ended in confusion with many human casualties when the bear broke loose into the crowd. There was some suspicion that the King had condoned, or even arranged, this threat to his humbler subjects, in contrast to Queen Elizabeth, who is recorded as having cried out, when a baited bear once broke loose at Whitehall, 'Spare my people, spare my people!', being delighted that no one was killed. The French 'safety record' for public spectacles was appalling, and Catherine de' Medici's husband, Henri II, had been killed accidentally in a tournament in 1559.

In scale and splendour, however, these festivities were overwhelming. A 'Triumph' at the Louvre in which Charles IX and his two brothers sat on top of three great silver rocks drawn on wheels probably outshone anything Sidney had seen before, even when the Queen came to Oxford in 1566. Splendid masques followed, but their connotations were ominous. In an allegorical show on the third day of feasting, Henri of Navarre was driven to hell by the Valois brothers, seated in heaven; the Protestants were confined in 'hell' for a whole hour, which must have generated some tension. In the fourth and final day's masque the Valois brothers and the Duke of Guise were disguised as Amazons, defeating Henri of Navarre and the Huguenots, dressed as Turks. Sidney was to put his own romance hero, Pyrocles, into Amazon disguise, though with less sinister implications. His recollections of the foppish Valois in Amazonian costume were probably vivid. The identification of the Huguenot nobility with the pagan and all-dreaded Turks was not a good sign for the future, and it is surprising that they were willing to adopt this rôle even in sport.

On 22 August the most eminent Huguenot in Paris, Admiral de Coligny, came away from watching the King and the Duke of Guise playing tennis. As he strolled along the street he was struck by an assassin's shot from a window. His assailant's aim was poor, and only his hand and arm were injured. Messages of sympathy from the King provided temporary reassurance, and many visitors, both Catholic and Protestant, came to condole with Coligny in his house in the Rue de Béthisy. Sidney may well have been among their number. However, the leaked news that the would-be assassin was an employee of the Duke of Guise raised the temperature to a fearsome level. During the weekend of 24 August, St Bartholomew's Day, the organized massacre of Protestants began. Guise's mercenaries broke into Coligny's house and finished off what the previous assassin had bungled. Thousands of Huguenots, high, low, men, women and children, were slaughtered all over Paris. A domino effect provoked massacres of Protestants in other large French towns during the next fortnight. For Protestant visitors to Paris, Sunday, 25 August, was a terrifying time. On the Queen Mother's orders church bells were rung from the early hours of the morning, a terrible signal that the killings were to begin. Leading Huguenots were dragged from their houses and slaughtered openly in the streets and squares. Some bodies were strung up on gibbets, others thrown into ditches or into the River Seine. In the courtyard of the Louvre there was a heap of two hundred corpses of Huguenots who had supposedly been enjoying royal protection. Inevitably, the crowds got out of control, and plunder and random killing were added to the sectarian violence. Wherever Sidney had been lodging previously, he certainly took refuge at this stage in Walsingham's house. A young English medical student, Timothy Bright, recalled having met him there when they both fled from the terror.[45] Bright was to be the author of a classic *Treatise on Melancholy* (1586), inventor of the earliest English system of shorthand, and also author of an abridgement of John Foxe's accounts of the sufferings of the English Protestants under Mary Tudor. He dedicated this last to Walsingham, acknowledging that he owed his life to his protection, without which 'myself, with a number more, should at that butchery of Paris now long ago been martyred'.[46] Without Walsingham's protection, Sidney too might well have been killed.

For all the Englishmen staying in Paris, the events of August 1572 must have been memorably terrifying. The casualties included some of Sidney's new friends. The distinguished logician Pierre de la Ramée at first took refuge in a bookshop just off the great booksellers' street, Rue St Jacques. Thinking all was now safe, he returned to his lodging at the Collège de Presles on Tuesday, 26 August, where he was repeatedly stabbed as he knelt in prayer, his body being thrown into the street below. Many such chilling stories could be told. Estimates of the total numbers killed vary, but they were certainly no fewer than three thousand. Fortunately the English ambassador and those taking refuge with him had one protector among the Catholic aristocracy. The Duke of Nevers, whose outdoor dinner party in June has already been mentioned, made himself responsible for shepherding Englishmen away from danger zones, and offered courtesy and protection to Walsingham. His motives may have been prudential. If English visitors had been killed, the sharp frost that descended on Anglo-French relations when news of the massacre reached Elizabeth would no doubt have been an ice age.

Back in England, Sidney's anxious family seem to have assumed and hoped that these events would bring a speedy end to the boy's Grand Tour. On 9 September the Privy Council wrote to Walsingham instructing him to procure a safe conduct for Sidney's return home. However, by the time the letter reached Paris, in mid-September, it seems that Sidney and his party, augmented by a new travelling companion, John Watson, the Dean of Winchester, were already on their way to Germany. It is difficult to know whose decision this was. Sidney must have guessed that his family would want him to return home, and it could certainly not be said that the condition set out by Leicester for his tour – 'His father and I do intend his further travel if the world be quiet' – had been fulfilled. However, there may have been an atmosphere of some urgency, and Walsingham may have seized the first opportunity to get the English party out of Paris, accepting a French safe-conduct for them as soon as he could, and sending them on the route along which many other Protestants were fleeing. If Sidney himself had been desperate to turn back for England at this point, he could surely have waited longer at Walsingham's house in the hope of finding some means of doing so, or he could have taken a route back home by way of Germany. It seems that he was not so shaken by the horrors he had witnessed as to have lost his appetite for travel. Paris, to which he never returned, had shown him some revolting spectacles of bigotry, hypocrisy and cruelty. In 1580, dissuading the Queen from her threatened marriage to Alençon, he was able to remind her 'that his brother made oblation of his own sister's marriage, the easier to make massacres of all sexes'.[47] But the stay in Paris had also brought him certain benefits. Though the French title of 'Baron' had no value in England, it was not without its pleasing side. More importantly, Sidney had made an enormous number of new acquaintances and friends, from the King of Navarre downwards. He may have encountered some of the leading Renaissance poets of the age. Pierre Ronsard and Salluste du Bartas were both in Paris at this time. Young friends whom he first got to know there included Philippe du Plessis Mornay, the Huguenot aristocrat and theologian, and the young Count of Hanau, both of whom also fled to Germany from the massacre, and with both of whom he sustained particularly warm friendships. Older friends, besides the murdered Ramus, included the Strasbourg lawyer Jean Lobbet, who was to become a frequent correspondent, and concerned himself closely with the education of Philip's brother Robert; and probably the former Chancellor of France, Michel de l'Hôpital, an intellectual and poet who sought common ground between Catholics and Protestants. L'Hôpital was not well known in England as a poet, but Sidney paid handsome tribute to him in the *Defence of Poesy* as pre-eminent among 'grave counsellors' who had also been poets:

> than whom (I think) that realm never brought forth a more accomplished judgement, more firmly builded upon virtue.[48]

L'Hôpital may have been one of the 'graver sort of courtiers' who, according to Bryskett, particularly enjoyed conversing with Sidney. He died in 1573.

Another older friend was the distinguished printer and bookseller Andreas Wechel. He had already been driven out of Paris once, in 1568, but was re-established there from June 1571. Like other printers and booksellers of the period, Wechel included among his activities the provision of accommodation for scholars, on generous terms, and Sidney may have lodged with him for a while in Paris, as he was later to do in Frankfurt. During the St Bartholomew's Day Massacre many Protestant booksellers were killed and their stock burnt. Wechel, too, lost his stock, but managed to escape to Frankfurt with the help of yet another of Sidney's older friends, the diplomat Hubert Languet. Languet was to preside genially and protectively over Sidney's career for the next ten years, extending the limited political horizons offered by his previous 'Dutch uncles' with his deep knowledge of the affairs of Europe. On Languet's side, at least, the friendship took on the warmth of a love affair. Though Sidney often felt stifled and irritated by Languet's emotional demands, he may initially have found his intensely expressed affection and solicitude much more congenial than the severe and patronizing exhortations of his father and uncles. By the autumn of 1572, marriage and domesticity were no longer in prospect for Sidney; he was in for a long spell of the kind of relationship to which he was most accustomed, with a new father-figure who was determined to do all he could to put a wise head on his young shoulders. He was also in for a great deal of travelling.

4
1572–5
SIDNEY'S GRAND TOUR

Hard sure it is to know England, without you know it by comparing it with others.[1]

Through many a hill and dale,
Through pleasant woods, and many an unknown way,
Along the banks of many silver streams
Thou with him yodest [travelled]; and with him didst scale
The craggy rocks of th'Alps and Apennine,
Still with the Muses sporting, while those beams
Of virtue kindled in his noble breast
Which afterwards did so gloriously forth shine.[2]

The song I sang old Languet had me taught,
Languet, the shepherd best swift Ister knew ...[3]

Even to contemplate Sidney's European travels is exhausting. After his hasty departure from Paris in September 1572 he travelled over an extraordinarily wide area of central Europe, visiting some cities, such as Strasbourg, Heidelberg, Frankfurt and Vienna, several times. The powers of horsemanship suggested by his Christian name, Philip, or 'horse-lover', were called upon to the full. He did not generally travel by the shortest possible route, and sometimes doubled back or took detours to include visits to the houses and estates of his new-made friends among the German aristocracy. At times he may, as in the joking fancy at the beginning of the *Defence of Poesy*, have 'wished himself a horse' rather than endure the leg sores, constant shaking and exposure to the elements to which his human condition condemned him. Sidney's itinerary as shown on the map (see pp. 66–7) does not indicate the actual routes he covered, only the major cities he visited. For instance, from November 1573 until August 1574 he was based in Venice and Padua, moving between the two

Venice, *circa* 1570 from Braun and Hogenberg, *Civitates orbis terrarum*, Cologne 1575–99 (Mansell Collection)

cities at least ten times, and often spending little more than a fortnight in one before going back to the other. Though this was a journey of little more than fifteen miles, and probably undertaken by barge rather than on horseback, each transfer entailed the usual business of packing up, securing lodgings (in Venice, at least – in Padua he seems to have kept the same lodgings in the Pozzo della Vacca), paying reckonings, and arranging for correspondence, which was fast becoming voluminous, to arrive at the right place. Even if Lodowick Bryskett, Griffin Maddox and John Fisher saw to most of these practical details, the continual upheaval must have been disruptive to concentration.

We have no direct reminiscences by Sidney of his travels. But the long second book of the 'New' *Arcadia*, where Musidorus tells Pamela, in successive instalments, about the past adventures of himself and Pyrocles, may partly reflect his own journeyings. If we place the fiction beside the documented actuality, however, we can see that a transforming alchemy has been at work. The Arcadian princes are shown as having encountered dragons, tyrants, shipwrecks, misers, civil wars and lustful women, proving themselves adroit and courageous in meeting all these challenges. Sidney, on the other hand, encountered enormous numbers of learned men, and frequently had to call upon social skills of a less dramatic kind in playing them off against each other. While the Arcadian heroes are shown as splendidly in control, heroes of their own tales, who through valour and effortless superiority are able to sort out the affairs of many misgoverned states, Sidney, during his most extended period of travel, was still a student, and under the control of others. Judging by the copious correspondence surviving from these years, his chief problem was not how to ward off the advances of amorous female rulers but how to placate and reassure the numerous old men eager to advise him. Throughout the period of the Grand Tour Sidney seems to have been dodging some older men while consorting with others. The independence and freedom of Pyrocles and Musidorus were what he longed for, but rarely achieved.

In addition to his long-term educational itineraries, to Vienna, then to Venice, back to Vienna again, and then to Prague before a gradual return home in the spring of 1575, Sidney made three excursions to more challenging destinations. They were not as challenging as he would have liked – he wanted to get both to Rome and to Constantinople – yet each had the character of an escapade. In each case he covered several hundred miles for a surprisingly short visit. The first was in August 1573, when he went to Pressburg (now Bratislava) in Hungary, enjoying feasts and 'carousals' with the learned Dr George Purkircher.[4] One of his companions was probably the distinguished botanist Charles de l'Ecluse, or Clusius (1526–1609), whom he had met in Vienna. De l'Ecluse was gardener to the Emperor Maximilian II, and sustained a vigorous correspondence with Sidney in later years on matters of friendship, current affairs and rare plants. John Buxton describes Sidney's visit to Hungary as a 'holiday' from Hubert Languet's 'oppressive paternalism'.[5] It is characteristic of Sidney's long-term interests that for him a holiday spot was a landlocked battle zone. The trip took him close to the Ottoman Turks, against whom he hoped one day to fight, perhaps under the leadership of the famous Hungarian general and military theorist Lazarus Schwendi.[6] As he recalled in his *Defence of Poesy*, Hungary offered threefold pleasures of drinking parties, songs and perpetual battle-readiness:

> In Hungary I have seen it the manner at all feasts, and other such meetings, to have songs of their ancestors' valour, which that right soldierlike nation think one of the chiefest kindlers of brave courage.[7]

The second excursion is the most thought-provoking from the point of view of Sidney's aesthetic development. In March 1574 he went to Genoa and Florence from Venice, returning within a little over four weeks. It may have been to this journey that Bryskett referred in remembering how he and Sidney scaled 'The craggy rocks of … Apennine, / Still with the Muses sporting …'

Carrickfergus
Galway
Dublin
Shrewsbury
Kenilworth
Oxford
London
Thames
Wilton
Plymouth
Antwerp
Bruges
Brussels
Paris
Seine
0
300 Mls
0
500 Kms

Cologne
Eisenach
Leipzig
Weimar
Dresden
Rhine
Frankfurt
Prague
Nuremberg
Heidelberg
Brno
Cracow
Passau
Danube
Ortenburg
Vienna
Pressburg
Wiener
Neustadt
Innsbruck
Bad Villach
Klagenfurt
Udine
Verona
Padua
Venice
Genoa
Florence
N
Sidney's 'Grand Tour'
May 1572 June 1575
Journey by boat

Genoa was the homeland of Bryskett's family, and for him it may have been a moving return to his roots. Regrettably, however, we know very little about the excursion from Sidney's point of view, except that once again, as when he went to Hungary, Languet reproached him bitterly for slipping the leash. Sidney's third excursion, in the autumn of 1574, was from Vienna to Cracow, where he had at one point hoped to see the installation of the French Crown Prince, Henri of Valois, as King of Poland. However, by the time he set out, Charles IX had died suddenly, and Henri had fled to secure the throne of France. A legend originating apparently in the early seventeenth century that Sidney himself hoped to become King of Poland is unlikely to have any basis in fact. Certainly a letter to Leicester written immediately after his 'Polish journey' gives no hint of this, offering only some rather complacent reflexions on the confusion of affairs there:

> The Polacks heartily repent their so far-fetched election, being now in such case [as] neither they have the king, nor anything the king with so many oaths had promised.[8]

Osborn calculated that the round trip from Vienna to Cracow amounted to about 550 miles, requiring 'close to forty miles in the saddle for each of fourteen days'.[9] If Sidney and Bryskett were indeed 'Still with the Muses sporting' as they trotted up and down central Europe, it is no wonder that Sidney wrote in *Astrophil and Stella* that his Muse

> Tempers her words to trampling horses' feet
> More oft than to a chamber melody . . .[10]

The melancholy lethargy of his *alter ego*, Philisides, whom we first see 'lying upon the ground at the foot of a cypress tree, leaning upon his elbow', could be partly a product of the sheer exhaustion of jogging hither and thither. Like Philisides, Sidney returned eventually to England/Arcadia as an alienated 'stranger', mysteriously weary and preoccupied, and in no mood to receive yet more advice from pompous old men.[11]

Yet it is clear that Sidney intensely enjoyed travelling, and was eager to extend his knowledge of men and cities. This eagerness, heightened by the respect and admiration with which he was received by dozens of eminent men, outweighed the inevitable aggravations of fatigue, illness, shortage of money and repeated episodes when he was robbed or cheated by landlords or travelling companions, or believed that he had been. He had resisted an appeal by his family to return home directly after the massacre in Paris, and he probably resisted subsequent appeals. None of his father's letters to him during this period survives. Sidney outstayed the leave of absence given on his passport by a whole year, and there is no evidence that he was given an extension. Even when he neared the end of the third year Sidney was not in a hurry to return home, for in the spring of 1575 he hoped to stay long enough in Frankfurt to have another extended meeting with Hubert Languet.[12] But by the time Languet reached Frankfurt, instructions had arrived from Leicester that Sidney was to go home by the most direct route, via Antwerp, pausing only long enough to meet the English envoy Thomas Wilkes in Heidelberg. By this time, Sidney was deep in debt to many of his continental friends, and had been persuaded by Languet to accept his life savings. Fynes Moryson estimated that £50 or £60 a year should suffice for a gentleman's travels in Europe; but he was only a 'private gentleman', not a leading courtier.[13] Sidney got through five or six times this sum in each of his three years abroad. Part of his trouble, financially, was that he needed 'spare' money to give away or lend, so that he could present his new acquaintances with an appearance of munificence, or even of 'magnificence'. It has been nicely suggested that for the Elizabethans the distinction between these two Aristotelian virtues was that the second was 'practised by the very rich, instead of by the moderately rich, man'.[14] An appearance of 'magnificence' would certainly not have been attainable on Sir Henry Sidney's allowance alone, though he seems to have been as generous to his son as his limited means allowed.

However eager continental noblemen and humanists were to make the young Englishman's acquaintance, it seems that, like the wealthy Portia in Shakespeare's *Merchant of Venice*, many of them expected some show of munificence from him in the initial stages. Sidney told his brother that 'much expense' was one of the means to the friendship of 'worthy men', and that in Italy this would be his largest outlay.[15] One documented instance of a 'worthy man' whose attachment was consolidated in the early stages with a gift of money suggests that there may have been many others. Théophile de Banos, minister of the Huguenot church in Frankfurt, was a friend and devoted disciple of the murdered logician Ramus. In a fulsome dedication to Sidney of his own commentaries on Ramus in 1576, prefixed by a biography of him, de Banos stressed Sidney's love and admiration for the dead scholar. Voluminous letters from de Banos to Sidney both before and after publication reaffirm his respect for him. However, it should also be noticed that in April 1575 de Banos had written to thank Sidney for what seems to have been a very handsome present of money, dispatching the normal token of esteem offered by the less wealthy to the more wealthy, a ring.[16]

No doubt Sidney's personal charm, learning and interest in Ramus and Ramism all played a part in persuading de Banos to dedicate his book to an Englishman of only twenty. But it is impossible to avoid a suspicion that a display of 'magnificence' at a crucial stage of Sidney's travels, when he was particularly anxious, having consorted with Catholic exiles in Venice, to signal his Protestant allegiance, helped to consolidate de Banos's attachment. Then, as later, Sidney felt it important to give money away even though his immediate resources were all but exhausted. John Buxton claimed that de Banos 'neither expected nor received any payment' for his dedication.[17] But the letter in which he thanks Sidney for his munificence, comparing him with Alexander the Great, had not then come to light. Sidney seems also to have given de Banos an inflated notion of his own aristocratic status and connexions, which led to embarrassment after his return to England. He implored de Banos to modify the emphasis, in the floridly complimentary printed dedication, on his descent from the Earls of Warwick. But de Banos still did not get Sidney's English status (or lack of it) quite right, addressing a letter to him at Court as 'Monseigneur Philippe Comte de Sidne'.[18] Youthful shows of 'magnificence' on the Continent had eventually to be paid for in the damper, more constrained climate of England.

Sidney's attitude to money was humanly inconsistent. While he seems to have expected that Languet, Leicester, or other older men would eventually settle the money debts he ran up during his travels, he did sometimes press continental friends for repayment of his loans/gifts to them. For instance, in the summer of 1577 he used Languet, rather embarrassingly, as a debt-collector, in trying to recover some money from a Bohemian nobleman, Michael Slavata.[19] His anxious insistence on this suggests that the sum was a large one.

Both practically and intellectually, Hubert Languet was the presiding influence over Sidney during his Grand Tour. Born at Vitteaux in Burgundy in 1518, Languet had for some years been in the employ of the Elector of Saxony. He was at the forefront of political and religious thought among continental Protestants. It was under his influence that his pupil Philippe du Plessis Mornay wrote the famous treatise *De Vindiciae contra Tyrannos*, suggesting circumstances in which it was lawful to resist monarchical rule or tyranny. These theories had special and urgent relevance to the increasingly concerted rebellion against Spanish rule in the Netherlands, a topic of absorbing interest to Sidney. Languet spoke no English, so his face-to-face meetings with Sidney must have kept the latter's French in excellent repair, while their regular correspondence served, among many other functions, to maintain his fluency in Latin. Languet effected many introductions to individuals who were to become Sidney's friends. He advised Sidney on his academic studies and transmitted up-to-date news and opinions on political and military matters. His exact status in relation to Sidney is not clear. Previous biographers have claimed, following Fulke Greville's account of Sidney and Languet 'chancing' to lodge together in Wechel's house in Frankfurt, that Languet spontaneously decided to undertake the rôle of intellectual mentor to the promising and attractive young Englishman.[20]

However, other assertions made by Greville are demonstrably false, such as his claim that Languet was Sidney's companion throughout the three years. His suggestion that the friendship sprang from a chance meeting, though flattering to Sidney's charm, is questionable. It seems more likely that Walsingham, acting on the instructions of Leicester, set up the initial meeting between Languet and Sidney, either in Paris or in Frankfurt, on the understanding that Languet would take on his tutelage. He may even have been paid a retaining fee. Sir Henry Sidney's confidence, some years later, that Languet would perform practical services for Robert Sidney implies this.[21] In this period friendships, like marriages, were rarely the product of unrehearsed impulse. Sidney's frequent restiveness is most readily explained if his friendship with Languet was an extension of that Polonian control over his education and development exercised by his English advisers.

There is no doubt that Sidney liked and admired Languet, and enjoyed the social and intellectual worlds to which he gave him access. But he also found many of his exhortations wearisome, and politely disregarded them. Some of them were tediously familiar. For instance, Languet sent him back yet again to the study of Ciceronian style, of which, after Shrewsbury and Oxford, he was surely weary.[22] His polite echoing of Languet's praise of Cicero, taken in conjunction with the presumably more candid attack on Ciceronianism in writing to his brother (see above, p. 39), calls in doubt the sincerity of many of his dutiful responses to Languet. His repeated 'slipping of the leash', when he went on excursions of which he knew Languet would disapprove without telling him his plans, is rather noticeable.

As well as advising Sidney on reading and study, Languet also undertook to shape his career in a broad way, trying to steer him away from two opposite courses of action. One was retirement from Court, which he felt would waste his political and diplomatic talents; the other was active military service, which would jeopardize his health and survival. In later years Sidney succumbed to both these temptations. He indulged in prolonged spells of withdrawal from Court, staying with his sister; and he also, four years after Languet's death, engaged in active military service, which did indeed imperil his life. These were by no means the only exhortations from Languet which Sidney resisted. During the years of the Grand Tour he was exposed to a constant barrage of kindly advice, both in letters and through direct contact. Osborn estimated that the two men spent at least forty weeks in each other's company. Languet also wrote to Sidney every week when they were apart, and of his letters written during this period more than forty survive. From them we can learn much about what Sidney was like at this time, or at least how he came across to older men.

Languet felt Sidney to be too solemn for his years. (We may recall Sir Henry Sidney's advice to his son, aged eleven, to 'give himself to be merry'.) By frequent ironical or jesting sallies he tried to stimulate Sidney to levity. Not knowing the English language or English culture at first hand, he may often have struck the wrong note when attempting this delicate task, misjudging the kind of thing Sidney found funny. For instance, in January/February 1574 Languet gave a facetious account of dozing off and allowing the book he was reading, Humfrey Lhuyd's treatise on ancient Britain, to fall into a candle and be burnt. He suggested that Sidney should commission his Welsh servant Griffin Maddox to solemnize Lhuyd's funeral, the book standing for the man. Sidney dutifully reported that Griffin had made a funeral oration in Welsh, at which he himself assisted 'with laughter'. But he probably felt uncomfortable about this, for Lhuyd had been a protégé of Sir Henry Sidney, who had paid for the posthumous completion of the book whose claims for the antiquity of Celtic culture Languet found so absurd.[23] Sidney also reported, 'joking apart', that Griffin Maddox had defended some parts of Lhuyd's scholarship, and supported this with his own opinion; Languet was compelled to concede the point.[24] Languet seems to have been unimaginative about how deeply even the most sophisticated Elizabethans were attached to Tudor claims for the

Celtic roots of British culture, and his attempt to make Sidney laugh may have served only to make him bristle, touchy as he was on questions of lineage.

Other exhortations missed their mark. For instance, Languet was anxious that Sidney should learn German, urging him to improve both his spirits and his language skills by 'playing and jesting' with Matthaus Delius, a former pupil of Philip Melanchthon. This time Sidney was frank about his reluctance to co-operate. He disliked the peculiar 'harshness' of the German language, and deflected Languet's jest with another, saying that he would practise the language with Delius 'particularly while I am toasting him'.[25] Since the convention was to use the Latin *Prosit* when exchanging toasts, such conviviality was not likely much to advance Sidney's fluency in German.[26] It may be a reflexion of Sidney's attitude to the language that one of the few German words to find its way into his writings is a term of abuse, *Schelm* or 'rascal'.[27]

Sidney's excursion to Genoa and Florence in the spring of 1574 was undertaken in direct contravention of Languet's advice. Languet thought that the only part of Italy deserving of his charge's study was the Venetian republic, and feared that other Italian states would prove dangerously corrupting. Sidney did not fulfil Languet's very worst fears by visiting Rome, but it may have been practical considerations, rather than obedience to the old man's wishes, that held him back.

Languet also fussed over more trivial matters. He worried about Sidney's tendency to eat what he regarded as excessive amounts of fruit, and to drink too much water in hot weather.[28] These habits, he felt, threatened serious digestive disorders to Sidney's slender frame. It may also have been with Sidney's health in mind that Languet advised him to travel by coach or covered waggon, which was a normal mode of transport in Germany and Bohemia at the time.[29] Though safer and more comfortable than riding on horseback, this method of transport was a good deal slower, and given the number of miles Sidney regularly covered it is unlikely that he availed himself of it. Also, he may have considered it unmanly. According to Aubrey:

> I have heard Dr Pell say that he has been told by ancient gentlemen of those days of Sir Philip, so famous for men at arms, that 'twas then held as great a disgrace for a young gentleman [cavalier *deleted*] to be seen riding in the street in a coach, as it would now for such a one to be seen in the streets in a petticoat.[30]

Dr Pell's mother, Mary Holland, came from Halden in Kent, where the Sidneys owned land; he may have had access to accurate recollections of Sidney and his circle. A belief that coaches were fit transport for women and old men (like Languet) but not for vigorous young 'cavaliers' is also indicated in the 'New' *Arcadia* when the elderly Basilius, his wife and younger daughter ride in a coach, accompanied by the 'cavalier' Pyrocles, who is indeed in a 'petticoat', or at least Amazon attire.[31] This situation is one of the feminizing humiliations that ensue from his disguise.

Advice with more far-reaching implications was Languet's repeated entreaty to Sidney to marry. Some passages in the letters convey a generalized wish that Sidney should reproduce himself.[32] Others clearly allude to particular women, but are hard to decode.[33] There may be some reference to an abortive scheme for Philip, and possibly also Robert, to marry one of the daughters of Henry, Lord Berkeley, nicknamed 'Henry the Harmless'. Not much is known about this project, which derived from a desire to end a long-running feud between the Berkeleys and the Dudleys. If it had come off, it would have made Sidney chief heir to the enormous Berkeley estates. It would also have given him a powerful mother-in-law, Catherine Howard, sister of the executed Duke of Norfolk. She was a fluent linguist, a stickler for protocol and so addicted to falconry that her dresses were covered with bird-droppings.[34] However, the birth of a son, Thomas, to the Berkeleys on 11 July 1575 made the daughters no longer such attractive prospects, and in any case the Sidney–Berkeley project seems to have collapsed by then.[35] Sidney was out of England for the whole time that it was under consideration. When pressed hard on the subject of marriage, he was able to point out that Languet himself had never married. He took no decisive steps towards matrimony, despite repeated pressure from Languet and others, until two years after Languet's death.

Given all these instances of Sidney's resistance to Languet's advice, it is difficult to know how wholeheartedly Sidney responded to Languet's devotion. If, as I have suggested, the friendship was not spontaneous in its early stages, Sidney's guarded responses to Languet's emotional demands are partly explained. In Languet's effusive declarations of attachment he may have detected an element of emotional blackmail which would, if accepted, deprive him of new and precious independence. Much of the surviving correspondence is taken up with anguished complaints by Languet that he has received no letter from Sidney for far too long, and self-righteous counter-claims by Sidney, pleading sometimes that he has been overwhelmed by business, at others that he has been consumed with lethargy. After his return to England he allowed a whole five months to elapse before writing to the old man, despite receiving letters from him as regularly as usual. Even allowing for the fact that fewer of Sidney's letters have survived, the balance of the correspondence is heavily on Languet's side. Languet's letters are also longer and more carefully written. Though it was Sidney himself, writing from Venice in December 1573, who first proposed that they should exchange letters once a week,[36] he seems to have made this proposal chiefly to reassure Languet, who was already, at this very early stage of their friendship, accusing him of dereliction. For a variety of reasons, Sidney was quite unable to sustain the commitment to write to the old man every week, especially when his correspondence with other continental friends had begun to proliferate. Those other friends became increasingly important to him, and it is they who account for Sidney's intense enjoyment of travel and reluctance to return home.

It was not primarily a search for the picturesque that drew Sidney to the great cities of central Europe. He cannot have failed to observe the splendour of many Renaissance palaces, the paintings and artefacts they contained, their ornate gardens and exotic menageries, their great banqueting halls and council chambers – not to mention the marvels of Gothic castles and cathedrals, and even such mechanical wonders as the astronomical clocks to be seen in the town squares of several cities, such as Strasbourg and Prague. Indeed, he certainly did notice such things, for visual details in the 'New' *Arcadia* can be seen to reflect his response to these material wonders. Yet he may also have viewed the Ruskinian splendours of pre-Baroque Europe with a loyal Tudor Englishman's eye, like that of Fynes Moryson. Summing up what he had seen during travels even more extensive than Sidney's, Moryson ranked the tomb of Suleyman the Magnificent in Constantinople in third place, after the tomb of Henry VII in Westminster Abbey and the sepulchre built by Cardinal Wolsey in St George's Chapel, Windsor.[37] The praise of Kalander's house in the 'New' *Arcadia*, which has often been plausibly linked with Sidney's native Penshurst, suggests a positive distaste for architectural elaboration:

> The house itself was built of fair and strong stone, not affecting so much any extraordinary kind of fineness, as an honourable representing of a firm stateliness ... all more lasting than beautiful, but that the consideration of the exceeding lastingness made the eye believe it was exceeding beautiful.[38]

When advising his brother Robert on travel, Sidney dismissed the claims of architecture on his attention, saying that 'houses are but houses in every place', differing only in size.[39] In a letter now lost, he gave a disparaging account of the city of Venice, which has enchanted so many other English travellers, and there is no evidence that he was distressed or in any way moved by the burning of the Doges' Palace in 1574. When he had his portrait painted by Paolo Veronese, his interest in it, at least as communicated to Languet, did not extend beyond the question of how long the sittings would detain him in Venice when he was impatient to return to Padua. People and ideas, not buildings, were what Sidney found most interesting. At the beginning of the 'Old' *Arcadia* he is scathing about Pyrocles' apparent interest in architecture and painting, provoked by a sight of a portrait of Philoclea:

> Desirous he was to see the place where she remained, as though the architecture of the lodges would have been much for his learning; but more desirous to see herself, to be judge, forsooth, of the painter's cunning.[40]

Art-appreciation here takes second place to an intense interest in human individuals, and this is apparently how it was for Sidney. He wrote to Languet from Venice just before Christmas 1573, anticipating a meeting with him in the spring: 'I shall take more delight in one conversation with you than in the magnificent magnificences of all those magnificoes.'[41] But since Languet was so fearful that Sidney might succumb to the Siren-like charms of Italy, it was particularly important for him to convince the old man that he was immune to them. With hindsight, we can detect more interest in art and architecture on Sidney's part than we would ever guess at from his letters. Subtly observed references to the art of painting in the 'New' *Arcadia* show that the secular and mythological paintings of Titian, Tintoretto, Veronese and the central European Mannerists were not lost on him.[42] But his responses to visual experience were not communicated to Languet, nor was it for the sake of such experience that he travelled. His quick visit to Florence, for instance, was governed by an interest in its political system, not in the art of Giotto and Brunelleschi.

Unlike painting and architecture, literature is something which we can be sure preoccupied Sidney. Yet this, too, was an interest which he did not choose to share with his mentor Languet. Most of the allusions to poetry in the Sidney–Languet correspondence concern either political verses or the relationship between the two men. For instance, Languet himself, not noted as a poet, wrote some Latin verses in praise of Sidney, inspired by an image of him made by the Imperial portrait medallist Antonio Abondio.[43] Sadly, neither the portrait nor the verses are known to survive. Hints of Sidney's own dawning interest in literature are given by his tendency to illustrate his letters to Languet with literary analogies, often from the plays of Terence, or from Virgil, Xenophon, Ovid or Aristotle's *Rhetoric*. Languet's references are more often to philosophers and historians. Reading between the lines, we may see that Sidney's literary interests were wider than Languet's, and it may be that the works he cited apparently for rhetorical purposes often meant as much to him as the political and historical writings which he explicitly discussed with Languet.

But one literary pleasure which Sidney did share with Languet was book buying. Together they attended the Frankfurt Book Fair in the spring of 1573. Later correspondence shows his continued interest in this great twice-yearly book market. Only one of Sidney's purchases abroad is now known to survive, a copy of Guicciardini's history of Italy, bought in Padua on 20 June 1574, and now in the Widener Library, Harvard.[44] But numerous allusions to book buying indicate that the collection Sidney gathered during his Grand Tour must have been substantial. Early on in his friendship with Languet, for instance, he offered him a choice of five handsome volumes published in

Venice, including Girolamo Ruscelli's beautifully printed *Imprese Illustri*. This contained at least one device relating to a new friend and kinsman of his, the Catholic Richard Shelley, showing an eagle releasing a dove from its claws, with the motto FE Y FIDALGUIA. It is not clear whether the five books Sidney enumerated were ones that he had already bought, or books that he planned to buy on Languet's behalf, on the understanding that the latter would foot the bill. Most probably he had already purchased them, for in the same paragraph he lavishly offered to pay five times the normal price for Amyot's translation of Plutarch.[45] His eagerness to acquire so many volumes suggests that he was little constrained either by a wish to economize or by a need to travel light. Amyot's version of Plutarch (from which 'Shakespeare's Plutarch', Sir Thomas North's English translation, derives) consists of two large folios. The elegance of Venetian printing, with its use of italic typefaces and many emblematic initials and ornaments, must have contributed to Sidney's pleasure in acquiring these books, which he called 'choice' or 'elegant'.

According to a recent theory, another elegant book that Sidney purchased in Venice was Jacopo Sannazaro's verse-and-prose romance *Arcadia*, in Sansovino's 1571 edition, which has numerous attractive woodcuts.[46] This purchase was momentous for Elizabethan 'Golden' literature, for it determined the title and genre of Sidney's own *Arcadia* and also, if the theory is correct, the format, at least, of Spenser's *Shepheardes Calender* (1579), designed to recall to its dedicatee, Sidney, the Sannazaro volume. Later allusions firmly establish Sidney's knowledge and appreciation of Sannazaro's romance, and his failure to mention it to Languet may confirm our suspicion that there were large areas of literary and aesthetic experience which he did not choose to share with his distinguished mentor. Despite his barrage of heavy-handed teasing, Languet took Sidney's career extremely seriously, and his plans for him probably left little room for pastoral and amorous poetry in a language with which he was unfamiliar.

Some broader bookish interests were shared between Sidney and Languet. In particular, they had a common acquaintance with a number of distinguished scholar-printers. The learned Andreas Wechel, already mentioned, was host to both Languet and Sidney in his 'white house' in Frankfurt, and possibly earlier in Paris. An even more remarkable scholar-printer, the French humanist Henri Estienne (Henricus Stephanus), met Sidney in Heidelberg, Strasbourg and Vienna, and paid the high compliment of dedicating his edition of the Greek New Testament to him in 1576. On their second meeting, in Strasbourg, he gave him a collection of Greek maxims penned by himself, which regrettably does not survive.[47] This probably consisted of selections from his *Apothegmata Graeca*, printed in 1568. Estienne, perhaps the most distinguished Greek scholar of his own or any generation, praised Sidney's intellectual growth between their three meetings, and anticipated that he would appreciate the physical appearance of both the handwritten and printed Greek, as well as grasping its meaning. Whether Sidney went to 'much expense' to secure the attachment of Estienne, we do not know. Estienne's claim that Sidney's Greek was so good that he had no need of translations[48] seems exaggerated, and it is a little surprising that such a significant work as Estienne's edition of the New Testament should be dedicated to a twenty-one-year-old Englishman who as yet lacked aristocratic status. He addresses Sidney as a young man 'in all ways most generous', which may indicate that he is using the Latin *generosus* in its more modern sense of 'lavish', as well as the older 'noble-minded'. But perhaps in this instance Sidney's own learning, his Protestant allegiance and the recommendation of Languet were enough to secure the dedication, without a great display of 'magnificence' on Sidney's part.

The rest of Sidney's continental acquaintance has been amply chronicled by Buxton and Osborn. Buxton explored Sidney's patronage with elegance and authority, and Osborn documented his correspondence and personal meetings in somewhat wearisome detail. In some ways Sidney's Grand Tour is *too* well documented, through surviving letters many of which are now in the Osborn Collection at Yale. A full catalogue of all those Sidney met, met again and corresponded with is beyond the scope of the present study. In any case, relatively few of those 'persons of importance in their own time' with whom Sidney parleyed can be shown definitely to have influenced his own writings. There is no doubt that his circle was extraordinarily wide. His friends ranged from princes and noblemen such as the future French King, Henri of Navarre, the Palatine Prince John Casimir, and the Count of Hanau; English Catholics, such as Edward, Baron Windsor, and Sir Richard Shelley, both resident in Venice; eminent scholars and academics, such as Crato von Crafftheim, the Emperor's physician, Jean Lobbet, professor of law at Strasbourg, and Johann Sturm, also of Strasbourg. Sidney's circle included also many envoys and ambassadors, such as Wolfgang Zündelin, a German agent based in Venice, and Jean de Vulcob, a French agent at this time based in Vienna. There are also some less distinguished persons who figure in the correspondence about whom one would like to know more. One such is the amiable-sounding man with whom Sidney lodged in Strasbourg, the bibulous Hubert de la Rose.[49]

But surviving documents, though copious, are often disappointing in terms of what they tell us about Sidney's personal development. Many of his most faithful foreign correspondents are more than a little tedious, dispatching flowery and calligraphically penned epistles in which remarkably little seems to get said. No doubt many of these letters are exercises in diplomacy rather than expressions of personal feeling. Many Protestant intellectuals were genuinely anxious to strengthen their links with someone whom they perceived (perhaps mistakenly) as a significant figure at the English Court, but the rhetorical nosegays they tossed across the Channel were apt to be rather dry and artificial. It is not surprising that Sidney soon began to fall behind with his replies to these epistles, and disappointed his friends with the shortness and infrequency of his own letters.

There remains a small handful of friends encountered by Sidney during his travels whose literary interests do seem to anticipate his own. The most obvious of these was his gentleman-companion Lodowick Bryskett, with whom he did not need to correspond, for they were together almost throughout the three years. Bryskett was a linguist, scholar and poet, and acted as Sidney's courier and guide, travelling with him on almost equal terms, and commanding the respect of many of Sidney's new humanist friends.[50] There were other Italians whose writings Sidney may have admired. For instance, Languet at several points commended to him the epistolary style of Pietro Bizzari (1530–86), a historian who was a native of Perugia. Bizzari was among that group of Protestant scholars sheltered by Walsingham during the Parisian massacre, who must have felt themselves bound together as veterans of that fearful time. He was a passionate Anglophile who had visited England in 1565, and dedicated a collection of essays and poems to Queen Elizabeth in the same year. Other English dedicatees in Bizzari's volume include the Earl of Bedford, the Marquis of Northampton and the Earl of Leicester. In a longish poem Bizzari celebrated the beauty and virtues of Anne Russell, on the occasion of her marriage to Sidney's uncle the Earl of Warwick.[51] In spite of his praise of his style, Languet seems not altogether to have liked Bizzari, finding his language too ornate and his manners too obsequious.[52] Perhaps he was also rather jealous of him, for Bizzari was a paid agent of the English Crown, receiving a salary of 'one hundred talers' in return for which he sent regular newsletters to Burghley,[53] as well as a rival 'elder statesman' figure in young Sidney's affections. Bizzari was a fluent occasional poet in Latin, using pastoral dialogue and other forms of lyric poetry for oblique political comment. His Italian account of the Hungarians' battles against the Turks must also have interested the battle-hungry Sidney.[54] However, like Languet, he may have found Bizzari in person rather wordy and embarrassing, perhaps one of those Italians he warned his brother against:

> For the men you shall have there [in Italy], although some indeed be excellently learned, yet are they all given to so counterfeit learning, as a man shall learn more false grounds of things, than in any place that I do know, for from a tapster upwards they are all discoursers [chatterers].[55]

An Italian friend whose interests were more exclusively literary, and whom Sidney may have found more congenial, was Cesare Pavese. He lived in

Venice, and was a close friend of the poet Bernardo Tasso, father of the more famous Torquato. Bryskett's decision to base his two elegies on Sidney on poems by the elder Tasso may hark back to the time he and Sidney spent together in Venice, with Cesare Pavese a 'missing link'. The timing of their respective visits to Paris and Venice makes it unlikely that Sidney and Torquato Tasso ever met in person,[56] but Pavese, friend of both the Tassos, could provide Sidney with indirect knowledge of them, and of the younger Tasso's great work in progress, *Gerusalemme Liberata*. The two surviving letters to Sidney from Pavese are mainly concerned with practicalities. He seems to have been responsible for forwarding Sidney's letters and belongings from Venice, and to have tried to liaise with Bryskett on these matters. Pavese's connexion with the Tassos, combined with his own literary productions, makes it probable that he was also a partner in some of Sidney and Bryskett's poetic 'sports'. Pavese is respectfully mentioned in the preface to Torquato Tasso's *Rinaldo* (1562), and he himself, under the pseudonym 'Pietro Targa', composed a delightful collection of verse fables, in Italian, derived from Aesop and others. They are set out in the manner of an emblem book, each headed by a lively woodcut. The third fable is one to which Sidney alludes several times, in which an ass, jealous of the affection lavished on a little dog, leaps up on his master's lap, but is beaten back.[57] Another story important for one of Sidney's early poems appears only three pages later, based on the Aesop fable in which the frogs ask Jove to give them a king. This is among several models for Sidney's own political beast fable (*OA* 66). No doubt he was already familiar with Aesop, but Pavese's attractively amplified and illustrated version may have given a particular stimulus to his interest in those poets who

> sometimes, under pretty tales of wolves and sheep, can include whole considerations of wrong-doing and patience.[58]

Pavese also wrote a preface and notes to an Italian translation of Statius's *Thebaid* (Venice, 1570), in which the classical epic, rendered into *ottava rima*, is accommodated to the form of an Ariostan Italian romance, and dedicated to two ladies of the Este family, Lucrezia and Leonora. This work, newly published when Sidney was in Venice, may have contributed to his incipient interest in the vernacular 'heroic poem' as a genre which carried serious import in a medium attractive and accessible to a female readership.

Sidney's closest Italian friends were charming and thought-provoking 'discoursers'. But more weighty literary and intellectual preoccupations were sustained by some of his French friends. Chief among these was the great Protestant theologian and political theorist Philippe du Plessis Mornay. Mornay was completing his own Grand Tour, which included visits to London and Rome, just as Sidney was in the earliest stages of his, and they probably first met at the time of the Parisian massacre. Their common experience of the horrors of August 1572 was only one of many bonds between them. Another was their interest in Ramist logic, for Mornay had been one of Ramus's pupils. Another, and closer, bond was the tutelage of Languet, whose relationship with Mornay was even deeper than that with Sidney. Yet another bond was Sidney and Mornay's shared knowledge of the cultivated society to be found in the French embassy in Venice, presided over by the enlightened Arnault du Ferrier. Du Ferrier was a man of breadth and tolerance, and at one point Du Plessis Mornay almost succeeded in converting him to Protestantism, or so his loyal wife claimed.[59] French Protestant intellectuals found shelter in the embassy, and one of them, François Perrot de Mésières, became a friend and correspondent of Sidney. In one of his six surviving letters to Sidney, from Venice, 26 November 1574, he mentions both a satiric poem on the state of Poland and some 'Italian verses' of his own which he sends to Sidney at his request.[60] These were almost certainly some of his verse epitomes of the Psalms, which were published as *Perle Elette* ('Chosen Pearls') in 1576, and dedicated to the Senate of Venice. Alternatively, they may have been some of his full metrical versions, half of which were published, as *Settacinque Salmi di David*, in 1581.

Perrot, born in about 1530, led a colourful life. As a very young man he had fought with the forces of Suleyman the Magnificent against the Persians. Early in life he decided that his true vocation was to be a poet, but his father forbade him, directing him instead to the study of law. Something similar had happened to Sidney's companion Bryskett, who had been attracted early on to the study of literature, but was compelled by his father to study medicine:[61] both were later to 'sport with the Muses' in Sidney's company. In 1564 Perrot was studying theology in Geneva when his wife died, and he had to go to Paris to establish the legality of his Protestant marriage and his own claim for custody of his infant daughter, Esperance. He was successful, and dedicated the French version of *Perle Elette, Perles d'Eslite*, to Esperance, by then aged about twelve, in 1577.[62] Perrot had to go to Geneva to arrange publication of all these works, which would not have been acceptable to Catholic censors either in Paris or in Venice, where the singing of vernacular Psalms was forbidden. Like many of Sidney's continental correspondents, he looked to England for protection, and perhaps an ultimate haven from persecution. But he was unlucky with his crowning achievement, a complete Italian version of the *Salmi di David*. It was published in Geneva in 1603 and dedicated to Queen Elizabeth, but by the time it appeared she had just died.[63] Though Perrot's six lengthy letters to Sidney are largely occupied with news and current affairs, especially concerning France, the single allusion to his 'Italian verses' makes it clear that he also shared with him in literary projects. Yet another bond between Perrot and Sidney was formed by the writings of Du Plessis Mornay, for Perrot translated Mornay's *De la vérité* into Italian, and Sidney began, at least, to translate it into English.[64]

The courage and tenacity of Huguenot writers such as Du Plessis Mornay and Perrot de Mésières must have been inspiring to Sidney, though the consistently serious tenor of their projects, undertaken in circumstances of considerable danger and discomfort, may also have been more than a little daunting. At the very same time that Sidney was completing his first draft of the *Arcadia* in the comfort and seclusion of Wilton House, Du Plessis Mornay, hampered by serious illness and exiled from his estates in France, was labouring over his *De la vérité*, a treatise which justified the Christian religion on a broad, ecumenical base, with much reference to the ancient philosophers and the Church Fathers, as well as to common sense and reason. Though it was probably not until almost a decade after the end of his Grand Tour that Sidney began work on his own translations of *De la vérité* and of the Psalms, his encounters with Mornay and Perrot in the early 1570s were seminal, providing him with models of Protestant poetics which he hoped ultimately to emulate.

Of the many surviving letters which Sidney received from continental friends, only one actually includes a poem. It is from a young German, Johann Wacker (or von Wackenfels), who studied at Strasbourg, Geneva and Padua, coinciding with Sidney at the last. He wrote Latin dramas, and seems to have enjoyed or anticipated some form of patronage from Sidney, whom he addressed in February 1575 as his 'most excellent future Maecenas'.[65] In December of the same year Wacker wrote a long letter to Sidney, by then settled back at the English Court, to which he appended a Latin poem addressed to God in the time of his recent prolonged sickness.[66] The content of the poem is wholly conventional, but its metrical form is unusual and ambitious. It is written in 'phaleuciacs', a difficult hendecasyllabic metre used by Catullus. Sidney wrote some English 'phaleuciacs', which appear in the Second Eclogues of the 'Old' *Arcadia*, and their clumsy military imagery and metrical imperfection may indicate that they were composed when Sidney was making his very earliest attempts at English verse in classical measures.[67] Nothing in their content relates specifically to the plot material of the *Arcadia*, and they may be an early experiment undertaken in emulation of young Wacker. The same metre was used with assurance by Tennyson three centuries later, as a display of virtuosity calculated to confound his critics:

> Look, I come to the test, a tiny poem
> All composed in a metre of Catullus,
> All in quantity, careful of my motion,
> Like the skater on ice that hardly bears him.[68]

Sidney's footing across the same metrical thin ice is exceedingly leaden:

> Her loose hair be the shot, the breasts the pikes be,
> Scouts each motion is, the hands the horsemen,
> Her lips are the riches the wars to maintain,
> Where well couched abides a coffer of pearl;
> Her legs carriage is of all the sweet camp ...[69]

If Sidney wrote these English hendecasyllabics in emulation of Wacker's Latin ones, before the larger concept of his pastoral romance had taken shape, their uncharacteristic ineptitude would be partly explained.

There is one further companion of Sidney's on the Continent who was of undoubted importance for his literary development. For the first two-thirds of his Tour, it was an Anglicized Italian, Lodowick Bryskett, who was his companion. But Bryskett went back to Venice, where his brother Sebastian lived, when Sidney began the return journey. On the final, homeward, lap Sidney's chief companion was an Italianate Englishman, Edward Wotton (1548–1626). Wotton had spent three or four years among Spanish residents in Naples.[70] He was employed by Walsingham as an agent, and at the time when Sidney first met him, in the autumn of 1574, he was working as a secretary to the English embassy in Vienna. Wotton was an excellent linguist, who had considerable personal charm and panache, enjoying a long and prominent career as a diplomat and courtier. He appears to have been a stylish dresser, for when he was made Controller of the Royal Household at Christmas-time 1602/3 he was praised for raising its sartorial tone by being always 'freshly attired', often in white from head to foot.[71] Though no writings by Wotton himself survive, his name is dropped in a significant manner in the first sentence of Sidney's *Defence of Poesy*, in which he recalled the winter of 1574–5:

> When the right virtuous Edward Wotton and I were at the Emperor's Court together, we gave ourselves to learn horsemanship of John Pietro Pugliano ...[72]

Wotton's friendship with Sidney, as this passage implies, was both intellectual and practical. Judging by Sidney's account, the two behaved like arrogant, over-confident young men at the Imperial Riding School, mocking the eminent Pugliano and his excessive devotion to horses, while being slow in learning his lessons and settling his bills. Wotton was undoubtedly drawn into Sidney's vexed financial affairs, for he acted as witness to the deed in which Languet made a loan/gift of his life savings to Sidney in January 1575. Sidney probably chose to mention Wotton in the opening words of the *Defence*, however, not just because they had shared riding lessons and other practicalities in Vienna, but also because the treatise is connected with him at some deeper level. He may have been in effect its dedicatee. His younger half-brother, Henry Wotton, owned a manuscript of Sidney's translation of the first two books of Aristotle's *Rhetoric*, which he probably obtained from Edward.[73] In a letter to Languet from Court in October 1577 Sidney was to make rather sharp use of a passage from Book II of the *Rhetoric* about the feeble passions of old men.[74] It is possible that his own translation of the *Rhetoric* was begun during his residence at the Imperial Court with Edward Wotton, and that his later, independent, treatise on rhetoric and poetry grew out of conversations with Wotton during the same period. With a true 'Renaissance' breadth, Wotton and Sidney participated both in elaborate feats of equine display and in rhetorical and poetical exercises, curvetting on horseback and on paper.

Edward Wotton was not a major literary patron, and no poetry by him is known to survive. Yet there is no doubt that he had marked literary and intellectual tastes. It was he who first set John Florio to translating the essays of Montaigne,[75] and in 1599 he had a chivalric romance dedicated to him, L.A.'s translation of *The eighth booke of the myrrour of knighthood*. In about 1610, in a sonnet appended to *Homer, Prince of Poets*, George Chapman addressed Wotton as the 'quick part' of his dead friend Sidney, by whom he had been 'eterniz'd'. This presumably refers to the immortality conferred on Wotton in the opening sentence of the *Defence*. While many other friendships initiated on the Grand Tour faded away in subsequent years, Sidney's friendship with Wotton endured. On his death-bed he made Wotton a bequest of 'one fee buck, to be taken yearly out of my park at Penshurst',[76] and Wotton was, with Dyer and Greville, one of the pall-bearers at Sidney's funeral. It was in Wotton's company that Sidney returned to Court in the first week of June 1575. He was no longer 'somewhat raw', as he had been when he set out, but a confident man of the world, keen and eager to embark on a career of foreign service similar to Wotton's.

At one point Sidney had hoped to travel back slowly through France. He certainly hoped to spend a last longish spell with Languet in Frankfurt; and at the very least, he intended to make a visit to his young friend the Count of Hanau on his way from Dresden to Frankfurt. None of these detours turned out to be possible, for, as he said in a letter to Hanau, 'I was compelled to travel with such haste, by the command of the Queen and my family ...'[77] After some delay in Antwerp, which kept him there for the better part of a month, Sidney reached England on 31 May 1575. His family must have found him greatly changed. As he later said to his brother:

> all of us come home full of disguisements, not only of our apparel, but of our countenances.[78]

Physically, he looked remarkably different from the spotty seventeen-year-old whom they saw off in 1572. He may well have grown several inches, reaching his adult stature. Under Wotton's guidance he was sprucely and expensively dressed. His speech and manners were transformed, enriched by many new words, aphorisms and social flourishes. His bearing was that of a young princeling, accustomed to being treated with respect and affection by eminent scholars and statesmen. The transition to the patronizing and heavy-handed guidance of his father, his uncles and the Queen must have been very disagreeable. When abroad, he had found himself in a position of glorious authority, in which in his own slender person he was felt to encompass all that was best about the younger generation at the English Court. Once back at Court, however, his position again became one of frustrating dependence, as one among numerous young aspirants to favour and employment. Also, he now had to account for his activities, including his lavish expenditure, to an unsympathetic older generation. We do not know whether, among these expenses, he had remembered to bring presents back to his nearest and dearest, but possibly he had not. In 1580 Sir Henry Sidney wrote to his younger son, then on his Grand Tour, thanking him for a forthcoming present of 'marten skins', and adding 'It is more than ever your elder brother sent me ...'[79] Robert's education, along with that of a young Bohemian, Johannes Hàjek, whom he had brought back from Prague at the request of Charles de l'Ecluse, was one of Philip's added responsibilities on his return home. Though he told Hanau, in the letter quoted above, that he had returned to find his family well, his mother was in fact never in good health or spirits, and his younger sister Ambrosia had died in February, to the great grief of her parents. Soon after his return to England Sidney himself became ill for a while, as he re-acclimatized himself to life with his family and at Court before setting out on yet another journey.[80] This time his destination was the English Midlands, where he had spent his schooldays. No longer did he trace the majestic waters of the Seine, the Danube or the Rhine, but the quieter streams of Thames and Avon. The Queen was going on her summer progress.

5

1575–6

WAITING AT COURT

Wait: To be in readiness to receive orders; hence, to be in attendance as a servant; to attend as a servant does to the requirements of a superior.[1]

Those that, having long followed one (in truth) most excellent chase, do now at length perceive she could never be taken; but that if she stayed at any time near her pursuers, it was never meant to tarry with them, but only to take breath to fly further from them.[2]

Full little knowest thou that hast not tried
What hell it is, in suing long to bide;
To lose good days, that might be better spent;
To waste long nights, in pensive discontent;
To speed one day, to be put back tomorrow;
To feed on hope, to pine with fear and sorrow;
To have thy prince's grace, yet want her peers';
To have thy asking, yet wait many years;
To fret thy soul with crosses and with cares;
To eat thy heart through comfortless despairs;
To fawn, to crouch, to wait, to ride, to run,
To spend, to give, to want, to be undone.
Unhappy wight, born to disastrous end,
That doth his life in so long tendance spend.[3]

In the two years between his return from the Continent in June 1575 and his departure as an ambassador in March 1577 Sidney completed his growing up. His way of life changed radically. He was no longer a peripatetic student, but an up-and-coming English courtier, full of 'good hope'.[4] He seems to have spent much less time reading than formerly. He certainly spent less time

Woodcut of royal hunting picnic, 1575, from *The Noble Arte of Venerie* (Bodleian Library)

writing letters, to the grief of his many continental friends. Much of his time was now taken up with 'waiting' on the Queen, as he participated in court festivities and ceremonials which enabled him to display his talents to those who had power over his future. He was also engaged for the first time in serious administrative and military duties, as a kind of apprentice to his father. It was almost certainly during this period that Sidney embarked on his earliest experiments in English poetry. These may be connected with newly forged bonds with his own close family, and also with a new English mentor and friend, Edward Dyer.

The first question to be addressed is why Sidney came back when he did. Why was it so urgent for him to return to England by the fastest route in the spring of 1575? Some reasons are fairly obvious. His passport had expired, and he risked severe royal displeasure if he outstayed his leave yet further. Also, his loving family must have been eager to see him again, and to discover how he had weathered the dangers and excitements of the last three years. More covertly, however, momentous struggles were going on in which Sidney's rôle might prove to be crucial. Both his father Henry Sidney and his uncle the Earl of Leicester were at points of crisis in their careers, and needed him badly. Among much contemporary rumour and modern speculation, it is hard to know quite what to believe about the year when Elizabeth most famously visited Kenilworth. But some broad issues are clear.

Sidney's father, that supposedly staunch public servant, was at this period something of a court malcontent. Ever since completing his second term of office as Lord Deputy Governor of Ireland in the summer of 1571 he had continued to be closely concerned with Irish affairs. While extremely bitter at the lack of remuneration or honour that had followed his time there, he was increasingly confident of his own ability to 'manage' Ireland, both militarily and economically, if only he could be given adequate resources. Though he claimed to dread a return to Ireland, finding his continuing post as Lord President of the Marches of Wales far more congenial, he was making a powerful and insistent bid for a return. In October 1574, for instance, he set out some detailed demands with conditions to be met 'in case he were sent again to be Lord Deputy'.[5] His brother-in-law Sir William Fitzwilliam had succeeded him as Lord Deputy in January 1571, and was becoming desperate to be recalled.[6] With the Queen's blessing, Walter Devereux, Earl of Essex, was attempting a 'plantation' of Antrim and some other parts of Ulster. This extremely bloody, near-genocidal campaign was achieving little stability. Essex and Fitzwilliam, at odds with each other, seemed between them to be mismanaging Ireland hopelessly.

Henry Sidney's backhanded bids for recall to the Deputyship of Ireland occasioned some strange undercurrents at Court. In a hitherto unnoticed note from Philip II to his Secretary of State, the King of Spain reported a conversation between Henry Sidney and the Spanish agent Antonio de Guaras:

> [Sidney] had asked to see Guaras and spoken in great secrecy to him, and offered that he had a way to serve His Majesty with six thousand chosen English soldiers; and since Guaras expressed two or three times his belief as to the difficulty of doing so with the Queen's will, and even more without it, he replied as many times that His Majesty should have knowledge of this his good desire, and that as security for the fulfilment of it he pledged his only heir who is also heir to the Earldoms of Warwick and Leicester and whose name is Philip whom His Majesty lifted from the font.[7]

De Guaras's letters, whose sensational contents the King summarized, were dated 11 and 29 April 1574. At this time Philip Sidney was in the final weeks of his sojourn in Padua and Venice, and may not even have been told of this extraordinary scheme, if indeed de Guaras understood it correctly. The King clearly had his doubts about it. Like other Spanish ambassadors, de Guaras may genuinely have misunderstood or deliberately have exaggerated what was being proposed. Yet that some conference between him and Sir Henry Sidney did take place, the subject being Sidney's next period of command in

Ireland, seems reasonably certain, especially since successive Spanish envoys had reported conversations with Henry Sidney. In the earliest years of Elizabeth's reign, de la Quadra found that he could talk fruitfully with both Henry and Mary Sidney, while despairing of getting any sense out of her brother, Lord Robert Dudley (later Earl of Leicester), whom he described in 1560 as 'the worst and most procrastinating young man I ever saw in my life, and not at all courageous or spirited'.[8] Henry Sidney he found 'a sensible man, and better behaved than any of the courtiers'. A remark by him that Sir Henry Sidney 'is not at all well informed on religious matters'[9] may indicate that the elder Sidney was, in fact, prudently non-committal, waiting to see which way the wind blew. King Philip went further in 1574, saying that Henry Sidney was 'held to be Catholic'.[10] If reverberations or rumours of these (imagined?) Spanish schemes reached Elizabeth, perhaps we have one clue to the puzzling question of why she was so reluctant to promote or reward either Henry Sidney or his son. Wallace dismisses as 'absurd' rumours in 1569, during the rebellion in Munster, 'that Leicester was to be King of England and Sir Henry Sidney King of Ireland'.[11] No doubt such rumours were still absurd in 1574–5. Yet Sidney and Leicester were indeed working strenuously to consolidate their power bases in those two countries. Perhaps they were eager to serve their Queen. But they also wanted her to give them the means to exercise some autonomous regality. Even if Sir Henry Sidney did not seriously intend to 'pledge' his son and heir to the King of Spain, he at least wanted his support and companionship at this time. Philip was also needed to act as head of the family when his father went once more to Ireland, whence he might not return alive.

Leicester was in even deeper trouble than his brother-in-law. His unique position of closeness to the Queen was under threat from several sides. Her courtship by Catherine de' Medici's ugly youngest son, François-Hercule, Duke of Alençon, looked like taking a serious turn. The French ambassador Mauvissière was in attendance throughout the 1575 Progress, ready to promote this match. In August 1574 a widowed baroness, Douglass Sheffield, with whom Leicester may have had a liaison for some years, bore him a son, Roberto. His affair with another lady, Lettice, Countess of Essex, may have already begun in 1575; certainly she was present at Kenilworth. In the face of these threats to his position as top favourite, Leicester was desperately anxious to make a fresh bid for the Queen's approval, and possibly even for her hand in marriage. As Roger Kuin puts it:

> The Earl knew what the Queen as yet did not: that his personal position was mortgaged to Douglas[s] Sheffield and to any enemy cunning enough to ferret out even a rumour of the truth.[12]

Leicester did not acknowledge the alliance with Lady Sheffield as a marriage, though she was to claim many years later that it had been one. But clearly if and when the Queen got to hear of it, his position in her favour would be severely compromised. He now had what all Elizabethan noblemen, and very notably the Dudleys, longed for: a direct male heir. But at present this heir was an appalling embarrassment rather than a source of joy and confidence in the future. The return of his nephew Philip could help Leicester considerably. As heir apparent to his estates and titles young Sidney was a vital component in Leicester's plan to show himself to the Queen as deserving of the very highest favour. If Philip could be well to the fore when Leicester entertained Elizabeth at Kenilworth, she might not listen to rumours that he had another heir, or believe that Philip had been displaced from his privileged position as 'sister's son'. No matter that Leicester did not actually like Philip much: his talented nephew could do much to help his image.

For us, since it is plain that Elizabeth never did marry either Leicester or Alençon, it is easy to say with hindsight that she never seriously intended to marry either of them. This was not so clear at the time, though there were some contemporaries who suspected it. One such was the shrewd Sir Henry Sidney, who had said back in 1565 'that he was always sure the Queen did not mean to marry', though he believed her to be 'so greedy of marriage proposals that she would be glad to have an offer from Don John of Austria'.[13] But Leicester also believed that he knew Elizabeth well, and commentators on his 1575 Kenilworth entertainments may be right to detect in them a bid not merely for restoration to favour, but ultimately for a position as her consort.[14] The further implications, from Sidney's point of view, would have been dizzying. Elizabeth was approaching her forty-second birthday. Even if she could eventually be persuaded to accept Leicester as her husband, the chances of her giving birth to an heir were not good. Many courtiers, including Sidney, expressed pious hopes of her childbearing capacity at the time of the second Alençon courtship in 1581–2, but it must in truth have seemed exceedingly doubtful even in 1575. If the Queen were to marry Leicester and produce no child, Sidney's position would become princely. It might even be constitutionally possible for Elizabeth to nominate him as her successor. No one at this time reckoned on Elizabeth's longevity. In their wilder imaginings, the younger members of the Sidney–Dudley circle may even have looked forward to a time when, with Philip II ruling in Spain, his godson Philip Sidney might rule in England. Such an Anglo-Spanish axis would neutralize the power of France. Elizabeth's wise determination never to name a successor until she was near death left the field wide open for such fantastic private imaginings, though to utter them openly would be treason. In the 'Old' *Arcadia* there is a popular movement, after the Duke's death, to make his chief counsellor, Philanax, 'lieutenant of the state'.[15] But soberer courtiers may have seen Leicester's courtship of the Queen at Kenilworth chiefly as a stratagem to block the French proposals.

Of Sidney himself we know surprisingly little during the summer months of 1575. He received many letters from the Continent, from Languet, de Banos, Lobbet, Zündelin and others, but seems to have taken a long vacation from letter-writing. He may have decided not to deal with his correspondence until he got back to London. No letters written by him between June 1575 and November 1576 survive, and letters from his correspondents suggest that though he did answer some letters during this period, his replies were often cursory. In Languet's opinion, Sidney had given up the later part of 1575 to unproductive idleness:

> Though a letter from you arrived yesterday [2 December 1575] it does not convince me that I was unjust in finding fault with your negligence, because a full five months have passed since you last wrote. You offer as excuse for your idleness attendance on the progress of the Court and your accompanying his Excellency your father ... I beg you, please, ponder the implications of not having wished in all that time to devote one hour to true friends who love you dearly ... You could have more than satisfied us merely by giving up one dance a month. A year ago you were with us for only three or four months. Recall how many excellent writers you read through in that short time, and the profit you gained by reading them.

Languet warned him not to squander all he had learned by 'immersing yourself in pleasures from top to toe'.[16] He goes on to consider the possibility that Sidney may still be continuing with his studies, even though he is neglecting his correspondence, but sounds on balance convinced that Sidney had abandoned himself to 'pleasures'. He was probably right. But what Languet cannot have understood were the political implications of these 'pleasures', and the importance of Sidney's participation in them.

Large-scale building work had been going on at Kenilworth for more than four years. Leicester changed the approach from south to north, building a 'magnificent Gate-house'. As Master of the Horse and expectant host to a huge party of carriages, he seems to have built the large stable block just inside the north wall known as 'Leicester's Barn'. He erected two large towers, one commanding a view of the tiltyard, and the other, Mortimer's Tower, suggesting his medieval aristocratic heritage. The castle had been his only since 1563, but by the time of this, the Queen's third visit, it had been transformed into a 'prodigy house', combining much fake medievalism with the latest technological advances in glazing and waterworks. The park was greatly extended for the purposes of hunting. There was a raised mound from which floating spectacles on the huge artificial lake, or 'Mere', could be viewed.

Many an 'R.L.' over doors and fireplaces asserted Leicester's dominance over the palatial residence, which had at one time belonged to John of Gaunt.[17] Large glass windows gave the castle an appearance quite novel in the English Midlands: people living within sight of it were amazed at its appearance by night, brilliantly lit up from within. The improvements at Kenilworth are said to have cost Leicester £60,000; his annual income was only about £5,000.[18]

Despite the lavishness of its architectural features, Kenilworth Castle was not able to accommodate the whole of the Queen's retinue, most of which was lodged five and a half miles away, at Warwick, 'thus causing a constant stream of horse and cart service in both directions over the road between the two towns'.[19] Part of the problem must have been the great size of Leicester's own retinue, whose residence at the castle was essential to support the feastings and spectacles of those eighteen July days. However, there can be no doubt that Leicester's sister Mary Sidney and her family stayed on the premises. The Privy Council doorkeeper, Robert Langham, whose serio-comic *Letter* (?1576) is one of the prime sources of information about the Kenilworth entertainments, boasted that

> sometime [I am] at my good Lady Sidney's chamber, a noblewoman that I am as much bound unto as any poor man may be unto so gracious a lady.[20]

When the Privy Council met in London Langham's duties included providing the council chamber with fresh boughs, flowers and silk cushions, and making sure that the fire-irons were in good repair. It is pleasant to think that for once Lady Sidney, who so often complained of her physical discomfort at Court, was well looked after: presumably this was the point of Langham's visits. The comfort of her lodgings must have been of particular importance to her because her scarred appearance made her reluctant to attend large public gatherings. As Fulke Greville put it:

> she chose rather to hide herself from the curious eyes of a delicate time than to come upon the stage of the world with any manner of disparagement.[21]

We may conjecture that she watched much of what went on at Kenilworth – the fireworks over the water, the country wedding, the bear-baiting – from her windows. She seems to have received the Queen in her chamber, for the Sidney accounts for the summer refer to an expense of £5 13s. 6d. 'when the Queen was with her'. Perhaps Elizabeth spent one of the wet afternoons in her old friend's room. Robert Langham, whose visits ensured that the room was well provided, had probably known the Sidneys from earliest years, for he received his first education at St Antony's School, adjoining the London residence most often used by Mary Sidney (see above, pp. 25–6). In 1578/9 – as perhaps also on other occasions – Robert Langham brought Mary Sidney a New Year's gift from the Queen.[22]

For the Sidney family as a whole, the 1575 Progress was a strange and intensely exciting holiday, painfully overshadowed by Sir Henry's departure for Ireland. Like the guests at Kala's wedding in the 'Old' *Arcadia*, the Sidneys did not come to Leicester's house 'like harpies to devour him',[23] but made generous contributions to the provisions. Sir Henry Sidney's steward's accounts record his gifts to Leicester at Kenilworth of 'Two great fat oxen ... 100 fat muttons ... divers kinds of poultry', and 'driving and carriage of the same', to the sum of over £50.[24] An amount little short of this, £42 6s., was pledged on Philip Sidney's behalf to 'Richard Rodway, citizen and merchant tailor of London'.[25] This was presumably for clothes to be worn during the Progress. Leicester may have both chosen and paid for these garments, as he had done when his eleven-year-old nephew visited Oxford in 1566.

Philip was accompanied by his usual two faithful servants, Harry White and Griffin Maddox, who witnessed his tailor's bill. He probably also had with him Johannes Hàjek, the sixteen-year-old Bohemian, son of the Emperor's physician, who had been entrusted to his care by Charles de l'Ecluse. Young Hàjek turned out to be unreceptive to his studies at Oxford, but may thoroughly have enjoyed the Progress, especially if, like many Bohemians, he was fond of field sports. Though the literary records testify chiefly to the plays, songs, speeches and spectacles of the Progress, it should not be forgotten that a major part of the time during a Progress was spent in hunting. For the Queen herself, this was the most enjoyable part. While Langham's *Letter* and George Gascoigne's *Princely Pleasures of Kenilworth* are important testimonies to the man-made and 'literary' entertainments of July 1575, a second book by Gascoigne, lavishly illustrated, was published, probably in the autumn of 1575, as a celebration of the Queen's delight in hunting.[26] *The Noble Arte of Venerie*, which has been called the 'definitive' Elizabethan hunting manual, is based for the most part on a French treatise by Jacques du Fouilloux. However, it has some original elements, the most substantial of which is a verse account of 'the place where and how an assembly should be made, in the presence of some Prince, or some honourable person'. Both visually and verbally, this appears to be based on sports at Kenilworth. The poem describes an outdoor feast in terms of a comic battle between the Butler and the Cook, the one with ample barrels of beer, the other with

> cold loins of veal, cold capon, beef, and goose,
> With pigeon pies, and mutton cold, are set on hunger loose,
> And make the forlorn hope in doubt to scape full hard,
> Then come to give a charge in flank (lest all the mart were marred):
> First neats' tongues powdered well, and gambons of the hog,
> Then sausages and savoury knacks, to set men's minds on gog ...

The Butler and his supporters triumph, but all are soon put to flight by the huntsmen, whose spokesman, possibly Gascoigne himself, invites the Queen to come to the chase, dinner being over. The woodcut of the 'assembly'[27] shows Cook and Butler left and right at the bottom of the picture. The Queen, top left, in a high plumed hat, is flanked by two bearded courtiers with garters on their left legs. These could represent Sidney's father (he was Royal Cupbearer) and perhaps Leicester, holding a napkin. A group of courtiers sitting and picnicking to the right ought, if precise identifications are intended, to include Sidney. The most noticeable of the group, and the youngest-looking, bears some slight resemblance to the 1577 portraits of Sidney. He is shown, unglamorously, about to stuff a large piece of meat into his mouth. Two lordly-looking little boys in the foreground, one quaffing from a flagon, the other eating, could represent young Robert and Thomas Sidney, then aged eleven and six. Sir Roy Strong has suggested that the woodcut is designed by the distinguished woman limner Levina Teerlinc, and that it is based on 'direct observation'.[28] This may overstate the case for its lifelikeness. Both Gascoigne's poem and its enclosing woodcuts – the next[29] shows Elizabeth casting an expert eye over some 'fewmets', or deer-droppings, presented to her by a kneeling huntsman (sometimes wrongly described as Elizabeth being presented with fruit) – are surely idealized, symbolic depictions of what ought to have happened at Kenilworth, rather than literal records of what did. The mock battle of Cook and Butler seems to have been among the many entertainments planned for Kenilworth which, for one reason or another, were not performed.[30]

There is no doubt that a great deal of hunting went on that summer, and that the Sidney family participated in some of it. The Queen was late arriving at Kenilworth on the evening of 9 July because she had enjoyed a long day of feasting and hunting en route, at Leicester's estate at Long Itchington, seven miles away, where a large pavilion had been erected. Langham gives a somewhat idealized account of the Queen's hunting on the third and fifth days at Kenilworth. On the Monday, a hot day, he describes the 'pastime delectable' of an evening expedition to hunt 'the hart of force' – a stag in its greatest fatness – which was successfully killed. On Wednesday, says Langham, a stag was driven into the water, and as the huntsmen held it up on each side the Queen exercised her royal prerogative by requesting that its ears be cut off 'for a ransom', and the animal 'pardoned'. From Langham's account we might imagine that relatively few deer were actually killed. But Leicester's gamekeeper tells a different story. His tally of deer killed at Kenilworth confirms that one buck was 'pardoned' by the Queen, but also that it 'died', presumably of shock and terror, after the amputation of its ears. The Queen personally dispatched at least half a dozen deer in the course of her stay, out of the grand total of ninety-nine dead by the end of the summer; and among many individuals listed as killing single deer in Rudfyn, or Redfern, Park, a mile or so north-west of the castle are both 'Mr Philip Sidney' and 'My Lady Sidney', his mother.[31]

It was probably politically essential that Leicester's heir made such public displays of his 'manhood'. We are not obliged to believe that he enjoyed doing so. Moffet wrote of the 'negligent' manner in which Sidney participated in school games (see above, p. 28). His hunting – or delivery of the death blow to a driven deer – may have been similarly half-hearted. In his literary works Sidney shows hunting as a recreation of old men, who lament the lack of interest shown in it by the younger generation. The benign old Kalander, in the 'New' *Arcadia*, recommends 'the sport of hunting' to his young guests, telling them

> how much, in the comparison thereof, he disdained all chamber delights; that the sun, how great a journey soever he had to make, could never prevent him with earliness, nor the moon with her sober countenance dissuade him from watching till midnight for the deer's feeding.[32]

Yet he acknowledges that 'activity and good fellowship' are no longer appreciated by younger men. When the deer is at bay, he has to prevent 'some of the younger sort' from killing it unsportingly with their swords. Old Kalander himself

> with a crossbow sent a death to the poor beast, who with tears showed the unkindness he took of men's cruelty.[33]

The unresponsiveness of the fictional young men to Kalander's eulogy of hunting, combined with the narrator's empathy with the deer's suffering, may indicate that Sidney himself, as Harington later remarked, disliked hunting. To a modern taste, there were even worse sports than killing deer. A particularly revolting passage in Langham's *Letter* is his oft-quoted account of the baiting of thirteen bears, which is described in terms of a legal dispute:

> if the dog in pleading would pluck the bear by the throat, the bear with traverse would claw him again by the scalp; confess and a list, but avoid a could not, that was bound to the bar.

That is, the maddened bear was chained to a stake, like the 'bear and ragged staff' in Leicester's coat of arms. Leicester liked to refer to himself and his brother Ambrose as the Queen's *ursus minor* and *ursus major*, her little and large bears. It would be nice to think that Sidney was able to avoid attending such spectacles, but since the Queen particularly enjoyed bear-baiting, preferring it to stage plays,[34] it is unlikely. Her host's heir would have to be in attendance when the 'bear and ragged staff', the Dudley badge so obsessively stamped on all Leicester's possessions, was cruelly brought to life in the courtyard of Kenilworth Castle.

If Sidney found hunting and animal-baiting old-fashioned and distasteful, one wonders how he felt about the more 'literary' entertainments presented at Kenilworth. Leicester had rounded up a positive 'Dad's Army' of middle-aged academics, elderly schoolmasters and professional entertainers to divert the Queen during her visit. First to greet her was Sybilla, perhaps played by one of the boys of the Chapel Royal, whose Master, William Hunnis, had written the speech. Hunnis was the author of such improving works as *A hivefull of Honey* (1578), a neat versification of the first chapter of Genesis, and *Seven Sobs of a Sorrowful Soul* (1583), versions of the Penitential Psalms. He had shown loyalty to the Princess Elizabeth during the reign of her sister Mary. Next came John Badger, Beadle of the University of Oxford. Sidney probably remembered him, for he was at Christ Church from 1550. He delivered a comic speech in the person of Hercules, pretending at first to bar the Queen from entering the castle:

> ... My friends, a Porter I,
> no Poper, here am placed;
> By leave, perhaps, else not,
> while club and limbs do last.
> A garboil this indeed!
> What, yea, fair dames? What, yea?
> What dainty darling's here?
> Oh God, a peerless pearl!
> No worldly wight no doubt,
> Some sovereign goddess sure ...

Similarly naive astonishment at the beauty of the Queen and her ladies was expressed by subsequent performers, such as the 'Savage Man', enacted by George Gascoigne, who got Echo to explain the first day's spectacles to him, as if to a well-meaning dolt. He concluded by giving notice of some future entertainments, thus revealing himself to be less ignorant than he had pretended:

> On Thursday next (think I)
> here will be pleasant dames,
> Who bet than I may make you glee
> With sundry pleasant games.

Gascoigne noted that these verses were devised and performed 'upon a very great sudden'. They read like it. It should be borne in mind, however, that unpredictable English summer weather, in conjunction with the Queen's even less predictable whims, made the detailed planning of entertainments extraordinarily difficult. There were a considerable number of elaborate shows which never came to fruition at Kenilworth, including a night battle on the lake and Gascoigne's play *Zabeta*. *Zabeta* was 'prepared and ready (every actor in his garment) two or three days together, yet never came to execution'. Gascoigne attributed its non-performance to 'lack of opportunity and seasonable weather'. Modern commentators have suspected that it was its unambiguous recommendation of marriage –

> Yet never wight felt perfect bliss
> but such as wedded been –

that made it unperformable. Some of the entertainments which did take place must have struck Sidney, with recent memories of pageantry in Paris, Venice and Vienna, as excruciatingly inane and provincial. They included a 'Hock Tuesday' play about an English victory over the Danes, performed by a group of citizens from Coventry who were strongly loyal to Leicester; a comic country wedding between a clod-hopping rustic and an ugly middle-aged bride; and such rustic sports as morris dancing and tilting at the quintain. Coarseness and clumsiness were all part of the joke, as when, some days later, an 'ancient minstrel' prepared to sing a dreary ballad of King Arthur. First he was 'sweetened' with some sack and sugar, and then

> after three lowly curtsies, cleared his voice with a 'hem' and a retch, and spat out withal, wiped his lips with the hollow of his hand, for filing his napkin ...

that is, he spat into his hand to avoid making his handkerchief dirty. The Queen seems to have enjoyed these 'popular' entertainments quite as much as the more courtly ones, and things which went wrong only added to the fun. At the end of the first day's hunting, for instance, Gascoigne as the 'Savage Man' threw down a branch which accidentally startled the Queen's horse:

> See the benignity of the prince! As the footmen looked well to the horse, and he of generosity soon calmed of himself, 'No hurt, no hurt!' quoth Her Majesty. Which words, I promise you, we were all glad to hear, and took them to be the best part of the play.[35]

On a later day, according to a manuscript source,

> There was a spectacle presented to Queen Elizabeth upon the water, and amongst others Harry Goldingham was to represent Arion upon the Dolphin's back, but finding his voice to be very hoarse and unpleasant when he came to perform it, he tears off his disguise, and swears he was none of Arion, not he, but e'en honest Harry Goldingham: which blunt discovery pleased the Queen better than if it had gone through in the right way.[36]

Whether young Sidney was equally pleased by these entertainments seems doubtful. Leicester had chosen his poets and performers for their proven loyalty to Elizabeth and likely ability to amuse her, and he chose them well. But his twenty-year-old nephew must have thought again and again how much better it could all be done, and, perhaps, that in future he would make contributions in a more elegant style. Many poetic genres and motifs which occur in the Kenilworth entertainments were adopted and refashioned by Sidney in the next few years, some publicly, others more privately. It may have been the expensive, showy but verbally unsophisticated works commissioned by his uncle that set Sidney off on some of his earliest poetic experiments. For instance, rather than presenting clowns who spat and retched in the monarch's presence, he was to show, in *The Lady of May* and in the 'Old' *Arcadia* Eclogues, rustics whose clumsiness was verbal rather than physical, and who could not always be condescended to by courtiers. While the rustic wedding at Kenilworth was designed to gratify the audience's sense of their own superior refinement, Sidney described in his Third Eclogues a rustic wedding whose dignity, beauty and correctness is an implicit reproach to the lawless decadence of the aristocratic characters. Some of his attempts to discover whether he could do better than Leicester's Kenilworth poets may have been undertaken almost immediately. The Savage Man's dialogue with Echo may well have stimulated what Ringler describes as 'one of Sidney's earliest experiments in measured verse', the dialogue between Philisides and Echo in the Second Eclogues.[37] Though Gascoigne's is probably the earliest 'echo' poem in English, it left plenty of room for improvement. Each verse falls into two lumpish, heavily caesuraed lines of poulter's measure. Echo's response is often absurdly predictable, being anticipated by Sylvanus:

> . . . And who gave all these gifts,
> I pray thee, Echo, say?
> Was it not he who but of late
> this building here did lay?
> *Echo*: Dudley.
>
> O Dudley, so methought;
> he gave himself and all,
> A worthy gift to be received,
> and so I trust it shall.
> *Echo*: It shall.[38]

And so on. For Gascoigne's 'Drab' poulter's measure, Sidney substituted far more exacting classical hexameters, though, as Ringler points out, he had not yet perfected his technique in writing them. This may have been his first extended attempt. Sidney made some, at least, of Echo's responses pointed and witty:

PHILISIDES:
What great name may I give to so heav'nly a woman?
ECHO:
A woe-man.

PHILISIDES:
Woe, but seems to me joy, that agrees to my thought so.
ECHO:
I thought so.

PHILISIDES:
Think so, for of my desired bliss it is only the course.
ECHO:
Curse.[39]

Whether Sidney's poem was written originally for performance, we do not know. In its context in the Second Eclogues he refers to the ingenuity with which Philisides raised the pitch of his voice for Echo's replies. Within the 'Old' *Arcadia*, the poem is a piece of calculated self-concealment, for Philisides has been invited by the Duke 'to declare the discourse of his own fortunes, unknown to them as being a stranger in that country'. It was as a 'stranger', who had been out of England for three years, that Sidney attended the 1575 Progress, and there may have been many who expected him to tell traveller's tales. Instead, all he was prepared to do was to suggest that he was melancholy and alienated, while showing himself a much better poet than George Gascoigne. In the Second Eclogues the echo poem forms part of the celebrations of the Duke's birthday. It is likely that Sidney gathered up into these Eclogues some verses originally composed for royal entertainments. If the echo poem was immediately stimulated by Gascoigne's, it could have been composed for celebrations of Elizabeth's forty-second birthday, on 7 September 1575, when she was on her way to Woodstock.

Sidney left the Progress in early August. His father was formally appointed Lord Deputy Governor of Ireland at a Privy Council meeting held at Lichfield, the Queen's next stopping place after Kenilworth. Father and son travelled together at least as far as Shrewsbury, scene of Philip's schooldays, where the corporation spent 7s. 2d. on 'wine and cakes' in entertaining them.[40] On 21 August Sidney was one of nine witnesses of his father's will. It is not clear at what point he parted from his father, but it may have been soon after this date. For such a seasoned traveller the journey back from Shrewsbury to Woodstock – next major stopping place of the Royal Progress – would take only a few days. His group would not need to go at the stately pace of the Queen's carriage party. Sidney probably rejoined the Progress either at Worcester or at Woodstock some time in early September, meeting up there with his sister Mary, his brothers Robert and Thomas, and his mother.

If Sidney presented himself about this time in the melancholy persona of 'Philisides', he was by no means the only courtier to make a public display of unhappiness. From the Queen's point of view, afternoons of hunting were doubtless the most enjoyable part of a Progress; but from the point of view of many participants, chasing deer was less enthralling than what Sidney in *The Lady of May* called 'one most excellent chase' – the pursuit of the Queen herself.[41] The Queen was rarely able to move about a park for long without being besieged by importunate nymphs, fairies, pages, shepherds, Wild Men or woodland deities. Beneath these disguises lay attempts at emotional blackmail by discontented courtiers or aspirants to courtiership for whom the 1575 Progress offered a chance to capture the Queen's attention. One of Leicester's literary protégés, the soldier-poet George Gascoigne, whose collection of poems *A Hundreth Sundrie Flowres* (1573) had been found offensive by the Privy Council, used the Progress and its aftermath for an all-out bid for favour and protection. Not only did he compose and perform many of the Kenilworth pieces, writing the whole thing up after the event, along with the hunting manual already mentioned; he also translated a Woodstock entertainment, *The Tale of Hemetes the Hermit*, into Latin, Italian and French, presenting his elegantly handwritten copy to the Queen as a New Year's gift in 1575/6.[42] The manuscript is illustrated with four emblematic pen drawings, the first of which shows Gascoigne kneeling before the Queen in the Presence Chamber, a laurel wreath suspended hopefully above his head. Though he seems to have achieved no formal position as 'laureate', Gascoigne was successful in acquiring state employment, being dispatched to observe affairs in the Netherlands in the summer of 1576.[43] His vigorous literary, dramatic and graphic efforts eventually paid off.

While Gascoigne, Robert Langham and some other non-aristocratic aspirants to favour were eager to identify themselves by name, to make sure that the Queen remembered who they were, more eminent suppliants veiled their identities. At Kenilworth, for instance, as the Queen was preparing to leave, she was led to an arbour made of holly bushes. From the prickly middle of the largest bush someone calling himself 'Deep Desire' gave utterance. He is described as 'that wretch of worthies, and yet the worthiest that ever was condemned to wretched estate'. He clearly represents a specific courtier who felt himself neglected:

> he was such an one as neither any delay could daunt him: no disgrace could abate his passions, no time could tire him, no water quench his flames: nor death itself could amaze him with terror.

His primary function was to lament Elizabeth's imminent departure from Kenilworth, on behalf of all those who had entertained her. But he was almost certainly enacted by or on behalf of an individual courtier who sought restoration to favour. Gascoigne may have known who he was, but not thought it proper to identify him to the reading public.

At Woodstock another neglected courtier cried out to Elizabeth from the middle of a tree, this time a trusty oak. The printed account of the Woodstock entertainment (1585) does not name the singer in the oak, who called himself 'Despair', but this one can be identified with some confidence. He was the Somerset gentleman Edward Dyer, family friend of the Sidneys, who was soon to assume a mentor and 'best friend' rôle in Sidney's life. The 'Song in the Oak' is attributed to Dyer in a manuscript whose ascriptions are generally correct,[44] and Dyer had good reason to appeal passionately to the Queen at this particular time and place. In June 1570, when he was only twenty-six, Dyer had been granted the stewardship and other offices at Woodstock, one of the Queen's favourite estates, 'for life'. This was a mark of high favour and confidence. But after only a year he fell from grace with the Queen, transferring most of his patents at Woodstock to an intermediary through whom they were soon passed to Sir Henry Lee. Lee, Royal Champion and prime mover of the Accession Day Tilts, was to be Ranger of Woodstock for nearly forty years.[45] It is not clear whether it was simply financial necessity that caused Dyer to part so swiftly with his royal gift, or whether the Queen herself or her advisers put pressure on him to do so. Nor do we know why he fell from grace. The time of his fall might make one suspect some association with the 'Ridolfi plot', the conspiracy to put Mary Queen of Scots on the throne which led to a death sentence on the Duke of Norfolk in January 1571/2. But there is no evidence for Dyer's implication in this. Perhaps some maladroitness or misjudgement in his dealings with the Queen was his undoing. If so, it is rather surprising that Dyer undertook, in October 1572, to advise that very accomplished courtier Christopher Hatton on how to handle the Queen.[46] He may have felt that he had gained wisdom from bitter experience. Whatever the cause of his disgrace, Dyer retained a physical toehold at Woodstock, and Henry Lee, who had so successfully replaced him in office there, probably felt obliged to help him in his struggle to attract the Queen's attention.

Edward Dyer's 'Song' at Woodstock struck a characteristically gloomy note. It came at the end of a festive afternoon during which the 'Queen of Fayry' had presented the Queen with a rich gown, ornate emblematic pictures devised by various noblemen had been admired, and coloured nosegays with greetings-card-like verses attached to them had been presented to seventeen ladies who attended the Queen. These included Sidney's fourteen-year-old sister Mary, whose verses ran:

> Though young in years, yet old in wit, a gest due to your race,
> If you hold on as you begin, who is't you'll not deface?

On the way back to Woodstock Palace, as the Queen rode in her coach, Dyer's self-pitying song was heard, beginning:

The man whose thoughts against him do conspire,
In whom mishap her story did depaint;
The man of woe, the matter of desire,
Free of the dead that lives in endless plaint:
His sprite am I . . .

Being 'Despair', he does not even lay claim to hope:

I am most sure that I shall not attain
The only good wherein the joy doth lie . . .

and ends with a somewhat blasphemous echo of a Biblical text often applied to Christ on the Cross:

O ye that here behold infortune's fare:
There is no grief that may with mine compare.[47]

Dyer was in a particular sense 'free of the dead', for his surname suggested a perpetual state of 'dying'. Most of the small surviving corpus of his poems contain punning allusions to his status as 'one of the living dead'. A particularly gloomy character in the *Arcadia*, Coredens, is, like Philisides, a 'stranger shepherd'. The name means 'Heart eating', and it may be that, as one who is perpetually 'eating his heart out', he is based on 'Dyer'. The heart-eating metaphor may have had special application to the miseries of waiting fruitlessly at Court, as in the passage from Spenser's 'Mother Hubberds Tale' quoted at the head of this chapter:

To eat thy heart through comfortless despairs . . .

Like Gascoigne, Dyer eventually reaped the reward of his dressing up and singing, for in January 1576 the Queen gave him a 'licence to pardon and dispense with tanning of leather'.[48] The Queen liked puns, too, and her choice of a monopoly to bestow on Dyer may have been stimulated by another sense of his name, as one who 'dyes'. Others used this play on Dyer's name; John Florio, for instance, complained of the untrustworthiness of 'Dyers' in an extended passage in his *First Fruites* (1578), and in his manuscript collection of Italian proverbs, *Il Giardino di Recreatione*, Florio's friend Matthew Gwinne called Dyer '*Tinctor*'.[49]

Young Sidney, who was often accused of being too solemn for his years, clearly found the gloomy Dyer/'Despair' most congenial. He paid explicit tribute to him both as a friend and a fellow poet, and veiled references to him are probably contained in his fictional presentations of Coredens, Klaius and others. In Sidney's eyes, Dyer's first recommendation was probably the fact that he was a good friend to his mother. In September 1574 Lady Sidney wrote to her husband's secretary, Edmund Molyneux, about the perplexing question of whether Sir Henry was or was not going to be sent to Ireland:

In all your proceedings in my lord's causes, take the wise, noble Master Dyer's friendly counsel, who I know doth tender my lord's honour and well doing as much as a faithful friend may do.[50]

Socially, Dyer was evidently not such a gloomy fellow as his poetic persona might suggest. Indeed, a disparity between the self-pitying songster and the amusing man of the world may have made the pose particularly arresting. Sir John Harington, to whom Dyer acted as a kind of guardian while he was at Cambridge, called him a person 'of great wit and mirth'.[51] There is an anecdote attributed to Francis Bacon which shows Dyer in later years neatly deploying his wit to strengthen his position with the Queen:

Queen Elizabeth, seeing Sir Edward [Dyer] in her garden, looked out at her window, and asked in Italian, 'What does a man think of when he thinks of nothing?' Sir Edward (who had not the effect of some of the Queen's grants so soon as he had hoped) paused a little, and then made answer, 'Madam, he thinks of a woman's promise.' The Queen shrunk in her head: but was heard to say, 'Well, Sir Edward, I must not confute you.'[52]

When Sidney first got to know Dyer well, during the summer of 1575, it was probably a delight to discover in this loyal family friend not only a person of 'wit and mirth', but someone with an interest in the reform of English poetry. Gabriel Harvey's account, in a letter to Spenser of early 1580, of the collaboration of Sidney and Dyer is typically egotistical and exaggerated, yet surely had a foundation in truth:

I cannot choose but thank and honour the good angel (whether it were Gabriel or some other) that put so good a motion into the heads of those two excellent gentlemen Master Sidney and Master Dyer, the two very diamonds of Her Majesty's Court for many special and rare qualities, as to help forward our new famous enterprise for the exchanging of barbarous and balductum rhymes with artificial [i.e. artful] verses, the one being in manner of pure and fine gold, the other but counterfeit and base ill-favoured copper.[53]

What Harvey was specifically praising was the shared interest of Sidney and Dyer in writing in classical measures in English. There seems little doubt that experiments in classical verse forms, like the Philisides–Echo poem quoted above, which is in hexameters, were among Sidney's very earliest poems. The 'Ottley manuscript', which contains over forty of Sidney's poems, written probably between 1575 and 1579, includes also his account of 'Rules in measured verse in English which I observe', suggesting a systematic programme of innovation.[54] Dyer seems to have been involved in Sidney's verse experiments more as a patron or spectator than as a participant. The older man presumably watched with excitement as the much more talented Sidney made English poetry and the English language over anew. No experiments in quantitative verse by Dyer have survived, and the poems of his which we have are in conventional metres used by many other poets of the 1560s and 70s. Yet Sidney was consistent in paying tribute to Dyer as *'il miglior fabbro'*, to use T. S. Eliot's epithet for Ezra Pound. In *Certain Sonnets*, for instance, there is a pair of sonnets by Dyer and Sidney, perhaps early poetic 'sports'. Dyer's is about a naive satyr who was so attracted to fire, newly brought down from heaven, that he kissed it and burnt his mouth. Sidney's sonnet concerns another naive satyr, who ran away terrified 'With sound of horn which he himself did blow'. Both may relate to the dangers and frustrations of the pursuit of royal favour; but the conclusion of Sidney's is a graceful compliment to his friend:

> ... And thus might I, for fear of 'maybe', leave
> The sweet pursuit of my desired prey.
> Better I like thy satyr, dearest Dyer,
> Who burnt his lips to kiss fair shining fire.[55]

This ending has ensured that Dyer's sonnet, awkward and old-fashioned though it is compared with Sidney's, has to be included in any text of *Certain Sonnets*. A poem in the First Eclogues of the 'Old' *Arcadia* also includes a compliment to Dyer. Geron ('Old man') tries to persuade Philisides to join in the general merriment and forget about love. A misogynistic outburst, ending with the line

> And to conclude, thy mistress is a woman[56]

provokes a third speaker, Histor ('Narrator'), to interrupt, identifying the line as a quotation from Dyer ('No women angels be, and lo! My mistress is a woman') which he re-interprets:

> These words did once the loveliest shepherd use
> That erst I knew, and with most plaintful muse;
> Yet not of women judging as he said,
> But forced with rage, his rage on them upbraid.

That is, Dyer was not really misogynistic, but was momentarily enraged by special circumstances. The quoted line comes from one of Dyer's longest and most wallowingly miserable poems, 'A Fancy', which begins:

> He that his mirth hath lost, whose comfort is dismayed,
> Whose hope is vain, whose faith is scorned, whose trust is all betrayed;
> If he have held them dear, and cannot cease to moan,
> Come, let him take his place by me: he shall not rue alone.

Sidney accepted Dyer's invitation to 'take his place' at his side, joining him in 'plaintful' and melancholy verses. He was unwavering in his respect for him. In the penultimate year of his life, in the autumn of 1585, Geffrey Whitney was assembling a large collection of emblems for dedication to Leicester, then on the point of taking up his command in the Netherlands. On mentioning to Sidney that he proposed to dedicate an emblem celebrating literary fame to him, Sidney insisted that this tribute to the leading English poet was due to Dyer, not himself.[57] Whitney solved this dilemma by dedicating the emblem to Dyer, as bidden, but devoting most of the long accompanying poem to praise of Sidney. No one else seems to have seen quite what Sidney did in Dyer's verses.

Clearly Sidney's friendship with Dyer was vital to his own birth as a poet. The attempt to write English poetry in classical measures may now be seen as a dead end. Sidney himself moved on to much more fruitful innovations in accentual lyric forms, especially the sonnet. Yet the classical experiments played an important part in the complex process of unlocking English poetry from some worn-out metrical conventions, and as midwife to Sidney's classical poems Dyer is a crucial figure in the history of English poetry. If the identification of Dyer with 'Coredens' is correct, Sidney saw him as Languet's successor as chief mentor and friend. In the 'Ister bank' poem he says that when Languet was forced to part from him on the banks of the Danube ('Ister'),

> To worthy Coredens he gave me o'er.[58]

Initially, the transfer was involuntary on Languet's part. As we have seen, he received no letters from Sidney in the later months of 1575, and cannot have known of the new rôle played by Dyer. Wearying of Languet's 'oppressive paternalism', which he continued to exercise through long, though unanswered, letters, Sidney turned eagerly to the more congenial guidance of Dyer. Languet had taught him a great deal about European politics and moral and political wisdom, with a bias towards philosophy and history. But, as we have seen, he took little interest in poetry or aesthetics. Also, he was an old man, and his tenacious emotional demands were often tedious. Dyer was only eleven years older than Sidney, was amusing company, wrote poetry and had immediate experience of the pleasures and pains of life as an English courtier. He was closely attached to Sidney's mother, and may also have paid poetic court to his sister as 'Amaryllis'. He was not distinguished for his learning, but his pragmatic approach to life at Court may have been just what Sidney needed at this time. Dyer's biographer detects a compliment to him in a passage on the nature of true eloquence in the *Defence of Poesy*:

> Undoubtedly ... I have found in divers smally learned courtiers a more sound style than in some professors of learning.[59]

If this is right, Sidney revealed, to those who picked up the allusion, a preference for the conversation of Dyer, Henry Lee and the like to that of Languet and his humanist colleagues.

By the time Sidney returned to London for the autumn and winter of 1575/6, his rôle as a courtier had become prominent. The Queen had had ample opportunity to appraise his talents. His career as a tilter, probably initiated at Woodstock in September, may have continued in the Accession Day Tilt on 17 November. On 27 October he assisted his aunt, the Countess of Warwick, at a splendid christening at Westminster Abbey (see above, pp. 11–12). His brother's Oxford tutor, Robert Dorset, wrote to him frequently in terms which suggest awed admiration for Leicester's nephew and heir.[60] From his uncle's grand household Sidney was able to catch up at last on correspondence, see to such family affairs as his brother Robert's education, and continue, in spare moments, with poetic experiments, some for private amusement, some for use in court spectacles. Leicester House, as surviving inventories show, was extremely lavishly furnished, and had a remarkable collection of paintings, tapestries and works of art. Some were clearly imported from the Continent, and it is possible that one of Sidney's tasks during his Grand Tour had been to purchase works of art for the collection.[61]

On 30 November 1575 Sidney came of age, reaching his twenty-first birthday. He was exactly half the age of the Queen on whose favour so much depended. Whatever he may have said publicly about Elizabeth's beauty and youth in poems and entertainments, Sidney's personal correspondence makes it clear that he viewed her (hopefully) as having one foot in the grave. While waiting for the old woman to die, he did not really want to 'wait' at Court for long periods, much though he clearly enjoyed participating in tilts and entertainments, showing off his skills in both horsemanship and poetry, the two arts he celebrates in the opening of the *Defence*. He really wanted action, if possible out of England. One strange opportunity occurred in the spring of 1576. The Queen's French suitor Alençon, who was later to find Sidney a fierce enemy, invited him to join him in leading a rebellion of *politiques* near the Loire. Like Sidney, the unprincipled Alençon was in search of an autonomous power base.[62] A letter from Languet of 28 May 1576 suggests that Sidney found the proposition tempting. Alençon's shifting allegiance, vanity and cruelty were not yet fully apparent. But it seems highly unlikely that the Queen would have given Sidney leave for this expedition, and in any case commitments nearer home had a prior claim. In the summer of 1576 he joined his father in Ireland.

In the summer of 1575 Languet had reprimanded Sidney for spending hours in dancing and other courtly pleasures which could have been better spent in writing to his friends. In the following summer he discovered fresh cause for reproach. He had reason to believe that Sidney was communicating with some other friends, but not with himself:

> From your letter of June 21 sent from London I infer that you did not intend to inform me of your Irish expedition unless you received a letter from me on the eve of departure. Yet you had earlier written detailed plans of the journey to other friends who told me about them ... Perhaps you feared I should not wish you success, and considered the good will of others to be stronger than mine.[63]

Once again, Languet's suspicions were justified. He was not alone in finding Sidney's letters both infrequent and uncommunicative. Jean Lobbet, writing from Strasbourg, made exactly the same complaints.[64] But there seems little doubt that Languet was being fast relegated to a fairly lowly position in the ranks of Sidney's advisers. This was noticed by others at the Imperial Court. The distinguished botanist Charles de l'Ecluse, for instance, sending him a copy of his elegant study of rare plants of Spain in March 1576,[65] enclosed a letter from Languet, and took occasion to implore him to put things right with his old mentor:

> It has been a long time since we have heard any news of you, and Monsieur Languet has often complained about this to me; he tells me you have grown idle ... You will send him your answer when it is convenient, but I would be glad if you would do this at the first opportunity, in order to dissuade him from that idea.[66]

Sidney's failure to keep Languet fully informed about his Irish journey has the drawback that many details about it are also inaccessible to the biographer. He probably did indeed suspect that Languet would not approve of the expedition, for several reasons. The cultivated old Burgundian saw the Celtic parts of Britain as threateningly savage and dangerous, as he went on to say in the letter already quoted:

> ... When I turn my mind to the high rugged mountains of Wales, to the stormy Irish sea, and to the consistently unhealthy autumn season I feel unusual concern about you. Hence, by the love which you once felt for me, I beg you earnestly to report that you are safe once you have reached the happy haven of your court ... Doubtless you will write to us punctiliously describing the Irish miracles and will send specimens of the birds which reportedly grow on trees there.[67]

The characteristic attempt to arouse Sidney's interest by means of sardonic banter fails to mask Languet's intense anxiety about the physical dangers of the Irish journey. He would have been even more worried if he had known that one of Sidney's chief companions was a man already seriously ill, who was to die of dysentery a few weeks later. This was Walter Devereux, first Earl of Essex, father of Sidney's 'Stella', who had already shown favour to Sidney in his schooldays (see above, p. 33). Sidney may have had a chance to renew his acquaintance with the Devereux children when the Royal Progress stopped at Chartley in August 1575. Essex himself had come back to England in the winter of 1575–6 to persuade the Queen to give him money and support for his Antrim 'plantations'. These costly bastions against the Scots had consumed both his funds and his health. Elizabeth had withdrawn her support for his enterprise in May 1575, but this did not prevent Essex from further military outrages, culminating in the massacre of all six hundred inhabitants of Rathlin Island. His attempt at 'plantation' had resulted in terror and depopulation.

In his quest for renewed favour from the Queen, Essex had some success. In May 1576 Elizabeth confirmed 'for life' his post as Earl Marshal of Ireland, and granted him extensive Irish estates, to compensate for the English estates she had claimed back in payment of his debts to her. In consequence, he was now committed irretrievably to a future in Ireland. As it turned out, this future was to be extremely brief, which was probably just as well for the native inhabitants of his newly acquired lands.

It was almost certainly with Essex and his party that Sidney travelled to Ireland, in July 1576. If so, he had another chance to meet the Devereux children at Chartley on the way. Penelope was now thirteen, and her father hoped for a marriage between her and Philip. As son of the Lord Deputy of Ireland and heir to the Earls of Leicester and Warwick, Philip was clearly a very attractive prospect to such an impoverished family as the Devereux had now become. But there were difficulties in the way of this marriage, not least the fact that Sir Henry Sidney could not abide Essex. Philip's own attitude to the scheme will be discussed later. Meanwhile, how he reconciled his own friendship with Essex and his father's dislike of him is hard to conjecture. Osborn suggests that he acted as a diplomat, trying to reconcile them,[68] which may be right.

In view of his friendship with Essex, it is not likely that Sidney's view of Ireland and the Irish was much more enlightened than that of his contemporaries. To most Elizabethans, Ireland was a country

> Where every prospect pleases,
> And only man is vile.

John Derricke, in his descriptive poem *The Image of Ireland*, dedicated to Sidney in 1581 but written in 1578, compared the country to a beautiful bride with an ugly husband. The bride was the soil itself, the bridegroom the 'wood kern', or poor natives. Foundations for still-continuing anguish were laid down in this period by the policy, in which Sir Henry Sidney was a firm believer, of 'planting' settlements of imported Protestants, while often treating the 'wild' or native Irish with outrageous cruelty. In the *Chronicles of Ireland* John Hooker used highly coloured language, calling the native Irish 'bare-arsed rebels', only to be subdued by means of unremitting severity:

> Withdraw the sword and forbear correction, deal with them in courtesy and entreat them gently, if they can take any advantage, they will surely out, and as the dog to his vomit and the sow to her dirt and puddle they will return to their old and former insolency, rebellion and disobedience.[69]

Nicholas Malby, a man much loved and promoted by Sir Henry Sidney, who appointed him Governor of Connaught, used another image of the Irish:

> knowing that he should have to do with a sort of nettles, whose nature is, that being handled gently, they will sting; but being hard crushed together, they will do no harm.[70]

With such metaphors did successive English governors legitimate their policies.

There was, however, a radical difference between Henry Sidney's strategies and those of Essex. While Essex was above all a soldier, who used military, and often treacherous, measures to subdue his territories in Ulster, Henry Sidney was a thoroughgoing and largely peace-loving administrator. Dividing Ireland into shires under a series of local governors was one of his chief objectives. He also proceeded judicially, holding a series of courts in each place where he stopped during his extensive journeys round the country. Though he was by no means gentle in his measures, Henry Sidney's preference for legal and diplomatic resolution of Irish resistance, and his willingness, sometimes, to hear complaints and deal with them within a legal framework, must have contributed to his popularity and partial success, relative at least to some other governors of the period. Economic rather than military problems were to be his undoing: the local governments he set up were extremely expensive to sustain. In the woodcuts illustrating Derricke's *Image of Ireland*, Henry Sidney is consistently shown in half armour only, with a soft hat rather than a helmet, and in Plate IX, depicting a military encounter with 'wild' Irish soldiers, he is nowhere to be seen. Major military operations tended to be delegated to others. It was, for instance, his friend Nicholas Malby who suppressed the rebellion of the Earl of Clanricard in Connaught in the winter of 1575–6.[71]

On 10 August Philip met up with his father at Kilcullen, twenty-eight miles from Dublin. Essex brought Henry Sidney welcome news of the Privy Council's approval 'for his diligence and execution of justice in all places'. Father and son spent a fortnight together at Dublin Castle before setting off for the west in search of further pockets of resistance led by the two sons of the Earl of Clanricard. As Osborn observes, this was not at all the kind of service Philip had hoped for:

> any military experience which Philip had gained in Ireland would have been in the

futile pursuit of guerillas, and not in regular military engagements or in the storming of fortresses that he would have observed had he joined General von Schwendi [to fight the Turks].[72]

Hunting out the often starved and ragged 'wood kern' was a miserable business. Perhaps it was more to Sidney's taste than hunting deer, but not much.

A consolation, however, was the sense that Ireland was a land full of marvels. One such was the native Irish love of music and poetry. Ireland offered vivid proof that poetry could do even more than 'hold children from play, and old men from the chimney corner'.[73] In that country poets could exercise the power of life or death. During Sir Henry Sidney's first term as Lord Deputy, in 1566, he had decreed

that whosoever could take a Rimer (which were a kind of superstitious prophesiers of Ireland) should spoil him, and have his goods, without danger of law.[74]

In revenge, the 'prophesiers' threatened to 'rhyme to death' Nicholas Malby and others at Kilkenny, a threat which was taken extremely seriously. Turned to virtuous ends, how much this poetic power might accomplish. Sidney placed the Irish bards in a wider and more positive context in his *Defence*:

In our neighbour country Ireland, where truly learning goeth very bare, yet are their poets held in a devout reverence.[75]

He did not forget the threat posed by the Irish bards to his father and others, but turned it into a joke against the enemies of poetry, whom he will not wish 'to be rhymed to death, as is said to be done in Ireland'.[76]

Most writers on Ireland, from Giraldus Cambrensis onwards, saw it as an island like Prospero's, 'full of wonders', though its 'sounds and strange airs' might well be hurtful. Languet jokingly asked Sidney to report on the 'barnacle geese', birds mentioned by Giraldus and faithfully reported by many later writers. They were supposedly generated, not from eggs, but from excrescences on trees. But Sidney actually met with a more interesting wonder than the barnacle geese. This was the legendary woman chieftain, Grania or Grace O'Malley. Our knowledge of the encounter comes from a long autobiographical letter written by Sir Henry Sidney to Walsingham in March 1583, when agreement had just been reached for a marriage between Philip and Walsingham's daughter Frances:

There came to me also a most famous feminine sea-captain, called Granny O'Malley, and offered her services unto me wheresoever I would command her, with three galleys and two hundred fighting men, either in Ireland or Scotland. She brought with her her husband, for she was as well by sea as by land more than master's mate with him ... This was a notorious woman in all the coast of Ireland ... this woman did Sir Philip Sidney see and speak with; he can more at large inform you of her.[77]

To a young man who was to show himself, in the *Arcadia*, fascinated by images of Amazons and sexually ambivalent warriors, it must have been a memorable episode, though there is no evidence that he was, as has been claimed, 'captivated' by Grace.[78] His father's suggestion that he will tell the tale to his future father-in-law suggests that even seven years later Philip was 'dining out' on his strange meeting in Galway. He may have felt considerable admiration for Grace O'Malley, as one of those 'heroically minded' women able to exercise authority effectively.[79] Like the Queen, Grace O'Malley offered an uncomfortable challenge to current male assumptions about gender rôles. Sidney's meeting with her may also have sparked off a curious passage in the 'Old' *Arcadia* in which Pyrocles, himself disguised as a woman, tries deliberately to degrade himself in the eyes of the amorous Gynecia. He describes himself as fighting successfully against the Amazons, until

> I (hoping to prevail against her) challenged an old woman of fourscore years to fight on horseback to the uttermost with me: who, having overthrown me, for saving of my life made me swear I should go like an unarmed Amazon till the coming of my beard did with the discharge of my oath deliver me of bondage.[80]

This is a ridiculous tall story, and even Gynecia does not quite believe it. But the Irish chieftainess – aged about fifty, not 'fourscore', when the Sidneys met her – was genuinely a force to be reckoned with. Sir Henry Sidney decided, probably wisely, to make a treaty with her. He also knighted her husband, Richard Burke, nicknamed 'the Devil's Hook', conversing with him in Latin, as he had no English. This was surely good strategy. Later English governors, like Richard Bingham, who imprisoned Grace O'Malley and threatened her with execution, had much trouble with her many supporters.

A more workaday commodity offered by Ireland was its horses, believed to be originally imported from Spain. Sidney acquired ten or more Irish horses. We know the names of two of them, Pied Peppered, 'sent into England with Mr Philip Sidney', and Grey Synnot, 'given to Mr Philip Sidney'.[81] By the time he travelled back with Pied Peppered there were graver matters to attend to than the welfare of horses. As already mentioned, the Earl of Essex died in Dublin Castle on 22 September after a month or more of illness. He was only thirty-five. Leicester's enemies laid the death at his gate, claiming that he had arranged for Essex to be poisoned so that he could marry his widow. This seems extremely unlikely, but rumours of poisoning made it essential for Henry Sidney to look into the matter and report his (negative) findings.[82] John Hooker, basing his account on reports by Essex's faithful secretary Edward Waterhouse, added that 'some inward grief of the mind and secret sorrow of the heart' hastened Essex's end.[83] This hinted at his dissatisfaction with the Queen's limited support for him. Whatever the truth of the matter, Essex's death stimulated a great deal of pious myth-making that strangely foreshadowed Sidney's. Even the date was prophetic, for Essex died ten years to the day before Sidney received his leg wound. Edward Waterhouse and others used the supposed godliness of Essex's end, as later writers were to use Sidney's, to cast a rosy glow back over his previous career. He is described as engaging in godly conversation, and

> The nearer that death drew, the more fervent he was in prayer, and requested all his company to do the like, and the very last words that he spoke was, 'The lord Jesus'. And when his tongue gave over to speak any more, he lifted up his hands and eyes to the Lord his God.[84]

Like Sidney, he is said to have called for a song, asking his musician William Hayes to accompany him on the virginals while he himself sang a penitent ditty of his own composition, beginning:

> O heavenly God, O Father dear, cast down thy tender eye
> Upon a wretch that prostrate here before thy throne doth lie . . .[85]

Actually, the song is the work of a friend of George Gascoigne's, Francis Kinwelmarsh, and the anecdote, along with the rest of the account, is probably a fabrication. It is hard to believe that a man who was having forty or more stools a day could die with such composure. We can, if we like, believe that this bloodthirsty soldier, who was capable of inviting a clan to dinner and then having the whole lot slaughtered, 'made a good end', as Mistress Quickly claimed of Falstaff. But it seems much more probable that Waterhouse's and Henry Sidney's accounts of Essex's serene piety were fictions intended for the edification of readers in England. In relation to the Queen, service in Ireland was 'subject to the ear', not 'object to the eye', as Henry Sidney's secretary Edmund Molyneux put it.[86] This had some advantages. The Queen was not expected ever to visit Ireland, and though she was, of course, no fool, careful control of what news of Irish affairs reached her could be used to shape the judgements of her ministers in England.

Quite what part Sidney played in the aftermath of Essex's death is not clear. He certainly seems to have spent a lot of time with the dead Earl's secretary, Waterhouse, who spoke very highly of the younger Sidney's gifts and desirability as a husband for the now orphaned Penelope Devereux. By 4 November Sidney was at Greenwich, making arrangements for the reception of his Irish horses. But his most important task was to reinforce the 'received version' of Essex's death at Court, and in particular to report on the success of his father in pacifying the greater part of Ireland. In so doing, he had an excellent opportunity to display his own maturity, tact and verbal skill. The Queen must have been impressed, for in the winter of 1576–7 she gave him his first and most congenial piece of state employment. He had not waited in vain.

6
1577
SIDNEY AS HE LIVED

The inheritors of unfulfilled renown ...
Sidney ... as he lived.[1]

Who gives himself may well his picture give
Else were it vain, since both short time do live.[2]

1577, when Sidney was sent to the Holy Roman Emperor, was the best year of his life. It is also unusually well documented, both visually and verbally. It was in June of this year that the best-known portrait of him was painted.[3] The artist is unknown, though attempts to identify him either with Frederico Zuccaro, Antonius Mor or Cornelius Ketel all suggest a recognition of the high quality of the painting. Yet another possible artist is the Serjeant-Painter, George Gower, who worked both for Leicester and the Queen. Which of three or four early versions is the original for which Sidney himself posed is also not certain, but it may be the exemplar now at Longleat, which was formerly at Wilton. Uniquely, the Longleat version has a couplet inscribed on it:

Who gives himself may well his picture give
Else were it vain, since both short time do live.

Robert Sidney adapted the first line in an incomplete 'crown of sonnets' within his sequence of poems:

Who gives himself may ill his words deny.[4]

Probably Philip himself wrote the original couplet, attaching it to the copy of his portrait given to his sister, the newly married Countess of Pembroke, perhaps as a wedding present. He was soon to 'give himself' to her over again in that rich, complex, highly entertaining delivery of thoughts bred in his 'young head', the 'Old' *Arcadia*, which he began writing in the autumn at her request.

Meanwhile, the portrait, also dedicated to her, is a speaking likeness (see dust-jacket). It presumably shows how Sidney wanted to be seen by his family and friends after the successful completion of his mission to the Emperor. Probably by design, it reveals a contrast between youth and vulnerability in the face and an aura of considerable importance emanating from clothes and bearing. Languet had complained in 1574 that Veronese's portrait made Sidney look far too young – no more than twelve or thirteen, though he was actually almost twenty.[5] Perhaps Sidney actually did look rather young for his years, and continued to do so, for the 1577 portrait shows him as a distinctly youthful twenty-two, beardless, short-haired and slender. This is most marked in the Warwick Castle version. Arrogance, pensiveness and keen expectancy are blended in the finely carved features. We should not be surprised that no pock-marks or pimples are shown. Though the pose, right hand on hip, left hand on sword handle, is conventional, it also has symbolic connotations appropriate to Sidney at this moment. He is only partly armed, prepared immediately for court ceremonial rather than military action. Yet the shadowy left hand, half closed around the sword hilt, points discreetly to a further ambition. His readiness with the sword in the limited arena of Elizabeth's Court was soon to get Sidney into trouble, while the serious military experience which he craved continued to be denied him. Meanwhile, in 1577, there was much to enjoy in the peaceful pleasures of court life, travel, diplomacy, friendship and study.

Not only do we first see an image of 'Sidney as he lived' in 1577, it is also in this same year that we first hear his voice. To it belong several accounts of his conversation, both formal and relaxed, as well as some occasional poems, three or four substantial letters, and a short political piece defending his father, the *Discourse on Irish Affairs*. Both this *Discourse* and the long letter in which he reported on his mission to the Emperor are in Sidney's own hand. This gives unusual freshness and immediacy to our perception of his thought processes, despite the fact that both documents were damaged in the Cotton fire. In effect, it was not to his sister only that Sidney 'gave' himself in 1577; he also bequeathed numerous images of himself to the scrutiny of after-comers. These images are sharper than those of subsequent years because so many of them are products of Sidney's own youthful 'self-fashioning', not as yet fully heightened by his fictive imagination, nor obscured by the propaganda or myth-making of others.

The year began well. The Sidney family (except Sir Henry, who was still in Ireland) participated in Christmas festivities at Court. There was much talk of marriage. Sidney's possible union with Penelope Devereux was still occasionally mentioned, but the increasingly evident poverty of the Devereux children made it less and less likely. As mentioned earlier, Sir Henry Sidney did not share Leicester's enthusiasm for the Devereux family. If we give literal credence to Sidney's later self-portrayal as 'Astrophil', his own disinclination may also have made him reluctant: 'I liked, but loved not.'[6] Also, Sir Henry Sidney was soon going to have to find upwards of £3,000 for the marriage of his daughter.[7] In December 1576 this was being actively spoken of, and by February 1577 it was a settled thing: the fifteen-year-old Mary Sidney was to marry Henry Herbert, second Earl of Pembroke, at Easter.[8] Though the Earl was almost forty, recently widowed by the death of his second wife, Catherine Talbot, the match was a great thing for the Sidney family. After only a year and a half of attendance on the Queen, young Mary was to become 'Lady of Wilton',[9] the great house and estate in Wiltshire where she would for many decades preside over her own small court or 'college'. It was a cheerful and hopeful winter for the younger Sidneys. Philip continued to take charge of his younger brother's education and welfare, and made sure that he was smartly enough dressed when he came from Oxford to Court for Christmas. The accounts of Robert Sidney's tutor Dorset mention, on 26 December 1576, 'a velvet hat with a gold band and a gold feather', and two further feathers, one white, one blue, purchased 'By Mr Philip Sidney's appointment against Christmas'.[10] What his uncle had done for him in earlier years, he was now doing for young Robert: making sure that he was turned out in the splendid style the Queen expected.

After the fatigues and miseries of the Irish journey Philip was able again to enjoy the security and comfort of England. He had leisure to catch up with letters, make new friends and pursue some absorbing interests. One of these, almost certainly, was 'chemistry', which for Elizabethans at this date most often denoted alchemy and mineralogy. Moffet particularly stresses young Sidney's interest in the subject:

> Led by God, with Dee as teacher and with Dyer as companion, he learned chemistry, that starry science, rival to nature. The variety of opinions, the tricks of the teachers, the high costs, the uncertainty of results, somewhat oppress the weakness of minds endeavouring to proceed so far ... Yet so far did he have an unexhausted eagerness for complete (or rather for only the accepted) learning that he leaped over all these obstacles at one bound.[11]

What Moffet's eulogy glosses over is the fact that Sidney, intelligent and questioning in so many matters, was as naive as the next man when it came to prospects of gold. Many people of good sense in this period were beguiled by the notion of the 'philosopher's stone', which could supposedly transmute base metal into gold. Among those so beguiled were Sidney's mother and her good friend Edward Dyer, who may have been bonded partly by their shared enthusiasm for alchemy. In October 1576 she made passionate pleas to Sussex for mitigation of the treatment of an alchemist called William Medley, once held in high esteem by Burghley, Leicester and others, but now discredited and imprisoned in the Counter.[12] Medley had a scheme for transmuting iron into copper by the use of vitriol. However, another investor, Sir Humphrey Gilbert, seems to have exposed this as fraudulent.[13]

Probably correctly, Moffet associates Sidney's interest in chemistry with both Dyer and Dr John Dee. On 16 January 1576/7 Leicester, Sidney, Dyer and others had a conference with this famous magus, who had long enjoyed the favour and protection of the Queen and had acted as a tutor to some of the Dudleys. It is not clear where this meeting took place, whether at Dee's house at Mortlake or, as seems more probable, at Leicester House.[14] Dee's areas of expertise were numerous, and the exact purpose of the meeting can only be conjectured. It has been thought to relate to Sidney's forthcoming mission to the Emperor Rudolph II.[15] Certainly Dee was a practised traveller, and had himself been to the Imperial Court in 1564, when he dedicated his *Monas Hieroglyphica,* a philosophical alchemical treatise, to Rudolph's father Maximilian.[16] But it is by no means clear that Sidney's appointment to the mission had yet been decided,[17] and it seems quite likely that the meeting had something to do with journeys in a quite other direction. Dee's *General and Rare Memorials pertaining to the Art of Navigation,* which went to press on 19 August 1577, must have been in active preparation during the previous winter. It was a preliminary fragment of a much larger work on navigation and exploration whose ultimate object was nothing less than the establishment of a British Empire, Protestant and peace-loving, which would rival the Spanish/Hapsburg Empire in the New World.[18] While the Spanish commanded territories in South America, English merchant venturers had high hopes of the northernmost parts of Canada, known as 'Meta Incognita'. Sidney's possible journey to the old 'Holy Roman' Empire may – if known about – have seemed of secondary interest to the exploration of 'Meta Incognita' and the transforming possibilities this appeared to offer. His uncle, Ambrose Dudley, had been the chief backer of Martin Frobisher's 1576 voyage in search of the North-West Passage which supposedly gave access to the fabulous wealth of Cathay, and Sidney, his mother and Dyer had each invested £25 in it. Now a second voyage was being planned, and Dee's opinion on the wisdom of investing in it must have been sought. Though Frobisher had not found the North-West Passage, one of his sailors had brought back a piece of black pyrite from Northern Labrador. After an Italian goldsmith called Agnello contrived (by a trick) to get gold out of it, the whole Court, from the Queen downwards, was in a fever.[19]

This time, the search for Cathay was given lower priority than mineral exploration. Frobisher's instructions directed him rather towards 'searching more of this gold ore than for the searching any further discovery of the passage'.[20] The Queen herself provided a ship, the *Aid*, and £2,000. The Dudleys, Sidney and Dyer were all substantial investors, doubling their previous contributions, though £50 was a sum Sidney could ill afford. Dyer also had a personal stake in the expedition, for his brother Andrew was master of the *Aid*. If all went well in the North Atlantic – if, as Sidney claimed to Languet, 'the island is so productive in metals as to seem to surpass the country of Peru'[21] – unlimited wealth and power seemed to be within reach. Many were in a Faustian mood:

> O, what a world of profit and delight,
> Of power, of honour, of omnipotence,
> Is promis'd to the studious artisan!
> ... his dominion, that excels in this,
> Stretcheth as far as doth the mind of man:
> A sound magician is a demi-god ...[22]

John Dee, regarded by the highest in the land as the 'sound magician' *par excellence*, could offer an expert opinion on the wisdom of backing Frobisher's second voyage, as well as on the smaller matter of Medley the alchemist. Mineralogy and geography were fields in which he excelled. As Peter French has shown, Sidney and his friends shared many sophisticated aims and ideals with John Dee: British colonial ambitions; schemes for religious union; connected plans for the reformation of vernacular music and metrics; an interest in Ramist logic, in Hermeticism and in Platonism.[23] But without substantial wealth many of these ideals, especially the colonial ones, would be doomed to perish in the scholar's study. Money, and plenty of it, was the first and most pressing need of Sidney and his friends. Frobisher's next journey seemed to offer glittering possibilities, especially if someone so knowledgeable as Dee was prepared to give it his blessing. Sidney may even have hoped to go to Meta Incognita in person. He was certainly very excited about it – unwisely so, in Languet's view.

Meanwhile we know that Sidney was also pursuing quieter studies. He spent some time during this same winter studying the first three books of Livy's *Roman History* with the handsome and learned Cambridge academic Gabriel Harvey, who noted the fact in the margin of his own copy of Livy.[24] At the time of his meetings with Sidney, Harvey was making a somewhat desperate bid for renewal of his Fellowship of Pembroke and his University Praelectorship in Rhetoric, both of which had lapsed in 1576. He also rather hoped to be sent abroad in some capacity, perhaps in Sidney's retinue.[25] In two of his printed orations, the *Rhetor* (delivered in spring 1576, printed in November 1577) and *Ciceronianus* (delivered in spring 1576, printed in June 1577), Harvey claimed that his Cambridge lectures attracted audiences of several hundred, while some senior academics lectured to empty rooms. This may well have been true, but it was scarcely tactful to make the point in print. Throughout his life Harvey had a unique capacity for making enemies. In the late 1570s he assiduously cultivated leading courtiers, having got himself intensely disliked at his Cambridge college. Even the powerful support of the Earl of Leicester failed to persuade the Master and Fellows of Pembroke to re-elect him, and eventually he was elected to a Fellowship at Trinity Hall, where he claimed kin with the master, Henry Harvey. Most famously, in the 1590s, when Harvey left Cambridge for a career as a lawyer in London, he became the butt of Thomas Nashe's richly inventive wit. Nashe acknowledged that Harvey had once enjoyed Sidney's favour and protection, but suggested that this was quite brief:

> ... Sir Philip Sidney (as he was a natural cherisher of men of the least towardness in any art whatsoever) held him in some good regard, and so did most men ... but afterward, when his ambitious pride and vanity unmasked itself so egregiously, both in his looks, his gait, his gestures, and speeches, and he would do nothing but crake and parrot it in print, in how many noblemen's favours he was, and blab every light speech they uttered to him in private ... then Sir Philip Sidney (by little and little) began to look askance upon him, and not to care for him, though utterly shake him off he could not, he would so fawn and hang upon him.[26]

Nashe also claimed that the arrogant Harvey

> would make no bones to take the wall of Sir Philip Sidney and another honourable knight, his companion, about the Court yet attending.

It is difficult wholly to separate the young Gabriel Harvey who enjoyed a brief intimacy with the young (and as yet unknighted) Philip Sidney from the ridiculous figure lampooned by Nashe, whose extended verbal portrait is reinforced with a woodcut of Harvey about to make water, a small, pompous figure in a silly ruff. There is no doubt that Harvey did indeed become too big for his buskins, and wrote hugely inflated accounts of his favour at Court. He probably exploded his chances of continued favour in the summer of 1578, when he published the overwritten and tactless *Gratulationes Valdinenses*.[27] But in the winter of 1576–7 his indiscretion was not yet apparent. His sound Latinity was never in question, and just as Dee's opinions on exploration and mineralogy were well worth having, so were Harvey's on Roman history. There was much in Livy's first three books to interest Sidney, and Harvey was well equipped to expound them to him, as he later expounded them to Sidney's friends Edward Denny and Edward Dyer.[28]

It is interesting that one of the complaints made about Harvey at Pembroke was that he spent the Christmas season studying rather than being sociable and playing cards.[29] Sidney, too, may have preferred to spend much of the Christmas holiday in study. It was presumably in Sidney's lodgings at Leicester House that the sandy-haired young courtier and the swarthy, moustachioed academic bent together over Livy's *Roman History*. There Sidney would have read, almost at once, about the vanity of consulting oracles, in the story of Titus and Aruns, who made a journey to Delphi to learn who would be the next king of Rome. They misinterpreted the oracle, but their companion, Brutus, pretending to be a fool, got it right and succeeded to the throne. He would have read, too, of repeated political disasters precipitated by sexual passion in groups or individuals – the rape of the Sabine women, Tarquin's rape of Lucretia, Appius Claudius's attempt to rape Virginia. Brutus, in Books 1 and 2, offered an austere image of the justice and impartiality which were perceived as most characteristic of ancient virtue when he condemned his own sons to death for their part in a conspiracy. Livy, whose 'pathetical spirit in moving affections' is praised by his Elizabethan translator, Philemon Holland, gives a touching account:

> Which suffering of theirs was the more notable, for that the father, by his place and virtue of his office, was bound and charged to see execution done upon his own children: and he who otherwise ought not to have been a spectator and looker on, even he (such was his fortune) was forced of necessity to be the principal actor in this tragical execution.[30]

All these motifs – an oracle sought and misinterpreted, the state shaken by sexual passion, the fortitude of a judge who condemns his own children – were to appear prominently in the *Arcadia*. Without knowing it, the unfortunate Gabriel Harvey was helping to determine the subject-matter of the first major work of English fiction. For all his manifest failings, he deserves some credit for this. Since he undoubtedly also acted as midwife to Spenser's *Shepheardes Calender* and *Faerie Queene*, he should be given a significant place in the history of Elizabethan literature, quite apart from his comic fame as Nashe's victim.

Spenser himself may first have become acquainted with Sidney about this time. He, too, was a graduate of Pembroke College, Cambridge, and may possibly have worked later this year as a secretary or courier for Sir Henry Sidney. Harvey could have brought him to Sidney's notice, as his best Cambridge 'familiar', or college friend. Both men hoped for diplomatic employment, and both had schemes for epic poems. However, at this early date Gabriel Harvey's grandiose scheme for an English epic praising Elizabeth, *Anticosmopolita*, probably seemed more impressive than Spenser's for his *Faerie Queene*, both because it was further advanced – Spenser was a notoriously slow writer, Harvey a flamboyantly quick one – and because it was more ostentatiously 'learned'.[31] That Sidney's recognition of the true worth of Spenser's poetry was delayed is suggested by Aubrey's anecdote:

Among others, Mr Edmund Spencer made his address to him, and brought his *Faerie Queene*. Sir Philip was busy at his study, and his servant delivered Mr Spencer's book to his master, who laid it by, thinking it might be such kind of stuff as he was frequently troubled with. Mr Spencer stayed so long that his patience was wearied, and went his way discontented, and never intended to come again. When Sir Philip perused it, he was so exceedingly delighted with it that he was extremely sorry he was gone, and where to send for him he knew not. After much enquiry he learned his lodging, and sent for him, mightily caressed <him>, and ordered his servant to give him [...] pounds in gold. His servant said that was too much; 'No', said Sir Philip, 'he is ...', and ordered an addition. From this time there was a great friendship between them to his dying day.[32]

Aubrey himself had his doubts about this story. If the incident happened at all, it was probably in 1580 or later. Yet the general notion that Sidney's appreciation of Spenser's worth as a poet was slow in coming but, once attained, was warm and generous may be correct. Even initially, Harvey cannot have made as good an impression on Sidney as he hoped, for he was not included, as he surely would have liked to be, in the very large party which was assembled during February 1576/7 to travel with Sidney to the Imperial Court. His period of strong favour with Sidney may have been, as Nashe claimed, extremely brief. By the time of the *Three Letters*, in which Harvey boasted of his and Spenser's familiarity with Sidney and Dyer, Spenser had easily overtaken him, which may have been one of Harvey's foolish reasons for flaunting his own supposed favour.

It was in early February that Sidney's appointment as ambassador was made.[33] Preparations for the mission forced him to abandon the contemplation of ancient Rome in favour of more practical matters. Clothes, horses, gifts and necessaries needed to be assembled, and financial and family affairs to be set in order. These tasks included making sure that his old nurse, Anne Mantell, got her salary (see above, p. 8). The ostensible purpose of the mission was to carry the Queen's condolences to the Emperor, Rudolph II, for the death of his father, Maximilian, and also to the two Counts Palatine, Ludwig and Casimir, for the death of their father, Frederick. But there was a further, much more ambitious, covert aim: to sound out Protestant princes about the possibility of a defensive league which would gather together widespread, but scattered, resistance to the powers of Rome and Spain.

Shifting the balance of power in central Europe at a time of great turbulence sounds like a big job to entrust to a twenty-two-year-old, yet Sidney was not uniquely young for such an appointment. His own father had been sent to France to mediate 'for composing the wars between [France] and the Emperor' when he was almost exactly the same age.[34] What was needed for such missions was a fluent linguist with considerable social skills, who could be trusted to carry out the Queen's instructions faithfully. Of Sidney's social and linguistic skills there could be no doubt. If some doubt attached to his youth and impetuosity, the presence of older and more experienced men in the party ought to act as a safeguard. These included the Queen's Champion, Sir Henry Lee, and Sir Jerome Bowes, who had been a member of the mission with which Sidney travelled to France in 1572. Soon after his return from Prague, Bowes got into trouble for slandering the Earl of Leicester;[35] but he later achieved distinction as an exceptionally pugnacious ambassador to Muscovy.[36] Among others in the party Sidney's close friends Edward Dyer and Fulke Greville were included, as was Henry Brouncker, mentioned by Moffet as one of Sidney's best friends.[37] There was also a young man called George More who was later to become the hostile father-in-law of the poet John Donne.[38] Sidney's female relations and younger brothers must have watched him go with considerable pride. But as so often, his absent father was rather out of touch. On 4 February Sir Henry wrote begging Leicester to send Philip to help him in Ireland – 'there was never father had more need of his son than I have of him' – and he seems not to have learned of his departure for the Continent until well after the party had left.[39]

Sidney and his companions set out at the very end of February. By 4 March they had arrived in Brussels, where the English ambassador, Dr Thomas Wilson, entertained them. During the three months of this mission Sidney encountered a greater number of eminent figures than he had done during the entire three years of his previous continental journey, at least if princes and statesmen are reckoned to be more eminent than scholars. The first such luminary he encountered was Don John of Austria, bastard brother of Philip II, and victor of the great battle of Lepanto against the Turks in October 1571. Now he was Philip's Vice-Regent of the Netherlands. Wilson arranged the meeting, which took place in Louvain on 6 March. Little is known of what passed. According to Greville, who was probably present, Don John (himself aged only twenty-eight) initially showed contempt for Sidney's youth, 'in his Spanish hauteur', but soon became deeply impressed by his gifts.[40] Dr Wilson reported that Sidney's 'plain speech had fair and sweet answers'. This 'plain speech' concerned English Catholic exiles who were hovering in Don John's Court.[41] However, as will be seen, Sidney's private attitude to such exiles may have been rather complicated.

The next stop was Heidelberg. Here Sidney met the younger Palatine prince, John Casimir, and we have his own account of the meeting in a letter written to Walsingham on 22 March. It is too long to quote in full, but passages in it show Sidney's increasing powers of vivid expression. For instance, in reporting on Casimir's loyalty to Elizabeth, he says: 'This he did in very good terms, and with a countenance well witnessing it came from his heart.' There was a widening split between Casimir and his older brother Ludwig, who had turned from Calvinism to Lutheranism. Sidney's account was characteristically optimistic:

[Casimir] is resolved if his brother do drive away from him the learned men of the true profession, that he will receive [them] to him, and hereof something may breed gall betwixt them if any do. But the best is to be hoped, considering Prince Lodovick is of a soft nature, led to these things only through conscience, and Prince Casimir wise, that can temper well with the other's weakness.[42]

These are confident character assessments coming from a twenty-two-year-old. Though many others considered Casimir to be a somewhat hotheaded and unreliable leader, Sidney got on well with him, and was keen to persuade the Queen to be generous in supplying him with money for his 'reiters', or cavalry.

To Sidney's next stop, Nuremberg, belongs the most extended account we have of his table-talk. It is in Latin, as doubtless Sidney's conversation was too, especially since he could not speak German. The party arrived there on 29 March and were soon joined by Sidney's old tutor Hubert Languet, who had hurried over from Frankfurt. Languet was present at a dinner party described by the Protestant scholar Philip Camerarius, who was a councillor for the Landgrave of Hesse, one of the noblemen with whom Sidney was to discuss the possibility of a Protestant league.[43] The Camerarius family may themselves have been the hosts on this occasion, for in May 1578 Sidney thanked Philip and his elder brother Joachim for their kindness to him in Nuremberg.[44] Finding the right topic for dinner-table conversation in large international gatherings, when profound religious and political differences might lie only just below the surface, was not easy. An Italian courtesy book translated into English in 1576, Giovanni della Casa's *Il Galateo*, gives numerous amusing examples of what not to do when at table. Gentlemen should not eat their food greedily,

and with both their cheeks blown (as if they should sound a trumpet, or blow the fire) not eat, but ravin: who, besmearing their hands, almost up to their elbows, so bedaub the napkins that the cloths in the places of easement be other while cleaner.

While at table, they should not sleep, pare their nails, sing or fidget. Speech should be neither scurrilous nor blasphemous; neither 'too deep and too subtle', nor melancholy, nor boastful.[45] Sidney's dinner-table topic was perfect:

uncontroversial, mildly patriotic, easy to follow and entertaining. On being asked why there were no wolves in England, he gave an extended historical explanation. Wolves, he reported, had once been 'as common in England as in Germany', and even fine English sheepdogs were unable to protect the fine English sheep.[46] However, at some unspecified date long ago there had been a law enabling criminals to avoid punishment on presentation of a specified number of 'tongues and heads' of wolves, which eventually eradicated the species. Sidney proved that there was no natural antipathy between English soil and wolves, as some believed, for

> in divers places of the country there are of them to be seen in the parks of great lords, who send for them out of Ireland and other places, to make a show of them as of some rare beast: but it is forbidden upon grievous penalties to let them escape out of their enclosure.[47]

Some wolves still remained in Scotland, but they too were securely contained both by 'great store of dogs' and by natural geographical features. Sidney seems also to have given an account of the British Isles, for the speech about wolves was

> accompanied with other memorable speeches touching Ireland, where his father governed; and of St Patrick's Hole, much esteemed when time was (at this day little set by) . . .

The discourse was 'very pleasing to the company that sat at table with him, and no man would make any question thereof, especially when we saw it approved by Hubert Languet . . .' When at home, Sidney was apt to complain of England's peaceful torpor, but at this gathering in Germany he evidently gave a positive account of its peace and prosperity, with its important wool manufacture unthreatened by the depredations of wolves. Also, without boasting crudely of his own position, he had managed to introduce a reference to the fact that his father 'governed' Ireland. Almost certainly one or more of his uncles were among the 'great lords' who kept wolves in their parks. It was vitally important for Sidney to affirm his obliquely aristocratic status. A tablet declaring his relationship to the 'Pro-Rex' of Ireland and the Earls of Warwick and Leicester was hung outside his lodgings throughout this journey,[48] which may have been standard diplomatic practice. But Sidney's youthful appearance and lack of any personal title made it essential for him to draw repeated attention to the high status of his close relations, lest it should seem that the Queen was insulting the nobility of Europe by choosing a mere boy to represent her.

On 4 April, which was Maundy Thursday, Sidney and his party arrived in Prague, where the new Emperor held his Court. Holy Week and Easter celebrations occupied the next four days. There must have been a chaplain in the English group, but his identity is not known. The 1559 Book of Common Prayer required that 'every parishioner shall communicate at the least three times in the year, of which Easter to be one'. Despite Archbishop Grindal's attempts in 1570 to displace Easter from its pre-eminent position in the Church's year,[49] there seems little doubt that Sidney and his friends would have kept it solemnly according to the English rite. Their first complete day in Prague was Good Friday, when they would have prayed to God to 'have mercy upon all Jews, Turks, infidels, and heretics, and take from them all ignorance, hardness of heart, and contempt of thy Word'. This plea would have had far more immediacy in Prague than in London, for Prague had a substantial Jewish community, and the Ottoman Turks were being actively fought in neighbouring Hungary. The new Emperor's attitude to the war with the Turks was one of the topics on which Sidney reported, finding him 'wholly given to the wars'. The Turks posed a potential threat to Prague itself; the chauvinist Fynes Moryson said that the stink of the city alone was enough to keep the Turks at bay.[50] Whether all the English visitors would have viewed Catholic members of the Imperial Court as 'heretics' is more dubious. There is reason to suspect that Sidney found the brand of Catholicism to be met with there distinctly attractive. The late Emperor, Maximilian II, had allowed considerable freedom of worship to his subjects, and his son's position was not yet clear. The Emperor's retinue of 'aulic Christians', courtiers who sat lightly to Catholicism, and cared little for Papal authority, were probably congenial to Sidney.[51]

Among Catholic priests in Prague there was an old acquaintance of Sidney's, Edmund Campion. Their paths had crossed at several points. As an outstandingly talented scholar of St John's, Campion had spoken and disputed before the Queen when she visited Oxford in 1566; eleven-year-old Sidney was presumably among the audience. There seems little doubt that Sidney later met Campion during his own undergraduate years and perhaps attended his rhetoric lectures. He may even have been among those students who called themselves 'Campionists' and imitated the speech, mannerisms and even the clothes of their master, a charismatic figure. Campion's Fellowship of St John's was funded by the Grocers' Company, of which at an unknown date Sidney became a member. After his refusal to make his exact religious position public by preaching at Paul's Cross, in London, Campion lost his Fellowship, but immediately came under the protection of Leicester and Sir Henry Sidney, spending more than a year in Ireland in 1570–71. Deep mystery attaches to the exact moment of Campion's 'conversion', or decision to 'come out' as a Catholic. But by the time Sidney met him once again, in Prague, he was a Jesuit, and had recently been appointed to a post at the Consistors' College.

He taught rhetoric, with much use of verse composition and literary exercise. For instance, he required his boy pupils to 'write a brief account of a garden, a church, a storm, or any other visible object'; they were also practised in epigram, elegy, dramatic composition and declamation. Indeed, despite their fundamental sectarian difference, Campion's teaching methods had much in common with those of Sidney's own Puritan headmaster, Thomas Ashton (see above, pp. 27–31).

There are three or four witnesses to Sidney's meetings with Campion. Though it must be borne in mind that the records of them are all Catholic, there is no reason to doubt that the meetings took place. Over fifty years later, another Jesuit, Father Thomas Fitzherbert, claimed that

> Sidney had the courage to confess in England that one of the most memorable things he had witnessed abroad was a sermon by Campion, at which he had assisted with the Emperor in Prague.[52]

This is a late and no doubt biased testimony. But Fitzherbert, too, was a contemporary of Sidney's at Oxford, and spent the later 1570s in London, where he could have heard about Sidney's verbal reports on his mission. Two witnesses much closer in time allude only to private meetings, but Sidney may also have heard a public sermon at which the Emperor was present, perhaps on Easter Day in St Vitus's Cathedral. The private meetings were not easy to arrange. According to Robert Parsons,

> Their meeting ... was difficult, for Sir Philip was afraid of so many spies set and sent about him by the English Council; but he managed to have divers large and secret conferences with his old friend. After much argument, he professed himself convinced, but said that it was necessary for him to hold on the course which he had hitherto followed; yet he promised never to hurt or injure any Catholic, which for the most part he performed ...[53]

The 'spies' who had been 'sent' by the Privy Council were presumably the older members of the party, men like Lee and Bowes. Certainly they would not have approved of the young ambassador's desire to see more of the brilliant English Jesuit. Yet there can be no doubt that Sidney did give them the slip and meet Campion, for Campion himself described this in a letter to his old tutor from St John's, also a Catholic and by now an exile, John Bavand, which survives in the archives at Stonyhurst. It is here translated by Richard Simpson, Campion's biographer:

> ... A few months ago Philip Sidney came from England to Prague, magnificently provided. He had much conversation with me – I hope not in vain, for to all appearance he was most eager. I commend him to your sacrifices, for he asked the prayers of all good men, and at the same time put into my hands some alms to be distributed to

the poor for him, which I have done. Tell this to Dr Nicholas Sanders, because if any one of our labourers sent into the vineyard from the Douai seminary has an opportunity of watering this plant, he may watch the occasion for helping a poor wavering soul. If this young man, so wonderfully beloved and admired by his countrymen, chances to be converted, he will astonish his noble father, the Deputy of Ireland, his uncles the Dudleys, and all young courtiers, and Cecil himself. Let it be kept secret.[54]

What are we to make of this? Previous biographers have seen Campion's account as a tribute to Sidney's personal charm and diplomatic skill, dismissing the claim that he was on the point of conversion as 'absurd'.[55] Yet there seems no reason why Sidney should have taken the risk of repeated meetings with the English Jesuit unless he wanted to discuss serious matters of religion with him. Given Campion's exceptional skill in arguing, Sidney may indeed have been all but persuaded. The allusion to Sidney's gift of money is entirely consistent with what we know of Sidney's usual practice when meeting clergymen abroad (see above, p. 70). As Wallace has shown, both Sidney and his father were apt to say one thing and do another in their dealings with Catholics.[56] No one disputes the fact that at a tricky stage of his career Campion enjoyed the protection of Sidney's father and uncle. It may have been precisely to allay suspicions that he was in fact a crypto-Catholic that Sidney felt obliged to introduce hard-line Protestant remarks into those of his writings that were to be read at Court. In the following autumn, for instance, he was to identify the worst characteristic of the Irish as their 'ignorant obstinacy in papistry'.[57]

One further near-contemporary document may allude to Sidney's admiration of Campion. In August 1581 Lord Vaux and Sir Thomas Tresham were among gentlemen apprehended for harbouring Campion during his mission to England in 1580–81. Tresham drafted what seems to be a speech he planned to use in his own defence, in which he expressed amazement that the learned and loyal Campion was now indicted as a traitor.[58] He would remind the court of Campion's orations before the Queen, the eulogy of him by Richard Stanyhurst in Holinshed's *Chronicle*, and of his personal reputation:

I never heard any ill of him, nor till this day did, but I have heard him well reputed of, and that by Protestants of good account that returned from the Emperor's court.[59]

This may be a reference to Sidney, whom it would not be tactful to name, but who was surely in this context a 'Protestant of good account' who had visited the Emperor's Court. There can be no doubt of Sidney's acquaintance with Tresham, who had been among a group of gentlemen knighted by the Queen during her visit to Kenilworth in July 1575. Tresham may have hoped to invoke the support of both the Sidneys, for Stanyhurst's introduction to Campion's *Description of Ireland* in Holinshed, in which he said that Ireland 'had great need of such a clerk as Master Campion', was fulsomely addressed to Sidney's father. Perhaps Sidney really was a discreet Catholic fellow traveller for a while after his meetings with Campion. It is certainly curious that his letter to the Catholic Lady Kytson, optimistically but mistakenly forecasting a 'general mitigation to be used in respect of recusants' in March 1581, is signed 'Your Ladyship's fellow and friend'.[60] There is no other correspondent to whom Sidney designated himself a 'fellow', nor is there any other surviving letter to an openly practising Catholic.

Naturally, no allusion to the meetings with Campion appears in Sidney's official account of his mission. His public business in Prague was conducted on Easter Monday and Tuesday. On Monday he had audience with the Emperor, probably in the council chamber at the end of the great Vladislav Hall in Prague Castle, which has exceptionally beautiful organic, tree-like rib-vaulting, and is big enough for the staging of indoor tournaments. The worn steps of its vast staircase testify to the trampling of armed knights. Sidney's account of his audience carefully follows the numbered points made in his instructions. These required him to convey the Queen's condolences, compliments and advice. Rudolph was only three years older than Sidney, but his enigmatic and eccentric personality was already apparent:

> He answered me in Latin with very few words ... the Emperor is wholly by his inclination given to the wars, few of words, sullen of disposition, very secret and resolute, nothing the manner his father had in winning men in his behaviour, but yet constant in keeping them. And such a one as though he promise not much outwardly, hath as the Latins say *Aliquid in Recessu* ['something in reserve'].[61]

The Latin tag may have been a reminiscence of conversations with Gabriel Harvey, for Harvey's marginalia in his copy of Sacrobosco's *De Sphaera*, one of which is dated 1580, and another of which alludes to Sidney, include the motto *Plus in recessu quam in fronte* ('More behind than shows before').[62] Its source is Quintilian's *Institutio Oratoria* I. iv. 2, where it is applied to the mysteries that lie hidden in poetry. In Rudolph's case, one of the important matters that lay hidden was his religious position, which continued to perplex his subjects for the next thirty years.[63] Another, at this early stage, was his passionate interest in alchemy, astrology and other arcane sciences. Immersed in his library and his collections of natural specimens and antique and modern artefacts, he neglected his political responsibilities, denying audience to many later ambassadors or answering them in very few words. He might, like Shakespeare's Prospero, have said:

> The government I cast upon my brother,
> And to my state grew stranger, being transported
> And rapt in secret studies.[64]

Like Prospero, he had eventually to yield up most of his authority to his younger brother, though this did not become formal until 1608. Sidney's description of Rudolph as 'secret' was prophetic.

On Easter Tuesday Sidney had audience with the Emperor's widowed mother and his younger siblings. In his account he drew attention to his own delicacy of feeling:

> Of the Emperor deceased I used but few words, because in truth I saw it bred some trouble unto her, to hear him mentioned in that kind [i.e. as dead]. She answered me with many courteous speeches, and great acknowledging of her own beholdingness to Her Majesty. And for her son, she said she hoped he would do well; but that for her own part she said she had given herself from the world and would not greatly stir from thenceforward in it.

Rudolph's younger sister Elizabeth was the young widow of Charles IX, from whom Sidney had received a barony in Paris five years before. His communication with her was even more restricted than that with her mother:

> Then did I deliver the Queen of France's letter, she standing by the Empress, using such speeches as I thought were fit for her double sorrow, and Her Majesty's good will unto her, confirmed by her wise and noble governing of herself in the time of her being in France. Her answer was full of humbleness, but she spake so low that I could not understand many of her words.[65]

Sidney reported also on the 'extremely Spaniolated' character of Rudolph and his three brothers. This was not surprising, for they had all been educated in the Court of Philip II.

Sidney told Walsingham nothing of his visual impressions of the Emperor and his Court. Yet he cannot have failed to observe Rudolph's rather comic appearance, his rubicund complexion, short stature and exaggeratedly jutting Hapsburg jaw. Seldom can such an unimpressive-looking man have been more splendidly and variously represented, in paint, cameo, medals, bronze, wax and stone.[66] A wax portrait now in the Victoria and Albert Museum of Rudolph with a favourite dog may be compared with a well-known portrait of the Earl of Leicester, also with a dog. The English courtier looks tall and handsome, towering masterfully over the faithful mastiff; the Hapsburg Emperor, dwarfish and lopsided, is completely upstaged by the rather handsome spotted dog which almost encircles his small frame. The best-known and most extraordinary portrait of Rudolph is Giuseppe Arcimboldo's composite head of the Emperor as the god Vertumnus (now in Skokloster, Sweden), an allegorical compendium of peace and plenty in which the monarch has cherries for lips, asparagus moustache, spiky wheat ears for hair, a pear nose, fig earring and cabbage-leaf epaulettes. Even in this extraordinary medium, Rudolph is curiously recognizable. T. DaCosta Kauffman has claimed that such pictures are not primarily comic, or, if comic, 'serious jokes'.[67] However, this mode of symbolism is difficult to translate into literary terms without humour. Of Sidney's attempts at composite portraits, one, Dicus's account of Cupid as a monster,[68] is explicitly satiric; another[69] may well be intended as a 'serious joke', but the effect is both ridiculous and repellent:

> thus her eyes
> Serve him with shot, her lips his heralds are,
> Her breasts his tents, legs his triumphal car,
> Her flesh his food, her skin his armour brave ...

Arcimboldo's paintings may have been among the influences that provoked Sidney to attempt such Mannerist effects.

Prague itself, in high spring, has a fairy-tale beauty, and had, in 1577, a pre-industrial freshness and clarity. At some point during his fortnight there Sidney went outside the city to the strange star-shaped hunting lodge (Hvêzda) built in 1559 by Rudolph's grandfather, Ferdinand of Tyrol. Though star-shaped buildings are not uncommon in the period, this is one of the most remarkable. It survives to this day, housing in its basement a scale model of the battle of White Mountain (1620), and the park is laid out in its original pattern, with six wide avenues raying out from the centre. The building seems to have prompted Sidney's account of the architectural fantasy of his own, fictional, superstitious monarch, Basilius:

> The lodge is of yellow stone, built in the form of a star, having, round about, a garden framed into like points; and beyond the garden, ridings cut out, each answering the angles of the lodge.[70]

The interior of the Bohemian Star Castle is richly encrusted with Italian stucco depictions of mythological scenes, which also survive. Sidney may particularly have noticed the central roundel, mid-point of the star, which shows Aeneas carrying his old father Anchises out of the flaming city of Troy. He used this motif as a key example of the didactic power of art in his *Defence*:

> Who readeth Aeneas carrying old Anchises on his back, that wisheth not it were his fortune to perform so excellent an act?[71]

Though Sidney was primarily defending poetry, not painting, the central position of Aeneas's display of filial piety in the Star Castle may have impressed on him its exemplary importance.

Altogether the 1577 mission was rich in visual experiences. For instance, on the return journey, as well as on the outward one, Sidney stopped in Nuremberg and met the Camerarius brothers, who must have owned many of the woodcuts and engravings of Albrecht Dürer. Their late father, Joachim I, had written a classic study of Dürer's life and work, in addition to translating his treatise on human proportion.[72] Travelling as an ambassador rather than as a visiting student, Sidney got to see far more of the insides of palaces and great houses than he had done before. The next stop was the beautiful city of Heidelberg, where he had audience with the elder Palatine prince, Ludwig, on 30 April. His purpose was to condole with him on his father's death 'and to persuade him to amity with his brother'. Ludwig's Vice-Chancellor made an inordinately long speech of reply on his behalf, which gave away very little. The discourse, said Sidney,

> fell into a commonplace of the necessity of brothers' love, but descended nothing into his own particularity or what he thought of him [i.e. John Casimir].[73]

Ludwig was even more non-committal on the question of tolerance for Calvinist scholars and Protestant churches, 'so notably established by his father'. Though Sidney

> laid before him as well as I could the dangers of the mightiest princes of Christendom by entering into like violent changes, the wrong that he should do his worthy father utterly to abolish that he had instituted . . .

even when the Vice-Chancellor was out of the room Ludwig would say no more than that he 'must be constrained to do as other princes of the Empire', whatever that might mean. Greville, who was present at these audiences, praised Sidney's effectiveness in stirring up the 'cautious and slow judgements' of 'that long-breathed nation', the Germans, to an awareness of the threat posed to them by the conjunction of Rome's power and Spain's.[74] But Greville clearly exaggerated Sidney's success in negotiating – the Queen sent two more envoys over during the summer, but still no Protestant League was formed. Greville's biographer, Rebholz, may be nearer the mark in calling the negotiations with German princes 'dismally unproductive'.[75] A sudden recall by the Queen prevented Sidney from a planned meeting with the Landgrave of Hesse at Kaiserslauten, and by the time he parted from Languet, at Cologne, his habitual depression had descended. Languet engaged in jesting with Pietro Bizzari (see above, p. 79), 'with a view to drive away your low spirits and my own', and tactlessly fell to speaking of a matter which he had intended to keep private to discuss with Sidney later. The unfortunate subject of banter may have been Sidney's marriage.[76]

Soon after his departure from Cologne things took a better turn for Sidney. A second messenger from the Queen reached him with instructions to visit William of Orange, whose leadership of resistance to Spanish rule was proving increasingly successful in the Northern Netherlands. Failing to find William at

Brussels, Sidney left Antwerp on 27 May and met up with him at the small fortress town of Geertruidenberg. Sadly, we lack Sidney's official account of this meeting, though his political discussions may be summarized in 'Certain notes concerning the state of the Prince of Orange, and the provinces of Holland and Zeeland, as they were in the month of May 1577'.[77] In a letter to Languet on 1 October he reported that 'I have a great regard for that prince, and have perhaps in some way been of more service to him than he is aware of.'[78] Wallace is probably right in describing his days with William of Orange as 'among the happiest that Sidney ever spent'.[79] There was much about the family to challenge prejudice. Both William and his third wife Charlotte of Bourbon had formerly been practising Catholics. Indeed, Charlotte had been set up by her family as the youthful Abbess of Jouarre, though she was later converted to Calvinism and escaped to Heidelberg. William's second wife, Anne, whom he had divorced for adultery in 1571, was still living. His beloved Charlotte brought him no dowry, and C. V. Wedgwood paints a vivid picture of her attempts to pull the household together on limited resources.[80] Their family home was at Middelburg, on Walcheren island, where, eight years later, Sidney was to come as Governor of Flushing.

After the splendours of the other German princes and their palaces, the shabbiness of William and his family must have been very noticeable. Sidney was all too familiar with the problems of trying to sustain an aristocratic way of life with slender means, and may immediately have felt at home. Fulke Greville, whose *Dedication* is not generally rich in visual description, was so struck by the plainness and casualness of William's dress that he described it in detail, though this account relates to his meeting with William in Delft in 1579:

> His uppermost garment was a gown, yet such as (I dare confidently affirm) a mean-born student in our Inns of Court would not have been well-pleased to walk the streets in; unbuttoned his doublet was, and of like precious matter and form to the other; his waistcoat (which showed itself under it) not unlike the best sort of those woollen knit ones which our ordinary watermen row us in; his company about him the burgesses of that beer-brewing town, and he so fellow-like encompassed with them as (had I not known his face) no exterior sign of degree or reservedness could have discovered the inequality of his worth or estate from that multitude.[81]

Shortly before Sidney's arrival William's beloved Charlotte had given birth to the second of their six daughters, and Sidney, deputizing for Leicester, stood godfather to her. For this occasion, at Middelburg, William doubtless put on something smarter than the woollen cardigan described by Greville. The Queen later sent christening presents of a jewelled dove for Charlotte, a gold lizard for William.[82] The second gift may relate to a story in Pliny of a dragon which rescued an Arcadian youth from robbers, to which Sidney alludes in the Third Song of *Astrophil and Stella*:

If love might sweeten so a boy of shepherd brood
To make a lizard dull to taste love's dainty food ...[83]

Like so many of the older men in Sidney's circle, William of Orange was on the lookout for a son-in-law. His favourite brother Louis had been killed near Maastricht in 1574,[84] and his son Maurice was aged only nine. It was not that he had great riches to bestow, but he badly needed an effective deputy who could hold the provinces of Holland and Zeeland together while he himself dealt with Don John in Brussels.[85] He also hoped for substantial financial and military aid from England. Even before they met, Sidney and William may have been considering a marriage alliance. Antonio de Guaras (see above, p. 88) reported from London to Don John as early as 1 June that Sidney

is busy arranging a secret marriage with the Prince of Orange's daughter by his first wife ... [William] will give him as dowry the government of the provinces of Holland and Zeeland.[86]

Marie of Nassau, William's daughter by his first wife, was about the same age as Sidney, and devoted herself to giving care and companionship to her father. C. V. Wedgwood describes her as 'fragile and sweet'.[87] She was clearly highly intelligent. Philip and Marie together would have been charismatic governors of the breakaway provinces, though holding rival factions together would never have been an easy task. As so often, we lack Sidney's own comments on this exciting project. But one of the occasional poems gathered up in *Certain Sonnets* reflects Sidney's near-connexion with the House of Orange. It is a neo-Platonic love lyric written 'To the tune of Wilhelmus van Nassau', that is, the battle hymn of the House of Orange. This catchy song was already popular among the Dutch rebels during Sidney's first visit to the Continent, and his meeting with William must have brought it to the forefront of his consciousness. Set to a popular French melody, the Dutch words by Marnix van St Aldegonde anachronistically celebrate William's loyalty to the King of Spain and defence of the Dutch 'Vaderlant'.[88] For Aldegonde's rousing battle cry, Sidney substituted a touchingly idealized, yearning declaration of devoted love, quite unlike the sexually charged, mannered and ironic style of the later *Astrophil and Stella*:

Look then and die, the pleasure
Doth answer well the pain;
Small loss of mortal treasure
Who may immortal gain.

Immortal be her graces,
  Immortal is her mind;
  They, fit for heavenly places;
  This, heaven in it doth bind . . .

But who hath fancies pleased
  With fruits of happy sight,
  Let here his eyes be raised
  On nature's sweetest light.[89]

Sidney's attachment to the simplistic patriotic melody of an idealized love song has often been thought puzzling, but the paradox is resolved if the poem was addressed to Marie of Nassau. The tune signals the poet's devotion to the House of Orange, while the words declare his absolute submission to the power over him of the eldest daughter of that house.

Sidney's happy visit to William of Orange lasted little over a week. By 5 June he was at Bruges, one of several cities which contend for the title of 'Venice of the North'; and by 10 June he was back at Court. Sidney's friends were anxious that the completed mission should be seen as an outstanding success. Edward Waterhouse wrote to Sir Henry Sidney of his son's triumph:

Mr Sidney is returned safe into England, with great good acceptation of his service at Her Majesty's hands; allowed of by all the Lords [of the Privy Council] to have been handled with great judgement and discretion, and hath been honoured abroad in all princes' courts with much extraordinary favour. The Emperor gave him a great chain, the Princess of Orange another with a fair jewel . . . God blessed him so, that neither man, boy or horse failed him or was sick in this journey; only Fulke Greville had an ague in his return at Rochester.[90]

Francis Walsingham, also writing to Sidney's father, was even more enthusiastic:

There hath not been any gentleman I am sure these many years that hath gone through so honourable a charge with as great commendations as he. In consideration whereof I could not but communicate part of my joy with your Lordship, being no less refreshing unto me in these my troublesome business than the soil is to the chafed stag.[91]

Nothing of William's offer to Sidney of the hand of his favourite daughter appears in the English reports, but during the next six months Hubert Languet made repeated glancing references to an important matter which they had discussed 'at the mouth of the Maine', i.e. at Mainz. This was evidently a marriage project. On the last lap of his journey Sidney had written a letter, now lost, to which Languet responded:

And now, forsooth, you have written me from Bruges that there are reasons which make you almost despair of the possibility of a successful issue, and you have asked me as far as I can to discourage the hopes of the other parties.[92]

Languet was almost certainly referring to an earlier project, that Sidney should marry a German princess, possibly John Casimir's sister or, more probably, Elizabeth of Anhalt.[93] A 'monsieur Ley', perhaps Sir Henry Lee, was privy to the scheme. The displacement of the other princess by William of Orange's daughter seems to be alluded to in Languet's next letter (23 September 1577), reporting

that both your reputation and my own have begun to suffer with our friends here. They are persuaded that you changed your mind in Holland, and that you preferred another proposal to that which was agreed upon between us.[94]

Languet was embarrassedly in the dark, for as so often he had received no word from Sidney during the summer, and was having to deal with rumours that he was ducking out of the German marriage negotiations without the benefit of any direct access to Sidney's current thoughts on the subject. Almost certainly, Sidney had indeed changed his mind in Holland. Perhaps he never was as much interested in the German princess as Languet hoped, and had the good sense to conjecture that such a marriage would never be allowed by the Queen. This might apply equally to the more tempting possibility of Marie of Nassau. However much Elizabeth approved in principle of their resistance to Spanish tyranny, she was to prove herself extremely reluctant to make any large commitment to the aid of either John Casimir or William of Orange. An alliance of the Dudley family – in the person of Sidney – with either of these foreign powers was an irreversible commitment of the kind that she would not countenance. Sidney's innermost feelings on the projected marriages are not available to us, but instinct may have told him that it would not be wise to invest much emotional capital in either of them. In the case of the German scheme he seems to have backtracked very rapidly, having been initially over-persuaded by Languet. Marie of Nassau was a different matter, and he may have been reluctant to abandon all hope of this match. Perhaps it contributed to his long delay in committing himself to marriage elsewhere. Marie herself did not marry until 1595, when she was about forty.

Despite the golden opinions broadcast by Waterhouse and Walsingham, Sidney fell almost immediately, after his return, into disappointment and disillusion. The portrait, begun in June and July, already reflects this, tempering an expression of lofty defiance with shades of defeat and sadness. The summer months brought Sidney some painful discoveries. The first related to his own status. He found that it was possible to be godson to the most powerful monarch in Christendom, nephew and heir to two Earls, one of them the Queen's longest-standing favourite, son of a Knight of the Garter who 'governed' both Ireland and Wales on the Queen's behalf, and to add manifest personal talent to all these unearned connexions – and yet receive no personal title. Now that he had proved himself as an ambassador he hoped for a knighthood, at least. But none was forthcoming. It may be that Sidney's very success with the German princes, especially William of Orange, counted against him in Elizabeth's eyes. She did not like foreigners telling her what to do with her own courtiers. But it may also be that someone in the mission reported to her on the meetings with Campion. Simpson, Campion's biographer, claims that these meetings were the reason why Sidney

> made no advance in his public career for several years, and held no trust or office except the nominal one of Royal Cupbearer.[95]

There may be something in this. There is reason to think that Elizabeth, while acknowledging Sidney's talent, never did quite trust him, and the Campion episode would give her good reason to hesitate. It should also be noted that Sidney derived the Cupbearer post from his father, who in turn had received it from Edward VI. Though it was a court post, the Queen played no part in placing Sidney in it. Sidney longed for honours which reflected his own achievements, not those of the previous generation. This is shown in what Molyneux recorded as his favourite motto, *Vix ea nostra voco* ('I scarcely call those things my own'), which he suffixed to his coat of arms. Like many of Sidney's self-definitions, it is at once modest and arrogant: a disclaimer of inherited honour whose sub-text is an assertion of his own individual worth. Sidney wanted a personal identity that was defined by his own achievements and associations, not those of his father and uncles. The old men's garments did not really fit. A bitter allusion to youthful heroism dressed up in worn-out inherited dignities comes in the 'New' *Arcadia*, when Musidorus rides at tilt dressed as the 'Black, or the Ill-apparelled Knight', with 'his armour of as old a fashion (besides the rusty poorness) that it might better seem a monument of his grandfather's courage'.[96] William of Orange or John Casimir of the Palatinate might offer Sidney new clothes and a new identity, but there was little hope that the Queen or his uncles would allow him to wear them.

Even more than after his Grand Tour, Sidney found being back home painfully frustrating. Abroad, once he had talked away his boyish appearance, he was fêted and treated with deference. In England he was kept on a relentlessly tight rein by an ageing monarch and her advisers. In her eyes, inherited honours counted for much, as Sidney was soon to discover. An Earl of Ormond or of Oxford was not to be lightly scorned by a mere 'Master', however superior his talents. In the summer and autumn of 1577 Sir Henry Sidney was in severe trouble with the Irish aristocracy. In an attempt to get adequate support for his administration he had extended the exaction of the 'cess', a land tax in kind or provisions, to those Irish lords living in the English 'Pale', the area around Dublin, who had hitherto claimed exemption.[97] Three spokesmen for the discontented lords were sent over to England in January 1577, and by the time Sidney returned to England the controversy was raging fiercely. At one point he hoped to join his father in Ireland,[98] but may have decided that he could help him more by staying at home. The Queen, strongly influenced by the Earl of Ormond,

> believed that Sir Henry was wasting her money and ill-treating her Irish peers; and Sir Henry, with prices constantly rising and a fear of invasion by James Fitzmaurice, was compelled to find some way of maintaining his troops.[99]

Unwisely, perhaps, Sidney 'took on' Ormond, nicknamed 'Black Tom', who was an Anglicized courtier, a senior Privy Councillor, and a close ally of Leicester's enemy the Earl of Sussex.[100] Plenty of bad blood had already flowed, for Sir Henry Sidney had on occasion favoured Ormond's deadly rival the Earl of Desmond. By mid-September things could not be glossed over, and Edward Waterhouse reported to Sir Henry Sidney:

> Some little occasions of discourtesies have passed between the Earl of Ormond and Mr Philip Sidney, because the Earl lately spake unto him, and he answered not, but was in dead silence of purpose, because he imputeth to the Earl such practices as have been made to alienate Her Majesty's mind from your Lordship ... The Earl of Ormond saith he will accept no quarrels from a gentleman that is bound by nature to defend his father's causes, and who is otherwise furnished with so many virtues as he knows Mr Philip to be; and on the other side Mr Philip hath gone as far, and showed as much magnanimity as is convenient, unless he could charge him with any particularities, which I perceive he yet cannot ...[101]

This sounds like a softened account of Philip's fury against Ormond, designed to reassure his father that no actual duel would take place. If the pen was not always, in this period, as mighty as the sword, it was at least a legitimate weapon for a young courtier to take up. Sidney now did so, writing a seven-part defence of his father's imposition of the cess, four parts of which survive.[102] Ormond is mentioned by name only in a marginal note, but a pervasive tone of sardonic contempt is no doubt directed chiefly towards him:

> ... this [exaction of cess] touches the privileges, forsooth; and privileged persons be all the rich men of the Pale, the burden only lying upon the poor, who may groan, for their cry cannot be heard. And, Lord, to see how shamefully they will speak for their country, that be indeed the tyrannous oppressors of their country! ... The means have been privileges granted by the Deputies of all times, whereby under colour of some good service (wherein, God knows, they are very barren) he should be exempted from any such charge ...[103]

The shift here from 'they' to 'he' indicates that though Sidney claims to generalize about the lords of the Pale, he is thinking chiefly of Ormond. Sidney's broader policy for the management of Ireland, which presumably reflects that of his father, is for a judicious alternation of 'force and gentleness', with the emphasis on the former:

> For until by time they find the sweetness of due subjection, it is impossible that any gentle means should put out the fresh remembrance of their lost liberty. And that the Irishman is that way as obstinate as any nation, with whom no other passion can prevail but fear, besides their story which plainly paints it out, their manner of life wherein they choose rather all filthiness, than any law, and their own consciences who best know their own natures, give sufficient proof of it. For under the sun there is not a nation which live more tyrannously than they do one over the other.[104]

A key example of the ungratefulness of the Irish to their English governors is the rebellion of 'all the Earl of Ormond's brethren'. In conclusion, Sidney praises his father as 'an honest servant, full of zeal in his prince's service', rounding off the piece with a saying which he may have remembered from Thomas Ashton's play *Julian the Apostate* in 1566:

> The Emperor Julian, to a busy accuser that told him, 'if he believed no accuser, no man should be condemned', made answer, 'if he believed all accusers, no man should be cleared'.

Edward Waterhouse praised Sidney's discourse as answering the complaints against Sir Henry Sidney 'the most excellently (if I have any judgement) that ever I read in my life ... let no man compare with Mr Philip's pen'.[105] The affair dragged on for another month, but on 1 November the Queen and Council conceded the lawfulness of Sir Henry Sidney's exaction of the cess, and the three complainants were committed to the Tower. Sidney had won this particular round of his battle to defend his father against what he saw as the malice of court favourites. But the conflict was exhausting and dispiriting, for it had revealed the extent of the Queen's reluctance to trust either of the Sidneys when their integrity was challenged by courtiers of higher rank.

Three unconnected events in the later part of 1577 opened up more cheerful prospects. Martin Frobisher returned from Meta Incognita with two hundred tons of (supposed) gold ore; George Gascoigne died; and Sidney's sister became 'Lady of Wilton'. Frobisher's return was in October, and the Queen ordered that his weighty cargo should be held under double lock in the ports where it was brought in, some in Bristol Castle, some in the Tower of London. Like Sidney on his return from Prague, Frobisher on his return from Canada had his portrait painted, by Cornelius Ketel, a tall, macho image of a man of action, large-boned and swarthy, which now presides over the Pro-Scholium of the Bodleian Library. Sidney's enthusiasm and excitement about Frobisher's return was explosive, and sage remarks by Languet, who once famously refused a chance of a trip to the North Pole proposed by the King of Sweden on the grounds that he preferred inhabited countries to empty ones, failed to dampen his ardour. Sidney expected a rich return on his investment, and hoped soon to go and see Meta Incognita for himself.

Meanwhile, in darkest Lincolnshire, one 'Drab' poet was staying with another. Leicester's protégé the soldier-poet George Gascoigne was guest of another soldier-poet, George Whetstone, on his estate near Stamford, and on 7 October Gascoigne died. Among those who wrote elegies on him was Sidney's acquaintance Gabriel Harvey, who noted that Gascoigne's 'want of resolution & constancy marred his wit and he undid himself'.[106] In his poem on him, Harvey imagines Gascoigne in Elysium being greeted by the pillars of English courtly poetry, Chaucer, Gower, Lydgate, Skelton, Thomas More and the Earl of Surrey. His eulogy teeters on the brink of ridicule, but it is hard to tell whether this is intentional or just the effect of Harvey's florid style. The fruition of Gascoigne's ambitions had been slow in coming, but since the great spectacles at Kenilworth in 1575 he had enjoyed a brief career as England's leading court poet, together with employment in the Netherlands. Perhaps as interesting to Sidney as any of his poems was a recent prose work, *The Spoyle of Antwerpe*, recording the horrors of the sack of the great and rich city by mutinous Spanish troops in November 1576. Gascoigne's sphere of connexions and interests matched Sidney's at many points – Gray's Inn, the Netherlands, English metrics, erotic prose fiction, courtly entertainment. But though Sidney must have been familiar with the man and his work for over a decade, it is unlikely that he felt much regret at his passing, and the absence of any allusion to him in the *Defence of Poesy* is noticeable.

The cultural vacuum created by Gascoigne's death came at just the right moment. Someone else was now needed to write and devise court entertainments for Leicester and the Queen, and indeed Sidney's new brother-in-law. On 21 April, while he was in Prague, Sidney's sister Mary had married the Earl of Pembroke. Together with his uncles and his brother Robert, he made his first visit to her at Wilton in late August and early September. After settling the affair of the cess and the Earl of Ormond during September and October, he wasted little time before returning once more to Wilton.[107] For ten days in December his uncles Leicester and Warwick also 'sported' and 'made merry' with their old friend the Earl of Pembroke.[108] But when they left to spend Christmas at Court they took a letter with them in which Sidney made his excuses to his uncle Sussex, as Lord Chamberlain:

> ... I am bold to trouble your Lordship with these few words, humbly to crave your Lordship's favour so far unto me, as that it will please you to let me understand, whether I may with your Lordship's leave, and that I may not offend in want of my

service, remain absent from the Court this Christmas time. Some occasions, both of health and otherwise, do make me much desire it.[109]

The vague reference to 'health' is unconvincing. The truth was that Sidney was enjoying himself at Wilton, and for the first time in his life was free from pressure to please and adapt to the whims of his father and uncles. Henry Herbert, the second Earl of Pembroke, was a convivial and easygoing host who loved dogs and horses and enjoyed outdoor sports. In 1583, for instance, he founded the Salisbury race, endowing it with a golden bell worth £50 as a prize.[110] Sidney could easily avoid any sporting activities he disliked. His chief companions were his sixteen-year-old sister and her female entourage, which included old Anne Mantell, who had been 'governess' to both Philip and Mary. This was the most congenial taste of family life he had had since his infancy at Penshurst. Nobody at Wilton badgered him to take an interest in European politics, or get married, or hang around at Court splendidly dressed in case the Queen wanted him. Here, among the pleasant Wiltshire Downs, he could play literary games, enjoy the affection and companionship of lively young women and choose his own rôle, instead of trying perpetually to be what others would have him.

The rôle he chose was that of the melancholy, love-lorn shepherd. This was a good way of channelling both his habitual low spirits and his sexual frustration. A charming poem survives from this period, released, perhaps, from among a collection of her brother's juvenilia, by the Countess of Pembroke for inclusion in the 1613 edition of the *Arcadia*.[111] The use of poulter's measure may reflect his assumption of Gascoigne's mantle, but Gascoigne never used the metre with such flexibility of rhythm and diction. *A Dialogue betweene two shepherds, utterd in a pastorall shew, at Wilton* is a whimsical, quaintly touching piece, in which an older shepherd, Dick, explains to a very naive younger one, Will, why he cannot sing, though 'others' expect it: he is in love. The context is a festive aristocratic gathering, probably Christmas at Wilton, 1577. The pastoral world is suggested in some detail:

A time there is for all, my mother often says,
When she with skirts tucked very high, with girls at stoolball plays.

Stoolball was a game rather like French cricket, played almost exclusively by women. Sidney's evocation of women enjoying themselves in country sports was apt for the dialogue's audience. Will is nicely characterized as a shepherd whose preoccupations are wholly material:

What? Is thy bagpipe broke, or are thy lambs miswent?
Thy wallet or thy tarbox lost, or thy new raiment rent?

He fails to gloss Dick's use of metaphor when the older shepherd describes his servitude to a cruel mistress, and his natural reaction is that women like her should be avoided:

> God shield us from such dames! If so our downs be sped,
> The shepherds will grow lean, I trow, their sheep will ill be fed . . .

Finally, the pair decide to exit, 'lest we great folks annoy'. Dick's final metaphor may have been selected to please the dog-loving Earl of Pembroke:

DICK:
> O hence! O cruel word, which even dogs do hate;
> But hence, even hence, I must needs go; such is my dogged fate.

It is tempting to imagine that Philip may have performed this dialogue with his younger brother Robert, then aged just fourteen, and that Dick's reluctance to go 'hence' mirrored Sidney's own reluctance to leave Wilton.

There is no doubt that Sidney did adopt a pastoral persona at this time, both at Court and at Wilton, choosing a rôle that released him from political pressures while liberating him to speak freely about private emotions. Of course, the emotions divulged are not of a Romantic literalness. In the play-world of Wilton, love melancholy may have functioned partly as an analogue to political dissatisfaction and alienation. If Sidney was going to be treated as an outsider – not taken seriously, not listened to, not given any substantial status or employment – he could at least play the outsider rôle for all it was worth, physically absenting himself from Court whenever possible, and presenting himself, even at Wilton, as an unhappy and lonely figure, ill-attuned to the very festivities to which he was contributing. In the course of the next three years Sidney was to discover that the pastoral rôle was even more liberating than at first appeared. It enabled him to create a whole new world which accommodated and transformed many components of the world in which he lived:

> Nature never set forth the earth in so rich tapestry as divers poets have done; neither with so pleasant rivers, fruitful trees, sweet-smelling flowers, nor whatsoever else may make the too much loved earth more lovely. Her world is brazen, the poets only deliver a golden.[112]

From the end of 1577 onwards we have evidence not just of how Sidney lived in a concrete sense – his appearance, his movements from place to place, his money troubles, his friendships – but also, increasingly, of how he felt, what he dreamed of and cared about.

7

1578–9

THE COURTIER POET

I will give you a nearer example of myself, who, I know not by what mischance, in these my not old years and idlest times having slipped into the title of a poet, am provoked to say something unto you in the defence of that my unelected vocation.[1]

Not long after his return from that journey, and before his further employment by Her Majesty, at his vacant and spare times of leisure (for he could endure at no time to be idle and void of action) he made his book which he named *Arcadia*, a work (though a mere fancy, toy and fiction) showing such excellency of spirit, gallant invention, variety of matter, and orderly disposition, and couched in frame of such apt words without superfluity, eloquent phrase and fine conceit with interchange of device, so delightful to the reader, and pleasant to the hearer, as nothing could be taken out to amend it, or added to it that would not impair it.[2]

There were many things that Sidney hoped to do soon after his return from Prague, and it is not clear that writing fiction was one of them. Though he was using a 'modesty topos' in describing his poetic vocation as 'unelected' and almost involuntary, it may in truth have been somewhat accidental:

as I never desired the title, so have I neglected the means to come by it. Only, overmastered by some thoughts, I yielded an inky tribute unto them.[3]

Molyneux's account of Sidney's dislike of idleness is surely correct. In the months immediately after his return from Germany Sidney was expecting continually to leave England once more. At various points, he hoped to respond to powerful appeals from John Casimir to assist William of Orange in fighting the Spanish, perhaps as the deputy of his uncle Leicester.[4] He hoped also to go to Ireland again to help his father, who was still having great difficulty in exacting the cess from the nobility of the Pale, and was exhausted

Emblem of porcupine from manuscript dedicated to Sidney (Bodleian Library)

and disheartened. Most of all, he hoped to go to the New World with Frobisher, and see for himself those seemingly golden islands off the coast of Canada. Even after Frobisher's two hundred tons of 'ore' had turned out to be 'worse than good stone', Sidney was convinced that the area was well worth further investigation, and in March 1578 he was contemplating an 'Indian project'.[5] None of these journeys took place, and by the end of 1579 he found himself instead dividing his time between the Court and Wiltshire, with ample time on his hands in which to write down his 'thoughts'. Though he clearly enjoyed writing, this was not the way of life he had anticipated.

Sidney's beginnings as a poet cannot be dated precisely. According to Lodowick Bryskett, he was already 'with the Muses sporting' on the Grand Tour, and I have suggested that some of the early metrical experiments may belong to this time (see above, pp. 82–3). If it is true that he purchased a copy of Jacopo Sannazaro's *Arcadia* in Venice in 1573, he may for some years have contemplated producing an English counterpart to this graceful and popular verse-and-prose romance. During the 1577 embassy he was complimented as a poet – or at least for his cultivation of the Muses, an ambivalent phrase – by a talented German poet, Paul Schede, who wrote under the name of 'Melissus', and was custodian of the Elector Palatine's magnificent library in Heidelberg. After praising Sidney for his notorious devotion to the Muses, Schede declared a longing to return to England with him, imagining 'Sidney's eloquence, which had charmed the Emperor, similarly assuaging the stormy seas'.[6] Schede was a close friend of Ronsard, and of the composer Orlando di Lasso. He was committed to the establishment of vernacular literature, and in 1572 had translated the first fifty Psalms into German, matching them to French chants.[7] It has been plausibly suggested that Sidney wrote some Latin poems which contributed to his reputation among continental humanists.[8] None has survived, and if they existed, it is likely that they were slight epigrammatic and occasional verses of the sort penned now and then by even the least poetical of humanists, like Languet (see above, p. 76), or we would surely know more about them.

When Sidney came to devote himself more fully to his 'unelected vocation' as a poet, he wrote entirely in English, thus excluding most of his humanist friends from his readership. Like Bembo in Italian, Ronsard in French, and Schede in German, he hoped to lay the foundations of a body of literature in his own language which might ultimately stand comparison with the Greek and Latin classics. In so doing, he was cutting himself off from direct communication with that commonwealth of letters composed by his central European friends, with whom he corresponded normally in Latin, occasionally in French or Italian, but never in English. Most notably, he was cutting himself off from Hubert Languet, who knew no English. Writing the *Arcadia* was to provide him with an escape, not just from the Queen and her Court, but also from the pressures placed on him by his other mentors, patrons and friends, some of whom were quite near at hand. During 1578–9 both Philippe du Plessis Mornay and John Casimir's friend Dr Butrech, nicknamed 'the equestrian doctor', were in London, and were warmly entertained by Sidney.[9] Yet it was not for their delectation that he embarked on the *Arcadia*. Even if his self-discovery as a poet was partly fortuitous, Sidney's choice of audience was surely conscious and deliberate. When writing at length, he chose to address himself to an audience of young women and 'smally learned courtiers', women like his sister, and men like Dyer, for whom Leicester apologized to William of Orange because he knew 'only Latin and Italian'.[10] Sidney's sister Mary, first and chief audience for the *Arcadia*, was better educated than this. Like Philip, she was fluent in French, as her published translations from Du Plessis Mornay and Garnier were to show. She also had excellent Italian, making a notably sensitive version of Petrarch's *Trionfo della Morte*.[11] She probably also had some Spanish. She may well have been familiar with Sannazaro's *Arcadia*, and perhaps, when she 'desired' her brother, some time in the winter of 1577–8, to write a romance for her, his brief was to imitate Sannazaro. In practice, Sidney's work took off in many directions unexplored by Sannazaro, having enormously more narrative coherence, fluency, variety, thematic profundity, humour and naturalism. Yet it may have been with Sannazaro that the project began.

Sidney's sister would not have 'desired' him to write a romance for her unless she had reason to think him capable of doing it: unless, that is, she had already seen evidence of his fluency and inventiveness in poetry and fiction. This evidence was provided largely by courtly entertainments. In addition to the rather 'domestic' Dick and Will dialogue performed at Wilton, Sidney displayed his skills more publicly during 1577–8. Between his two visits to Wilton in August and December 1577, and after resolving his differences with the Earl of Ormond, he made his début as a tilter at Whitehall. Mary did not witness this, remaining at Wilton, so it may have been partly for her benefit that he wrote up his first tiltyard appearance in the collection of early poems included in the 'Ottley manuscript'. Elizabeth's Accession Day, 17 November, fell this year on a Sunday. By the second half of her reign the day was regularly celebrated with bell-ringings, sermons, distribution of alms to the poor, bonfires, fireworks and a tournament at Whitehall.[12] The special character of 17 November 1577 as a 'sabbath' was underlined by Sidney. The Queen's Champion, Sir Henry Lee, acted as master of ceremonies, and it was probably under his direction that Sidney devised his own appearance as 'Philisides, the shepherd good and true'. Accompanied by a troop of gentlemen clad as rustics, he brought a characteristic note of faux-naif realism to the occasion. The first of two songs describes Philisides' appeal to 'Menalcas the husbandman' to abandon his ploughing 'with horse and man', in order to celebrate this, 'the chief of Cupid's sabbath days':

> Menalcas, who of long his thoughts had tilled
> With fancy's plough, that they might pleasure bear,
> And with his love the empty furrows filled
> Which always sprang to him again in fear,
> Was well content the plough and all to yield
> Unto this Sabbath day, and sacred field.

'Menalcas' was presumably a friend and fellow courtier – Fulke Greville, the Earl of Arundel and Baron Windsor were among Sidney's companions that day – whose 'ploughing' accoutrements complemented Sidney's 'shepherdish' ones. The poem suggests that Menalcas's mount resembled a 'till horse', or heavy horse used for ploughing. Though the central object of these courtiers' devotion was the Queen, Philisides first proceeded to the tiltyard 'With songs of love, and praise of Mira's hue'.[13] 'Mira', who figures in a handful of early 'Philisides' poems, is most plausibly identified with Sidney's sister Mary. Thomas Moffet, an employee and close associate, uses this name for her in *The Silkewormes and their Flies* (1599), and Fulke Greville, addressing himself to Sidney's sister, called himself 'Miraphill'. Privately, Sidney might dream of another Mary, Marie of Nassau, but this devotion was not one to wear on his sleeve, or helmet. His sister, as a newly married woman and a close relation, could be safely complimented without any compromising or risky commitment. Unquestionably Sidney really did love his sister: but she also provided him with a convenient emotional smokescreen. If he felt any inward stirrings of amorous attraction or marital ambition, he had no intention of proclaiming them publicly.

Philisides' second song, presumably sung as he and his company drew up in front of the Royal Box, placed Elizabeth firmly at the centre:

Sound up your pipes, do you not see
        That yond is she,
Even she, that most respecteth
        The faithful loving minds,
And no one thought rejecteth
        That upon honour binds? ...

Show forth your joy, let mourning stay,
        This is her day:
Her day, on which she entered,
        And with her entered Peace,
Which she hath not adventured [exposed to risk],
        But kept for our increase.

Let such a saint be praised,
        Which so her worth hath raised!
From them that would not thus,
        Good Lord, deliver us.

Sidney's adaptation of the Prayer Book Litany is a gentle secularization of words very familiar to his audience, for the Litany, with its response 'Good Lord, deliver us', was prescribed for use every Sunday, Wednesday and Friday. How Sidney and his companions looked is recorded in the account of the Iberian Jousts in the 'New' *Arcadia*, which contains clear allusions to the Accession Day Tilts:

Against him came forth an Iberian, whose manner of entering was with bagpipes instead of trumpets, a shepherd's boy before him for a page, and by him a dozen apparelled like shepherds for the fashion, though rich in stuff, who carried his lances, which, though strong to give a lancely blow indeed, yet were so coloured, with hooks near the morne [head of a tilting lance], that they prettily resembled sheephooks. His own furniture was dressed over with wool, so enriched with jewels artificially placed that one would have thought it a marriage between the lowest and the highest. His impresa was a sheep marked with pitch, with this word: 'Spotted to be known'.[14]

It becomes apparent a moment later that the Iberian's name is 'Philisides'. His opponent is one 'Lelius', 'who was ever known to be second to none in the perfection of that art'.

Because Philisides is a novice at tilting, Lelius deliberately swings his lance high up over his opponent's helmet, so that no breaking of lances takes place. Philisides is aggrieved at what he thinks is 'contempt of his youth' – like

Sidney, he wanted a proper fight – but Lelius explains that he has made a promise to tilt in this 'hurtless' manner to the 'nymph to whom he is chained' – perhaps the Queen, whose Champion he was. The whole account is probably a recollection of Sidney's début in the tiltyard, and his encounter there with Sir Henry Lee, known later in life as 'Hardy Laelius'.[15] Though Sidney often exploited his own youth as a deliberate rhetorical strategy, it is characteristic that he was nevertheless affronted by being treated as young.

Professor Ringler found Sidney's poetry 'remarkable for what he did not write about'. In particular, he claimed that 'except for some passages in *The Lady of May* he never wrote in praise of the Queen'.[16] Perhaps he was a little too anxious to accommodate Sidney to a republican ideal, relegating his tiltyard poetry to 'dubious' categories. Actually, in the late 1570s and early 80s Sidney seems to have written a good deal in praise of the Queen, for use in public performance. As Molyneux recorded, he was a celebrated tilter:

> As time wrought alteration in his deep and noble conceit at jousts, triumphs, and other such royal pastimes (for at all such disports he commonly made one) he would bring in such a lively gallant show, so agreeable to every point which is required for the expressing of a perfect device (so rich was he in those inventions) as, if he surpassed not all, he would equal or at least second the best.[17]

Eulogy of Elizabeth was inseparable from participation in court tournaments. However, he also wrote a certain amount in dispraise of her, with varying degrees of explicitness. As 'Philisides', he performed a delicate balancing act between devotion either to an unnamed lady or to 'Mira', and loyalty to the Queen, which may reflect the balancing act he performed in real life as he moved to and fro between Elizabeth's Court and Mary Herbert's 'little college' at Wilton. The longest 'Philisides' poem, 'Now was our heavenly vault deprived of all light', which was to find a place in the Fourth Eclogues of the 'Old' *Arcadia*,[18] may originally have been a verse epistle addressed to his sister.[19] In it Sidney bluntly declared his preference for Mira/Mary over Elizabeth. Following a thinly veiled prose account of his own birth and education, the poem describes a surreal nocturnal vision. It marks a deliberate contrast to Philisides' other long poem, also a nocturnal vision, 'As I my little flock on Ister bank'.[20] While 'As I my little flock' is a political, social poem, associated explicitly with central Europe, the influence of Languet and with the burdens of authority – 'Then found I which thing is a charge to bear' – 'Now was our heavenly vault' shows Philisides alone, in England ('in fairest wood / Of Samothea land'), and in deep meditation on the eternal mysteries of life:

> ... What essence dest'ny hath; if fortune be or no;
> Whence our immortal souls to mortal earth do flow;
> What life it is, and how that all these lives do gather
> With outward maker's force, or like an inward father ...

These profound broodings are rudely interrupted by a noise like a vast explosion, as a chariot bursts out of the moon containing two squabbling, harridan-like women:

> Strange were the ladies' weeds, yet more unfit than strange.
> The first with clothes tucked up, as nymphs in woods do range,
> Tucked up e'en with the knees, with bow and arrows pressed ...
> The other had with art (more than our women know)
> As stuff meant for the sale, set out to glaring show,
> A wanton woman's face, and with curled knots had twined
> Her hair which, by the help of painter's cunning, shined ...

They turn out to be Diana and Venus; their waiting woman is a pearl-like 'virgin pure' called Mira. The middle-aged goddesses decide to resolve their disputes, in a version of the Judgement of Paris, by asking the 'lad' Philisides to award a 'crown of amber fair' to whichever of them he thinks worthiest. The loud quarrelsomeness of the goddesses, who both talk at once, and have a particularly feline way of calling each other 'dear', is amusingly evoked. Predictably, Philisides awards the crown to the young waiting woman, and is punished by the goddesses with fruitless, chaste passion for Mira. It has been suggested that the poem refers to Mary Sidney's position for two years as a maid of honour, and has some connexion with Dyer's *Amaryllis,* which describes a three-cornered relationship between two lovers, Coridon and Caramell, and the unattainable Amaryllis (Mary?).[21] This interpretation conforms with the poem's application to Sidney's own position. Court life, and in particular the insistent demands made of Sidney by Elizabeth, who was often celebrated as an embodiment of both Diana and Venus, were a rude interruption to Sidney's meditations and intellectual aspirations. Elizabeth, notorious for her lavish use of cosmetics and hair dye, and her fondness for exposing more, not less, of her body as years went by, seems clearly alluded to in Sidney's unsparing description. The society of his younger sister provided welcome respite from the humiliating and tedious aspects of attendance on the ageing Queen.

Successful courtiership required great versatility, bordering on insincerity. How successful Sidney really was as a courtier is open to question. Certainly he was never one of Elizabeth's 'minions'. She does not seem to have flirted with him or given him a nickname, and postponed knighting him for as long as she possibly could. Yet there is no doubt that his poems show him to be extremely adept in shifting rôles and attitudes for the requirements of different occasions. The marked lack of gallantry with which Sidney described the middle-aged goddesses in 'Now was our heavenly vault' is in complete contrast to his direct treatment of Elizabeth in his next surviving public entertainment,

The Lady of May. While the 'Old' *Arcadia* and its Eclogues were directed to a circumscribed audience which did not include the Queen, *The Lady of May* was written specifically for her amusement during a visit to Leicester's house at Wanstead, in Essex, in May 1578, part of a leisurely Progress through East Anglia which continued until mid-September.[22]

Unlike the *Dialogue betweene two shepherds* and the Accession Day appearance, *The Lady of May* has no rôle for Sidney himself. Elizabeth is praised, not by a Sidney-figure, but by two women, a mother and a daughter. The dilemma of the drama concerns the daughter's choice between two suitors, a lively but lawless forester and a rich but ineffective shepherd. Like the authors of the Kenilworth entertainments, Sidney used a spontaneous opening to capture the Queen's attention:

> Her most excellent Majesty walking in Wanstead Garden, as she passed down into the grove, there came suddenly among the train one apparelled like an honest man's wife of the country; where, crying out for justice, and desiring all the lords and gentlemen to speak a good word for her, she was brought to the presence of Her Majesty ...[23]

Both the nameless woman and her nameless daughter, who has been chosen as May Queen, praise the Queen's beauty as superior to their own, before appealing to her wisdom and clemency. It is unlikely that they were represented by real women. The play proper opens with some knockabout humour, as six foresters engage in a tug-of-war with six shepherds, pulling the May Lady first to one side, then another. A pedantic schoolmaster, Rombus, trying to sort out the dispute, receives 'many unlearned blows'. This is rough schoolboy stuff, and probability favours its enactment by child actors, either from Leicester's own company or from the Queen's. The performers may have been the very company who played at Kenilworth in 1575, the Children of the Chapel Royal, now under the direction of Richard Farrant, at Blackfriars, rather than William Hunnis, and augmented by boys from St George's Chapel, Windsor.[24] Despite his Puritan allegiances, Leicester was a generous friend and patron to actors and musicians, and seems to have taken this company in particular under his wing.[25] Considerable professionalism would be required for what Ringler calls *The Lady of May*'s 'operatic combination of song and spectacle'. His suggestion that Rombus was played by Leicester's servant the comic actor Richard Tarlton, to whose son Sidney was godfather in 1582, is attractive.[26]

Much has been made of the deeper meaning of *The Lady of May*. Ringler and others have argued that the real point at issue is 'whether England should actively support the cause of continental Protestantism by giving military aid to the Netherlands'. Louis Adrian Montrose, on the other hand, sees it as a debate between two kinds of courtiership or clientage, 'the pliable placeman and the impetuous free spirit'.[27] Both interpretations lead to a conclusion that in choosing, as she did, the harmless shepherd Espilus rather than the active forester Therion, the Queen was denying Sidney's own aspirations, and turned the occasion into something of a fiasco or disappointment. Though such political symbolism can never be wholly ruled out, I find both of these interpretations unconvincing. In broad terms, it seems unlikely that Sidney would be so rash as to use his uncle's public entertainment of the Queen to force a statement from her on such grave matters. In any case, in May 1578 he was still confidently expecting to go to the Netherlands in the near future, so from his own point of view the matter appeared to be settled. More narrowly, I think several details make it both apt and predictable that the Queen should choose Espilus, the inoffensive shepherd, rather than Therion, the active forester. On a literal level, could he have expected the Queen to reward a violent poacher?

Therion doth me many pleasures, as stealing me venison out of these forests, and many other such like pretty and prettier services; but withal he grows to such rages, that sometimes he strikes me, sometimes he rails at me.

In wooing the May Lady Therion seems to have taken liberties with Leicester's property, or the Queen's, in stealing deer; and a young man who was capable of hitting a girl before he was married to her was scarcely a promising prospect for matrimony. Even in sport Sidney, whose first fiancée was so disastrously married to the violent Earl of Oxford, would surely not have considered such a match desirable. Those who have discussed *The Lady of May* in political terms have seen it as a confrontation between the radical and headstrong Sidney and the cautious and compromising Queen. Yet much of Sidney's explicit political advice was actually conservative, pleading against violent changes, such as the French marriage, where he strongly defends the *status quo*:

... a man might well ask: 'What makes you in such a calm to change course? To so healthful a body, to apply such a weary medicine? What hope can recompense so hazardous an adventure?' Hazardous indeed, were it for nothing but the altering of a well-maintained and well-approved trade. For as in bodies natural any sudden change is not without peril, so in this body politic, whereof you are the only head, it is so much the more, as there are more humours to receive a hurtful impression.[28]

His fictional counsellor, Philanax, also urged his monarch not to make any radical change.[29] Close in time to *The Lady of May*, perhaps even while he was writing it, on 25 April 1578, he remarked sententiously to his father that it is 'most noble to have always one mind and one constancy'.[30] To Edward Waterhouse, a few days later, he wrote of his own stoical constancy:

I, of myself, thus much: always one, and in one case; *Me solo exultans totus teres atque rotundus.*[31]

He was quoting here from memory from Horace's *Satires* II. vii, a passage on the true freedom of the wise man who scorns passion and ambition, 'so that nothing from the outside can rest on the polished surface, and against whom Fortune in her onset is ever maimed'. To Languet he had written in March of his desire to cultivate his mind and become a 'stoic' or even a 'cynic'.[32] If Sidney was cultivating these stoical reflexions in the spring of 1578, he was probably not minded at present to provoke the Queen to declare a commitment to radical change. On the contrary, he may have been setting up a situation in which she would give public approval to his own current life of contemplation rather than action. Her choice of the inoffensive Espilus rather than the dangerous Therion conformed to one of his own favourite sayings, recorded by two close associates, Sir Roger Williams and Lodowick Bryskett. Williams, describing the qualities needed in a good military commander, said that an open-handed and constant leader should

not be condemned without great faults; as noble Sir *Philip Sidney* was wont to say, *Let us love him for his small virtues, for a number have none at all.*[33]

Elizabeth may also have been aware of Sidney's distaste for hunting. In addition, the playlet may contain some private allusions which she correctly glossed. Though many literary pastoral names were available to Sidney for his shepherd-suitor, he may have had a special reason for using, instead, the odd, untraditional name of 'Espilus', or 'felt-presser'. In 1561 and 1562, when Leicester was recovering position after the setback of Amy Robsart's death, the Queen enriched him by giving him four licences to 'export woollen cloth unwoven' (i.e. felt), which he made over to the Merchant Adventurers' Company for the extraordinarily large sum of £6,266.[34] In choosing the gentle felt-presser, Elizabeth may have been aware that she was expressing a preference for her old favourite and his nephew, as against other, more threatening, advisers or even consorts.

In Rombus's valedictory speech, which seems to have been added to *The Lady of May* at the last moment, a deliberately scaled-down, domesticated picture is given of Leicester and his benevolence:

So it is that in this our city we have a certain neighbour, they call him Master Robert of Wanstead. He is counted an honest man ... and when he comes to his aedicle [little house] he distributes *oves, boves et pecora campi* largely among the *populorum* [i.e. he makes a great feast for all his tenants].[35]

A joke is made of Leicester's religion. He is supposedly stained 'with the papistical enormity', but this turns out to mean only that he is obsessed with

Elizabeth, using a string of round agates as a rosary on which he repeatedly adds 'and Elizabeth' to the Lord's Prayer. Rombus pretends to have confiscated the necklace from Master Robert's cell, presenting it, of course, to the Queen. In using the imagery of Catholic devotion Sidney was steering very near the wind. After his conferences with Campion and, more recently, his tiltyard appearance in the company of two notorious Catholic aristocrats, Lord Arundel and Lord Windsor, there may have been a few seconds of 'double-take' when the Queen heard Rombus's regretful announcement that Master Robert was 'a huge Catholicam', quickly followed by relief and gratification as his picture of Leicester as Elizabeth's beadsman was unfolded. As in the *Discourse on Irish Affairs* six months earlier, Sidney may have been keen to show the Queen how ready he was to dismiss, or even jest about, Catholic devotion, in order to allay her suspicions. This was vitally important if, as he believed, she was about to send him on another mission to the Continent following up the idea of a Protestant League. If it was indeed Richard Tarlton who acted Rombus and therefore made the final speech and presentation, he may have been chosen to keep the occasion on an even keel, for Tarlton 'was credited with the power of diverting Elizabeth when her mood was least amiable'.[36]

In asking the Queen for judgement, the May Lady says that 'in judging me, you judge more than me in it'. It is this line that has encouraged modern commentators to look for a political sub-text. Yet the further judgement required of the Queen may have been relatively simple: she was being asked to spot which suitor could be best identified with the Dudley faction. It is true that the Dudley faction favoured active participation in the Netherlands, but it does not follow from this that in playing the rôle of the gracious guest the Queen was either endorsing or denying such specific policies. After all, she sometimes accepted hospitality from known Catholics, like the Norrises at Rycote; but in doing so she was not expressing support of their beliefs. With her fluent Greek and her pleasure in nicknames, she may quickly have discovered a Leicester-figure in the wealthy and innocuous 'felt-presser', showing her approval of him in his Essex retreat in just the way that was hoped. In so doing she may also, though perhaps unknowingly, have given oblique approval to Sidney's recent drift towards contemplation and away from an active political life at Court. At Wilton, Sidney, like his fictitious shepherds, had discovered the joys of retirement:

> ... where it is lawful for a man to be good if he list, and hath no outward cause to withdraw him from it; where the eye may be busied in considering the works of nature, and the heart quietly rejoiced in the honest using them. If contemplation, as clerks say, be the most excellent, which is so fit a life for a templer as this is, which is neither subject to violent oppression, nor servile flattery?[37]

It was neat and ingenious to manoeuvre the Queen, who was by no means proof against flattery, into giving her approval to a way of life which was free of it. The pastoral contemplation described here closely resembles Philisides' meditation in 'Now was our heavenly vault', where, of course, it was rudely interrupted by two Elizabeth-like figures. In *The Lady of May* the shepherds' passionless life is explicitly contrasted with the 'doleful agonies' of courtiers struggling to pursue the favour of a mistress (the Queen) who can always outwit them, and is capable of 'extreme cruelty'. In declaring Espilus the winner, Elizabeth was in a sense endorsing the value of a life away from herself.

The Earl and Countess of Pembroke probably witnessed *The Lady of May*. In April 1578 Sidney received them at Penshurst, when £7 18s. 7d. was spent in entertaining them, together with many neighbouring Kentish gentry.[38] The whole party may then have joined the next stage of the Queen's Progress. By now Sidney had begun the habit of filling in odd moments with pastoral verses and metrical experiments, and may have started to plan the framework of his romance. But the distracting conditions of royal progresses, combined with the expectation from week to week that he would soon be taking the Queen's financial and military support to Prince Casimir, made it hard to do very much. Even as Philisides hovered gloomily in the margins of his pastoral romance, so his own poetic career still seemed marginal, not central.

Sidney's restless, fiery temperament did not equip him well for the rôle of Elizabethan courtier. Though he had inherited his father's affability and charm with close friends and dependants, he was also under the influence of his mother's almost paranoid bitterness and insecurity about the position of the Dudley family at Court. To this was added his own peculiar volatility of temperament, in which periods of melancholy lethargy alternated with bursts of manic energy. In 1577–8 he appeared to be performing his expected duties as a courtier more than adequately. As we have seen, he participated in the Accession Day Tilt in November 1577. At New Year he gave the Queen 'a smock of cambric, the sleeves and collar wrought with black work, and edged with a small bone lace of gold'.[39] Clothes seem to have been 'in' as gifts this year, for Sidney's mother gave the Queen a doublet embroidered with gold and silver, Edward Dyer gave her a gold-embroidered kirtle, and Fulke Greville gave her a cambric smock embroidered with 'Spanish work of roses and trees'.[40] *The Lady of May* showed Sidney's willingness to deploy his verbal and inventive skills in the service and celebration of the Queen, and should have gained him some 'brownie points', especially since it flattered the Queen so skilfully in creating a set-up in which she rejected flattery.

But the strain of not knowing whether, when and with what status he would be sent to the Netherlands, together with a consciousness that his father's service in Ireland was still not being properly appreciated by the Queen, was beginning to tell. At the end of May he penned a much less amiable piece than his pastoral playlet, the savagely threatening letter to Edmund Molyneux quoted above (pp. 22–3). It was presumably written at the current stopping place of the Progress, for 'Court' was wherever the Queen was. Molyneux's reply reveals his astonishment at receiving a death threat for carrying out his duties as Sir Henry Sidney's secretary:

I have received a letter from you, which, as it is the first, so the same is the sharpest that ever I received from any: and therefore it amazeth me the more to receive such a one from you, since I have (the world may judge) deserved better somewhere, howsoever it pleaseth you to condemn me now ... Mine innocency I hope in the end shall try mine honesty, and then I trust you will confess you have done me wrong.[41]

Sidney's letter was literally 'sharp', for he had threatened to 'thrust [his] dagger' into the unfortunate Molyneux, whom he suspected, wrongly, of complicity with the Earl of Ormond and his faction. If Sidney was not allowed to attack Ormond directly, he was determined to vent his rage on someone.

Violence often lies just below the surface in Sidney's fiction, and he may have been in the habit of using menacing language rather freely. A joking remark by Languet in a letter of 2 May 1577 suggests as much:

If you marry a wife, and if you beget children like yourself, you will be doing better service to your country than if you could cut the throats of a thousand Spaniards or Frenchmen.[42]

The Queen objected strongly to quarrels and duelling among her courtiers. Sidney's outburst against Molyneux reflected a pattern of behaviour which she cannot have failed to notice. She must have felt grave misgivings about letting someone so explosive loose in the Netherlands. Her general reluctance to commit herself definitely to the Dutch struggle for independence was compounded by extreme anxiety about how Sidney, in particular, might exploit such an opportunity. The very eagerness with which he was asked for seemed suspicious. Had he presented himself to Orange and Casimir as a person of higher status than he really was?

On 25 April 1578 Casimir sent letters to the Queen and to several leading courtiers. In his letter to Sidney he claimed that the Queen herself had made a proposal:

that I should march into Flanders with moderate forces, which I should be glad to see augmented by a force from England [and] I have begged her to appoint some gentleman to be attached to me to assist me in her name ... I have desired that this should be yourself, for the singular opinion that I have of your virtues and the pleasure I should receive from often conference with you ...[43]

In May Casimir repeated his assertion that the Queen herself had requested him to march into the Low Countries, together with his demand for Sidney to be sent over at the head of English reinforcements. Nothing, as it turned out, could be further from Elizabeth's intention. While she did eventually, in July, give Sidney leave to go,[44] it was as her envoy only, not as a military leader. He was to carry with him letters in which she explicitly disclaimed any responsibility for Casimir's arrival in the Netherlands. Leicester, reporting on this to Walsingham, believed that his nephew's departure would now do more harm than good:

> ... This earnestly has she commanded Philip to say to him, writing such a letter besides of cold comfort that when I heard of both, I did all I could to stay him at home; and with much ado I think I shall, seeing I know not what he should do there but bring discouragement to all her best friends. For my part I had rather he perished in the sea than that he should be instrument of it.[45]

Leicester's letter was written on 1 August from Bury St Edmunds, some miles south of the Queen's continued stately Progress through East Anglia. His vehement tone suggests that he was having some difficulty in persuading his impetuous nephew not to rush off to the Netherlands, the Queen's discouragement notwithstanding. Sidney continued to toy with the idea of an autonomous involvement in the wars in the Netherlands, for on 22 October Languet gave him a firm and lucid exposition of the distinction between lawful and unlawful killing.[46] To kill a man in battle without the express authority of one's sovereign was tantamount to murder. But Languet was equally worried at the prospect of Sidney's retirement from Court:

> I am especially sorry to hear you say that you are weary of the life to which I have no doubt God has called you, and desire to fly from the light of your court and betake yourself to the privacy of secluded places to escape the tempest of affairs by which statesmen are generally harassed ... I confess that in the splendour of a court, there are so many temptations to vice that it is very hard for a man to hold himself unspotted by them, and keep his feet on so slippery ground. But you must stand firm on your principle and strength of mind against these difficulties ...

Languet may have misinterpreted or glossed over the true reasons for Sidney's weariness with a life at Court, which had more to do with frustration at the Queen's treatment of him than with resisting temptation.

Though Sidney's courtiership failed to impress the Queen – failed, at least, to impress her sufficiently for her to give him his head – he was by this time becoming a considerable patron of the arts. Greville for once hardly overstates the case:

> The universities abroad and at home accounted him a general Maecenas of learning, dedicated their books to him, and communicated every invention or improvement of

knowledge to him . . . his heart and capacity were so large that there was not a cunning painter, a skilful engineer, an excellent musician or any other artificer of extraordinary fame that made not himself known to this famous spirit and found him his true friend without hire, and the common rendezvous of worth in his time.[47]

The letter to Sussex in which Sidney begged leave of absence from Court at Christmas 1577 had included a postscript pleading for Sussex's continued generosity to 'the poor stranger musician', presumably one of the many Protestant refugees who arrived in England at this time. Among books and manuscripts dedicated to Sidney during the period when it was believed that he was about to take up a command in the Netherlands may be one particularly splendid volume penned by a young protégé, Abraham Fraunce, who was an undergraduate at St John's College, Cambridge. It consists of a summary of Ramist logic and a collection of *imprese*, or personal emblems.[48] The coloured binding shows a scene from the *Aeneid* in which the castaway Achaemenides, left with Polyphemus by Odysseus, pleads to be rescued by Aeneas and his companions. The schematized, helmeted Aeneas, a dominating figure on the departing sailing ship, is clearly a representation of Sidney himself, and the symbolic identification of Achaemenides with Fraunce is indicated by the placing of his initials, A.F., between his feet. The back cover has acrostic valedictory verses praising Sidney's wisdom, strength and eloquence, and the first of the *imprese* is a porcupine, borne by Louis XII of France, but also by the Sidney family, whose crest it was.[49] Clearly Fraunce was bidding Sidney farewell as he went off on some expedition which he himself would have liked to join, and this may be the expected mission to the Netherlands.

A work praising Sidney which undoubtedly does belong to the second half of 1578 is even more extravagant. At the end of July the Queen stayed at Audley End, in Essex, where she was lavishly entertained by dignitaries of the University of Cambridge. Among them was Sidney's old friend Gabriel Harvey, who participated in disputations on questions of whether 'clemency was more praiseworthy in a magistrate than severity' and whether 'the stars do not impose necessity'.[50] The poet and diplomat Giles Fletcher the Elder presided over the three-hour debate. Harvey made much of his participation in this royal visit. He presented a handsome manuscript collection of Latin verses to Burghley to commemorate the occasion,[51] and may have distributed other such manuscripts to eminent visitors. This was normal and acceptable practice. But in September 1578 he had the verses printed as part of a more ambitious work, *Gratulationes Valdinenses*, in which in many respects he went too far. He made embarrassingly over-elaborate play with the fact that he had kissed the Queen's hand, and that she had remarked that he looked like an Italian. He drew a rather tricky comparison between the integrity of the Earl of Leicester and the wicked ways of the Machiavel (probably standing for the Duke of

Alençon), and urged Leicester to marry Elizabeth. The full ghastliness of this blunder can only have hit him when it later emerged that Leicester had been secretly married to Lettice Knollys that very month. In a final section he offered encomia on three leading courtiers, Oxford, Hatton and Sidney. Sidney cannot much have relished being bracketed with Oxford, and Harvey's knowing reference to Sidney as being on the point of departure rubbed salt in a wound, since, as we have seen, he did not in fact leave England, much to his chagrin. But there was worse than this. Harvey, as Nashe was mercilessly to point out, stressed the closeness and length of his friendship with Sidney, '*mihi multis nominibus longe charissimum*', using language that transgressed the capacious boundaries of courtly eulogy, for it suggested homosexual passion. Nashe quoted and translated thus:

I have perused verses of his, written under his own hand to Sir Philip Sidney, wherein he courted him as he were another Cyparissus or Ganymede; the last Gordian true love's knot or knitting up of them is this:

> Sum iecur ex quo te primùm, Sydnee, vidi,
> Os oculosque regit, cogit amare iecur.
>
> All liver am I, Sidney, since I saw thee;
> My mouth, eyes, rules it, and to love doth draw me.[52]

The liver was believed to be the seat of sexual passion, and it is unlikely that Sidney relished this style of compliment. Like his own hero Pyrocles, he could have said that 'there is nothing I desire more than fully to prove myself a man'.[53] Avuncular emotional blackmail from Languet in private correspondence was one thing; declarations of sexual attraction in print from an eccentric Cambridge academic whose job was running out were another. In an almost equally ill-advised publication late in 1580, *Three Letters*, Harvey claimed that he and Spenser both enjoyed the favour of Sidney and Dyer. But by this time Spenser, though absent in Ireland, had far outstripped Harvey and was probably being exploited by him to suggest to the reading public that Harvey, too, was still intimate with 'those two odd gentlemen you wot of'.

The poem which opened in such an embarrassing manner introduced two further poems, *Aulicus* and *Aulica*. Heavily based on Castiglione, they itemized the qualities and gifts required in the ideal courtier and courtly gentlewoman.[54] Purely in terms of his talent and versatility, there is no doubt that Sidney did come nearer than most to fulfilling the Castiglionian ideal. But as we have seen, this did not ensure that his actual position at Court was a distinguished or comfortable one, and by the end of 1578 it was severely jeopardized. Much of his status at home and abroad derived from his being heir to Leicester. By no means the least important aspect of this was his credit-worthiness. His father's finances never recovered from the double blows of having to pay £3,000 for his daughter's dowry and £840 for his son's expenses in travelling to Germany, both in the spring of 1577.[55] From September 1577, if not before, Philip, too, was perpetually in debt. He was slow in producing his contributions to Frobisher's expeditions, and was borrowing sums of £200–300 from various moneylenders.[56] So long as he was heir apparent to the wealthy Earl of Leicester, creditors may have been loath to press him too hard. But on 20 September 1578 Leicester 'quieted his conscience' by marrying the widowed Countess of Essex, Lettice née Knollys. The ceremony was conducted at Wanstead by an old friend of Gabriel Harvey's, Humphrey Tyndall, who recorded that the bride had been wearing a 'loose bodied gown'. Coupled with Leicester's reference to his conscience, this implies that she was pregnant. Though this infant does not seem to have survived, it must have become apparent to Sidney in 1578–9 that his special position of favour and expectation was under threat. It is noticeable that acute money worries crop up continually in his correspondence from this time on.

At what stage Sidney learned of his uncle's marriage is unknown. He is not among the small group of named witnesses. But he was probably aware of it many months before the Queen, who learned of it only six months later. With Leicester's marriage still a well-kept secret, New Year 1578/9 seems to have passed off cheerfully at Court, with the customary exchange of extravagant gifts. Leicester gave Elizabeth a tiny gold clock decorated with diamonds and rubies, 'and upon each side a lozenge diamond, and an apple of gold enamelled green and russet'.[57] Perhaps the apple alluded to the Judgement of Paris, in which the golden apple was awarded to Helen of Troy. The Queen's return gift to Leicester of 100 ounces of gilt plate suggests undiminished favour, for her gift to him the previous year had been similar, 100 ounces of silver gilt.[58] For the first time, Sidney's name appears at the head of the list of 'Gentlemen'; he gave his monarch 'a waistcoat of white sarcenet, quilted and embroidered with gold, silver, and silk of divers colours', which must have cost him a pretty penny.[59]

The most expensive court celebrations, however, were yet to come. Weary of trying to whip up support for his campaign through letters and envoys, Prince Casimir decided to visit England in person, 'to persuade the Queen to give him substantial and open assistance'.[60] Very much at the last minute, Hubert Languet, recovering from a prolonged illness, decided to seize this opportunity to see for himself how his young charge was getting on as an English courtier, and joined Casimir's party at Ghent. The Queen deputed Sidney and his father (recently returned from Ireland) to meet Casimir on arrival at the Kent coast, probably at Dover. Casimir was disguised as a merchant, but as he approached London no doubt donned court dress. The party travelled together up the Thames, arriving at the Tower of London on 22 January. According to Camden it was 'a sharp winter, full of snows'.[61] Despite the cold, three weeks of junketings followed, with feasting, civic receptions, hunting, a tournament and tourney, and a visit to Paris Gardens, presumably to watch bear-baiting. Both Court and City welcomed Casimir warmly, the latter presenting him with a gold collar and gold goblets 'in the whole to the value of 2,000 crowns', as Leicester reported to William Davison, then English agent in Antwerp. Socially, the visit was a huge success: 'as he is liked here, so he liketh his entertainment, and taketh in very good part the great courtesy he findeth'.[62] The Queen was a generous hostess, bearing the whole cost of his lodging, at Somerset House; and on 8 February she showed her special favour to him by making him a Knight of the Garter, putting the Garter on his leg with her own hands. Yet politically nothing was achieved. Casimir did not get the money, soldiers or assurances of support that he had come for, nor was his offer to the Queen of 'a large area of the Belgian coast' accepted. He must have been extremely disgruntled, for his party decamped, on 14 February, in such a hurry that Languet had no chance to say goodbye to Sidney and Dyer, and nearly got left behind for want of a horse. For once, Languet had to apologize to Sidney, rather than the other way round:

> ... I am sorry that I could not let you see even tears and sighs, as pledges of my great regard for you; but it was not my fault, for our party was hastening away, as if they were taking leave of enemies, not of friends, and I should have given great offence, if I alone had behaved with common sense, instead of being mad with the rest.[63]

Once Languet did manage to rejoin his party, which now included Fulke Greville and young Robert Sidney, they had a difficult crossing, but embarked in bad weather rather than over-tax the attentions of Sir Henry Sidney, who came to see them off.

Sidney's reactions to the visit of Casimir and Languet are unrecorded. He must have been embarrassed by the Queen's failure to give Casimir any of the help he had come for. Languet, whose first and only visit to England this was, later conveyed rather mixed impressions. He had enjoyed making the acquaintance of Sidney's friends Dyer and Greville, and seeing for himself that Sidney was 'high in favour';

> But to speak plainly, the habits of your court seemed to me somewhat less manly than I could have wished, and most of your noblemen appeared to me to seek for a reputation more by a kind of affected courtesy than by those virtues which are wholesome to the state, and which are most becoming to generous spirits and to men of high birth. I was sorry therefore, and so were other friends of yours, to see you wasting the flower of your life on such things, and I feared lest that noble nature of

yours should be dulled, and lest from habit you should be brought to take pleasure in pursuits which only enervate the mind.[64]

It would be nice to know precisely what 'pursuits' Languet had in mind. He may have been thinking of English court ceremonial. During the three weeks of Casimir's visit Sidney may frequently have been called upon to exercise his function as Royal Cupbearer, with much ritual hand-washing, carrying of napkins, toasts, and general bowing and scraping.[65] Elizabeth liked foreign dignitaries to see her courtiers elaborately displaying their loyalty to her. Languet, fresh from the unpretentious household of William of Orange, may have been repelled by such spectacles. He may also have felt that tilting, an activity in which Sidney now delighted to participate, was an appalling waste of time and money. It was embittering to see so many resources going into tournaments at Whitehall, and so few to the grave conflict in the Netherlands.

Languet soon had cause for serious anxiety. The courtly ladder that Sidney had struggled to climb, through his diplomatic mission, his participation in court festivities, and his attendance on the Queen as her Cupbearer, was wobbling badly. Languet had probably brought with him from Ghent a commendatory poem by the Anglo-Dutch envoy Daniel Rogers which gave a syrupy account of Sidney's relationship with the Queen:

... whether she walks with wandering steps through the green fields which one sees from the nearby Court of Richmond, or whether she takes a walk through the sunny gardens, you are there, faithfully ready to wait upon Her Majesty. If it pleases the goddess to ride into the gay fields, you will mount your horse, and presently keep your Mistress company. And when an ambassador from a distant country arrives she first commends him to your good care. And whatever you are doing, you must be close to the Queen, whether she is seriously occupied or pleases to be merry. O fortunate man, who as the servant of Eliza can mix with Stars – yea, goddesses. And need I speak of how often she merrily chirps with you, and of how that Royal Nymph delights the company with her ready wit. By condescending to favour your wishes, how much your obedient services must please her![66]

In reality, new developments threatened the position of the whole Dudley network at Court, and Sidney, its youngest and most talented member, soon found himself its 'fall guy'. The Queen's courtship of the Duke of Alençon, or 'Monsieur', who had now become heir to the throne of France, had ticked over quietly for some years. Suddenly, as Alençon prepared to fill the military vacuum in the Netherlands, his wooing of Elizabeth gained intensity. Alençon's new agent, Jean de Simier, initiated this new, more urgent phase of wooing when he came over to London in January 1579, a few days before Casimir. Camden described Simier as 'a refined courtier, who was exquisite in the delights of love, and skilful in the ways of courtship'.[67] To the horror of many of her advisers, Elizabeth seemed, after twenty-one years as a Virgin Queen, to be seriously contemplating marriage. What was really going on in what Antony Bacon was to call 'that deep and inscrutable centre of the court, which is Her Majesty's mind', we shall never know.[68] Political considerations were no doubt uppermost. If England, through Elizabeth's marriage, could gain control over Alençon's activities in the Netherlands, French dominance might be effectively neutralized, and French resources, in terms of wealth and soldiers, might be exploited in the English interest. A dreaded alliance between France and Scotland could be deflected. But Elizabeth played the love-game alarmingly well, being apparently enchanted by her proxy-wooer, Simier, who soon became her '*singe*, or pet monkey'. She was eager for the arrival of her true 'frog', Alençon.

Months of controversy and tension ensued. The anti-marriage faction, which was led by Leicester, Walsingham, Pembroke and Hatton, and included many leading churchmen, outnumbered supporters. But the latter had at their head two of the Queen's most trusted advisers, Burghley and Sussex, and their hangers-on included Sidney's old rival the Earl of Oxford. Early in July Simier pulled out a trump card, revealing to Elizabeth that Leicester had been secretly married for over six months.[69] The rage which fell on Leicester extended to his family circle. Sidney's mother seems to have withdrawn from Court, and no doubt Sidney's own position was severely shaken. If the Queen already suspected the Dudley–Sidney faction of playing various double games, this revelation provided ample confirmation. There is little doubt that she also felt personally piqued, for Leicester had been a friend since childhood, and she was deeply attached to him. It also happened that Leicester's new father-in-law, Sir Francis Knollys, was another strong opponent of the French marriage. Simier's revelation had made the Queen's marriage to Alençon more likely by silencing some of the strongest voices raised against it. Walsingham had already voiced cautious and sensible arguments against the marriage during prolonged meetings of the Privy Council; Leicester was now removed from the arena, though he seems to have been no further away than Greenwich. New anti-marriage spokesmen were needed.

On 17 August 1579 Elizabeth's 'frog' hopped across the Channel, with no retinue, and no aim except flamboyant flirtation. Elizabeth had always maintained that she could not marry a man she had not seen – her father's disastrous marriage to Anne of Cleves taught her that – so with the removal of this impediment, marriage came a stage nearer. Despite Alençon's small stature, pock-marked complexion and bulbous nose, Elizabeth revelled in love-games with her 'frog', who was, as H. R. Woudhuysen has pointed out, rather more cultivated and intelligent than his enemies allowed. Popular opinion, in this period when overt satire of public figures was largely forbidden, seems to have found oblique expression in the revival of an old song about a frog who would a-wooing go. On 21 November 1580 a ballad, no doubt already in circulation, was licensed called 'A most strange wedding of the frogge and the mouse'. No copies survive, and it may be significant that it was not until eight years after Elizabeth's death that an 'up-market' version was produced, by Thomas Ravenscroft in his *Melismata* (1611).[70] But a direct, unsparing attack on the proposed French marriage was delivered by a courageous Puritan gentleman, John Stubbs. It was written and published at high speed at the time of Alençon's visit. *The Discoverie of a Gaping Gulfe whereinto England is like to be swallowed by an other French marriage* is a powerful, still stirring piece of propaganda. Stubbs saw many sinister connotations in Alençon's wooing. Whereas in later versions of the ballad, froggy went wooing 'whether his mother would let him or no', in Stubbs's account Alençon's mother, Catherine de' Medici, was plotting

> so she might have this land another while for her stage. She is dressing her Prologue to send him in; trust him not. The players be tragical, though he [Alençon] wear peaceable laurel on his head.[71]

Stubbs made many allusions to Elizabeth's 'years', claiming that Alençon showed 'a very French love' in proposing marriage to her at just the time when, given her age, childbirth was most likely to be fatal to her. Really, Stubbs suggested, Alençon hoped to marry the Queen of Scots once Elizabeth was dead, thus gaining control of the whole of mainland Britain. He drew attention to Alençon's diseased and ill-shaped body, the 'crew of unruly youths' who surrounded him, and his poor record as a military commander. Though too young to have participated in the St Bartholomew's Day Massacre, he had proved himself a false friend to the reformed Churches in France, committing 'abominable and beastly disorders' in La Charité and Issoire.[72]

It was rumoured in France that Stubbs had been set up by Walsingham. If so, Walsingham failed to come to his defence when, on 3 November, Stubbs and the publisher, William Page, had their right hands struck off. Walsingham did, however, plead successfully on behalf of the printer, Hugh Singleton, so he may indeed have been in some way 'behind' *A Gaping Gulfe*. The condemnation of the three was based on the questionable revival of an Act passed by Mary Tudor protecting the Queen's husband from libel, now adapted to apply to the Queen's suitor. The propaganda effect of the punishment appears to have been the reverse of what the Queen and Burghley hoped. The chronicler John Stow, who was present, recorded that the crowd were silent with fear and pity for Stubbs, 'whom they reputed honest'. Stubbs himself, in a splendid gesture of martyred loyalty, immediately after his right hand had been struck off with a butcher's cleaver, raised his hat with his left and cried out 'God save the Queen!' before fainting away and being taken to prison, where he remained for the next year and a half.[73]

Perhaps about the same time as the inflammatory *Gaping Gulfe*, addressed to a wide readership, a much more tactful treatise was penned for consideration by the Queen and her immediate circle, Sidney's *Letter to Queen Elizabeth touching her marriage with Monsieur*, as it is called in some of the many manuscripts. Common ground between the *Letter* and *A Gaping Gulfe* suggests common origins in the Leicester–Walsingham circle, or the influence of one on the other. In mid-August Leicester returned to London, and presided over some sort of secret conference, in which Sidney and his father also participated, at the Earl of Pembroke's London house, Baynard's Castle.[74] It has been suggested that among the number of 'other friends and relatives' present was the poet Edmund Spenser, who may at this time have been in Leicester's employ.[75] Sidney's *Letter* was almost certainly the product of the meeting. A comment on it by Languet in October – 'you were ordered to write as you did by those whom you were bound to obey'[76] – suggests this. Sidney was a rapid and fluent writer, and it may not have taken him long to put his piece together, assimilating arguments already made by Walsingham and others. He showed diplomatic as well as rhetorical finesse in his handling of the themes most likely to enrage Elizabeth. For instance, he made no allusion either to the twenty-year disparity in age between Alençon and Elizabeth, or to the risk of her dying in childbirth, but wrote as if any marriage she made could be fruitful:

> Nothing can it [marriage with Alençon] add unto you, but only the bliss of children: which, I confess, were a most unspeakable comfort, but yet no more appertaining to him, than to any other to whom the height of all good haps were allotted, to be your husband.[77]

This almost sounds as if Sidney himself (not yet twenty-five) would have liked to marry Elizabeth. Warned, possibly, by the reception of Stubbs's pamphlet, he refrained from extended personal attacks on Alençon yet said enough to draw attention to the widely held belief that he was syphilitic:

> I will not show so much malice as to object the universal doubt of all that race's unhealthfulness; neither will I lay to his charge his ague-like manner of proceeding, sometimes hot and sometimes cold in the time of pursuit, which always likely is most fervent; and I will temper my speeches from any other unreverent disgracings of him in particular, though they might be never so true.[78]

Without larding Elizabeth with amorous eulogies, he included delicate references to 'the perfections of your body and mind'. Stubbs had made much of Alençon's Catholicism and his proven unreliability as a champion of Protestants, but Sidney dealt with the religious question in more cogently psychological terms:

He of the Romish religion, and if he be a man, must needs have that man-like disposition to desire that all men be of his mind.[79]

The thrust of Sidney's argument was that Elizabeth's already long reign, her personal gifts and her Protestantism all combined to make her popular and the country secure. Marriage with Alençon would throw all this into confusion, damaging the deep love that her subjects at present had for her. She should not listen to rumour or calumny, but rest secure in her 'standing alone ... as a singular honour God hath done unto you, to be indeed the only protector of his church';[80] and

Lastly, doing as you do, you shall be as you be: the example of princes, the ornament of this age, the comfort of the afflicted, the delight of your people, the most excellent fruit of all your progenitors, and the perfect mirror to your posterity.[81]

In the final phrase, Sidney suggests implausible confidence that the forty-six-year-old Elizabeth will indeed have children, though not by Alençon. Sidney served his party brilliantly. The case against the marriage could not have been more adroitly made. Yet the courtship dragged on, and a Royal Proclamation against criticism of Alençon on 27 September, followed by the punishments meted out to Stubbs and Page, ensured that no more such pleas could be voiced.

Unlike the unfortunate Stubbs, Sidney kept all his limbs intact. Elizabeth's response to his *Letter* is something of an enigma. According to Fulke Greville, who was closely involved in the anti-marriage faction and had spent three months as personal assistant to Walsingham in the Netherlands, the Queen treated Sidney generously. Answering a suggestion that it was 'an error, and a dangerous one, for Sir Philip, being neither magistrate nor counsellor, to oppose himself against his sovereign's pleasure', Greville declared that Sidney's 'worth, truth, favour and sincerity of heart' privileged him to write the *Letter*. Also, he had addressed the Queen herself, 'to whom the appeal was proper'; he had not (like Stubbs?) sought to stir up sedition. Greville went on to say of Sidney after the composition of the *Letter*

that howsoever he seemed to stand alone, yet he stood upright; kept his access to Her Majesty as before; a liberal conversation with the French, reverenced among the worthiest of them ... In this freedom, even while the greatest spirits and estates seemed hoodwinked or blind, and the inferior sort of men made captive by hope, fear or ignorance, did he enjoy the freedom of his thoughts, with all recreation worthy of them.[82]

Greville's chronology is different from that of modern biographers, for he went on to describe Sidney spending his post-*Letter* 'freedom' playing tennis at Court, quarrelling with Oxford, and only then being called to account by the Queen.[83] His narrative is infuriatingly opaque, but it is notable that he does not suggest that Sidney endured definite royal disfavour or banishment from Court even after the quarrel with Oxford. Since Sidney did not withdraw to Wilton for another six months after the tennis-court quarrel, Greville may be right, and the later tradition that Sidney retreated as a direct consequence of his boldness in advising the Queen may be wrong. If Greville's account of the order of events is correct, the second half of August 1579 was crowded with incident. On the 17th Alençon arrived, privately, or 'as it were in a mask', as Stubbs put it. A day or so later Leicester, the Sidneys and the others had their emergency conference at Baynard's Castle. Sidney would need to have written his *Letter* immediately to give time for the Queen to respond to it and allow him his customary 'freedom' for some days before the quarrel with Oxford, which must have taken place a day or so before 28 August, for on that date Sidney wrote about it to Sir Christopher Hatton:

> As for the matter depending between the Earl of Oxford and me, certainly, Sir, howsoever I might have forgiven him, I should never have forgiven myself, if I had lain under so proud an injury as he would have laid upon me, neither can anything under the sun make me repent it, nor any misery make me go one half-word back from it. Let him, therefore, as he will, digest it. For my part, I think tying up makes some things seem fiercer than they would be.[84]

Though the timing is constricted, this may, indeed, have been the order of events. Sidney was an extremely rapid writer, as some of his longer letters show. There had been six months or more during which the anti-marriage party were assembling their arguments, and a single day may have sufficed for Sidney to assimilate these into his *Letter*.[85] The matter was one of the utmost urgency, given Alençon's arrival in person, and the *Letter* may have been written in white heat – a fevered excitement that Sidney attempted to allay, perhaps, with a relaxing game of tennis among his friends.

There is, presumably, some connexion between Sidney's opposition to the Alençon marriage and his quarrel with Oxford, for the latter was one of its supporters. Yet Greville made no explicit allusion to this; his account makes it chiefly a battle for personal space and social precedence. According to him, Sidney, 'in this freedom of heart' – i.e. the liberty that the Queen allowed him after the delivery of the *Letter* – 'being one day at tennis', probably at Greenwich Palace, Oxford,

> born great, greater by alliance, and superlative in the prince's favour, came abruptly into the tennis-court, and speaking out of these three paramount authorities, he forgot to entreat that which he could not legally command.[86]

On Sidney's calm refusal, Oxford grew heated, and

commands them to depart the court. To this Sir Philip temperately answers that if his lordship had been pleased to express desire in milder characters, perchance he might have led out those that he should now find would not be driven out with any scourge of fury. This answer, like a bellows blowing up the sparks of excess already kindled, made my lord scornfully call Sir Philip by the name of puppy.[87]

Both sides now became 'loud and shrill', and the sound unfortunately attracted members of the French delegation, who 'had that day audience' with the Queen. Sidney asked Oxford 'with a loud voice' to repeat what he had just said; Oxford again called Sidney 'Puppy', and Sidney, in front of the numerous witnesses, 'gave my lord a lie impossible ... in respect all the world knows puppies are gotten by dogs and children by men'. Even in Greville's doubtless biased account, Oxford won the day, for Sidney and his friends 'abruptly' left the tennis-court. A day or so later a 'gentleman of worth' – perhaps Walter Ralegh – delivered a challenge. It was then that the Queen intervened, expounding to Sidney

the difference in degree between earls and gentlemen; the respect inferiors owed to their superiors; and the necessity in princes to maintain their own creations, as degrees descending between the people's licentiousness and the anointed sovereignty of crowns.

As we have seen, Oxford held the premier Earldom in England. Sidney, on the other hand, despite Greville's backdated 'Sir Philip', was not yet even a knight. To be reminded of this so bluntly must have been painful. According to Greville, Sidney pointed out to the Queen that although Oxford was great by birth and through his alliance with the Cecils, yet he was 'no lord over him, and therefore the difference of degrees between free men could not challenge any other homage than precedency'.[88] Whatever Sidney really said to the Queen, there is no doubt that she compelled a stand-off between these two fierce young men, and showed her preference for Oxford.

Though the Alençon marriage was a matter of national importance, and the quarrel with Oxford a relatively parochial affair, it may have been the latter that most preoccupied Sidney during the later part of 1579. Conditioned as he was by his mother to be acutely aware of the dignity of his lineage, he found the Queen's command to stand down because of his inferior rank exceedingly painful. The slight injured the whole family, and it may have been Philip's defeat in the Oxford affair that provoked both Leicester and Sir Henry Sidney to commission family pedigrees from Robert Cooke, Clarenceux King of Arms, at about this time.[89] With the help of four forged deeds, Cooke traced the Sidneys back to a supposed chamberlain of Henry II, William de Sidne.[90] Oxford's hereditary position as Lord Chamberlain may have stimulated this exercise in creative genealogy. Cooke eventually got a bad name among his fellow heralds for prostituting 'his office in the vilest manner for money'.[91]

What is not clear is whether Sir Henry Sidney, praised by Molyneux and others for his love of antiquities, knew what he was doing, and deliberately briefed Cooke to up-grade the Sidneys. Their eminence actually went back only to his own grandfather, Nicholas Sidney, who improved his standing by marrying Anne Brandon. Philip was throughout his life preternaturally sensitive to any suggestion of 'want of gentry',[92] and may have been persuaded by his father that the Sidneys really were courtiers of two centuries' standing.

Despite their difference in rank and political allegiance, Sidney and Oxford had had uncomfortably much in common. Both, as adolescents, enjoyed the patronage of Cecil and anticipated marriage to his daughter Anne; then, as now, Oxford won the day. They belonged to the same 'London club', Gray's Inn. Both spent a large proportion of their money on literary patronage. Both wrote and participated in court entertainments; Oxford had, for instance, collaborated in devising a Shrovetide show in 1579.[93] Most perplexingly, both were associated with Catholic courtiers such as the Howards. Oxford seems to have been a crypto-Catholic; Sidney's position is problematic, and may have undergone several changes.

Though no duel took place, the Oxford quarrel dragged on for many months. In mid-November Languet reported that Casimir was extremely concerned to hear about it, and was willing to 'assist' Sidney.[94] Oxford was a murderous enemy, and Sidney's continued defiance of him was rash to the point of foolhardiness. Oxford is said to have bragged when drunk that he would 'murder Sidney in his bed' at Greenwich Palace, or 'make away Philip Sidney', afterwards fleeing by barge on the Thames, well armed with pistols.[95] He may also have given vent to his feelings in some curious verses, perhaps those later referred to as 'a pleasant conceit of Vere, Earl of Oxford, discontented at the rising of a mean gentleman in the English Court *circa* 1580'.[96] Like many Elizabethan lyrics, it is a poem about not being able to write poetry. As an expression of murderous rage, however, it is unique in the period:

Fain would I sing, but fury makes me fret,
And rage hath sworn to seek revenge of wrong.
My mazed mind to malice so is set
As death shall daunt my deadly dolours long;
    Patience perforce is such a pinching pain
    As die I will, or [before I] suffer wrong again.

I am no sot, to suffer such abuse
As doth bereave my heart of his delight,
Nor will I feign myself to such a use
With calm content to suffer such despite.
    No quiet sleep shall once possess mine eye
    Till wit have wrought his will on injury.

My heart shall fail, and hand shall lose his force,
But some device shall pay despite his due;
And fury shall consume my careful corse
Or raze the ground whereon my sorrow grew.
Lo, thus in rage of ruthful mind refused,
I rest revenged of whom I am abused.
Finis Earl of Oxford[97]

If Sidney issued a comparable poetic challenge to Oxford, it has not survived. But a poem called *Speculum Tuscanismi* by the ever-unwise Gabriel Harvey was interpreted by Oxford's protégé John Lyly as a personal attack on the Earl. Despite vigorous denials by Harvey in later years, Lyly was probably right, as Harvey in private jottings seems to have acknowledged.[98] In the poem Harvey drew a crude portrait of a ridiculously foppish Italianate courtier:

... With forefinger kiss, and brave embrace to the footward,
Largebellied codpieced doublet, uncodpieced half-hose ...
A little apish hat, couched fast to the pate like an oyster,
French cambric ruffs, deep with a whiteness, starched to the purpose ...

The best-known portrait of Oxford shows him with just such an 'apish hat'. His reaction, as reported by Harvey in *Pierces Supererogation* (1593), suggests that Oxford felt, indignantly, that the hat fitted. In framing *Speculum Tuscanismi* Harvey said that the poet could have written far better had he had as model some of the work of Sidney and Dyer – perhaps a signal that the poem depicted their enemy.

The book in which *Speculum Tuscanismi* appeared, *Three Letters* (1580), reflects Sidney's transition, during 1579–80, from the world of active politics to that of literature. Though he was not explicitly banished from Court, he was tied up, if not muzzled, and had for the time being to abandon hopes for advancement in rank or a posting abroad. At Leicester House, Baynard's Castle and Wilton, Sidney withdrew from the Queen's presence, attaching himself, instead, to the society of his sister and the increasingly absorbing literary pursuits which he shared with her.

8
1580
THE COTERIE POET

Here now have you (most dear, and most worthy to be most dear, lady) this idle work of mine, which I fear (like the spider's web) will be thought fitter to be swept away than worn to any other purpose ... Now it is done only for you, only to you; if you keep it to yourself, or to such friends who will weigh errors in the balance of goodwill, I hope, for the father's sake, it will be pardoned, perchance made much of, though in itself it have deformities. For indeed, for severer eyes it is not, being but a trifle, and that triflingly handled.[1]

In the winter of 1579–80 Sidney and his sister Mary were both pregnant. She was about to produce a longed-for male heir for the Earls of Pembroke, a boy who would live to be the friend and patron of Shakespeare. Sidney's longer gestation was eventually to produce a work in which, as Virginia Woolf said, 'all the seeds of English fiction lie latent'.[2] He called it his 'child which I am loath to father', the almost involuntary product of an over-active imagination:

... a young head not so well stayed as I would it were (and shall be when God will), having many many fancies begotten in it, if it had not been in some way delivered, would have grown a monster.[3]

For eighteen months or so, from the autumn of 1579 until the spring of 1581, writing the *Arcadia* was his chief preoccupation. It is unlikely that it was written wholly at Wilton, as tradition has had it. Sidney said only that 'most' of it was written in his sister's presence, the rest, 'in loose sheets of paper ... sent unto you as fast as they were done'. The paucity of letters from Sidney during this period, with two notable exceptions which will be discussed, is explained by the fact that so much of his writing energies were now going into his romance.

Despite the continuing controversy over the Alençon courtship and the

Pyrocles disguised as an Amazon, from the title page of *The Countesse of Pembrokes Arcadia*, 1598 (Bodleian Library)

Oxford quarrel, Sidney remained at Court for some months. Perhaps to publicize their forced rapprochement, both he and Oxford, together with the Catholic Lord Windsor, participated in the 1579 Accession Day Tilt; it is a pity that further details are not known.[4] In the rather short New Year gift-list that survives for 1579/80 Sidney's name appears at the very end, which may reflect his current loss of favour.[5] His present, 'a cup of crystal with a cover', refers uncontroversially to his continued post as Cupbearer. Edward Dyer's gift, 'a pillar of gold enamelled, garnished with small opals and small rubies', may be more political, symbolizing Elizabeth's unmarried strength, which Sidney in his *Letter* celebrated as her 'standing alone'. In a later poem Sidney gave a pillar this meaning:

> His mark a pillar was devoid of stay,
> As bragging that, free of all passions' moan,
> Well might he others bear, but lean to none.[6]

Leicester's gift was, as ever, splendid, consisting of two jewel-encrusted gold bodkins (or small daggers). Though bodkins were quite common as gifts, these may have been a gesture of submission, implying that Elizabeth could, if she wished, stab him. A decoration of thirty-six 'true-love knots and ragged staffs' indicated his continued devotion to her, while reminding her of the number of years of their friendship. Meanwhile, riding high on the ocean of royal favour were the Earl and Countess of Oxford, who gave the Queen respectively a jewelled ship and a pair of bracelets adorned with 'six cloud stones or shells of the sea'.

The tortured ingenuity with which courtiers signalled their devotion to Elizabeth contrasts with the spontaneous warmth of Sidney's fraternal relationships. There is probably a connexion between his deteriorating position at Court, where he had acquired such formidable enemies as Ormond, Oxford and Alençon, and the noticeable strengthening of bonds with his own immediate family and friends. Two long 'familiar' letters belong to the period 1579–80, one to his brother Robert, one to a friend, Edward Denny. Both show Sidney at his very best: warm, intelligent, amusing and affectionate. They reveal that though he was denied serious responsibility by the Queen, he was rightly regarded within his own circle as an authority on politics and learning. In contrast to the heavy-handed and patronizing letters of advice that Sidney himself had received as a boy, the letters to his younger brother Robert, who was committed to his tutelage during Sir Henry's prolonged absences, are beguilingly informal. An extended letter of advice about travel belongs presumably to the later part of 1578; Robert set out on his academic peregrination in February 1579. Understandably, it became a model for such letters, achieving wide manuscript circulation and being printed as early as 1633.[7] Philip's second letter to Robert is also a classic of its kind, and was quoted by Walter de la Mare in his marvellous anthology *Come Hither*.[8] It reveals a warm complicity between the brothers, ranging agreeably in subject-matter from the mundane to the intellectual and back again:

> My dear brother: for the money you have received, assure yourself (for it is true) there is nothing I spend so pleaseth me as that which is for you. If ever I have ability you will find it; if not, yet shall not any brother living be better beloved than you of me ... Look to your diet (sweet Robin), and hold up your heart in courage and virtue. Truly, great part of my comfort is in you ... For the method of writing history, Bodin hath written at large; you may read him, and gather out of many words some matter ... In that kind [narrative history] you have principally to note the examples of virtue or vice, with their good or evil successes; the establishments or ruins of great states, with their causes ... Besides this, the historian makes himself a discourser, for profit, yea, a poet sometimes, for ornament: an orator, in making excellent orations *e re nata*, which are to be marked, but marked with the note of rhetorical remembrances; a poet, in painting forth the effects, the motions, the whisperings of the people, which though in disputation one might say were true, yet who will mark them well shall find them taste of a poetical vein, and in that kind are gallantly to be marked, for though perchance they were not so, yet it is enough they might be so ... This write I to you in great haste, of method, without method ... My time exceedingly short will suffer me to write no more leisurely. Stephen can tell, who stands with me while I am writing ... I write this to you as one that, for myself, have given over the delight in the world; but wish to you as much if not more than to myself ... My toyful book I

will send, with God's help, by February, at which time you shall have your money. And for £200 a year, assure yourself, if the state of England remain, you shall not fail of it; use it to your best profit. My Lord of Leicester sends you forty pounds, as I understand by Stephen, and promiseth he will continue that stipend yearly, at the least ... In any case write largely and diligently unto him, for in truth I have good proof that he means to be every way good unto you. The odd £30 shall come with the hundred, or else my father and I will jarl [quarrel]. Now, sweet brother, take a delight to keep and increase your music; you will not believe what a want I find of it in my melancholy times. At horsemanship, read Grison, Claudio, and a book that is called *La gloria del cavallo* withal, that you may join the thorough contemplation of it with the exercise, and so shall you profit more in a month than others in a year; and mark the bitting, saddling and curing of horses. I would, by the way, your worship would learn a better hand, you write worse than I, and I write evil enough. Once again, have a care of your diet, and consequently of your complexion: remember, *gratior est veniens in pulchro corpore virtus.*

Now, sir, for news, I refer myself to this bearer; he can tell you how idly we look on our neighbours' fires, and nothing is happened notable at home, save only Drake's return, of which yet I know not the secret points; but about the world he hath been, and rich he is returned... And to conclude, my eyes are almost closed up, overwatched with tedious business. God bless you, sweet boy, and accomplish the joyful hope I conceive of you. Once again, commend me to Mr Neville, Mr Savile and honest Harry White, and bid him be merry. When you play at weapons, I would have you get thick caps and bracers, and play out your play lustily, for indeed ticks and dalliances are nothing in earnest ... use as well the blow as the thrust, it is good in itself, and besides exerciseth your breath and strength, and will make you a strong man at the tourney and barriers ... Lord, how I have babbled! Once again, farewell, dearest brother. At Leicester House this 18 of October 1580.

Your most loving and careful brother
Philip Sidney.

Even a greatly shortened version of this letter reveals much about Sidney during the period of the composition of the 'Old' *Arcadia*. He was thinking about the exemplary power of poetry, as the comment on the value of 'poetical' passages in historical writings shows. He regretted what he considered to be his own limited understanding of music, a lack which he may have felt especially keenly when he wrote and framed those lyrics in the *Arcadia* which were designed to be sung. He regarded himself as having withdrawn from 'delight in the world', by which perhaps he meant the active world of courtly politics and ambition. Meanwhile, the composition of his 'toyful book', the *Arcadia*, was reaching its final stages, and Robert, like Mary, was to receive a copy. Though he was at Leicester House, not Wilton, he seems to have been working on it.

We do not know if Edward Denny was also among the privileged few for whom the first version of the *Arcadia* was written. He certainly had copies of some of Sidney's literary compositions, for in the penultimate sentence of his letter of advice to him Sidney enjoined him:

that you remember with your good voice to sing my songs, for they will one well become another.[9]

A copy of Sidney's long letter to Denny came to light only in 1972.[10] Style and detail leave no room for doubt as to its authenticity. As a communication written from Wilton on 22 May 1580, during the intensest phase of Sidney's work on the *Arcadia*, it is exceptionally interesting. The background to it is Lord Grey's imminent departure for Ireland, where he was to succeed Sir William Drury as Lord Deputy Governor. This appointment marked yet another foundered hope for Sidney, who had believed, perhaps rather unrealistically, that he himself might succeed to this post. In writing to Denny, who was serving under Lord Grey, he is magnanimous about it:

... very willingly do I bear the preferring of the noble Lord Grey, since so I prefer him to myself, as I will ever be most glad to do him service with affectionate honour, which, truly, I am but to very few.

Again, at the end, he refers to his 'impudence' in offering advice to one who 'hath my Lord Grey's company'. Among others departing with Grey was the poet Edmund Spenser, but, sadly, no reference to him can be detected in Sidney's letter.[11] Though seven years older, Denny regarded Sidney as his 'master', and had written to ask him to direct his studies. It may seem strange that someone preparing for military and administrative service in Ireland should be planning such a substantial programme of reading, yet the careers of Geffrey Fenton, Edmund Spenser, Lodowick Bryskett and many others show that Irish service was frequently combined with literary pursuits. Sidney's letter combines moral uplift with detailed suggestions for reading and method:

You will me to tell you my mind of the directing your studies. I will do it as well as the haste of your boy, and my little judgement, will able me. But first let me rejoice with you, that since the unnoble constitution of our time doth keep us from fit[ter] employments, you do yet keep yourself awake with the delight of knowledge; one of the notablest effects of that which makes us differ from beasts. Resolve therefore upon that still and resolve thus; that whensoever you may justly say to yourself you lose your time, you do indeed lose so much of your life ... Neither let us leave off because perchance the right price of these things is not had, without we should wish ourselves asses because some folks know not what a man means.

The last sentence indicates that Sidney knows that many people hold intellectual pursuits in contempt, but Denny, like Sidney, should persevere undaunted. 'Ned Denny' is a mature man, not a child; nor is he a University student, but a man of action. Sidney claims to moderate his recommendations accordingly, but the result is none the less daunting. He begins with study of the Bible:

> The knowledge of ourselves no doubt ought to be most precious to us; and therein the Holy Scriptures, if not the only, are certainly the incomparable lantern in this fleshly darkness of ours. For (alas!) what is all knowledge, if in the end of this little and wearisome pilgrimage, Hell become our schoolmaster? They, therefore, are diligently to be read.

Denny is to supplement this with study of the ancient moral philosophers: Aristotle, 'but he is something dark, and hath need of a logical examination', Cicero and Plutarch. Next, Denny, who is particularly inclined to 'soldiery', needs to study history, geography and cartography. Sidney knows that 'You have already very good judgement of the sea maps' – Denny had been on several expeditions to the New World, most recently with Sir Humphrey Gilbert and Sir Walter Ralegh.[12] This he should supplement with study of 'an Ortelius'. Sidney himself possessed a copy of Ortelius's *Theatrum Orbis Terrarum*, for he ordered one from its printer, Christopher Plantin.[13] The reading list which follows runs to a total of twenty-three historical writers, some ancient, such as Herodotus and Xenophon, some modern, such as Froissart, Guicciardini and Holinshed. Sidney admits that this list of ancient writers 'might seem too long, though indeed not so long as a man would think'. He then outlines a specific timetable for study:

> But now may you ask me: 'What shall I do first?' Truly, in my opinion, an hour to your Testament, and a piece of one to Tully's *Offices*, and that with study. Plutarch's discourses you may read with more ease. For the other matters, allot yourself another hour for Sacroboscus and Valerius, or any other of geography, and when you have satisfied yourself in that, take your history of England, and your Ortelius to know the places you read of; and so in my conceit you shall pass both pleasantly and profitably. Your books of the art of soldiery must have another hour, but before you go to them you shall do well to use your hand in drawing of a plot [map] and practice of arithmetic. Whether now you will do these by piecemeal, all in a day, or first go through with one, you must be your own judge, as you find your memory best serve. To me, the variety rather delights me than confounds me.

This programme reveals much about Sidney's own use of time. If Denny, whose vocation was to be a soldier, was to practise drawing maps and diagrams for an hour or two each day in the intervals of his historical studies, Sidney, whose 'unelected vocation' was to be a poet, may similarly have fitted in his hours of writing piecemeal, in the midst of other pursuits. At Wilton, in spring and summer, such pursuits were often out of doors. A great-uncle of John Aubrey's, who lived near Wilton,

remembered him [Sidney], and said that he was often wont, as he was hunting on our pleasant plains, to take his table book out of his pocket, and write down his notions as they came into his head, when he was writing his Arcadia.[14]

This may well have been the kind of variety of occupation that delighted him – the more so since he did not much like hunting.

The end of Sidney's letter to Denny is more personal:

I will end with these two remembrances: 1. that you forget not to note what you conceive of that you read. And 2. that you remember, with your good voice, to sing my songs, for they will well become another. My Lord of Pembroke, my sister, and your charge thank you with many thanks, and your cakes are reserved against all the parish come to dinner. Remember your last promise, and farewell from my heart. At Wilton, this Whit Sunday. 1580.

Your master in name but true friend indeed.

The jolly-sounding occasion at which Denny's cakes were to be eaten was a party for the christening of young William Herbert, to whom Sidney's sister gave birth on 8 April 1580. They were probably large fruit cakes, such as one described by Eleanor Fettiplace, 'big enough to cut into well over a hundred slices', rich in currants and spice, and raised with a barm of yeast, ale and butter.[15] We do not know to whom Sidney was referring as Denny's 'charge', nor what his 'last promise' was. But these personal greetings reinforce the sense of affable intimacy conveyed by the letter as a whole. Not much more is known of Sidney's friendship with Denny. Gabriel Harvey knew of Sidney's advice to him, perhaps from this letter, or perhaps from conversation.[16] It seems to have been thanks to Harvey's friend Humphrey Tyndall, who later became Master of Queens' College, Cambridge, that the letter has survived.[17] Sidney's continued goodwill towards Denny is shown in his trying, unsuccessfully, to procure the Irish estate of Powerscourt for him in October 1581.[18] Writing to Walsingham at this time Denny called Sidney 'the most worthy young man in the world'.[19] Denny also shared with Sidney the uncomfortable distinction of being one of those the Earl of Oxford said he wanted to kill.[20]

Though not all of the *Arcadia* was written at Wilton, much of it was, during the spring and summer of 1580. After Shrove Tuesday, 20 February, court festivities ceased for Lent, and Sidney was at last able to get away. It must have been an enormous relief. The coldness of the Queen towards himself and his family, her continued dalliance with Alençon, the intemperate rage of Oxford and his cronies, and the vast expense of a courtier's life all made attendance at Court extremely disagreeable. But more positively, as we have

1 Philip's mother, Lady Mary Sidney, *née* Dudley, by Hans Eworth (*Petworth House, Sussex*)

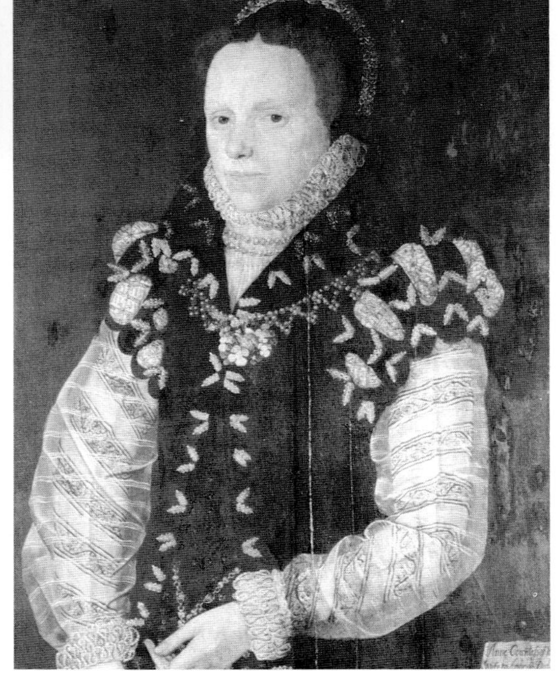

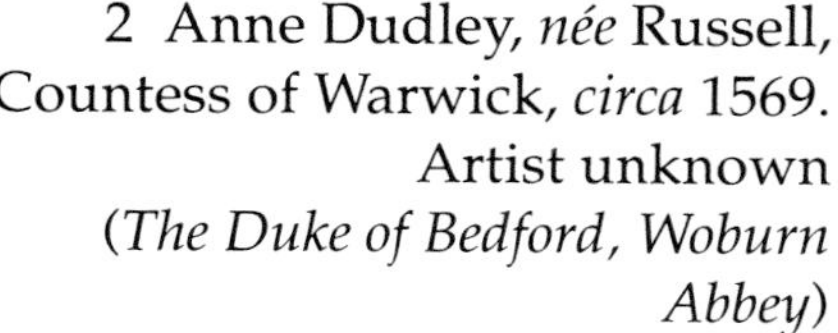

2 Anne Dudley, *née* Russell, Countess of Warwick, *circa* 1569. Artist unknown (*The Duke of Bedford, Woburn Abbey*)

3 Frances Sidney, Countess of Sussex, *circa* 1580. Artist unknown (*Sidney Sussex College, Cambridge*)

4 Lettice Dudley, *née* Knollys, Countess of Leicester, *circa* 1585, by George Gower (*The Marquess of Bath, Longleat, Wiltshire*)

5 Woodcut of Sir Henry Sidney riding out of Dublin Castle, from John Derricke, *The Image of Irelande*, 1582 (*Bodleian Library*)

6 Robert Dudley, Earl of Leicester, *circa* 1575.
Artist unknown (*National Portrait Gallery*)

7 William Cecil, Lord Burghley, riding a mule. Artist unknown (*Bodleian Library, Oxford*)

8 Edward de Vere, 17th Earl of Oxford, in his 'little apish hat'. Artist unknown (*Duke of Portland, Welbeck Abbey; on loan to the National Portrait Gallery*)

9 Composite portrait of Rudolph II, Holy Roman Emperor, as Vertumnus, *circa* 1591, by Giuseppe Arcimboldo (*Skokloster Castle, Sweden*)

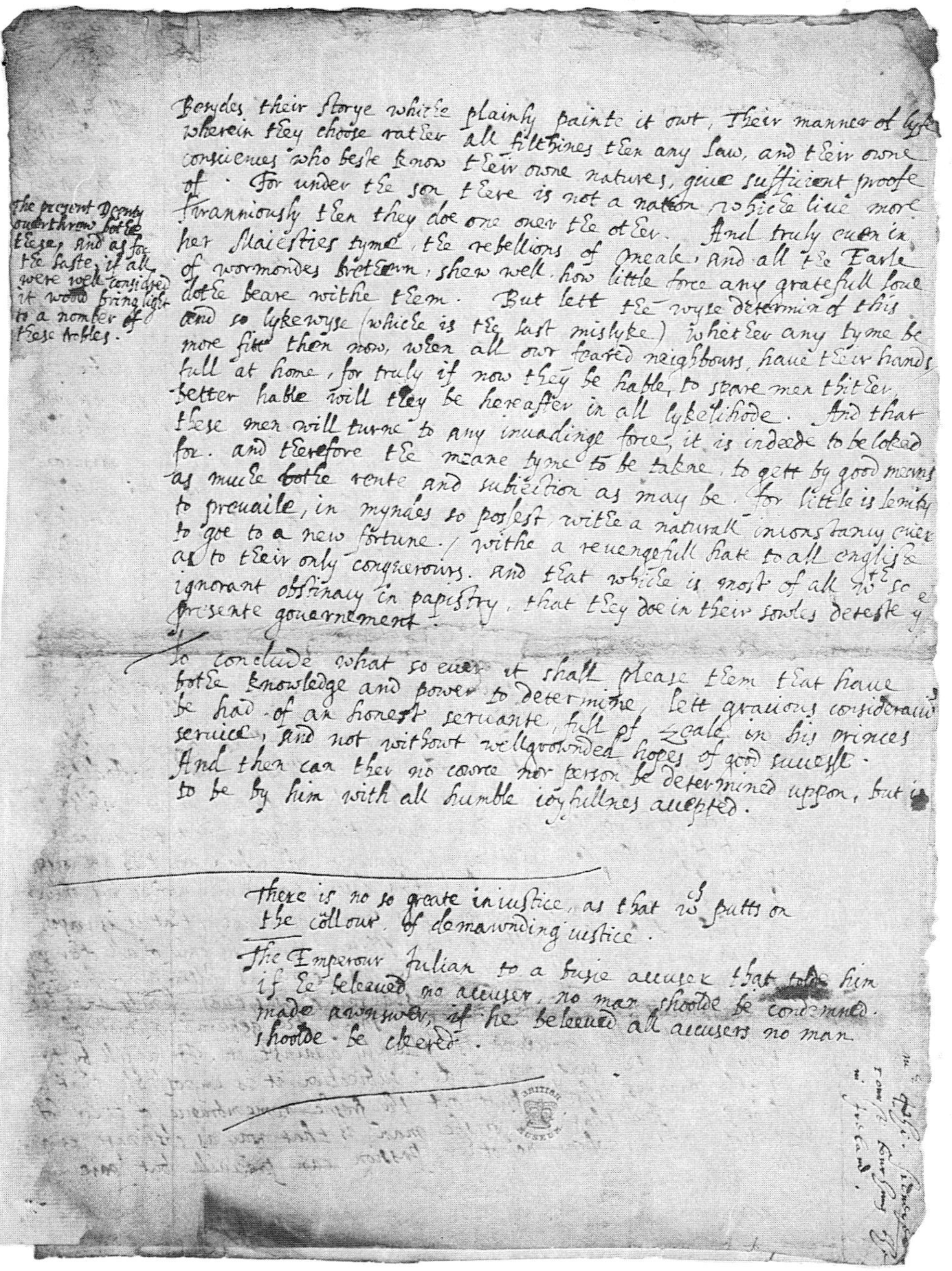

The present Deputy overthrow bothe these, and as for the laste, if all were well considered it wold bring light to a nomber of these troubles.

Besydes their storye which plainly painte it owt, Their manner of lyfe wherein they choose rather all filthines then any law, and their owne consciences who beste know their owne natures, giue sufficient proofe of. For under the son there is not a nation which liue more tyrannously then they doe one over the other. And truly even in her Maiesties tyme, the rebellions of Oneale, and all the Earle of wormondes bretherin, shew well how little force any gratefull loue dothe beare withe them. But lett the wyse determin of this and so lykewyse (which is the last mislyke) whether any tyme be more fitt then now, when all our feared neighbours, haue their hands full at home, for truly if now they be hable to spare men thither, better hable will they be hereafter in all lykelihode. And that these men will turne to any inuadinge force, it is indeede to be loked for. and therefore the meane tyme to be taken, to gett by good meanes as muche bothe rente and subiection as may be. For little is lenity to preuaile, in myndes so possest, withe a naturall inconstancy ever to goe to a new fortune, withe a revengefull hate to all english as to their only conquerours. and that which is most of all withe so ignorant obstinacy in papistry, that they doe in their sowles deteste ye presente gouernment.

To conclude what so euer it shall please them that haue bothe knowledge and power to determine, lett gracious consideration be had of an honest seruante, full of zeale in his princes seruice, and not without wellgrownded hopes of good succeste. And then can ther no course nor person be determined uppon, but is to be by him with all humble ioyfullnes accepted.

there is no so greate iniustice, as that which is putt on the collour of demaunding iustice.

The Emperour Julian to a busie accuser that tolde him if he beleeued no accuser, no man shoulde be condemned, made awnswer, if he beleeued all accusers no man shoulde be cleered.

10 Final page of Sidney's defence of his father's administration in Ireland, written in September 1577, autograph (*British Library*)

11 William of Orange by Adriaen Key (*Mauritshuis, The Hague, Netherlands*)

rain ſeigneur noſtre ſainct Pere le Pape, me ſemblé qu'a plus forte raiſon le treſ-
chreſtien Roy, premier filz de l'Egliſe a treſque iuſte cauſe de ſe leuer contre les
ennemis du ſainct ſiege Apoſtolic, meſmement en aiant eſté ſupplié de ce faire.
¶ S'il a defendu comme Vicaire du ſainct Empire les Allemagnes contre l'opreſſe
de l'Empereur, il a maintenant beaucoup meilleure, cauſe comme filz de defendre
noſtre ſainct Pere, & auroit (otées toutes les autres iniures) cette cy ſeule aſſes
d'argument pour rompre la Trefue, mais les aduerſaires premiers par leurs pratic-
qees l'ont enfrainćte,

FIN.

sleep Baby myne desyre, nurse beauty singeth
Thy cryes o Baby sett my hedd on akinge
The Babe cryes way thy love doth keep me waking
Lully lully my babe, hope cradle bringeth
unto my babies allway good restt takinge
The babe cryes way thy love doth keepe me wakinge
since Baby myne frome me thy watching springeth
sleep then a little pap content is makinge
The Babe cries nay for it abyde I wakinge

12 Sidney's *Certain Sonnets* 6, 'Sleep baby mine, desire', written out in his own hand (*Biblioteca Bodmeriana, Cologny, Geneva*)

13 Double portrait of Penelope and Dorothy Devereux, *circa* 1581. Artist unknown (*Marquess of Bath, Longleat, Wiltshire*)

14 Effigy of Robert Dudley, Baron Denbigh, 'the noble impe', died 19 July 1584 (*Beauchamp Chapel, St Mary's Collegiate Church, Warwick; photograph by C. R. Richards*)

15 Illustration of the opening scene of Sidney's 'New' *Arcadia*, 1629, showing the shepherds Strephon and Klaius rescuing Musidorus from drowning, by Matthaeas Merian. Just above Musidorus' feet Pyrocles can be seen in the water, waving his sword *(Dr B. E. Juel-Jensen)*

To the Angell spirit of the most excellent
Sr Phillip Sidney

To thee pure sprite, to thee alone's addrest
this coupled worke, by double intrest thine:
First raisde by thy blest hand, and what is mine
inspird by thee, thy secrett power imprest.
So dard my Muse with thine it selfe combine,
as mortall stuffe with that wch is diuine,
Thy lightning beames giue lustre to the rest,

That heavens King may daigne his owne transform'd
in substance no, but superficiall tire
by thee put on; to praise, not to aspire
To, those high Tons, so in themselues adorn'd,
wch Angells sing in their cælestiall Quire,
and all of tongues with soule and voice admire
Theise sacred Hymmes thy Kinglie Prophet form'd.

Oh, had that soule wch honor brought to rest
too soone not left and reft the world of all
what man could showe, wch wee perfection call
This halfe maim'd peece had sorted wth the best.
Deepe wounds enlarg'd, long festred in their gall
fresh bleeding smart; not eie but hart teares fall.
Ah memorie what needs this new arrest!

16 Scribal copy of the opening of the Countess of Pembroke's poem addressed 'To the Angell spirit' of her brother Philip (*Dr B. E. Juel-Jensen*)

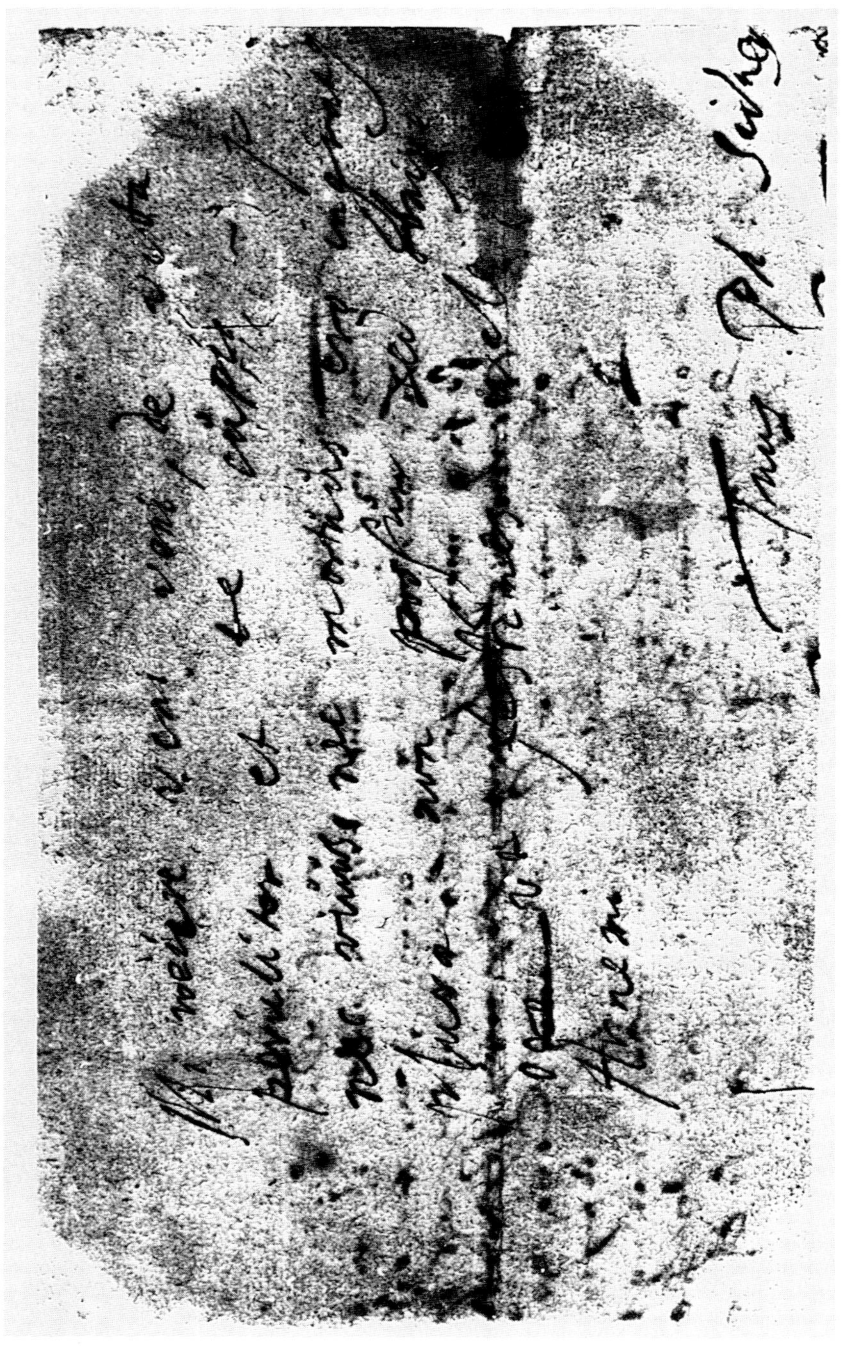

Mi Weiere veni, veni. De vita
periclitor et te cupio.
Nec vivus nec mortuus ero ingratus.
Plura non possum sed obnixe
oro ut festines.
Vale
Tuus Ph. Sidney

17 Sidney's last letter, written to Dr Jan Wier on the evening of 16 October 1586 (*Public Record Office, London*)

seen, the Pembroke household was congenial to him. Though Aubrey sentimentalized and exaggerated Sidney's devotion to the 'romancy' countryside of Wiltshire, he did not invent it. The letter to Denny from Wilton, just discussed, radiates ease and cheerfulness, and those poems which have explicit references to Wiltshire reflect appreciation of its distinctive and remarkable features. *Certain Sonnets* 22, perhaps an early, non-Arcadian poem written for his sister, opens with an account of Stonehenge:

> Near Wilton sweet, huge heaps of stone are found;
> But so confused, that neither any eye
> Can count them just, nor reason reason try
> What force brought them to so unlikely ground.

'Lamon's Tale', a poem which opens with a detailed account of country pursuits and Maytime rituals, also uses a scene observed in Wiltshire to illuminate its narrative. In a game of 'barley-break', the love-lorn shepherd Strephon runs desperately after his beloved Urania,

> Who nothing earthly, but of fire and air,
> Though with soft legs, did run as fast as he.
> He thrice reached, thrice deceived; when her to bear
> He hopes, with dainty turns she doth him flee.
> So on the downs we see, near Wilton fair,
> A hastened hare from greedy greyhound go,
> And past all hope his chaps [jaws] to frustrate so.[21]

The confidential 'we see' marks the poem as belonging to that substantial body of Sidney's writing which he shared with his sister. It also lends some support to Aubrey's uncle's anecdote, for it shows the poet as a spectator of hunting rather than a participant. Perhaps, while others hunted, he withdrew to watch and write.

There is no doubt that in reality, as well as in his own 'Philisides and Mira' myth, Sidney was devoted to his sister. Still unmarried at the advanced age of twenty-five, he was deeply preoccupied with Mary's welfare as she prepared to give birth. Languet's felicitations after the happy event, written on 6 May 1580, must reflect Sidney's anticipatory anxiety:

> I hear that your noble sister has been safely delivered of a beautiful boy, and so has made her husband and all of you her near relations happy. I rejoice that she is relieved from danger, and you all from your anxiety, and I congratulate you on the happiness which I am sure possesses you. In truth some share of the happiness reaches even me; for her singular excellence and her generosity to me, though she never knew me, made me not a little anxious on her account, until the news was brought me of her safe delivery.[22]

Like her elder brother, Mary Herbert was physically as well as mentally energetic. Even in her mid-fifties she amused herself, when on holiday at Spa, shooting at targets with pistols.[23] Her extensive literary labours in the 1590s, and her vigorous litigation, travel and house-building during the two succeeding decades, all show that like her brother Philip she 'could endure at no time to be idle' (see above, p. 141). In 1580 she was only eighteen and a half, and must have found the long weeks of lying down imposed on her by obstetric practice of the time exceedingly irksome. Instalments of the *Arcadia* delivered while it was in process of composition beguiled the tedium and anxiety of this time. It should be remembered that for Elizabethan mothers the period after delivery of a baby was even more dangerous than the later stages of pregnancy, because of the risk of puerperal infection. Elizabethan midwives were great believers in clean air, and mothers were often removed from home to give birth in supposedly more salubrious surroundings; few, however, fully understood the importance of clean hands. A letter of Sidney's from Clarendon, a smaller house in a large park to the north of Wilton, may indicate that she gave birth there. Written on 2 August 1580, it shows his relief that, four months after giving birth, his sister is at last fully recovered:

> I have now brought home my sister, who is well amended both of her pain and disease.[24]

'Disease' means here, probably, not a separate illness, but 'dis-ease', such normal post-natal discomforts as painful breasts, or bleeding.

It is not possible to identify specific passages of the *Arcadia* with which Sidney amused his sister during her lying-in. Probably the parts written earliest were the Eclogues, which incorporate pastoral poems directly modelled on Sannazaro, early metrical experiments undertaken with friends like Bryskett and Dyer, such as the 'phaleuciacs' discussed above (pp. 82–3) and verses composed for court entertainments. There was much in the Eclogues that was of intense interest to the founders of the 'New Poetry', such as Spenser. Mary Herbert's use of quantitative metres in her versions of the Psalms shows that she, too, eventually participated in this movement. Many of the Eclogue poems were probably already written by 1580, though perhaps not yet fully framed or organized. At some stage, perhaps soon after the hectic events of August 1579, Sidney decided to make prose narrative, which in Sannazaro is slight and static, a dynamic vehicle for entertainment and moral exemplification. His dedicatory letter suggests that he found, once embarked on writing the romance his sister requested, that his head was buzzing with 'fancies'. Cryptic references in the *Defence of Poesy* – 'Only, overmastered by some thoughts, I yielded an inky tribute unto them'[25] – also claim that his pen ran away with him. There may have been some truth in this, though, as eventually fashioned, the 'Old' *Arcadia* was extremely carefully structured – Edmund Molyneux was to praise its 'orderly disposition'.[26]

Writing the *Arcadia* offered both an escape from recent disappointments and a way of obliquely commenting on them. It is neither a *roman à clef* nor a literal transcription of events in Sidney's life, but an exemplary fable which includes many themes of immediate relevance to his own situation. The whole story hinges on the capriciousness of an ageing monarch who disregards advice given by a loyal courtier, and is unable to control his own undignified and inappropriate sexual passions. Basilius is not precisely an Elizabeth-figure, any more than Arcadia is precisely England. The *Arcadia* is a genuine work of fiction, in which Sidney has fashioned some 'forms, such as never were in nature'.[27] Yet at several points the fictional Arcadia matches England as it was in 1579–80. Arcadia, like England, is at peace, while the countries that surround it are at war. It enjoys stability under an unusually long-reigning monarch, who is

> of sufficient skill to govern so quiet a country where the good minds of former princes had set down good laws.[28]

We should notice that on a first reading this may sound like praise. On reflexion, after a reading of the whole, it will be seen that the narrator is saying only that little skill is needed to govern Arcadia, so Basilius, who has little, nevertheless has enough. This is one of many subtly cynical observations about the relations of monarchs to their people. After Basilius's death, for instance, the extravagant grief of his subjects, who give him 'the sacred titles of good, just, merciful, the father of the people, the life of his country', is undercut by the narrator's interpretation of it as evidence

> that men are loving creatures when injuries put them not from their natural course, and how easy a thing it is for a prince by succession deeply to sink into the souls of his subjects.[29]

That is, the cult of the monarch tells us more about the natural goodness of humanity than about the actual gifts of the monarch. Though sceptical about Elizabeth's personal gifts, Sidney and his friends lived in perpetual fear of the chaos that might ensue should she die without naming a successor. Such fears are given substance in Book 4 of the *Arcadia*:

> There was a notable example how great dissipations monarchal governments are subject unto; for now their prince and guide had left them, they had not experience to rule, and had not whom to obey. Public matters had ever been privately governed, so that they had no lively taste what was good for themselves, but everything was either vehemently desireful or extremely terrible.[30]

At Elizabeth's Court, as at Basilius's, there was no such thing as 'open government'. Important changes of policy were often concealed even from her Privy Council. In particular, in the eyes of the Sidney–Dudley faction, Burghley had too much power, and loyal, disinterested advice, such as that given to the Queen in Sidney's *Letter*, was apt to go unheeded.

The *Arcadia* opens with a political fable that seems to arise in outline, though not in detail, out of the events of 1579. The Duke Basilius, whose two daughters have just reached marriageable age, makes a misguided attempt to delve into the future, 'desirous to know the certainty of things to come, wherein there is nothing so certain as our continual uncertainty'. He visits Delphos and receives an oracular prophecy which fills him with amazement:

> Thy elder care shall from thy careful face
> By princely mean be stolen and yet not lost;
> Thy younger shall with nature's bliss embrace
> An uncouth love, which nature hateth most.
> Thou with thy wife adult'ry shalt commit,
> And in thy throne a foreign state shall sit.
> All this on thee this fatal year shall hit.[31]

The narrator makes it clear that Basilius should never have gone to Delphos in the first place. But since he has done so, he is now in need of good advice about how to proceed. This is offered by 'one chosen friend, Philanax' ('Lover of his lord'), who is remarkable for his devotion both to Basilius personally and to the welfare of the state. Like Sidney's advice to Elizabeth, Philanax's to Basilius is for preserving the *status quo*:

> These thirty years past have you so governed this realm that neither your subjects have wanted justice in you, nor you obedience in them; and your neighbours have found you so hurtlessly strong that they thought it better to rest in your friendship than make new trial of your enmity ... Let your subjects have you in their eyes, let them see the benefits of your justice daily more and more; and so must they needs rather like of present sureties than uncertain changes. Lastly, whether your time call you to live or die, do both like a prince.[32]

It has been convincingly demonstrated that Sidney disliked superstition, and may have felt that Mortlake, where John Dee lived, was the Queen's 'Delphos'.[33] In Philanax's advice to Basilius he is clearly echoing his own recently written *Letter*. The last sentence quoted was in turn echoed by Webster, whose Duchess of Malfi, confronted by her murderous brother, says proudly:

> ... know, whether I am doomed to live or die,
> I can do both like a prince.[34]

Basilius, however, whose name's meaning of 'kingly' proves increasingly ironic as the narrative proceeds, lacks dignity both in life and death. All of Philanax's excellent advice goes unheeded, though Basilius at least has the good sense to leave Philanax as regent, while he retires to the country, commanding him 'especially to keep narrow watch of the frontiers'.[35]

Political ideas are deeply embedded in the plot structure of the 'Old' *Arcadia*, but they are not its main source of narrative energy. As befits the youthful writer and his even more youthful audience, love, not the art of government, is the dominant theme. The romance is composed as a whole of nine sections, five narrative 'Books, or Acts', divided by four sets of contemplative 'Eclogues'. The comic theme of love is arranged in a two-thirds/one-third proportion to the tragic theme of civil and moral chaos, for Books 1–3 with their accompanying Eclogues mainly treat of love, while Books 4–5 with their single set of dividing Eclogues explore the leaderless state and the disastrous consequences of human folly. Erotic passion pervades the first two-thirds of the romance. In the view of one distinguished critic, Sidney's artistic greatness is limited by his having confined so much of his writing to this single theme;[36] and the biographer Wallace was clearly embarrassed by his preoccupation with 'the facts of sex'.[37] Yet the treatment of love is extremely varied. At the top of the scale are the devoted shepherds Strephon and Klaius, who love the celestial-sounding Urania without rivalry and without lust. Sidney gave them more prominence in the revised version, but even in the 'Old' version their dignity and eloquence, above all in their intricate and moving 'double sestina', set them apart from other characters. Almost equally admirable is the unhappy Plangus, who is bent on rescuing Princess Erona from prison and a death sentence, and sees her suffering as a type of undeserved suffering. A model of true married love is given by the shepherd Lalus, who is not handsome, but has won the love of the prettiest girl in the village, Kala, through tactful and ingenious courtship, for instance by trimming the fleece of her favourite sheep into becoming shapes and fastening love poems to it.[38] Sidney's own fictive persona, Philisides, embodies devoted love to an absent and unattainable lady, but is shown as a remote, preoccupied figure who has only an accidental-seeming relationship with the main characters, being more a poet than a participant.

Centre stage are some examples of distinctly earthly passion. The aged Duke Basilius falls ridiculously in love with Prince Pyrocles, disguised as an Amazon, who is only eighteen and has very long blond hair. This dotage is not revelatory of latent homosexual passion, but a manifestation of Basilius's vanity, caprice and inability to form correct judgements, which has already provoked him to disregard Philanax and to appoint the clown Dametas as his elder daughter's guardian. *Mutatis mutandis*, this part of the story had some bearing on Elizabeth's flirtation with her frog-prince Alençon. While the *senex amans* is an evergreen comic figure, the Phaedra, or incestuously lustful middle-aged woman, is more often tragic, and so it is with Basilius's wife Gynecia, who quickly penetrates Pyrocles' Amazon disguise and falls desperately in love with him. An even more pathetic casualty of the princes' intrigues is the gullible peasant girl Mopsa, Dametas's daughter, who is encouraged by Musidorus to believe that he loves her, and hopes with his help to become 'the greatest lady of the world, and never after to feed on worse than frumenty'.[39]

Somewhere in the middle of the wide spectrum of love and lovers range the young princes, Pyrocles of Macedon and Musidorus of Thessaly. Their aristocratic bearing, their good looks, charm and eloquence are mediated through the narrator's apparently approving words in such a way that for much of the time the reader is persuaded that their love for Basilius's two daughters is noble and admirable. Strictly speaking (and strict judgements are eventually brought to bear on them in their trial in Book 5), it is not, for the end they aim at is sexual enjoyment, in pursuit of which they are willing to sacrifice every moral principle and to place everyone, including the princesses they supposedly love, in extreme danger. Fascinated uncertainty attaches throughout to the presentation of the princes, and Mary Herbert, herself married to a middle-aged man in poor health, probably enjoyed reading about these resourceful, charismatic and highly sexed young men. The only principal character untroubled by sexual feeling is the Tarlton-like clown Dametas, whose wife Miso's savage jealousy, deliberately provoked by Musidorus, is quite wide of the mark, for he is one who 'loves a piece of cheese better than a woman'.[40]

While political motifs in the 'Old' *Arcadia* can be definitely linked with Sidney's life and personal circumstances, amorous ones cannot. Despite the plenitude of his writings about love, Sidney's own sexual feelings remain invisible. Love could have been among those 'thoughts' that, as he said in the *Defence*, provoked him to become a poet, but we have no way of knowing whether it was. Certainly he gave the sexless-seeming word 'thought' inescapable erotic connotations in Song x of *Astrophil and Stella*. In the *Defence* he stressed the importance of poets' writing cogent, powerful love poetry that persuades the reader 'that in truth they feel those passions'.[41] Yet he did not say that in order to produce this result poets needed 'in truth' to be in love – only that they should have sufficient skill to persuade the reader of the reality of feeling within the poem. Ben Jonson summarized the situation concisely:

> No poet's verses yet did ever move
> Whose readers did not think he was in love.[42]

The emphasis is on 'think': what matters is the conviction produced in the reader, not the sincerity of the writer. As we shall see when coming to consider *Astrophil and Stella*, the reader of Sidney's best love poetry is placed in a double bind. His poetic theory directs us to look for 'forcibleness', or naturalism; yet the emotional naturalism frequently achieved may testify only to Sidney's brilliant mastery of the arts of persuasion, not to any real-life experience. There is no necessary continuity between literary subject-matter and the writer's life. As Giles Fletcher the Elder said a few years later:

> a man may write of love, and not be in love, as well as of husbandry, and not go to the plough: or of witches, and be none; or of holiness and be flat profane.[43]

For all we know, Mary Herbert may have recognized traits of her brother both in the languid love-melancholy of Philisides and the explosive sexual passion of Pyrocles. On the other hand, in locating such passion within characters who have manifest connexions with himself, Sidney may simply have used fictionally transformed self-images for literary purposes. Love, after all, was the dominant theme of his chief models, Chaucer's *Troilus and Criseyde*, Sannazaro's *Arcadia*, the Greek romance *Aethiopica*, the French *Amadis de Gaul* and the Spanish *Diana*.

In a period rich in scurrilous gossip, Sidney provoked no contemporary sexual scandal, unlike his brother Robert, who seems, in the mid-1590s, to have had a distinct reputation for amorousness and indiscretion.[44] Aubrey's allegation that Sidney had an incestuous love for his sister can be dismissed as a late and malicious embroidery of the published dedication of the *Arcadia*,[45] for Aubrey had a grudge against a later member of the Herbert family, and set out to defame them. Nearer in time to those who remembered Sidney, Ben Jonson in his drunken conversations with Drummond of Hawthornden revealed himself to be enviously obsessed with Sidney and his reputation, and would surely not have held back from sexual abuse if he could have thought of some. Yet the worst he could find to say about him personally was that he was red-faced and pimpled (see above, p. xii). There is no reason to think that Sidney ever made a girl pregnant, as so many aristocrats did; nor did anyone in the next generation claim him as father. Thomas Moffet, indeed, describes him as rebuking others for their sexual misdemeanours:

> As yet scarcely a man, he admonished in friendly fashion several men and youths who had been sticking in the same mire of avarice and licentiousness, and, so far as by his example and by his words he could, recalled them to a better mind.[46]

If this is right, Sidney's real-life behaviour was priggishly correct. Obviously, he may have nourished passions which were unfulfilled, but they may also have been unvoiced. Here, again, is a double bind. The fictional Philisides says of his love that 'I did with so much covering hide [it] that I was thought void of it as any man',[47] and the later persona Astrophil also stresses his sincerity as proved by the very fact that he displays none of the conventional signs of being in love. The less amorous these self-projections seem, the more it proves the validity of their love: 'They love indeed, who quake to say they love.'[48] If Sidney used this strategy in real life, his own closest friends may not have known whether or with whom he was in love. As a writer, he cultivated an air of mystery which at once invites and defeats enquiry. Repeated disappointments, both in marriage schemes and in projects for employment, may have taught him to construct an elaborate carapace about himself which effectively concealed his own weak and wounded spots. Whether he really was or had been in love, the important thing is that he knew how to write about love convincingly.

The coterie for which the *Arcadia* was written was predominantly female. Whatever Sidney's private feelings were, the *Arcadia*, as we saw in the first chapter, revealed him to be unusually perceptive and sympathetic in his literary presentation of women. On first mentioning Pamela and Philoclea his narrator says pointedly that

> they seemed to be born for a sufficient proof that nature is no stepmother to that sex, how much soever the rugged disposition of some men, sharp-witted only in evil speaking, hath sought to disgrace them.[49]

While eulogists of Elizabeth I commonly used the 'exceptional woman' formula, praising her virtues at the expense of the rest of her sex, Sidney suggests that the excellence of his heroines typifies general excellence in women. He delights in showing the princesses coming out strongly under pressure, yet allows them to make just enough mistakes to show that they, like the princes, are young and fallible. Pamela, the elder, is heir to the throne, and has appropriate qualities of dignity, eloquence and moral authority. Her weakness, suggested with delicacy, is that she is a little too queenly, a little too fond of hearing herself praised. Just as Pyrocles, though younger, is 'chiefer' of the two princes,[50] so the younger princess, Philoclea, is identified as the book's heroine:

> But alas, sweet Philoclea, how hath my pen forgotten thee, since to thy memory principally all this long matter is intended?[51]

The narrator has a special relationship with Philoclea, and appears to be envious of Pyrocles' eventual success in seducing her:

> ... he gives me occasion to leave him in so happy a plight, lest my pen might seem to grudge at the due bliss of these poor lovers whose loyalty had but small respite of their fiery agonies.[52]

When we read on to Book 4, however, we find that sexual fulfilment has had a disastrous effect on Pyrocles, who thinks he can solve his problems – adultery is a capital offence in Arcadia, we are now told – by committing suicide. Both symbolically and actually he is 'unmanned' by the loss of his sword, which Dametas took while he was asleep, and he uses casuistry to persuade himself that the suicide he proposes is acceptable in the eyes of Jove:

> Neither be offended that I do abandon this body, to the government of which thou hadst placed me, without thy leave, since how can I know but that thy unsearchable mind is I should do so, since thou hast taken from me all means longer to abide in it?[53]

Pyrocles falls at this point into Basilius's fatal error, of believing he has access to the workings of Divine Providence. Though he calls Jove's mind 'unsearchable', he has actually made up his mind about what Jove is to do next. Philoclea, on the other hand, from being a vulnerable girl whose 'virtue', with sexual connotations, never seemed secure, has grown overnight into an eloquent speaker and moralist. The loss of her physical 'virtue' has done no damage at all to her 'virtue' in a wider sense. On the contrary, rather like Shakespeare's Juliet after her wedding night, she has acquired adult poise and decisiveness. Virginia Woolf was disappointed, in reading the folio *Arcadia*, to find Sidney's apparent feminism undermined by his stereotypical male obsession with female chastity.[54] If Mrs Woolf had read the 'Old' version she might have reached a different conclusion. Philoclea, no longer a virgin, is more intelligent and beautiful than ever, and her lucid distillation of fragments of second-hand ethics picked up from 'my father and other wise men' ought to put the well-educated Pyrocles to shame. Among many surprises Sidney keeps in store for his readers in Books 4 and 5 this transformation is the most startling. Philoclea seems to have been reading Plato and St Augustine, revealing herself to be one of those virtuous pagans whom many theologians considered to have merited salvation:

> it is not for us to appoint that mighty majesty what time he will help us. The uttermost instant is scope enough for him to revoke everything to one's own desire . . . to prejudicate his determination is but a doubt of goodness in him who is nothing but goodness . . . That we should be masters of ourselves we can show at all no title, nor claim; since neither we made ourselves, nor bought ourselves . . .[55]

Though the *Arcadia* is set in a pre-Christian Greece, Philoclea's use of the word 'bought' shows that she has insight into the concept of 'redemption', through which one day God's Son will 'buy' salvation for mankind. Philoclea's determination to dissuade Pyrocles from his wretched and undignified attempt to kill himself with a rusty iron bar is not disinterested: she loves him, and cannot face a future without him. Yet in locating such authoritative speeches in the mouth of his youngest and weakest-seeming female character Sidney both directs his readers' attention to profound moral issues and suggests vividly that 'nature is no stepmother to that sex'. The fortitude and intelligence of women under pressure were clearly a theme he found intensely interesting, for he developed it at greater length in the 'New' *Arcadia,* though locating it this time chiefly in the more conventionally 'virtuous' Pamela. The bold use of the deflowered Philoclea as a figure of moral authority may have been one of the factors that made Fulke Greville consider the revised version 'fitter to be printed'.[56]

For Philoclea and Pyrocles, the 'Old' *Arcadia* has a happy ending. At the last minute everything is indeed 'revoked according to their desire'. Pyrocles and Musidorus are delivered from the death sentence pronounced on them by Pyrocles' father, the just magistrate Euarchus, and both couples are able to marry and live happily ever after. For Gynecia, mother of Pamela and Philoclea, no such journey into the sunset is possible. She has fallen desperately in love with her future son-in-law, Pyrocles, and her exceptional intelligence and self-awareness make her subsequent shame almost unendurable. The narrator describes her as having an exceptionally 'working mind', or active imagination, and her inner life is more deeply explored than that of any other character. She alone independently penetrates Pyrocles' disguise; she alone sees immediately the moral consequences of the passion that grips her, in another line that Webster was to pick up in *The Duchess of Malfi*:

O imperfect proportion of reason, which can so much foresee, and so little prevent![57]

and she alone dreams, a sinister, prophetic dream which has an effect of psychological horror rare in Elizabethan literature outside Shakespeare:

Newly was Philoclea departed out of the chamber when Gynecia, troubled with a fearful dream, frightfully awaked. The dream was this: it seemed unto her to be in a place full of thorns which so molested her as she could neither abide standing still nor tread safely going forward. In this case she thought Cleophila [Pyrocles in disguise], being upon a fair hill, delightful to the eye and easy in appearance, called her thither; but thither with much anguish being come, Cleophila was vanished, and she found nothing but a dead body which seeming at the first with a strange smell so to infect her as she was ready to die likewise, within a while the dead body (she thought) took her in his arms and said: 'Gynecia, here is thy only rest.'[58]

In a work whose tone is teasingly complex – we often cannot tell whether our own naivety is being mocked or that of the characters – Gynecia gathers around her some extraordinary narrative effects. It is easy to present the lustful mature woman as comic, as Shakespeare does much of the time with Venus in *Venus and Adonis;* but Sidney avoids this. At several key moments he invites his female readers to enter into her situation. For instance, he appeals to them for sympathy at the moment when Gynecia realizes that it is not the young Pyrocles, but her aged husband, who is about to make love to her:

In what case poor Gynecia was when she knew the voice and felt the body of her husband, fair ladies, it is better to know by imagination than experience.[59]

As women who were themselves very probably married to much older husbands they may have been all too well able to imagine this moment. Even when Gynecia tears her clothes open, exposing her breasts, in a desperate attempt to arouse Pyrocles' answering passion, the narrator will not allow us to laugh at her. Instead, he points out, with measured portentousness, that Pyrocles finds her distinctly attractive:

if Cleophila's heart had not been so fully possessed as there was no place left for any new guest, no doubt it would have yielded to that gallant assault.[60]

Rather than locating sympathy exclusively in male or female characters, Sidney's narrator shifts rapidly between the sexes, and in the scene just mentioned, after Pyrocles/Cleophila has embraced and 'once or twice' kissed Gynecia, persuading her, falsely, that he really loves her, the narrator makes a point of including everyone in her delusion:

For such, alas, are we all! In such a mould are we cast that, with the too much love we bear ourselves being first our own flatterers, we are easily hooked with others' flattery, we are easily persuaded of others' love.[61]

For Gynecia, there can be no happy ending. Her literary progenitrix is the tragic Phaedra. Sidney may have known her story best from Seneca's *Hippolytus*, rather than that of Euripides. Gynecia, however, is less faulty than Phaedra, and her punishment is the tragi-comic one of having to live on with an awareness of her own guilt. Indeed, she assumes to herself an excessive burden of guilt, too readily accepting responsibility for her husband's death. Her appearance at the trial in Book 5 is pathetic:

she had cast on a long cloak which reached to the ground, of russet coarse cloth, with a poor felt hat which almost covered all her face, most part of her goodly hair (on which her hands laid many a spiteful hold), so lying upon her shoulders as a man might well see had no artificial carelessness.[62]

She quietly acquiesces in the sentence imposed on her, to be walled up alive in her husband's tomb. Instead, with the revival of Basilius, Gynecia has to accept the sentence imposed on innumerable real-life women in the early modern period: to remain married to a foolish elderly man for the rest of his natural life, presenting the world with the misleading impression 'that she was the perfect mirror of wifely love'.[63]

It would be going too far to suggest that the 'Old' *Arcadia* offered a deliberate challenge to the concept of a patriarchal society. But like many Elizabethan writers, Sidney showed the disasters that ensue in such a society when the figure wielding most authority, the 'father of the people',[64] fails to correct his personal limitations by taking good advice. Women and young men alike suffer from the mistakes made by the older generation. For Basilius's wife and daughters the pastoral retreat is little better than a prison. The disguise and subterfuge of the young princes is in a sense forced on them by the security system set up by Basilius to frustrate the fulfilment of the oracle. But it is the suffering of the female characters that is made most interesting to us, because of the direct access to their thoughts given us by the narrator. Gynecia, indeed, threatens to leap out of the story's frame; she is a disturbing figure for whom readers will feel a nagging anxiety even when the book is finished.

It is in the Eclogues, rather than the Books, that the resentment of young men towards foolishly wielded patriarchal authority is most openly expressed (see above, pp. 42–3), and the manner in which this is done is often entertaining rather than threatening. In the First Eclogues Philisides is rebuked by Geron ('Old man') for his bondage to love in the poem which begins 'Up, up, Philisides, let sorrows go', and ends with Philisides rudely refusing to listen to his good advice.[65] However, the next poem, beginning 'Down, down, Melampus; what? your fellow bite?', to some extent restores harmony between the generations. Geron begins by sorting out a fight between his old dog, Melampus ('Blackfoot'), and his young one, Laelaps, and then discusses the younger generation with another old man, Mastix ('Scourge'). Mastix roundly condemns the time-wasting of young and old alike:

> As for the rest, how shepherds spend their days,
> At blow point, hot cockles, or else at keels,
> While, 'Let us pass our time', each shepherd says.
> So small account of time the shepherd feels,
> And doth not feel that life is naught but time,
> And when that time is past, death holds his heels.

But Geron, in turn, using a beast fable, condemns Mastix for his excessive bitterness, and his plea for restraint and self-examination on the part of the older generation – 'who makes us such judges over all?' – provides the last word in this section.[66]

Like many of Sidney's minor characters, the two old men with their dogs are pleasingly naturalistic. In placing his romance in ancient Greece Sidney ostensibly removed his narrative far away from Wiltshire in 1580. Fulke Greville was to use a comparable strategy in locating his two political tragedies in Turkey. But the setting enabled Sidney to write with considerable freedom, not just about large, potentially dangerous concepts, such as the weakness of a monarchical system unsupported by wise statesmen, but also about many concrete features of his own world. C. S. Lewis rightly said that as we read the *Arcadia* 'we must have in mind the ruffs, the feathers, the tapestries, the rich carvings, the mannered gardens, the elaborate courtesies' of the Elizabethan age.[67] Sidney's characters do not wear classical draperies, but an exaggerated form of sixteenth-century costume, the kind of symbolic dress worn in masques, jousts and other court entertainments. Pyrocles' Amazon costume is described in such detail that a masquing outfit could easily be based on it, and the title-page engraving of the 1593 *Arcadia* follows it closely. The slashed openings so typical of Elizabethan dress *circa* 1580 are often mentioned; Pyrocles wears

> a little short pair of crimson velvet buskins, in some places open (as the ancient manner was) to show the fairness of the skin[68]

and Philoclea's light taffeta dress is 'so cut as the wrought smock came through it in many places'.[69] The extent to which Sidney expected his audience to think of elaborately layered Elizabethan clothes is underlined when, in Book 5, he describes Pyrocles for the first time 'clothed after the Greek manner', in a long white velvet coat, 'without any collar', his fair neck 'not so much as hidden with a ruff'.[70] This emphasis suggests that most of the time it is to be taken for granted that these supposedly Greek characters, like Elizabethan gentry, wear ruffs.

The *Arcadia*'s world is heightened – as Lewis said, 'Its woods are greener, its rivers purer, its sky brighter than ours'[71] – and in some ways it is un-English. The weather, for instance, seems to be the unbroken sunshine conventional in Mediterranean pastoral. But it shares many properties of the 'real world'. Basilius, creeping out of the marital bedroom in the dark, thinks 'everything creaked under him', and finds himself bumping painfully into 'each coffer or cupboard'.[72] Though few meals are described, Musidorus at least remembers to provide a picnic of 'fruits and other cates' when he elopes with Pamela,[73] and graphic food images are used in the poem which provide an analogue to the erotic banquet enjoyed by Pyrocles. Claret, apples, wine, milk, cherries, liquorice, comfits set in marchpane, all serve to define the delectable components of a woman's body.

As well as being unusually naturalistic, Sidney was unconventional, as a writer of romance, in making no use of the supernatural. He took care to make his narrative perfectly coherent, and never solved plot difficulties by bringing in non-human intervention. A vital element in the plot is a supposedly aphrodisiac potion which Gynecia plans to give to Pyrocles. Basilius accidentally drinks it, and its effects appear to be fatal. Its being a poison is confirmed by a test:

Among other trials they made to know at least the cause of his end, having espied the unhappy cup, they gave the little liquor that was left in it to a dog of Dametas, in which within short space it wrought the same effect; although Dametas did so much to recover him that for very love of his life he dashed out his brains.[74]

The first-time reader will naturally conclude that Gynecia's potion has been proved to be a poison. Yet, of course, the dog has actually been killed by Dametas's clumsiness, and a couple of pages from the end we learn that the liquid was actually neither an aphrodisiac nor a poison, but a drink that provokes thirty hours of comatose sleep. It had once been used to good effect by Gynecia's grandmother, who managed with its help to marry a young nobleman whom she 'furiously' loved.[75] Like many of the subsidiary narratives, the story of Gynecia's grandmother is a shade fantastic; but for the purposes of narrative coherence, it is enough that 'it might be so'. Sidney used his own 'good invention'[76] to resolve narrative difficulties, not magic or divine intervention.

Various external events during 1580 impinged on Sidney's immersion in his own creations. England, unlike Arcadia, was having a spell of bad weather. On the evening of 6 April most of the country was shaken by an earthquake lasting for about a minute, which some attributed to the earth's having soaked up too much water – being like the tremor of a drunken man. In London, bells rang of their own accord, law students ran out from supper with their knives still in their hands, pieces of masonry fell off old buildings, and off the Kent coast ships were tossed about by turbulence.[77] It seems to have been felt most strongly in London and Eastern England. Spenser, in Cambridge, corresponded with Gabriel Harvey, in Essex, about its possible causes, Harvey concluding sensibly that it was a natural phenomenon unconnected with the heavy rain.[78] Its effects may have been less marked in the West Country, and Sidney, with his dislike of superstition, probably did not view the tremor as ominous for his sister's confinement, which occurred only two days later. It must nevertheless have contributed to the anxiety of this time. On 25 March Sidney had written a short, cheerful note to Leicester's secretary Arthur Atey, with 'no news but that all be well, which God keep, and thee too, my honest Atey'.[79]

In late May there was a jolly family party at Wilton for the christening of little William Herbert. Leicester deputized for the Queen as godmother. Sir Henry Sidney, possibly accompanied by his wife, came over from the Welsh borders to see his new grandson. The Queen, however, 'misliked' his attendance at these merrymakings. Ireland was once again in turmoil, with Munster in revolt, and substantial aid to the rebels from Spain and the Pope was expected momently. More directly within Sir Henry's sphere of responsibility, an important commission set up to reform 'recusants and obstinate persons in religion within Wales and the marches' appeared so far to have done nothing.[80]

In late June Edmund Campion arrived back in England as part of a courageous Jesuit mission; it was almost inevitable that he would eventually try to make contact with his old friends the Sidneys.[81] In August Walsingham warned Sir Henry that his position was in serious jeopardy:

Your Lordship had need to walk warily, for your doings are narrowly observed, and Her Majesty is apt to give ear to any that shall ill you. Great hold is taken by your enemies, for neglecting the execution of this commission [i.e. the commission for religious reform].[82]

The Queen was well aware that a new Sidney–Dudley axis had been formed with the Herberts in Wiltshire, awkwardly far away from her direct control, and she did not like it. While war raged in Ireland and the Welsh borders seethed with unreformed recusants, the Sidneys were thoroughly enjoying themselves dandling the new baby, eating Edward Denny's cakes, singing Philip Sidney's songs and plotting goodness knew what. However, Sir Henry fairly soon returned to his post in the Welsh borders, and from Denbigh in September he wrote a long letter of advice to Lord Grey about how to proceed in Ireland, advice which he acknowledged had to be pragmatic rather than idealistic:

Me thinks it is now out of season to make any treatise or discourse of a general reformation, for that were like as if a man seeing his house on fire, would set down and draw a plot for a new, before he would put his helping hand to quench the old.[83]

But he promised that further advice on problems as they arose would be as freely given as 'if Philip Sidney were in your place, who most earnestly and often hath spoken and written to do this loving office' – i.e. Philip would really have liked Lord Grey's job. Though only fifty-one, Sir Henry was suffering from a shaking hand, and his letter, like most from this date onwards, was dictated. By 1583 he was 'toothless and trembling'. Clearly the ageing Sir Henry would have liked young Philip at his side to help him with his responsibilities in Wales, but he remarks rather sadly to Lord Grey that he 'is not here'. In a letter probably belonging to the winter of 1580–81, in which he advised Robert to imitate the 'virtues, exercises and actions' of his elder brother, he lamented that 'I saw him not these six months, little to my comfort.'[84]

Torn between Ireland, Wales and the Court – his personal ambitions and his obligations to his father and his uncle – Sidney nevertheless remained at Wilton until the autumn. In the letter already quoted, in which he reported to Leicester on his sister's recuperation after childbirth, he went on to say:

For myself, I assure your Lordship upon my troth, so full of the cold as one cannot hear me speak: which is the cause keeps me yet from the Court, since my only service is speech, and that is stopped. As soon as I have gotten any voice I will wait on your Lordship if so it please you. Although it be contrary to that I have signified to Her Majesty of my want, I doubt not Her Majesty will vouchsafe to ask for me, but so long as she sees a silk doublet upon me Her Highness will think me in good case. At my departure I desired Mr Vice Chamberlain he would tell Her Majesty necessity did even banish me from the place. And always submitting myself to your judgement and commandment, I think my best, either constantly to wait, or constantly to hold the course of my poverty, for coming and going neither breeds desert nor witnesseth necessity.

Though he goes on to say that he hopes to shake off the cold 'within 3 or 4 days', it is clear that Sidney was reluctant to return unless he had the assurance of a large sum of money, either from Leicester or from the Queen. His letter ranges wittily from the relatively trivial affliction of a heavy cold to the graver one of loss of favour. He makes no allusion to his 'toyful book', which his uncle may not have known about, but his verbal fluency reflects the current phase of intense creativity. There is a bitter little joke in the remark that 'my only service is speech, and that is stopped'. He cannot speak because of catarrh: but his 'speech' in another sense, that is, his advice to the Queen, has also been suppressed. In any case, action, not speech, is the service he would prefer. A 'case' meant a suit of clothes as well as a situation; the pitiless Queen, judging from silk doublet alone, was apt to think Sidney in good enough 'case' without concern for his essential welfare. Clearly he had told Sussex that he wished to withdraw from Court indefinitely, and only the prospect of a large sum of money would persuade him to return.

We do not know how much it cost to get Sidney away from Wilton. By 18 October he was at Leicester House, writing the charming letter to his brother Robert quoted above, and continuing to work on the *Arcadia*. Though Sidney said in it that 'nothing is happened notable at home, save only Drake's return', this was a turbulent period, with the completion of the first circumnavigation of the world by an Englishman about the only piece of good news. Otherwise Protestant England seemed under threat. Portugal, long an ally of England, was about to be assimilated into the Spanish Empire. The Jesuit Robert Parsons had arrived in London, and was searching for a safe house for Campion. In September 600 Spanish and Italian troops landed at Smerwick, on the west coast of Ireland, where they occupied a large fortress built the previous year by James Fitzmaurice. If Sidney, not Lord Grey, had been appointed Lord Deputy Governor of Ireland he would have had to decide how to deal with this invasion. It is impossible to conjecture whether he would have acted as Lord Grey did. Though the besieged troops surrendered on 8 November, clearly displaying a white flag, all 600 were put to the sword, and many Irish men and women were brutally hanged. The Queen 'was delighted with what Grey had done, except that she doubted the wisdom of granting life to those spared by Grey'.[85] The poet Edmund Spenser justified the massacre in his *View of the Present State of Ireland*, claiming that 'there was no other way but to make that short end of them which was made'.[86] Sidney's opinion is unknown, but he may have shared the general approval of what Lord Grey had done. The modern reader must feel some relief that Sidney was still in London and immersed in his 'toyful book'. Otherwise two major Elizabethan poets, rather than just one, might have been implicated in this horrible episode.

True to his assertion that he preferred 'either constantly to wait [at Court], or constantly to hold the course of my poverty', Sidney seems, once back in London, to have remained there throughout the winter and spring of 1580–81. The coterie for which he wrote was expanding, and its existence was proclaimed to the book-buying public by the indiscreet Gabriel Harvey in a curiously elaborate publication called *Three proper and wittie, familiar Letters: lately passed betwene two Universitie men: touching the Earthquake in Aprill last, and our English refourmed Versifying*, to which was appended *Two other very commendable Letters*. It probably replaced a volume which Harvey had planned to dedicate to Dyer, and seems to have been published in August or September 1580.[87] Harvey's letters to Spenser, thinly disguised by the pseudonym 'Immerito', echo with dropped names, and are embarrassingly knowing in their allusions to 'those two excellent gentlemen Master Sidney and Master Dyer, the two very diamonds of Her Majesty's Court'.[88] His attempt to gratify Sidney by insulting the Earl of Oxford has already been mentioned (see above, p. 167). The *Letters* stress Sidney's and Dyer's commitment to the 'reform' of English versification, and include an oft-quoted remark by Spenser:

> And now they have proclaimed in their ἀρειοπαγω a general surceasing and silence of bald rhymers, and also of the very best, too: instead whereof, they have by authority of their whole senate, prescribed certain laws and rules of quantities of English syllables for English verse: having had thereof already great practice, and drawn me to their faction.[89]

By the time Spenser's letter, dated from Leicester House, 5 October 1579, appeared in print a year later, it was out of date, and its possibly jocular account of Sidney's and Dyer's 'areopagus', 'senate' or 'Faction' was extremely misleading. Spenser was by now away in Ireland with Lord Grey, and Harvey alone seems to have been responsible for this fascinating but foolish publication. Almost certainly he was considerably less intimate with Sidney and Dyer than he liked to hint. It was true that Sidney had drawn up 'rules in measured verse in English which I observe',[90] based on an earlier set of rules by Thomas Drant, domestic chaplain to Archbishop Grindal, and Spenser seems to have had a copy of these.[91] But the 'Old' *Arcadia* shows that by 1580 experiments with classical metres formed only a small part of Sidney's literary interests, one that he was fast outgrowing. Of seventy-seven poems in it, only ten are in classical, quantitative metres, and a debate about versification included in an early version of the romance concludes with a balanced judgement:

> Basilius, after he had moderated between them ... said that in both kinds he wrote well that wrote wisely.[92]

Sidney was not the kind of authoritarian extremist that Harvey's and Spenser's letters suggested, and in his *Defence of Poesy* he praised the English language especially because it was 'fit for both sorts' of versification.[93] Nor was his circle a formal academy or 'areopagus', but a loose-knit association which included the younger members of his family and such friends as Denny and Dyer. Spenser and Harvey may have had access to a collection of Sidney's early poems, such as those in the 'Ottley manuscript', some of which were later gathered up into the Eclogues. But the much more radically adventurous prose narrative of the *Arcadia*'s 'Books' was, as Sidney said to his sister, done 'only for you, only to you',[94] and it is unlikely that anyone else was shown it while it was still in process of composition. In publishing the *Letters*, in which he appeared to offer tantalizing glimpses of literary developments among leading courtiers, Harvey actually exposed his own marginal position in the Sidney circle. Though the publication may not actually have led to a spell in prison, as Nashe later alleged, it certainly did him no good. He failed to get the post he hoped for as University Orator, and when he returned to Cambridge in New Year 1580/81 he 'found he was sufficiently famous to be parodied in the comedy *Pedantius*'.[95]

Sidney, meanwhile, had at last returned to Court, emerging from what Languet had called 'a sort of cloud'.[96] If he was to remain there in any comfort he had to win back the Queen's favour. This he seems to have sought with a lavish and ingenious New Year's gift, consisting of

> a jewel of gold, being a whip, garnished with small diamonds in four rows and cords of small seed pearl.[97]

There is no doubt that this was a gesture of submission, for in his revised *Arcadia* Sidney made Musidorus, who had deeply offended Pamela, wear in his helmet 'a whip to witness a self-punishing repentance'.[98] The symbolism was more than inert, for in real life Elizabeth quite often did strike her courtiers. In 1579, for instance, young Gilbert Talbot inadvertently glanced up as he walked through the tiltyard, and saw the Queen at the window still in her nightgown. As he reported to his father,

> when she saw me at after dinner, as she went to walk, she gave me a great fillip [sharp blow] on the forehead.[99]

Not so playfully, in 1598, she boxed the ears of the Earl of Essex after he had insultingly remarked that 'her conditions were as crooked as her carcass'.[100] Sidney's gift of a jewelled instrument of punishment placed him symbolically at her mercy: she could strike him if she wished, so long as she also forgave him. He had abandoned his sister's court in favour of that of Elizabeth; let her do with him what she would.

9

1581–2

DASHED HOPES

Sir Philip Sidney, who was a long time heir apparent to the Earl of Leicester, after the said Earl had a son born to him, used at the next tilt-day following ~~SPERAVI~~ [I have hoped] thus dashed through, to show his hope therein was dashed.[1]

Within a year or so of Sidney's becoming an uncle, another boy baby was born in his family whose arrival had momentous consequences for his career. The exact birth-date of Robert Dudley, the Earl of Leicester's only legitimate child to survive infancy, is shrouded in mystery. Probably he was born some time between autumn 1580 and early 1581.[2] Stow describes him, at the time of his death on 19 July 1584, as being 'of the age of three years and somewhat more'.[3] Though Camden, in the quotation at the head of this chapter, says that Sidney proclaimed his displacement by little Robert 'at the next tilt-day following', he does not say when this tilt-day was. If he had, we would have a better idea of the boy's birth-date.

However, Camden had been a close observer and admirer of Sidney's ever since they had lodged together at the Deanery at Christ Church, and his account of Sidney's tiltyard motto is likely to be correct. It is given confirmation by Whetstone's reference to Sidney's using the motto *Spero* ('I hope'),[4] which would make the 'dashed hopes' motto especially telling. Once he had been a young hopeful; now he was nothing. His hopes were doubly negatived in the motto, by being put in the past tense, and by being visibly dashed through, in a line similar to those used on 'tilting cheques' to indicate the number of staves that had been broken.[5] 1581–2 was notable for the splendour and scale of its tournaments. It is possible that Sidney used the great *Triumph* of May 1581 as an occasion on which to indicate his private disappointment, alongside the more complex imagery and language with which he signalled his public

Title-page engraving of knights being rowed across water to fight outside Cecropia's fortress, from Jean Baudouin's French translation of the *Arcadia*, Paris, 1625 (Bodleian Library)

loyalty to Elizabeth, just as in the 1577 Accession Day Tilt he declared both private devotion to 'Mira' and public loyalty to Elizabeth[6] (see above, p. 144). But neither of the detailed accounts of this great spectacle mentions the ~~SPERAVI~~ motto, and such a personal message, beside the highly charged imagery of the 'Fortress of Perfect Beauty' and its besiegers, might be confusing and inappropriate. Camden's phrase 'the next tilt-day following' suggests, rather, a routine court tilt for one of the feasts with which they were regularly associated, of which the likeliest would seem to be Accession Day 1581, when Sidney had particular reasons for signalling his now hopeless condition.

Since the Queen was still angry at Leicester's marriage to Lettice Knollys, the birth of their son may have been initially concealed from her. This could explain the absence of any reference to the date of his christening. Also, the Earl and Countess seem previously to have lost one or two babies at birth or in very early infancy, and may have been reluctant to rejoice too soon at the arrival of this latest child. For the purpose of locating the period when Sidney's hopes were dashed, the crucial time to establish is not so much the date of the baby's birth as the time by which it seemed clear that little Lord Denbigh was robust, and might live to inherit Wanstead, Leicester House, Kenilworth and the rest, along with his father's title. My own surmise, which will be confirmed or denied should a record of Lord Denbigh's christening one day come to light, is that the child was born in the autumn or winter of 1580. I connect this with a specific disappointment, crucial to his development as a poet, which Sidney experienced in the spring of 1581. It was not by the birth of Lord Denbigh alone that Leicester's marriage to Lettice Devereux, formerly Knollys, had enlarged the family circle. She already had four children by her marriage to the first Earl of Essex, two girls, Penelope and Dorothy, and two boys, Robert and Walter; all of these were now Sidney's cousins. I have already mentioned that it was Essex's dying wish, as reported by his secretary, that Penelope should marry Philip Sidney. This wish was based partly on the high opinion Essex had of Philip's talent and maturity. As we have seen, he had shown favour to him as a schoolboy, giving him a present of a 'red horse' from Chartley (see above, p. 33). But the scheme must also have derived from awareness that his family resources had been virtually exhausted in the ill-conceived Ulster 'plantation'. As heir apparent to Leicester and Warwick, Philip Sidney promised position, wealth and security to Essex's bright little daughter Penelope. Though there seems never to have been a marriage contract, there must have been a continuing expectation in the family that Philip might marry Penelope when the time was ripe. This expectation could be among the reasons why his marriage was so long delayed.

How much Philip and Penelope saw of each other in their formative years is unclear. Though Ringler overstates the improbability of early meetings,[7] there is no doubt that for most of the years 1577–80 the Devereux sisters were at Ashby de la Zouch, in the custody of Sidney's aunt, the Countess of Huntingdon. But in January 1580/81 the Countess arrived at Court, bringing her charges with her. She was 'graciously received by the Queen on 29 January'.[8] A recently re-identified portrait, now at Longleat, shows the sisters about this time, in elegant red velvet dresses over white smocks edged with 'black work', and pearl and jet necklaces and hair ornaments.[9] Both girls have wavy, reddish-blond hair, and distinctively long upper lips which may conceal the large front teeth so characteristic of English girls. There has been some debate over which sister is the elder.[10] Probability, and the later placing of names above their heads, favours the girl on the left as Penelope, the one on the right as Dorothy, since pictures are normally 'read' from left to right. Also, the lack of any neck-covering on the girl on the right makes her look younger. The portrait, perhaps by George Gower, Cornelius Ketel or Leicester's mysterious employee 'Hubbard', marks the completion of the Devereux sisters' education and their arrival at marriageable age.

It may have been on 29 January that the Countess of Huntingdon formally presented her charges to the Queen, giving her also an amusing jewelled pendant which alluded to Elizabeth's affection for Alençon:

> one green frog, the back of emeralds, small and great, and a pendant emerald, with a small chain of gold to hang by.[11]

Sidney may have been present at this audience. In any case, he must about this time have had frequent opportunities of meeting Penelope and Dorothy, and reconsidering the possibility of marriage. Unfortunately, what we know of Sidney at this time sheds no light on his thoughts on the matter. He had just become Member of Parliament for Ludlow, and sat on two committees, one concerned with taking measures against possible foreign invasion and another committed to drawing up a bill 'against slanderous words and rumours and other seditious practices against the Queen's Majesty'.[12] Fulke Greville, now M.P. for Southampton, was a fellow member of the second committee. Sidney's current closeness to Greville is reflected in a second irate letter to Edmund Molyneux, written from Baynard's Castle on 10 April 1581, in which he implored him:

> I pray you, for my sake, you will not make yourself an instrument to cross my cousin Fulke's title in any part, or construction of his letters patents. It will turn to other bodies' good, and to hurt him, accordingly, were a foolish discourtesy.[13]

Greville was anxious to obtain the emoluments of the office of Clerk of the Signet to the Court of the Council in the Marches of Wales, part of a bureaucracy recently created by Sir Henry Sidney. By late July 1581 he 'received half the income from the Signet, while Fox and his clerks did the work'.[14] Though Sidney had not on this occasion offered any physical threat to Molyneux, the latter was, not surprisingly, rather wounded by his accusatory tone:

> Sir, it seemeth by your said letters, that you have been informed, that I either have already, or in some sort pretend hereafter, to be an adversary to Mr Greville in his suit here ...[15]

He assured Sidney that he respected Greville as Sidney's 'dear and entire friend', and in any case had no influence in the matter of the Clerkship to the Signet in Wales, 'having only to walk in the path I am directed'. As on the previous occasion, the subordinate Molyneux was unlucky enough to be at the receiving end of Sidney's anger, perhaps because this could not be vented directly on persons of greater authority, in this case, his own father, who was Molyneux's employer. The angry, assertive tone Sidney adopted with Molyneux is quite unlike the warm, personal manner in which he wrote to Leicester's secretaries, Arthur Atey and Jean Hotman.[16] It may be that Sidney's relationship with his father at this time was not altogether happy (see above, p. 121).

Sidney's irascibility in the matter of Fulke Greville's suit may also have been exacerbated by an unconnected personal disappointment. While he anticipated a period of weeks or months during which he could see more of Penelope Devereux, with a view to possible marriage, this option was suddenly removed from him. On 10 March the Earl of Huntingdon wrote to Lord Burghley:

> Hearing that God hath taken to his mercy my Lord Rich, who hath left to his heir a proper gentleman and one in years very fit for my Lady Penelope Devereux if with the favour and liking of Her Majesty the matter might be brought to pass. And because I know your Lordship's favour to the father gone, and also your favour to his children, I am bold to pray your furtherance now in this matter, which may, I think, by your good means be brought to such a pass as I desire. Her Majesty was pleased the last year to give me leave at times convenient to put Her Highness in mind of these young ladies, and therefore I am by this occasion of my Lord's death the bolder to move your Lordship in this matter. I have also written to Mr Secretary Walsingham herein.[17]

News had travelled fast, for the old Lord Rich had died on 27 February in Essex, and Huntingdon, who was Lord President of the North, wrote from Newcastle. Evidently marriages for both 'these young ladies' were under consideration, with the Queen's approval. The younger Robert Rich, aged about twenty, was, like his father, a zealous Puritan, whose extremism was soon to get him into trouble. In the Puritan Earl's eyes, as in those of her grandfather, Sir Francis Knollys, this was a point in his favour. Conversely, Sidney's friendships with Catholic courtiers may have counted against him. Also, the young man was aptly named 'Rich'. In finding such a marriage for Penelope Devereux Huntingdon clearly believed he was fulfilling the trust imposed on him by 'the father gone', Essex. If there had been an understanding that she was to marry his nephew Philip, it was too nebulous to stand in the way of the excellent alliance that had just arisen. This may indicate that Sidney was no longer heir apparent to his uncle Leicester, or his extensive expectations might have outweighed the cash-in-hand of Lord Rich. Once again, Sidney's deepest feelings are unavailable to us. His richly complex sonnet sequence *Astrophil and Stella* will be discussed more fully in the next chapter. But at this point the one sonnet, 33, which alludes to the missed opportunity of marriage should be quoted:

I might, unhappy word, O me, I might,
And then would not, or could not, see my bliss:
Till now, wrapped in a most infernal night,
I find how heavenly day, wretch, I did miss.
    Heart, rend thyself, thou dost thyself but right!
No lovely Paris made thy Helen his;
No force, no fraud, robbed thee of thy delight,
Nor Fortune of thy fortune author is,
    But to myself, myself did give the blow,
While too much wit (forsooth) so troubled me,
That I respects for both our sakes must show:
And yet could not by rising morn foresee
    How fair a day was near. O punished eyes!
    That I had been more foolish, or more wise.[18]

Ringler suggests that lines 9–11 'imply that [Sidney] actively furthered her marriage to Lord Rich, which now that he has become aware of the full noon-tide of her beauty, he bitterly regrets'.[19] However, it seems to me that Ringler's interpretation does not really work in terms of the poem's imagery. The contrast between 'rising morn' and 'fair day' indicates a substantial interval of time, during which Penelope/Stella grew from girlhood to womanhood. In 1581 she was eighteen, and the 'rising morn'/'fair day' contrast cannot readily be applied to the eight months which elapsed between her arrival at Court in January and her marriage on 1 November, during which her appearance can have changed little. The 'rising morn' image makes far better sense as alluding to a sight of Penelope in her girlhood, such as Sidney could have had when he was a schoolboy at Shrewsbury (see above, p. 33). According to Sonnet 33, Sidney/Astrophil's opportunity of union with 'Stella' was already lost by 1581. The suggestion that 'too much wit ... troubled' him is hard to decode; but it may imply that he was excessively cautious about the marriage scheme when it was being actively promoted in 1576–7. Now that he saw Penelope in her full beauty and maturity, the chance was lost.

As so often in Elizabethan marriages, money and rank played a larger part than questions of personal attraction. Huntingdon does not even mention the feelings of the young people whose future he controlled, being concerned only with the views of the Queen, Burghley and Walsingham. Five years earlier, when Penelope's father died, Sidney had offered excellent prospects as a future husband for Penelope Devereux. He was heir to his Dudley uncles, and his talent and energy promised a brilliant career. It appeared at that point more than likely that he would in due course succeed his father either in the Irish post or the Welsh one or both. He surely could not long remain plain 'Master Philip'. Instead, in the spring of 1581, Sidney still held no office of real weight or responsibility, he had no personal title, and his relationship with the Queen was distinctly uneasy. Almost certainly, through the birth of Lord Denbigh, he had also lost his position as Leicester's chief heir. It was a new version of an old story. Ten years earlier, just after his father had turned down a barony, he had lost his first fiancée to the high-ranking but unpleasant Earl of Oxford. Now Penelope Devereux, for whom he probably cared far more deeply than he had for Anne Cecil, was all of a sudden to marry someone richer, younger and of higher rank than himself. How they compared in appearance we do not know, but Sidney's remark that he was ousted by 'No lovely Paris' may refer obliquely to Rich as no Adonis. Perhaps if Sidney had been more decisive while his own value in the marriage market was high he could by now have been Penelope's husband.

Sonnet 33 cannot safely be taken to indicate what Sidney 'really' felt about his failure to marry Penelope Devereux, indicating only what he wished his readers, a couple of years later, to think he felt. But neither can it be totally removed from actuality, since Penelope herself was the first reader he had in mind, and must herself have known something of the order of events. As I shall suggest in the next chapter, it is possible that Sidney/Astrophil's devotion to Penelope/Stella was an elaborate act of reparation or face-saving. He may never have been very enthusiastic about the marriage, or never enthusiastic enough at the right moment:

> Never the time and the place.
> And the loved one all together.[20]

Whatever Sidney's feelings at different moments, whereas in Sonnet 33 Astrophil claims responsibility for failing to marry Stella – 'to myself, myself did give the blow' – in real life it was older people who took the crucial decisions. What dealt the decisive 'blow' to Sidney's chances of marrying Penelope Devereux may have been the birth of Lord Denbigh, not his own slowness to fall in love.

We do not know what stage the writing of the *Arcadia* had reached when news broke of Penelope Devereux's betrothal to Lord Rich. Though Sidney had promised his brother in October that his 'toyful book' should be finished by February 1581, it is probable, given his many concerns at Court during the earlier part of 1581, that completion took a good deal longer. A poem in the Third Eclogues, *OA* 71, may have a bearing on Sidney's alienated position at the time of Penelope Devereux's betrothal and marriage.[21] Old Geron urges a young shepherd, Histor ('Story-teller'), to imitate Lalus's example and get married, rather as Languet, in 1575, had urged Sidney to follow the example of Edward Wotton.[22] Histor has definite links with Sidney, for it is through him that Sidney pays tribute to Dyer as 'the loveliest shepherd ... That erst I knew'.[23] In reply to Geron's persuasions, he speaks bitterly of marital discord:

If many Kalas our Arcadia gave,
Lalus' example I would soon ensue;
And think I did myself from sorrow save.
But of such wives we find a slender crew;
Shrewdness so stirs, pride so puffs up their heart,
They seldom ponder what to them is due.
With meagre looks, as if they still did smart,
Puling and whimp'ring, or else scolding flat,
Make home more pain than following of the cart.
Either dull silence, or eternal chat;
Still contrary to what her husband says:
If he do praise the dog, she likes the cat ...
Let other fouler spots away be blown,
For I seek not their shame; but still, methinks,
A better life it is to lie alone.[24]

Geron counters this speech with an eloquent defence of women, based on long experience:

These fifty winters married I have been;
And yet find no such faults in womankind.
I have a wife worthy to be a queen,
So well she can command, and yet obey;
In ruling of a house so well she's seen.
And yet in all this time betwixt us tway,
We bear our double yoke with such consent,
There never passed foul word, I dare well say.

Histor's reply is guarded; he says that 'perchance' he will eventually marry, but meanwhile he is more interested in talking to Kala, the girl he would really have liked to marry. Sidney's latest experience of losing a long-expected marriage prospect may have been assimilated into his presentation of the embittered bachelor Histor, and Geron's observation that 'Riches of children pass a prince's throne' could bear a covert allusion to Penelope Devereux's married name, on which he punned so frequently in *Astrophil and Stella*.

Whether or not Sidney regarded it as 'A better life ... to lie alone', he continued to be unmarried during 1581. Court life kept him busy. On 22 January, a week before his aunt's audience with the Queen, he participated in a memorably splendid tournament. It was initiated by Philip Howard, who delivered a challenge, as 'Callophisus', on Twelfth Night. Son of the executed Duke of Norfolk, Philip Howard was in process of campaigning to establish his claim to his grandfather's Earldom of Arundel, and this doubtless had something to do with his challenge. At this time he appeared to be a fellow traveller rather than a committed Catholic. What exactly was going on among Catholic aristocrats is perplexing, but there is no doubt that they were conspicuous at Court at this time, and that both Sidney and his rival Oxford were visibly associated with them. Perhaps they thought, while the Alençon marriage was still in prospect, that they would soon receive support and encouragement at the highest level, that is, from the Queen's consort. It was not yet apparent that Catholic sympathies were incompatible with public office. The high profile of these Catholics is particularly odd since the session of Parliament of which Sidney was a member opened, on 25 January, with a rousingly anti-Catholic speech by Sir Walter Mildmay.[25] However, this was chiefly directed against the Jesuit mission, foreign invasion, and recusancy in the provinces. Whatever the deeper reasons, both Sidney and Oxford, together with the Catholic Lord Windsor, took part in the 'Callophisus' tournament. Oxford's participation is especially puzzling, since just before Christmas he had tried to betray three of his own Catholic associates to the Queen.[26] Yet for the time being this did not bring an end either to his favour with the Queen or to his association with other, more eminent, Catholics.

Several fragmentary records of the 'Callophisus challenge' survive, but it is not easy fully to reconstruct either its format or its meaning.[27] Clearly it showed its participants, young courtiers whose positions were in various ways insecure, in lively competition for the Queen's favour. Even more than most such tournaments, this one seems reminiscent of the courtship displays of exotic birds. Philip Howard, the 'fair-natured' Callophisus, declared himself in his challenge to be a prisoner to the Queen's beauty, 'finding the place of his imprisonment so strong as he cannot escape'.[28] He cannot have foreseen that he would spend the last ten years of his life literally a prisoner, 'at the Queen's pleasure', in the Tower of London.[29] He offered six propositions springing from his devotion to the Queen, corresponding with the six courses normally run by each contestant in a tilt.[30]

The challenge was disputed on 15 January 1580/81. The Earl of Oxford appeared splendidly arrayed as 'Knight of the Tree of the Sun'; he directly confronted Callophisus's second, the 'Red Knight', Sir William Drury (not the Lord Chief Justice of Ireland, who had died in October 1579, but a younger man). On the tilt-day itself Oxford had an elaborate pavilion of brown and silver taffeta, 'curiously embroidered with silver', and sat under a huge artificial bay tree 'the whole stock, branches and leaves whereof were all gilded over'.[31] Unfortunately, at the end of the tilt the tent and tree were torn to shreds by the crowd. Whether this was motiveless vandalism or sprang from Oxford's unpopularity we have no way of knowing. Oxford's second was the 'White

Knight', whom he described as 'to me ... unknown' but superior to the challengers 'in zeal and worthiness'.[32] This was Edward, Lord Windsor, whose 'white', or unengraved, armour alluded both to the fact that he was a novice at tilting and to the white unicorn which was the Windsor family crest. Actually, Windsor was well known to Oxford, being his nephew.[33] He was also well known to Sidney, who had seen a good deal of his father in Venice in 1573–4. At this time Windsor was just short of his twenty-first birthday, a little younger than Sidney had been when he made his tiltyard début in 1577. Young Windsor's entry may be recalled in the reference in the 'New' *Arcadia* to

> a great nobleman of Corinth, whose device was to come without any device, all in white like a new knight (as indeed he was) but so new as his newness shamed most of the others' long exercise.[34]

Callophisus's second supporter, the Blue Knight, appears to have been Sidney, who undoubtedly wore blue in the 'Four Foster Children of Desire' tournament four months later. The surviving speech bears many of the marks of Sidney's style and manner. The 'Blue Knight' criticized the White Knight's incorrect challenge of a challenge, as springing from a false claim to superior loyalty –

> where in truth he cometh far behind, and can no more compare with him than the wolf with the faithful spaniel, or as the ramage [wild, untamed] buzzard with the pilgrim falcon.

Animal imagery came easily to Sidney, who in *The Lady of May*, for instance, enforced the defence of Therion with analogous contrasts:

> ... let him also doubt that the well-deserving Therion is not to be preferred before the idle Espilus, which is even as much as to say that roes are not swifter than sheep, nor stags more goodly than goats.[35]

As well as employing animal images, the Blue Knight declared concern for real-life animals, requiring 'that whoso hurteth horse with spear or sword shall lose the honour and his pledge'. If the Blue Knight, like Callophisus, was called 'Philip', or 'Horse-lover', the condition gained extra meaning. None of the other speeches refers to horses. The speech ended with a 'figure', or *impresa*, by which he was to be recognized. It is included in the manuscript of the speeches, and consists of a two-branched tree with a broken hour-glass on the left, a laurel wreath on the right, probably indicating a determination either to win or to regard his time as lost. While the speech is in secretary hand, the signature, 'The Blewe Knight', is in an italic script not unlike Sidney's own, though the sample is too small to be identified with confidence.[36]

The 'Callophisus' tilt was a wholly artificial combat, for the supposed opponents were really on the same side. All sought to prove their passionate loyalty to the 'lady' whom the Blue Knight praised as one

that by remembrance of her name only stirreth up all desires to virtue, and by the perfections of her beauty and good graces subdueth the stoutest heart of her beholders.

Accounts of tournaments in the 'New' *Arcadia* reveal Sidney's ironical view of what was achieved by such combats. For instance, in Book 1, a skilful tilter, Phalantus, challenges all comers to tilt against him in defence of their mistresses' beauty. Though he has defeated a dozen knights in the past, carrying their mistresses' portraits as trophies, it is all an empty parade. Phalantus does not really love his own supposed mistress, Artesia, and is delighted to be rid of her when he is at last defeated by Musidorus, as the 'Ill-apparelled Knight'.[37] His spectacular challenge proves nothing about either Artesia's beauty or his own devotion to her.

Nevertheless, in real life, Sidney continued to use the tiltyard as a stage on which to display his gifts. If the sub-text of the 'Callophisus' tilt had to do with bids for royal acceptance by courtiers with Catholic sympathies, the next major tournament concerned a much larger issue. Plans for it were probably begun immediately after 22 January. The Queen's marriage to Alençon was once again under active discussion, and really seemed likely to take place.

Preparations were made to receive a large and distinguished French delegation. Stow describes the construction of a special banqueting house at Whitehall, built in only three weeks at the cost of £1,744 19s. It had ten banks of steps for spectators, and 250 glass windows. The ceiling was particularly ornate:

the top of this house was wrought most cunningly upon canvas works of ivy and holly, with pendants made of wicker rods, and garnished with bay, rue and all manner of strange flowers garnished with spangles of gold.[38]

In between swags of fruit, 'as pomegranates, oranges, pumpkins, cucumbers, grapes', were to be seen 'the clouds, with stars, the sun and sun beams'. It was begun on 26 March, and finished on 18 April, just in time for the arrival of the 500 French noblemen. While the carpenters, glaziers and painters were hard at work on the banqueting house, Sidney and his friends, Fulke Greville and Philip Howard – who on 18 March was reinstated in blood and succession to the Earldom of Arundel – were equally preoccupied with intellectual and practical preparations for another tournament, probably under the guidance of Leicester.[39] This time the Earl of Oxford did not participate, though he may have been involved in the earlier stages of planning, for Anne Vavasour gave birth to his child on 21 March, and both soon found themselves imprisoned in the Tower.

There has been some debate about the authorship of different parts of the texts that survive from the 'Four Foster Children' display.[40] They were promptly gathered up by one Henry Goldwell in a pamphlet entitled *A briefe declaration of the shews, devices, speeches, and inventions, done & performed before the Queene's Majestie, & the French Ambassadours, at the most valiant and worthye Triumph, attempted and executed on the Monday and Tuesday in Whitson weeke last, Anno 1581*. Like most such entertainments, the *Triumph* must have been a collaborative venture. For instance, it is not improbable that though Oxford was *hors de combat*, his protégé John Lyly, whose romance *Euphues* had been published in 1578, followed in 1580 by its sequel, *Euphues and his England*, had a hand in some of the speeches, perhaps under Oxford's direction. Sir Henry Lee, Queen's Champion, was already a veteran of the tiltyard, and some of the broad outlines may derive from him. Philip Howard, fresh from his 'Callophisus' invention, and first to enter the tiltyard on both occasions, surely contributed some ideas. It is also tempting to associate the syntactical contortions in certain passages with the characteristic style of Sidney's friend Fulke Greville. However, Edmund Molyneux paid special tribute to Sidney's inventiveness as a tilter:

> at jousts, triumphs, and other such royal pastimes (for at all such disports he commonly made one) he would bring in such a lively gallant show, so agreeable to every point which is required for the expressing of a perfect device, (so rich was he in those inventions) as, if he surpassed not all, he would equal or at least second the best.[41]

Much of the language and imagery of the piece connects so closely with other writings by Sidney that his hand and brain seem to dominate. For instance, in the opening challenge, delivered on 16 April, spoken by a page dressed in red and white 'as a martial messenger of Desire's fostered children', Elizabeth is complimented with a bold simplicity reminiscent of the opening of *The Lady of May*. There she had been addressed simply as 'Most fair lady; for as for your other titles of state, statelier persons shall give you . . .'[42] Here she is addressed:

> O lady, that doth entitle the titles you possess with the honour of your worthiness . . .[43]

Sidney's *Letter* seems to be recalled at the end of the challenge, when the page says he

> will daily pray that all men may see you, and then you shall not fear any arms of adversaries.

Sidney in his *Letter* had stressed that the Queen's safety from her enemies lay in her inherent 'perfections' which were visibly 'set to all men's eyes'.[44] The central conceit, in which the Queen was represented symbolically as an impregnable 'Fortress of Perfect Beauty', hopelessly besieged by loving courtiers, was a traditional one, even to such 'special effects' as cannons which shot out 'sweet powder' and 'sweet water', betokening Elizabeth's radiant bounty.[45] The French visitors would have been familiar with 'mounts' and 'forts' as symbols of the monarchy. But some of the more original images may derive from Sidney. In particular, the striking notion that Elizabeth's young courtiers were her 'children', half-weaned babies clamouring to return to the breasts of 'Desire' from the cruel nourishment of their other foster-mother, Despair, connects with many passages in Sidney's writings (see above, pp. 8–9). He had a distinctive fondness for foster-parent-and-baby imagery, often in unusual contexts. He was tempted to reject the *Arcadia*, for instance,

> as the cruel fathers among the Greeks were wont to do to the babies they would not foster.[46]

Among numerous other examples, in *Certain Sonnets* 10 he called pain the 'foster-child' of man's weakness; and in *Astrophil and Stella* 50 he described his own inadequate words about Stella as 'poor babes' which find 'death in birth'. Sidney's close involvement with his sister as she gave birth is all of a piece with his interest, as a writer, in viewing all sorts of abstract relationships in terms of the mother–baby–nurse triangle. He was probably the originator, therefore, of the complex central image of the 1581 *Triumph*:

> hereby ... there lies encamped the four long hapless, now hopeful, fostered children of Desire: who, having been a great while nourished up with that infective milk, and too too much care of their fiery fosterer (though full oft that dry nurse, Despair, endeavoured to wean them from it), being now as strong in that nurture, as they are weak in fortune, encouraged with the valiant counsel of never fainting Desire, and by the same assured that by right of inheritance, even from ever, the Fortress of Beauty doth belong to her fostered children; lastly, finding it blazed by all tongues, engraved in all hearts, and proved by all eyes, that this fortress built by nature is seated in this realm: these four I say, and say again, thus nourished, thus animated, thus entitled, and thus informed, do will you by me, even in the name of Justice, that you will no longer exclude virtuous Desire from perfect Beauty.[47]

The sentences are wandering and complex, and so are the images. Elizabeth is both the fortress to which they claim access and the source of their 'desire' for that fortress. She is at once cruel mother and cruel mistress. Her courtiers, bonded to her like unweaned babies, now seek to possess her, like masterful lovers, longing both for maternal comfort and for sexual fulfilment. They long in vain. Elizabeth, or the Fortress of Perfect Beauty, was not to be won, despite all their efforts, and after the traditional day of tilting followed by a tourney, or sword fight across barriers, on the second day, they made a rehearsed act of repentance. A page dressed 'in ash-coloured garments in token of humble submission' presented the Queen with an olive branch, and acknowledged on behalf of the four challengers

> this Fortress to be reserved for the eye of the whole world, far lifted up from the compass of their destiny ... They acknowledge they have degenerated from their fosterer in making violence accompany Desire.[48]

The sequence of violent sexual assault followed by painful retreat, self-reproach and repentance is close to the heart of Sidney's imaginative writings. Pyrocles and Musidorus both make assaults on the objects of their desire, and are ultimately compelled to acknowledge their errors. Astrophil kisses Stella while she is asleep, as Musidorus does Pamela, and longs, like Musidorus, to carry his assault further – 'Now will I invade the fort.'[49] At the end of the sequence of ten sonnets celebrating the kiss he comes to see that in threatening his rival, Stella's pet sparrow, he is also threatening himself, sharing both name and dishonourable intention with the lecherous bird:

> Leave that, sir Phip, lest off your neck be wrung.[50]

The word 'desire', given such special connotations in the *Triumph*, also pervades Sidney's other writings, occurring more than eighty times in his verse.[51] It is central to the first of the two palinodic sonnets which close *Certain Sonnets*, a rejection of earthly passion which leaves the speaker

> Desiring naught but how to kill desire.[52]

Though 'desire' and 'despair' are common words in Elizabethan love poetry, Sidney's distinctive interest in extending their range, in conjunction with foster-mother-and-baby metaphors, seems clearly to mark the 'fore-conceit' of the *Triumph* as his.

The *Triumph* was dense with subsidiary patterns of symbolism, few of which can now be recovered or understood. Goldwell omitted many speeches, 'for that some of them be mystical and not known to many'.[53] Among named participants whose outfits and speeches are not described are two good friends of Sidney's, Edward Denny and Henry Brouncker. Even the major entries described by Goldwell are not easy to interpret. On 15 May Sidney entered the tiltyard as third of the four 'children'. First to ride in was Philip Howard, now Earl of Arundel, wearing 'gilt and engraven' armour, with two gentleman ushers, four pages 'on four spare horses' – i.e. horses to be used in successive courses during the tilt – and twenty gentlemen dressed in crimson, yellow and gold. In heraldry, red and gold signified 'a desire to conquer', and this may be what Howard's liveries indicated.[54] Next came Lord Windsor, whose retinue were dressed in scarlet and 'orange tawny', with white feathers, and the family crest of 'the unicorn of silver plate on their sleeves'.[55] Sidney's entrance was equally spectacular:

Then proceeded Master Philip Sidney, in very sumptuous manner, with armour part blue, and the rest gilt and engraven, with four spare horses having caparisons and furniture very rich and costly, as some of cloth of gold embroidered with pearl, and some embroidered with gold and silver feathers, very richly and cunningly wrought. He had four pages that rode on his four spare horses, who had cassock coats and Venetian hose all of cloth of silver laid with gold lace, and hats of the same with gold bands and white feathers, and each one a pair of white buskins. Then had he a thirty gentlemen and yeomen and four trumpeters, who were all in cassock coats and Venetian hose of yellow velvet laid with silver lace, yellow velvet caps with silver bands and white feathers, and every one a pair of white buskins: and they had upon their coats a scroll or band of silver which came scarf-wise over the shoulder and so down under the arm, with this posy or sentence written upon it, both before and behind: *Sic nos non nobis.*[56]

Like the central image of Elizabeth as unassailable fortress, Sidney's personal imagery was ambivalent, perhaps conveying different meanings to Elizabeth, to the French delegation, and to his own friends. *Sic nos non nobis* was an adaptation of a motto, *Sic vos non vobis,* traditionally applied to unselfish labour, such as that of bees who toil to gather the honey that others consume; Sidney had already used it in this form in the 'Old' *Arcadia.*[57] The adapted version, 'Thus we [do or are] not for ourselves', could bear a wide range of meanings. Its primary implication was that Sidney and his retinue were engaging in the challenge not for selfish reasons, but for the sake of Elizabeth, or the good of the state, or both. In combination with the blue and gold of Sidney's armour and the gold and silver of his retinue the words could have other applications. The Sidney crest was a gold arrow-head on a blue ground. The motto might suggest that Sidney disclaimed his personal entitlement to these colours which he had not himself earned, rather as he is said by Molyneux to have disclaimed his family arms with the motto *Vix ea nostra voco,*

signifying thereby, that he would not call those his own which he knew not how worthy he was to bear, nor how long he should enjoy and keep them, sith that both states and persons are subject to time and mutation.[58]

Yet another, more intimate, meaning cannot be excluded. According to Gerard Legh, gold with azure meant 'to be trusted to keep the riches of the world for himself, and from another'; azure with gold meant 'the joyful pleasure of riches'.[59] Though Penelope Devereux was not yet Lady Rich, Sidney may have begun to play with her future married name, signifying cryptically that he and his followers looked rich, and yet lacked Rich; they were desirous of riches, yet denied both material wealth and the possession of her who was destined to be Rich. Molyneux's comment on Sidney's tiltyard activities, 'so rich was he in those inventions', seems unlikely to be innocent of the association, but may of course refer to later tiltyard appearances. The fourth challenger, Fulke Greville, appears to have been something of an 'also ran', with a smaller retinue than the other three. They were dressed in tawny and yellow, melancholy colours which prefigured the eventual defeat of the four 'children'. Perhaps they alluded also to the gloomy connotations of his name, 'grieve-ill'.

Ringler said that it would be 'futile' to try to identify a particular tournament as the one referred to in *Astrophil and Stella* 41.[60] Yet it seems highly probable that it refers to the 1581 *Triumph*. As Ringler himself stressed, Penelope Devereux was not at Court until late January 1580/81. The sensational spectacles on 15–16 May gave her her first chance to see a public performance by the man her father had hoped she would marry. Sidney's leading rôle in the *Triumph*, and the presence of the enormous French delegation, seem to be clearly alluded to. Though French spectators were also present at the Accession Day Tilt on 17 November, these now included Alençon himself, who could not so aptly be described as 'sent' from France, being a Crown Prince:

Having this day my horse, my hand, my lance,
    Guided so well, that I obtained the prize,
    Both by the judgement of the English eyes
And of some sent from that sweet enemy, France;
Horsemen my skill in horsemanship advance;
    Town-folks my strength; a daintier judge applies
    His praise to sleight, which from good use doth rise;
Some lucky wits impute it but to chance;
    Others, because of both sides I do take
My blood from them, who did excel in this,
Think nature me a man of arms did make.
How far they shoot awry! The true cause is,
    Stella looked on, and from her heavenly face
    Sent forth the beams, which made so fair my race.[61]

The sonnet is a cunning blend of arrogance and modesty. Sidney just stops short of boasting of his success, but he reports it, and reports also that it was achieved before a large audience. He collects up the comments of various spectators: 'Horsemen'; 'Town-folks' (presumably Londoners); a connoisseur of the art of tilting; cynics who think he had good luck; and others who remember that both his grandfathers, John Dudley, Duke of Northumberland, and Sir William Sidney, were active tilters, and believe he has inherited their skill. It is perhaps not accidental that the reference to his lineage comes last and occupies three lines, while none of the other comments goes beyond a line and a half. Though thinly veiled as 'Astrophil', the speaker identifies himself quite clearly as the descendant of the Dudleys and Sidneys. In the end, of course, the whole credit for the enterprise is assigned to Stella. Simply by her presence, he claims, she generated his success.

Superficially, the whole *Triumph* was also a success. It fulfilled its devisers' immediate aim of showing the French Commissioners 'that English court culture was as sophisticated as French'.[62] It was so striking a spectacle that it was recorded not only by Goldwell, but also by Stow, Holinshed and a French spectator called Nallot.[63] More than twenty-five years later the author of a fictionalized 'heroical epistle' from Sidney to Lady Rich included the *Triumph* as one of the most notable events in Sidney's career:

> When great Auvergne and Arthur Cossay came,
> With other peers of France of princely name,
> To great Elizabeth; to grace the French
> I amongst others framed a rolling trench,
> And undertook, enkindled by love's fire,
> The names of foster children to desire.
> Where what we did thereby can censure least,
> Since all my strength by seeing thee was blest.[64]

It is interesting that the unknown poet attributes most of the invention of the *Triumph* to Sidney, including the spectacular 'rolling trench', or movable mount, which physically represented the Fortress of Beauty. The poet also implies that this was the tournament alluded to in *AS* 41. However, as a political statement or challenge the *Triumph* achieved little, either for individuals or parties. His splendid and enormously expensive displays of loyalty in the tiltyard did not save Philip Howard from house arrest, after a visit by the Queen in 1583, which was followed eventually by lifelong imprisonment in the Tower for his Catholicism. Though the marriage negotiations did collapse during the summer of 1581, being replaced by a treaty which made no mention of marriage, it is unlikely that the *Triumph* played any significant part in Elizabeth's change of mood. In any case, from a political viewpoint, practically every element in the *Triumph* could be interpreted in at least two opposing ways.

This was doubtless intentional. Elizabeth, Fortress of Beauty, or the Sun, could not be won by her courtiers, and they acknowledged that it was misguided of them to try to 'destroy a common blessing for a private benefit'. This could indicate that Alençon had no hope of winning her in marriage. On the other hand, a French prince might succeed where four English courtiers had failed; if she was hard to win, his eventual success could be all the more impressive. Catholic sympathizers, noblemen and gentlemen, were shown as united in their challenge to the fortress, perhaps prefiguring a united Anglo-French Court in which all parties harmoniously supported Elizabeth and

Alençon. On the other hand, what united them was competition and conflict. Their playful but vigorous combats in the tiltyard could point to more serious struggles to come should the French delegates graduate from spectators to participants. The passionate 'desire' manifested by the courtiers expressed their love and loyalty, but also their anguish and frustration. They really did long to 'conquer' Elizabeth, that is, to bend her will in accordance with their own rather various aspirations. If she continued stubborn, mock combat might escalate to something more threatening. The combatants were simultaneously very strong – they were richly armoured and splintered their lances with vigour – and very weak, recognizing Elizabeth's absolute power over them. They were babies on horseback.

As at Kenilworth and Woodstock in 1575, there were undertones of conflict and unhappiness. Sir Thomas Perrot and Antony Cooke appeared in armour 'beset with apples and fruit', representing Adam and Eve, the latter having 'hair hung all down his helmet'.[65] This strange imagery seems to have supported the notion of Elizabeth as a sinless Eve, yet must inevitably have provoked thoughts of guilt and punishment. The Genesis story was too well known to be convincingly appropriated. Thomas Ratcliffe, as the 'Desolate Knight', supposedly lived in a wet cave by the sea:

> In this den he used for his bed moss, for his candle moss, for his ceiling moss, and unless now and then a few coals, moss for his meat. A dry food, God wot, and a fresh, but so moistened with wet tears, and so salt, that hard it was to conjecture whether it were better to feed or to fast.

Four sons of Sir Francis Knollys (uncles of Penelope Devereux) pulled out a challenge from the bosom of a dead companion, possibly an allusion to a death in the family, of yet another brother, Edward Knollys, who had died in 1580. The Knollys family, Elizabeth's cousins, had strong Puritan commitments, and it is striking to find them participating in a tilt which had been led off by the near-Catholic Howard and Windsor. Tone, as well as meaning, is elusive in many of the later inventions recorded by Goldwell. Such images as that of the 'Frozen Knight', Thomas Perrot again, who 'dissolves in drops' as he basks in the warmth of the Sun Elizabeth, sound to a modern reader rather comic. Yet in a culture collectively attuned to symbolic displays, it may not have been so. Sidney paid almost explicit tribute to Elizabeth's delight in tournaments and court spectacles in the 'New' *Arcadia* in his account of the peace-loving Queen of Corinth:

> she made her people by peace, warlike; her courtiers by sports, learned; her ladies by love, chaste; for, by continual martial exercises without blood, she made them perfect in that bloody art; her sports were such as carried riches of knowledge upon the stream of delight.[66]

As *AS* 41 suggests, Sidney knew that he was particularly good at tilting, and enjoyed displaying himself in this way, even if in other moods he saw the folly of it all. The *Triumph*, in which he played a starring rôle, brought together his many talents, literary, social and sporting. He showed physical prowess in tilting, probably once more opposite Sir Henry Lee, and exceptional imaginative power in devising much of the allegory. Yet his personal motto suggested, among other things, a kind of absent-presence at the occasion: thus he appeared, splendidly arrayed, but it did him no good personally. Though his appearance in the *Triumph* was memorable, it left him still without title, position or spouse. It also left him extremely short of money, though Leicester probably underwrote the tiltyard costumes, as he had helped Sidney with ceremonial clothes on previous occasions.

Events outside London claimed Sidney's attention during the summer. He may well have accompanied Leicester to Oxford in time for 27 June, when the latter, as Chancellor, presided at Commencement, or the great festive annual degree ceremony. As participants entered the University church they were startled to find more than four hundred copies of a new book laid out on the benches. This was Edmund Campion's *Decem Rationes*, privately printed in a lodge at Stonor Park, near Henley, under the patronage of Dame Cecilia Stonor. Its false 'Douai' imprint deceived few. Under ten headings Campion set out powerful arguments for the truth of the Catholic religion and the falsity of Protestant doctrine, ending with a plea to the Queen herself to turn back to the old religion:

> All hail, O holy Cross! The day will come, O Queen Elizabeth, that very day, I mean, when the veil of each man's actions shall be drawn aside, and when it will evidently appear whether the Society of Jesus, or the brood of Luther, did affect thee with Christian love and charity.[67]

It is highly likely that Campion's old friend Sidney was included among those to whom inscribed copies were presented. This carefully orchestrated public challenge to the Anglican settlement had considerable impact in a University where there was already a strong underswell of Catholicism, and where many remembered the charismatic Campion. As a public manifestation of the continued and increasingly successful Jesuit mission in England it left Elizabeth's advisers in an awkward predicament. It was still important for the pro-French faction to suggest that Catholics and Protestants could live together harmoniously, yet such open Catholic proselytizing could not be countenanced. Leicester had already received two letters from a Catholic informer, George Eliot, listing priests and Catholic gentry, which he had passed on to Burghley.[68] These, too, could not be ignored. The odious Eliot was provided with a warrant for Campion's arrest, probably by Walsingham. On 16 July 'more than sixty Catholics and Oxford students' assembled to hear Campion preach at Lyford Grange, in Berkshire, the house of Mr Yate, an imprisoned recusant. Yate's widowed mother, two priests and eight Belgian nuns lived there. After a search which lasted more than twenty-four hours Campion, two priests, and nine laymen were seized. On the early stages of the journey Campion was well treated, and friendly Oxford scholars came to talk with him at Abingdon. But when they reached the last lap the prisoners' treatment was changed, under instructions from the Privy Council. All had their arms bound and their legs tied under their horses' bellies, and Campion had a paper stuck into his hat – or rather Robert Parsons's hat, for they had exchanged hats at their last parting[69] – inscribed 'CAMPION THE SEDITIOUS JESUIT'.[70]

How all this affected Sidney it is hard to guess. There is much that is mysterious about the days immediately after Campion's arrest. In particular, one would like to know more of what passed on 25 July, when Campion was taken secretly from the Tower by barge to Leicester House, to be closely questioned by Leicester, the Earl of Bedford and others before what seems in effect to have been a meeting of the Privy Council. It emerged at the trial that the Queen herself had been present. It seems that Campion was being given an opportunity to save himself by declaring loyalty to the Queen and denying Papal authority. Though the Earls, 'who had known and admired him in his youth at London and Oxford',[71] were deeply impressed by his demeanour, they could not persuade him to make the crucial denials which would have won him his liberty. However, Leicester told the Lieutenant of the Tower, Sir Owen Hopton, to treat Campion better – he had hitherto been held in the narrow confines of Little-Ease. Sidney, who according to Parsons had promised Campion in Prague to help him if he were ever in trouble, may have played some part in this episode. There is no doubt that he mediated between Catholics and the Council on several occasions in the next few years,[72] and he may have exercised his diplomatic skills on this occasion also.

All that we know for certain of Sidney's involvement in religious matters at this time is that he was among those who supported Dr Tobie Matthew's candidacy for the Deanery of Durham in early December.[73] This may or may not be connected with the Campion affair. Matthew had been President of Campion's old college, St John's, from 1572 to 1576, and it was he who, perhaps under the direction of Leicester, led the reply to Campion's challenge in Oxford. On 9 October he opened the new academic year with a Latin sermon in which he refuted Campion's *Decem Rationes*.[74] Matthew's gentle but firm appeal to primitive Christianity, in which he studiously avoided the citation of Luther, contrasted with the brutal methods being used with Campion himself in the Tower.

As autumn drew on it became terrifyingly apparent that friends in high places, such as Leicester and Sidney, were not going to be able to save this courageous and brilliant man from the worst that the Elizabethan system of 'justice' had to offer. He was subjected to repeated rackings and interrogations during the month of August, followed by gruelling public conferences in the Tower Chapel, at which he had no forewarning of the topics to be discussed, no books to refer to, and not so much as a chair on which to rest his tortured limbs. Despite all these handicaps, he continued to acquit himself well. After a respite of a fortnight or so, another, less public conference was held on 18 September, on the question of whether the Church was visible or invisible, which was somewhat rambling and inconclusive. There was another on the 23rd, on the Real Presence, and one on the 27th, on the sufficiency of Scripture.[75] The authorities came to realize that these conferences achieved nothing, and it was Campion who through his dignity and steadfastness was winning the propaganda battle. As an anonymous poet put it:

> His reasons were ready, his grounds were most sure,
> The enemy cannot his force long endure;
> Campion, in camping on spiritual field,
> In God's cause his life is ready to yield.[76]

On 31 October Campion was racked once more; on 14 November he and his companions were arraigned before a grand jury on a charge of conspiracy to overthrow the Queen. Campion had been so severely racked that he was unable to raise his arm as he made his plea of 'not guilty'.[77] On 20 November he was brought to trial, and continued to deny any crime against the state:

> We are dead men to the world, we only travelled for souls; we touched neither state nor policy ...[78]

Though eleven years had passed since Pius V's Bull which declared Elizabeth excommunicate and deposed, the full extent to which Catholicism could be interpreted as a treason was only now revealed. Despite savage questioning by the prosecuting counsel, Edmund Anderson, Campion continued calm and composed. Many spectators assumed that he would be acquitted. While the jury retired a well-wisher brought Campion a reviving glass of beer. But the jury had been 'bought' – whether by threats or bribes is not clear – and returned after an hour with a verdict of 'guilty' on all the accused. After some postponements, Campion was taken to execution on 1 December, 'clad in the same gown of Irish frieze which he had worn at his trial'. A huge crowd assembled in wind and rain at Tyburn to see him hanged, drawn and quartered. Among officials present were Sir Francis Knollys, to whom he once again denied his treason, and Sidney's fellow tilter Sir Henry Lee.[79]

We do not know how much of this bad business Sidney witnessed. His fellow tilter Philip Howard was so moved by the conferences with Campion in the Tower in September that he decided from then on to live and die a Catholic.[80] Clearly this was not Sidney's response. However, the penultimate scene of his 'Old' *Arcadia*, in which Philanax acts as prosecuting counsel to secure conviction of the two Arcadian princes, has been plausibly compared with the invectives of Edmund Anderson, Q.C., against Campion.[81] It is possible that Sidney vented some of his own indignation at Campion's mistreatment in this unpleasant episode, in which Philanax's previously admirable loyalty to his prince develops into vindictive rage against his supposed murderers. If Campion's trial had an influence on the trial scene in the *Arcadia*'s first draft, Sidney was seriously behind schedule, having planned to finish the romance more than eight months earlier. Given his many preoccupations during 1581, this is possible. It may have been during his visit to Wilton at Christmas 1581–2 that he wrote the last part of Book 5,[82] which bears signs of haste, and lacks any concluding set of Eclogues. However, Sidney's unjustly condemned heroes enjoy a last-minute reprieve and amnesty; for Campion, there was no happy ending in this world.

While Campion languished in the Tower his old friend Sidney had been deeply involved in two royal visits. The first was from Dom Antonio, pretender to the throne of Portugal. Portugal had been thrown into confusion since 4 August 1578, when the young king Sebastian was killed at the famous battle of Ksar el-Kebir in a quixotic 'crusade' against the forces of Abdelmelec in Morocco. George Peele, who had been at Christ Church at the same time as Sidney, later wrote a splendidly swashbuckling play about the battle.[83] Among others killed in the African desert was the English adventurer Thomas Stukeley, who had at one time been favoured by Sir Henry Sidney in his suit for lands and office in Ireland.[84] Young Sebastian was briefly succeeded by an elderly great-uncle, Cardinal Henry. He died on 31 January 1579/80, when Philip II of Spain 'promptly assumed the sovereignty'.[85] The sudden enlargement of Spanish rule over Portugal and its colonies was alarming both to England and France, and many favoured the claims of the late Sebastian's bastard cousin Antonio, Prior of Crato. On 13 May Dom Antonio appealed to Sidney for assistance, writing from Tunis, and telling him about the fleet he was gathering in the hope of recovering his kingdom.[86] Clearly he hoped that Sidney would join his expedition, as well as supporting his cause in the English Court. Antonio arrived in England at the end of June, unable at first to have audience with the Queen because of 'lack of apparel'.[87] During the complex negotiations which followed, Elizabeth realized that a treaty with France against Spain on the Portuguese issue would give her the pretext she now sought for an alliance which did not include marriage.[88] It was all very delicate, and she was anxious not to provoke a Spanish counter-attack. Drake and Hawkins were at one point going to support Dom Antonio's fleet in the Azores, but then the Queen forbade them. Her support for Dom Antonio was definite, but not lavish. By early September he was on the point of departure, accompanied by a party which included the Earl of Oxford, Charles Howard and Sidney. But his ships were delayed by contrary winds for several weeks. On 26 September Sidney wrote impatiently from Dover to Sir Christopher Hatton:

Sir, the delay of this prince's departure is so long, as truly I grow very weary of it, having divers businesses of mine own and my father's, that something import me, and to deal plainly with you being grown almost to the bottom of my purse. Therefore your honour shall do me a singular favour if you can find means to send for me away, the King himself being desirous I should be at the Court, to remember him unto Her Majesty, where I had been ere this time, but being sent hither by Her Highness, I durst not depart without her especial revocation and commandment. The Queen means, I think, that I should go over to him, which at this present might hinder me greatly, and nothing avail the King for any service I should be able to do him. I find by him, he will see all his ships out of Thames before he will remove. They are all wind bound, and the other that came hither, the wind being strainable at the East, hath driven them toward the Isle of Wight, being no safe harbour here to receive them; so that he is constrained to make the longer abode, if it were but to be waft over. I beseech you, Sir, do me this favour, for which, I can promise nothing, seeing all is yours already.[89]

Hanging about with Dom Antonio, and perhaps even going to France and the Azores with him, was clearly not at all what Sidney wanted. He claimed that he could do the Portuguese pretender ('the King') more good by continuing to press his suits with the Queen. Actually, he may have suspected that Antonio's schemes were doomed to failure. The previous October he had reported tersely to his brother that 'Portugal we say is lost'.[90] He may have foreseen, as others did, that Antonio was mistaken in hoping for substantial aid from Catherine de' Medici. From a letter of William Herle's of 28 September we learn that Walsingham, like Sidney, was holed up at Dover, and Elizabeth and her chief ministers were rather scattered:

Anjou [Alençon] presses for marriage out of personal affection alone, and is coming to England. The Queen is at Nonsuch, Leicester at Kenilworth, Burghley at Theobalds, and Walsingham at Dover, detained by contrary winds ... There is treason in France prepared for [Dom Antonio], but he is obstinately bewitched to his evident ruin.[91]

By 10 October Sidney was back in London, desperately appealing to Burghley for help in obtaining a lucrative office and fresh sources of income.[92] As the Campion affair developed he may have grown increasingly anxious about his own association with Catholic sympathizers, and the further damage this might do to his already stagnant career. Whatever his private sympathies, if he was to have a political future he must be seen to align himself with those who trod the correct Anglican *via media*. Perhaps it was while he and Walsingham were marking time at Dover that a long-term solution appeared. Ever since they had been together in Paris at the time of the massacre Walsingham had liked and admired Sidney. His elder daughter, Frances, was still only about thirteen; but an eventual marriage between her and Philip would benefit both parties. Sidney would acquire excellent Protestant connexions and much-needed financial security, and Walsingham, who had no son, would strengthen his personal bonds with an exceptionally talented young man.

The fulfilment of this plan lay some way in the future, and it was not yet widely known. Meanwhile the Court was preparing for another royal visit, that of Alençon, which was to be far longer and more 'official' than his quick trip in August 1579. It was a source of embarrassment to many, since Elizabeth no longer claimed to want to marry him, but particularly so to Sidney, since he was well known to be hostile to him.[93] It was only one of several events displeasing to Sidney in the autumn of 1581. On 30 September Hubert Languet died at Antwerp. In some ways he and Sidney seem to have drifted apart, though it is hard to tell, since no letters survive from the previous ten months. But Sidney must have felt keenly the loss of his affection and encouragement at a time when his career seemed to be going nowhere. He may even have missed his banter. On or about 1 November, the very day that Alençon was due to arrive in London, Penelope Devereux's marriage to Lord Rich was solemnized. According to the man who later became her lover and second husband, Charles Blount, Penelope,

> being in the power of her friends, was by them married against her will unto one against whom she did protest at the very solemnity, and ever after: between whom from the first day there ensued continual discord, although the same fears that forced her to marry constrained her to live with him.[94]

Though Blount had a personal interest in invalidating the marriage, for he sought to prove the legality of his own union,[95] there is probably some truth in this. Royal wards, like Penelope, were notoriously allowed little say in their marriages, and even in a period when arranged marriages were the norm

> the subjugation of an heir or heiress to the dictates of the market place was distasteful.[96]

If Penelope Devereux's marriage had not been hateful to her from the outset Sidney could hardly have written so boldly as he did in *AS* 37:

> . . . of my life a riddle I must tell:
> Towards Aurora's court a nymph doth dwell,
> Rich in all beauties which man's eye can see;
> Beauties so far from reach of words, that we

Abase her praise, saying she doth excel;
Rich in the treasure of deserved renown;
Rich in the riches of a royal heart;
Rich in those gifts which give the eternal crown;
Who though most rich in these, and every part
Which make the patents of true worldly bliss,
Hath no misfortune, but that Rich she is.[97]

This sonnet was omitted from one manuscript and from the earliest printed text of *Astrophil and Stella*,[98] but it is included in another,[99] and is clearly an authentic part of the sequence as presented to Penelope Devereux herself, whose 'misfortune' in marriage formed its climax.

Begging letters punctuate the autumn, revealing Sidney as dispirited and nervous. In a long letter to Sir Christopher Hatton from Baynard's Castle on 14 November he pressed him for speedy completion of the documents entitling him to some unknown office. He hopes

that the suit is of such a nature, as I may have the means at the least, to show how ready I am to requite some part of your favours towards me.[100]

Wallace plausibly suggests that Sidney was offering Hatton a financial cut as a reward for his efforts.[101] His tone is anguished:

If you find you cannot prevail, I beseech you let me know it as soon as may be, for I will even shamelessly once in my life bring it to Her Majesty myself: need obeys no law, and forgets blushing: nevertheless, I shall be much the more happy, if it please you indeed to bind me for ever by helping me in these cumbers.

This letter was penned on the day of Campion's arraignment. Three days later Sidney was due to tilt once more opposite Sir Henry Lee, and in the presence of Alençon, for Accession Day, according to Robert Glover, Somerset Herald.[102] The tilt was again led off by Philip Howard and Lord Windsor, the former's conversion being not yet publicly apparent, and participants again included Sir Thomas Perrot, Thomas Ratcliffe, Fulke Greville, Antony Cooke and Henry Brouncker. It may have been on this occasion that Sidney publicly proclaimed his loss of position with the motto ~~SPERAVI~~. Self-presentation as a hopeless, alienated courtier would have been a way of dealing with his notorious enmity to Alençon, for if he showed himself publicly as out of favour, his opposition to Alençon could pose no threat.

But there is some doubt as to whether Sidney did, in fact, participate in the 1581 Accession Day Tilt.[103] He may have beat a hasty retreat to Wilton soon after 17 November. His sister had given birth to a daughter, Katherine, on 15 October, and he was eager to see her again. He wrote from Wilton to Walsingham on 17 December, recommending a nameless bearer:

that he may have some consideration for the packet he brought, because belonging to my brother Robert, a younger brother of so youngly fortuned a family as the Sidneys; I am sure, at least have very vehement conjectures, he is more stored with discourses than money.[104]

The stress on the poverty of the Sidneys may derive from his realization that the Dudley side of the family now promised much less than it had once done. The letter opens with greetings to his future mother-in-law and wife:

the country affords no other stuff for letters but humble salutations, which indeed humbly and heartily I send to yourself, my good Lady, and my exceeding like to be good friend.

Painfully, he was still appealing to Hatton for aid. Campion was dead, and the authorities were cynically accumulating more and more fines and goods from those who had the courage to continue to practise the old religion. Sidney could not afford to be too squeamish about this:

some of my friends counsel me to stand upon Her Majesty's offer, touching the forfeiture of Papists' goods. Truly, Sir, I know not how to be more sure of Her Highness in that, than I thought myself in this. But though I were, in truth, it goeth against my heart, to prevent a prince's mercy: my necessity is great: I beseech you vouchsafe me your honourable care and good advice: you shall hold a heart from falling, that shall be ever yours.

It seems that the earlier bid for an office had collapsed. Perhaps the Queen had deliberately substituted for it the offer of forfeited goods, to force Sidney into the anti-Catholic camp. He strongly disliked being in a position to 'prevent a prince's mercy', that is, to inhibit generous treatment of Catholics. Yet his position was miserable, and he could not live at the expense of his brother-in-law for ever. After Christmas he wrote two letters to Leicester. In the first, on 26 December, he excused himself from returning to Court for New Year, being

exceeding loath to deck my misfortune in any more disgraces, besides your Lordship knows the time was too short to provide anything, and to come unprovided will rather breed contempt than favour, where things past are so soon forgotten.[105]

He mentioned in a postscript that he has also written at length to Sussex, as Vice-Chamberlain, 'of my discomforts'. Presumably he was 'unprovided' of a New Year's gift for the Queen, but he may also have lacked money and inclination to devise a fresh outfit for participation in the lavish New Year's Tilt alongside Alençon.[106] The second letter, dated 28 December, is more complex.[107] It seems that Sidney's friends were still pressing him to accept money confiscated from Catholics, and he was in acute discomfort, feeling that he might still fail to get it, and so dirty his hands for nothing:

I know not truly what to say, since Her Majesty is pleased so to answer, for as well may Her Majesty refuse the matter of the Papists, and then have I both shame and scorn.

Presumably this means 'shame' for his willingness to profit from the persecuted Catholics and 'scorn' for his continued poverty. He went on to clarify his position:

But this I beseech your Lordship, without it be £3,000, never to trouble yourself in it, for my case is not so desperate, that I would get clamour for less. Truly I like not their persons and much worse their religions, but I think my fortune very hard that my reward must be built upon other men's punishments. Well, my Lord, your Lordship made me a courtier, do you think of it as seems best unto you.

Sidney made it bluntly apparent that he was prepared to sacrifice his principles, or, perhaps, his standing with Catholic friends, but only for a very substantial sum. Despite the conventional disclaimer – 'I like not their persons' etc. – he was worried about how his acceptance of such money would affect his image, and it is hard to see how he would 'get clamour' unless his circle did, in fact, still include some Catholics and Catholic sympathizers, as we know that it did. The letter shows Sidney to be unhappy and confused. His tone to his uncle is reproachful: Leicester has forced him into a courtier's life, while denying him the means to sustain it. He goes on to deny an allegation by Leicester's agent Sir John Huband that Sidney has accused Huband of 'unkindness':

... If any other words were but to this purpose touching Sir John Huband, as I shall much condemn my remembrance, so if they were, I assure your Lordship, they were not meant when they were written, but belike my mind was very much astray.

Sidney seems to have been writing too many letters too quickly, and in a state of extreme agitation. His relationship with his uncle, once pleasantly convivial, had become distinctly strained, and it is noticeable that he sent no greetings either to his aunt Lettice or his little cousin Robert. Leicester's middle-aged philoprogenitiveness had left him high and dry.

At the end of January 1582 Sidney's exclusion from inheritance became formal. Leicester drew up a twelve-page will, signed on each page by himself and Huband, in which Kenilworth and other large estates in the Midlands and elsewhere were bequeathed to his son, and his wife Lettice had a life interest in Leicester House. Some provision was made for 'my well beloved nephew Philip Sidney' in a separate document, which does not survive; but it seems to have been relatively modest – nowhere near the £3,000 he had asked for.[108] It was time to withdraw once more into the kingdom of the mind, as celebrated by his friend Dyer:

My mind to me a kingdom is,
Such perfect joy therein I find,
That it excels all other bliss
That world affords, or grows by kind ...[109]

After so many dashed hopes, only the sustenance of literary pursuits and congenial friendships could make yet another return to Court bearable.

10
1582–3
THE COURTLY NYMPHS

Because I breathe not love to every one,
 Nor do not use set colours for to wear,
 Nor nourish special locks of vowed hair,
Nor give each speech a full point of a groan,
The courtly nymphs, acquainted with the moan
 Of them, who in their lips love's standard bear:
 'What, he?' say they of me, 'now I dare swear,
He cannot love; no, no, let him alone.'[1]

A lady must now be provided for him, whose deserts eased him of the trouble of courtship. Many nobles of the female sex, venturing, as far as modesty would permit, to signify their affections unto him: Sir Philip will not read the characters of their love, though obvious to every eye. And now the sole daughter of Sir Francis Walsingham is preferred to be his consort, with great hope and expectation that the world should be enriched with a male-heir of these united perfections.[2]

To the years 1582–3 belong Sidney's two most perfect literary productions, the *Defence of Poesy* and *Astrophil and Stella*. Their completion is the more remarkable since during this time Sidney enjoyed no long settled spell away from court politics comparable with the summer of 1580 when he worked on the *Arcadia* at Wilton. He must have made a deliberate decision to seek in literature and literary patronage the fulfilment and autonomy that were lacking elsewhere, using every spare moment to this end. As poet and patron he was now a commanding figure, who fostered the work of others with generosity and discernment and by his own example showed how English poetry could be made new, fresh and important. But as a courtier and aspirant administrator he was still crushingly dependent on the uncertain favour of older people.

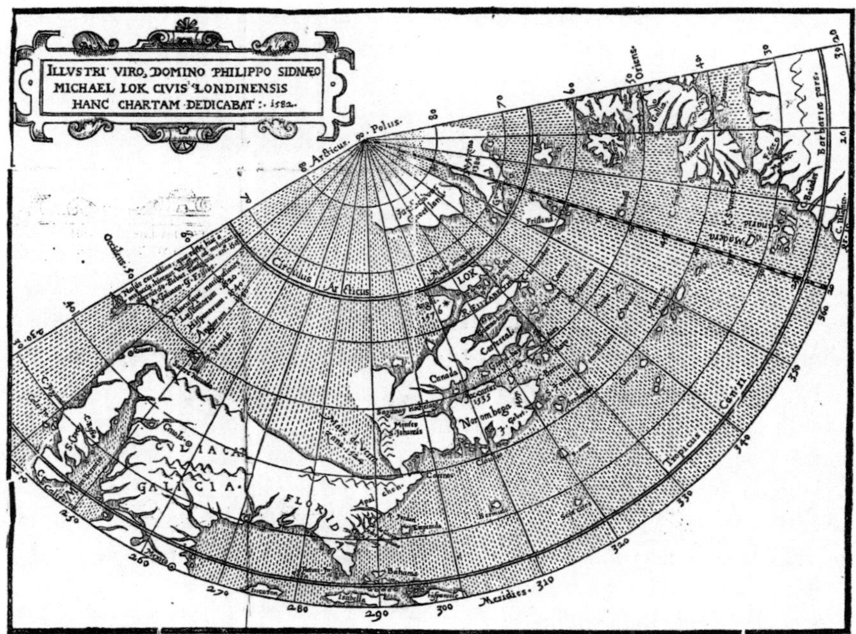

Map of the New World by Michael Lok, from Richard Hakluyt's *Divers voyages*, 1582 (Bodleian Library)

These years also raise inescapable, yet largely unanswerable, questions about his attitude to women, his sexuality and his particular attachments. The poetry he defended theoretically was above all heroic and didactic, yet the poetry he wrote was love poetry, of such a lively, complicated and individualistic kind that no reader comes away from *Astrophil and Stella* without feeling that it must derive from experience.

Externally documented events provide an unpromising context for these two brilliant works. Time-wasting and disappointment continued to dog Sidney's career. If he did not much enjoy hanging around at Dover with the ill-fated Dom Antonio, he must still less have relished participating in Elizabeth's lavish send-off to Alençon in January 1581/2. Marriage for the time being was 'off', but public flirtation was very much 'on', providing a cheap form of encouragement to Alençon as he set out to lead rebel forces in the Netherlands under the new title of Duke of Brabant. Like Sidney, Elizabeth was expert at the game of suggesting that the less passion she showed, the more profound were her true feelings:

I grieve and dare not show my discontent,
I love and yet am forced to seem I hate,
I do, yet dare not say I ever meant,
I seem stark mute but inwardly do prate.
I am, and am not; freeze and yet am burned,
Since from myself another self I turned . . .[3]

More than 600 English noblemen and gentlemen accompanied Alençon, the Queen herself escorting him as far as Canterbury. Her poem is associated with their parting, when she told him that he must 'address his letters to his wife the Queen of England'.[4] The emotional farewells of these two bewigged and painted figures, whose splendid clothes could not conceal the fact that one was nearly fifty and the other small and ugly, were a grotesque spectacle. The English party, well provisioned, with a supply vessel containing fifty beeves and 500 sheep, travelled on to Flushing and Middelburg, where they were welcomed by William of Orange, whom Sidney enjoyed introducing to Leicester. It was heartening to have another meeting with his favourite rôle model. He was also able to hear from him a personal account of the death of Languet, who had been lovingly tended in his last days by Mme du Plessis Mornay.[5] When the Anglo-French party reached the great trading port of Antwerp, the splendours and triumphs with which Alençon was greeted disgusted even the normally pageant-loving Leicester, and must have disgusted Sidney still more.[6] Another posting abroad was something he had long wanted, but not as a minor adjunct to Alençon's triumph.

Sidney was back in England by early March, and the search for office, above all for the emoluments of office, continued. Though the Queen always found Sidney useful when foreign dignitaries needed to be entertained, she showed little inclination to appoint him to any worthwhile or lucrative position, either at home or abroad. In late March bad news arrived from the Netherlands. William of Orange, on whose head a price of 25,000 *écus* had been set by Philip II, had been shot in the cheek by a Biscayan on 18 March. He had just returned home after felicitating Alençon on his birthday, which was celebrated with riding at the ring and the quintain and a dinner with 'eighteen meat courses'.[7] It was several weeks before it became apparent that William would recover, little impaired. His beloved wife Charlotte of Bourbon, the 'little nun', died suddenly after the strain and shock of this time.[8] In April a hope was expressed that Sidney might be sent over to the Netherlands at the head of a troop of English cavalry, but nothing came of this.[9] Nor did anything come of his bid to replace Sir Edward Horsey as Captain of the Isle of Wight in the spring of 1583,[10] though it was vigorously supported by Edward Dyer.[11]

If Sidney was ever going to get a job, it would have to be through nepotism. In the summer of 1582 he spent some weeks in Hereford and elsewhere with his father, hoping to be appointed to the Welsh Council, probably on the understanding that he would eventually succeed him as Lord President of the Marches. Provided that his son was appointed as his assistant and heir presumptive, and provided also that the Queen would give him a peerage and a grant of land to go with it, Sir Henry was willing to consider yet another term of office in Ireland, this time with the title of 'Lieutenant' rather than 'Deputy'.[12] This was remarkable in view of his failing health and the agonizing struggles over the cess that had overshadowed his last Deputyship. But no doubt the appearance of Leicester's new heir made Sir Henry anxious to set up some new form of inheritance for his son. He had drawn up a will in Philip's favour on 8 January, but had little to leave him except Penshurst and its contents.[13]

Neither the Welsh nor the Irish project succeeded. Instead it was through an uncle little mentioned up till now, Ambrose Dudley, Earl of Warwick, that Sidney did at last acquire some share of a post. Warwick had poor health, having never fully recovered from the leg wound he received at Le Havre in 1563. He had no children living, and when his oldest nephew was disinherited through the birth of his brother Leicester's son, it fell to him to salvage Philip's foundered fortunes. In the winter of 1582–3 Warwick petitioned the Queen for Sidney to be allowed to join him in the post of Master of the Ordnance, which he had held since 1560. Two letters survive from Sidney to Burghley in which he begged for his support in this suit. One was written from Court on 27 January 1582/3, the other from Wiltshire on 20 July 1583.[14] However, though he did get some kind of minor post in the Ordnance Office, Sidney had to wait two more years before being appointed Joint Master, alongside Warwick, with a salary of 200 marks and an allowance for secretaries and clerks.[15] During the period under discussion here Sidney continued to be effectively unemployed.

The final solution to Sidney's financial problems was marriage. Questions will be asked later about his deeper feelings. Meanwhile, it is clear that the Sidney family's appalling debts were the essential context to his union with Frances Walsingham. Sir Henry Sidney's great 'tragical discourse', as he called it, written to Sir Francis Walsingham on 1 March 1583, makes this abundantly clear. It was not simply to show what a good administrator he had been that Sir Henry catalogued his Welsh and Irish services. The essential point he wanted to get across was that his substance had been exhausted, through no fault of his own. The Queen and others had in the past accused him of extravagance, but this was quite unjust. He was anxious, first of all, to rebut the charge that he had been 'cold' in the matter of his son's marriage to Walsingham's daughter.[16] But he soon comes to the point:

> ... I find there is no hope of relief of Her Majesty for my decayed estate in Her Highness' service ... I know, Sir, that it is [for] the virtue which is, or that you suppose is, in my son, that you made choice of him for your daughter, refusing haply far greater and far richer matches than he ...

Sidney's merits were being traded for Frances Walsingham's dowry. In a lengthy account of his terms of office in Ireland, first as Lord Chief Justice, then as Lord Deputy, Sir Henry drew particular attention to the expenses he had incurred. For instance, he spent Christmas 1578 with the Earl and Countess of Desmond, 'and presented them both with silks and jewels, not a little to my cost'. The 'tragical discourse' is rich in graphic description, much of it horrifying, as when Alastair Og sent Sir Henry Shane O'Neill's head 'pickled in a pipkin', or when his nephew Sir Henry Harington was captured by Rory Og: Harington was slashed about with his own sword, his little finger was cut off, 'and in sundry parts of his head [they] so wounded him as I myself in his dressing did see his brains moving'. The miseries of winter campaigns, when he spent 'long and cold nights in cabins made of boughs and covered with grass', are reminiscent of the sufferings of Lear and his companions in the hovel on the heath. But money, or the lack of it, is the burden of his song. For instance, when he was sent to the Kent coast to see off Casimir in January 1579, 'well I remember allowance I had none, nor yet thanks'. His responsibilities are and have been great, yet he lacks

> one groat of pension belonging to the office. I have not so much ground as will feed a mutton ...

The apparently irrelevant passage about his wife's smallpox in 1562 has important financial implications. Since her illness, he explains, he and his wife have kept separate households, with a consequent doubling of domestic expenses. Her solitary life is

> more to my charge than if we had boarded together, as we did before that evil accident happened.

His house, in Ludlow Castle, is not a smart new mansion, such as many of Elizabeth's advisers enjoyed, but more than a hundred years old, and in constant need of repair. What the Sidneys can offer the Walsinghams is not money, but talent:

> I have three sons, one of excellent good proof, the second of great good proof, and the third not to be despaired of, but very well liked. If I die tomorrow next, I should leave them worse than my father left me by £20,000, and I am now fifty-four years of age, toothless and trembling, being five thousand pounds in debt, yea, and £30,000 worse than I was at the death of my most dear King and master, King Edward the Sixth.

Walsingham could be left in no doubt whatsoever that in acquiring Sidney as his son-in-law he was taking on a major responsibility. The marriage contract included the unusual provision that Walsingham would underwrite up to £1,500 of his son-in-law's debts.[17] He also bequeathed all his lands to Philip and Frances, and undertook for the time being to give them board and lodging. The Sidney family were looking for a fresh source of financial and political support outside the Dudley connexion, and in Walsingham it seems they found it.

Frances Walsingham's was not the only dowry offered to Sidney. Leicester's 1582 will, mentioned at the end of the last chapter, contained a curious clause:

> Where there hath been heretofore some talk of marriage between my well-beloved nephew Phil. Sidney and Lady Dorothy Devereux specially if my hearty and earnest wish was and if it should be so for the great good will and liking I have to each party, and for that the said P.S. is my nephew and nearest of blood next mine own brother, and failing any issue of mine own body is to be my next heir, I do most heartily desire that such love and liking might be between them as might bring a marriage, for which respect I will give and bequeath ... to be paid to the said Lady Dorothy and P.S. two thousand pounds over and besides her father's bequest.[18]

No allusion to this proposed marriage occurs elsewhere, and it may be that the 'talk' there had been of it was chiefly between Leicester, Huntingdon and Burghley, with little reference to the young people themselves. Though Leicester was eager to tighten the Dudley–Devereux bond which he had himself formed through marriage to Penelope's and Dorothy's mother, others apparently were not.

The reasons can only be guessed at. The likeliest explanation, supported by some evidence, is that Dorothy Devereux had ideas of her own. She had seen her sister forcibly mismatched to Lord Rich, and made up her mind to resist such an arranged marriage. The view of 'Philophilippos', quoted at the head of this chapter, that women were falling over each other in their eagerness to marry Sidney, may be further from the truth than Sidney's own suggestion, in the sonnet quoted, that many of 'The courtly nymphs' regarded him as rather a bore because of his refusal to flirt. The hitherto conventional idealization of Sidney would make it unthinkable that an eligible young woman should have disliked the prospect of marrying him, yet such may have been the case. Dorothy Devereux had set her heart on the Queen's 'fine Frozen Knight', Sir Thomas Perrot, whom she married in 1583 'without the consent of the Queen and her guardians',[19] but with the assistance and encouragement of her sister.[20] The story of Dorothy Devereux's marriage is a case of life imitating art, offering curious parallels to the elopement of Musidorus and Pamela in the *Arcadia*. She was spending the summer in the house of Sir Henry Cock at Broxbourne, in Hertfordshire. One morning in mid-July she got up much earlier than usual, and as Cock's daughter Mrs Lucy later testified:

put on her best apparel, bestowing great labour in trimming of herself ... [she said] 'I know you marvel why I am so trim this day; the cause is for that the Earl of Huntingdon will be here by and by.'[21]

This news sent Lady Cock hurrying to the kitchen to supervise the preparation of a special dinner for the Earl. Meanwhile Dorothy called for her lute, slipped out of the house, and went with Sir Thomas Perrot to an outdoor seat where she often used to sit in fine weather. The pair sat there in a leisurely manner, dispatching a servant for 'metheglin', or spiced wine, and other provisions for an outdoor breakfast. The lute was no doubt a deliberate ruse to prevent villagers from realizing the true object of her morning stroll. Dorothy next pretended to take an interest in seeing a mill which stood just by the church. The Vicar of Broxbourne was summoned and asked for a key of the church. Perrot showed him a marriage licence from the Bishop of London, and offered him a *rial*, or Spanish sixpence, to conduct the marriage ceremony. He refused, but Perrot had brought a minister of his own with him, and the service was rattled through with 'no bell rung nor surplice worn, but the minister married them in his cloak booted and spurred', while Perrot's servants guarded the church door with drawn swords to prevent any of the witnesses from leaving. When all this became known, the Bishop of London, John Aylmer, was naturally furious that his authority had been abused, and Perrot had a spell in the Fleet prison.

Since the marriage required Dorothy Devereux's active participation, for instance in her lie about her guardian's imminent arrival, there can be no doubt that this was a love match. Leicester may have been unaware of the affection between his niece and young Perrot. But another possibility is that he was perfectly well aware of it, and made the provision in his will in the hope of preventing what happened. If Leicester and the Queen both wished Sidney to marry Dorothy Devereux, this would help to explain the fury and disfavour that both young people endured after their respective marriages. But whether or not Leicester knew of Dorothy Devereux's affection for Sir Thomas Perrot, Sidney, much closer to them in age, must have been well aware of it. He realized that as far as marriage and a good financial settlement were concerned his best course was to wait for Frances Walsingham to reach marriageable age. In 1582 she was still only fourteen.

Lack of resources never prevented Sidney from spending money on things he considered worthwhile. One of these was patronage. As Fulke Greville put it:

his heart and capacity were so large that there was not a cunning painter, a skilful engineer, an excellent musician or any other artificer of extraordinary fame that made not himself known to this famous spirit and found him his true friend without hire.[22]

Some of those who approached him bear witness to his generous habits. For instance, the scribe and translator Richard Robinson recorded in 1599 that twenty years earlier he had dedicated a translation of Philip Melanchthon's prayers

> to the honourable and virtuous and renowned gent. Mr Philip Sidney Esquire, who gave me for his book 4 angels, and his honourable father gave me for his book [i.e. his copy of the same book] ten shillings. These two honourable personages many times benevolent unto my poor study.[23]

There can be no doubt that Sidney also rewarded a more distinguished writer, Edmund Spenser, for his dedication to him of *The Shepheardes Calender* in the winter of 1579–80, and continued to foster his larger poetic projects.

Some of the books dedicated to Sidney in this period refer to his expected employment in public affairs. John Derricke's handsomely illustrated *The image of Irelande* (1581) must be connected with his expected succession to his father as Lord Deputy. William Blandy's *The castle of pollicye* (1581) and Nicholas Lichefild's translation of Gutierres de la Vega's *De re militari* (dated 1 January 1582)[24] suggest practical military interests. Blandy gives an account of the recent exploits of Sir John Norris's regiment in Friesland, and Lichefild's book is a translation of a treatise pillaged from one of the Spanish soldiers slaughtered by Lord Grey's troops at Smerwick. Presumably both writers expected Sidney to go on active service in the Netherlands shortly. Though it turned out to be nearly four years before he did so, he probably studied *De re militari*, in particular, with interest. Its detailed descriptions, with diagrams, of Spanish battle formations both indicated what might be expected in the enemy and offered models to be imitated by English generals. A particularly large and striking plate shows 'The battle in form of a Moon, being of great force for the night'.

The book that struck closest to the heart of Sidney's current aspirations was Richard Hakluyt's *Divers voyages*, dedicated to him in the summer of 1582. He seems to refer to it two years later in a letter to Sir Edward Stafford:

> We are half persuaded to enter into the journey of Sir Humphrey Gilbert very eagerly, whereunto your Mr Hakluyt hath served for a very good trumpet.[25]

The fold-out map at the end of *Divers voyages* was also separately dedicated to him by the bankrupt merchant Michael Lok, who had ruined himself through his underwriting of Frobisher's voyages, and no doubt looked to Sidney to relieve himself, his wife and his fifteen children. Sidney's voice, if not his purse, may have aided his release from the Fleet prison. Greville praised Sidney as

> a man fit for conquest, plantation, reformation, or what action soever is greatest and hardest among men.[26]

At this time his interest in exploration and colonization was intense. One possibility offered by settlements in the New World was that of religious freedom, which seemed especially desirable during the crackdown which followed Campion's execution. Sidney and his father were involved with two gentlemen, Sir George Peckham and Sir Thomas Gerard, who in June 1572 had purchased the right to explore and settle parts of 'Florida', which corresponded with a much larger area than the modern state, and two offshore islands.[27] Gerard had lost most of his goods and undergone a spell of imprisonment for recusancy in the early 1570s, and Peckham seems to have been at least a Catholic sympathizer. Probably both hoped to practise their faith unhindered in the New World. All were strongly interested in Sir Humphrey Gilbert's project for a large English colony in North America. In June 1583 – the month of Gilbert's embarkation – Sidney purchased the right to settle, cultivate and trade in three million acres not yet discovered by Gilbert, and in the following month he covenanted these vast, but as yet purely notional, estates to Sir George Peckham.[28] It is difficult to size up Sidney's position. Did he really believe that his letters patent would one day make him master of a huge estate that would make up for the loss of his uncle's expected inheritance, or was this just another cynical scheme for making money out of beleaguered Catholics? It has been suggested that Walsingham saw grants of land in America as a device

> for ridding the realm of potentially dangerous Catholics without alienating them from England or causing them to emigrate to lands hostile to his own.[29]

Yet there is no doubt that Sidney himself longed to go to the New World, and in the summer of 1585 made a serious attempt to do so. It is conceivable that for Walsingham's son-in-law, as for Peckham and Gerard, freedom from the obligation to conform in matters of religion was among the many attractions of tnese new and unknown territories.

Meanwhile, he found himself exploring the more accessible, and in many ways no less liberating, kingdom of the mind. There is little doubt that the *Defence of Poesy* and *Astrophil and Stella* are closely connected to each other, and that both are rooted in the years 1582–3. The *Defence,* as has been said, includes tantalizing references to the speaker as 'overmastered by some thoughts' which have exacted 'an inky tribute'.[30] This may allude to the now completed 'Old' *Arcadia,* while also glancing at the origins of *Astrophil and Stella*. Sidney's parenthetical defence of love hints at his own current preoccupation with it:

> Alas, Love, I would thou couldst as well defend thyself as thou canst offend others. I would those on whom thou dost attend could either put thee away, or yield good reason why they keep thee.[31]

The phrase recurs in *AS* 10, when Stella's beauty proves 'By reason good, good reason her to love'.[32] An explicit allusion to the *Defence* comes in *AS* 18. 9–10:

> My youth doth waste, my knowledge brings forth toys,
> My wit doth strive those passions to defend ...

The word 'passions' could mean 'love poems', being used in this sense by Thomas Watson in his *Hekatompathia*. Numerous verbal and thematic parallels between the two works when taken together introduce unsuspected ironies. In the *Defence*, for instance, Sidney gives a contemptuous account of the star-gazer:

> by the balance of experience it was found that the astronomer, looking to the stars, might fall in a ditch ...[33]

The figurative use of the image in *AS* 19. 9–11 is self-deflating:

> For though she pass all things, yet what is all
> That unto me, who fare like him that both
> Looks to the skies, and in a ditch doth fall?

All the quarto editions of *Astrophil and Stella* give the sequence a sub-title, *Wherein the excellence of sweet Poesie is concluded*.[34] For late Elizabethan readers, it seems, Sidney's treatise established the theoretical value of poetry, and his sonnet sequence conclusively demonstrated it.

The immediate literary and personal origins of the two works are obscure. In neither case do we know precisely for what audience Sidney was writing. Nor can the date by which either was completed be definitely fixed. Ringler's attempt to confine the composition of *Astrophil and Stella* within the summer of 1582 is unsubstantiated, and probably derives from anxiety about the idea of Sidney writing would-be adulterous poems in the period immediately before his marriage. If 'this great cause', for which Astrophil begs release from Stella in Sonnet 107, could be identified, it would provide us with at least an imagined terminal date. But the phrase could refer to any of the postings for which Sidney hoped during 1582–3. Though the topical questions listed in Sonnet 30 seem to relate to the summer of 1582, there is no conclusive evidence that the entire sequence was completed within that period.

In its final form it must have taken a considerable time to complete. Not only are all the sonnets written in the exacting 'Italian' form, which is far more difficult to compose than the 'English', or 'Surreyan', form, but the work as a whole is extremely carefully structured, with many finesses which are still not wholly understood. It is only since the appearance of a computer-aided concordance, for instance, that it has been easy to discover that the word 'love' occurs 108 times, perfectly matching the total of 108 sonnets.[35] Sidney's brilliant effects of spontaneity and naturalism within a tightly organized framework must have been the product of prolonged toil. As Yeats, reflecting the Castiglionian ideal of *sprezzatura*, put it:

> A line will take us hours maybe;
> Yet if it does not seem a moment's thought,
> Our stitching and unstitching has been naught.[36]

The *Defence of Poesy*, on the other hand, bears signs of haste, and may have been completed within a relatively short time.

Probably the *Defence* was finished first, some time in 1582. It is rooted in a tradition of literary theory and defences of vernacular literature which was already flourishing in France, Italy and Germany.[37] Two recent works in particular may have set Sidney off on his

> pitiful defence of poor poetry, which from almost the highest estimation of learning is fallen to be the laughing stock of children.[38]

One was a book dedicated to him in the summer of 1579 by an Oxford scholar and dramatist, Stephen Gosson's *The Schoole of Abuse, conteining a pleasaunt invective against Poets, Pipers, Plaiers, Jesters, and such like Caterpillers of a Commonwealth*. Edmund Spenser, whose own *Shepheardes Calender* was dedicated to Sidney later that year, claimed that Gosson had blundered:

> New books I hear of none, but only of one, that writing a certain book called *The schoole of Abuse*, and dedicating it to Master Sidney, was for his labour scorned: if at least it be in the goodness of that nature to scorn. Such folly is it, not to regard aforehand the inclination and quality of him to whom we dedicate our books.[39]

If Sidney really 'scorned' Gosson, he did not make this immediately apparent. He must have given him his customary reward, for Gosson went on to dedicate his next book, *The Ephemerides of Phialo*, to him later that same year. But Spenser may have been aware that Sidney had found Gosson's onslaught on the 'abuses' of poetry extremely provocative. As Spenser knew, Sidney had already written up some of his reflexions on metrics;[40] he now began to think in much more radical terms about the worth of poetry. Lively controversy ensued from Gosson's book. It was immediately attacked in a pamphlet, now lost, called *Straunge news out of Affrick*; a counter-attack by Gosson was appended to his *Ephemerides*; Thomas Lodge rebutted this in his *Honest Excuses* (1579), and included a fresh attack on Gosson in his *An Alarum against Usurers* (1584), which was dedicated to Sidney.[41] Sidney did not participate directly in the battle, but enjoyed watching it from his superior vantage-point. His *Defence* is not a reply to *The Schoole of Abuse* – indeed, on the issue of the 'abuse' of the stage Sidney and Gosson seem to have held similar views – but shared phrases and quotations suggest that he had read Gosson's piece attentively.[42]

A more direct model for the *Defence* was provided by an old friend, the great French scholar Henri Estienne, in his *Project du Livre intitulé De la precellence du Langage Français* (1579). This brilliant work, dedicated to Henri III, and published at the time of Alençon's most active courtship of Elizabeth, may well have provoked Sidney to consider defending poetry in general and the English language in particular as part of a larger project to demonstrate the sophistication of English court culture during the years of the threatened French marriage (see above, p. 210). French models and French scholarship were appropriated to prove, chauvinistically, the superiority of English to French as a literary language. In addition to the 1579 treatise, Sidney also drew on Estienne's *Deux dialogues* (1578), his *Poesis Philosophica* (1573) and many of his editions of classical writers.

Despite the many ironical strategies used by Sidney in the *Defence*, we need not question his jokey assertion that the most powerful reason for writing it was 'self-love'. More than poesy was on trial: he was defending himself. Finding that he had 'slipped into the title of a poet' he sought to elevate the standing of this, his 'unelected vocation'. As he reached his late twenties and prepared to become Walsingham's son-in-law he was acutely conscious that 'my knowledge brings forth toys'.[43] Writing imaginative fiction and love poetry was not what he had been primarily groomed for by his 'Dutch uncles'. An inessential social grace in a courtier had become for him a serious and central activity, lacking that 'recklessness', or apparent carelessness, that should mark the incidental recreations of the true courtier.[44] But by demonstrating that the reading, writing and patronage of poetry were honourable and dignified pursuits, compatible with high civic office, he showed that his own recent absorption in literary activities was no disqualification for such office. Walsingham need not worry about his head being too full of poetic fancies for him to be a worthy successor to a vital post like his own First Secretaryship. On the contrary, 'kings, emperors, senators, great captains' had all in the past not only favoured poets, but written poetry. After invoking such figures as King David the Psalmist, François I of France, King James of Scotland and his tutor George Buchanan, Sidney chose his final example with care:

> ... so grave counsellors as, besides many, but before all, that Hôpital of France, than whom (I think) that realm never brought forth a more accomplished judgement, more firmly builded upon virtue.[45]

It was in Paris in 1572 that Sidney and Walsingham had first met, during the latter's years as Elizabeth's ambassador, Michel de l'Hôpital. He had been

Chancellor of France from 1560 to 1568 and represented the values of enlightened and tolerant Catholicism which had been hideously destroyed by the Massacre of St Bartholomew's Day. Although L'Hôpital was not killed in the massacre, his château was occupied by Guise's cavalry, he was menaced and mocked, and his Calvinist wife was compelled to attend Mass. This was testified by a good friend who came to visit them, Charlotte Arbaleste (Mme du Plessis Mornay).[46] L'Hôpital died, traumatized, six months later. Few English readers knew anything about him, and Sidney's invocation of his name as 'before all' suggests that Walsingham was the reader he had most prominently in mind when writing the *Defence*. The treatise displayed that 'virtue' which made the alliance worthwhile for Walsingham, while allaying doubts which might attach to his known fluency as a poet.

Sir Henry Sidney, drafting his lengthy self-testimonial for Walsingham, was able to list many positions held, military exploits performed and administrative reforms effected. His son had nothing comparable to offer. However, he had visited the Imperial Court, first as a student, then as an ambassador, and opened with a reminder of this:

> When the right virtuous Edward Wotton and I were at the Emperor's court together, we gave ourselves to learn horsemanship of John Pietro Pugliano . . .[47]

He also drew attention to his familiarity with the culture of Ireland and Wales,[48] and gave an eye-witness account of feasts in Hungary where 'songs of their ancestors' valour' were sung.[49] In his fictional writings Sidney buried his identity within fictitious names and narrative voices. Here he writes – or speaks, for the discourse is in the form of an oration – explicitly as the witty, charming, well-read Philip Sidney, Sir Henry Sidney's son. An anecdote of his father's is enclosed in the important passage in which he pleads for 'forcibleness' in love poetry:

> But truly many of such writings as come under the banner of unresistible love, if I were a mistress, would never persuade me they were in love: so coldly they apply fiery speeches, as men that had rather read lovers' writings – and so caught up certain swelling phrases which hang together, like a man that once told my father that the wind was at north-west and by south, because he would be sure to name winds enough – than that in truth they feel those passions, which easily (as I think) may be bewrayed by that same forcibleness or *energia* (as the Greeks call it) of the writer.[50]

He draws frequently on personal experience, using it to support claims for the didactic power of fiction:

> Truly, I have known men that even with reading *Amadis de Gaule* (which God knoweth wanteth much of a perfect poesy) have found their hearts moved to the exercise of courtesy, liberality, and especially courage.[51]

Despite his dazzling array of learning and easy familiarity with classical and humanist philosophy and literature, Sidney's range of reference is deliberately catholic (with a small 'c'). In a period when oral literature was little admired, he confesses to finding power even in 'the old song of Percy and Douglas'.[52] Homely Englishness is underlined with expressions like 'as if they overshot Robin Hood', and in a preference for natural speech over learned oratory:

Undoubtedly ... I have found in divers smally learned courtiers a more sound style than in some professors of learning; of which I can guess no other cause, but that the courtier, following that which by practice he findeth fittest to nature, therein (though he knoweth it not) doth according to art, though not by art.[53]

When he comes to discuss English poetry, however, he finds himself in difficulty. Recent examples of published poetry seem to him worthless:

Now, as if all the Muses were got with child to bring forth bastard poets, without any commission they do post over the banks of Helicon, till they make the readers more weary than post-horses.[54]

Modestly, he then includes himself in 'the company of the paper-blurrers', admitting that 'the very true cause of our wanting estimation is want of desert'.[55] However, he has not rushed into print, like the writers he most vigorously condemns, and his superior position is soon re-established when he distributes honours among English poets of the previous 200 years:

Chaucer, undoubtedly, did excellently in his *Troilus and Criseyde*, of whom, truly, I know not whether to marvel more, either that he in that misty time could see so clearly, or that we in this clear age go so stumblingly after him. Yet had he great wants, fit to be forgiven in so reverent an antiquity. I account the *Mirror for Magistrates* meetly furnished of beautiful parts, and in the Earl of Surrey's lyrics many things tasting of a noble birth, and worthy of a noble mind. The *Shepheardes Calender* hath much poetry in his eclogues, indeed worthy the reading, if I be not deceived. (That same framing of his style to an old rustic language I dare not allow, since neither Theocritus in Greek, Virgil in Latin, nor Sannazaro in Italian did affect it.) Besides these I do not remember to have seen but few (to speak boldly) printed that had poetical sinews in them; for proof whereof, let but most of the verses be put in prose, and then ask the meaning, and it will be found that one verse did but beget another, without ordering at the first what should be at the last; which becomes a confused mass of words, with a tinkling sound of rhyme, barely accompanied with reason.[56]

In not naming Spenser, who was a protégé of Walsingham as well as of himself,[57] Sidney respects Spenser's plea for anonymity for his work, some of which, particularly the ecclesiastical satire, was rather bold:

Go, little book: thyself present,
As child whose parent is unkent,
To him, that is the president
Of noblesse and of chivalry.[58]

Sidney's criticism of Spenser's use of 'an old rustic language' is a little inconsistent, for he himself had experimented with such language in two poems in the 'Old' *Arcadia* (64, 66). The comment may have been calculated to measure the social distance between Leicester's nephew and Lord Grey's secretary; or it may have been a piece of banter, mimicking the false pedantry of the commentator E.K.

Of all Sidney's works, the *Defence of Poesy* gives the most vivid impression of what it must have been like to meet him. It was rapidly written, in the 'extemporal vein' admired by Thomas Nashe. Quotations have not been checked, and mistakes such as 'Bubonax' for 'Hipponax' in the final sentence show that he was drawing examples from a well-stocked mind, not from a laboriously compiled notebook. The frequent use of 'truly', 'forsooth', 'marry' and the like mark the writing as very close to natural speech. According to Greville, Walsingham often told him

that his Philip did so far overshoot him in his own bow as those friends which at first were Philip's for the Secretary's sake, within a while became so fully owned and possessed by Sir Philip as now he held them at the second-hand, by his son-in-law's native courtesy.[59]

Reading the *Defence*, we can easily imagine how this might come about. Walsingham was a gifted linguist, a brilliant spy-master, and a man who combined political sophistication with unusual personal integrity. But he lacked the fire, charm and humour of his son-in-law, as expressed in many of the *Defence*'s most famous passages:

Only the poet, disdaining to be tied to any such subjection, lifted up with the vigour of his own invention, doth grow in effect another nature, in making things either better than nature bringeth forth, or, quite anew, forms such as never were in nature, as the Heroes, Demigods, Cyclops, Chimeras, Furies, and such like: so as he goeth hand in hand with nature, not enclosed within the narrow warrant of her gifts, but freely ranging only within the zodiac of his own wit. Nature never set forth the earth in so rich tapestry as divers poets have done; neither with so pleasant rivers, fruitful trees, sweet-smelling flowers, nor whatsoever else may make the too much loved earth more lovely. Her world is brazen, the poets only deliver a golden.[60]

Figurative techniques display the superiority of the poet to the historian or philosopher:

[The poet] doth, as if your journey should lie through a fair vineyard, at the first give you a cluster of grapes, that full of that taste, you may long to pass further. He beginneth not with obscure definitions, which must blur the margin with interpretations, and load the memory with doubtfulness; but he cometh to you with words set in delightful proportion, either accompanied with, or prepared for, the well-enchanting skill of music; and with a tale forsooth he cometh unto you, with a tale which holdeth children from play, and old men from the chimney corner.[61]

Some of the old men in Sidney's life, such as Walsingham, were surely kept from their chimney corners by the treatise itself.

Not all of the *Defence* is so positive, but the negative passages are no less entertaining. For instance, Sidney ridiculed popular drama for its defiance of the Aristotelian unities of place, time and action:

where you shall have Asia of the one side, and Afric of the other, and so many other under-kingdoms, that the player, when he cometh in, must ever begin with telling where he is, or else the tale will not be conceived. Now you shall have three ladies walk to gather flowers: and then we must believe the stage to be a garden. By and by we hear news of a shipwreck in the same place, and then are we to blame if we accept it not for a rock. Upon the back of that comes out a hideous monster with fire and smoke: and then the miserable beholders are bound to take it for a cave. While in the meantime two armies fly in, represented with four swords and bucklers: and then what hard heart will not receive it for a pitched field?[62]

Since only a few pages earlier he had defended metaphor and allegory with reference to the ease with which place-references in the theatre can be grasped,[63] this account seems rather severe. Sidney is good at making works he dislikes sound absurd. While praising his own protégé Spenser, he is dismissive of the Earl of Oxford's protégé John Lyly, whose *Euphues* and *Euphues and his England* are unmistakably described:

Now for similitudes, in certain printed discourses, I think all herbarists, all stories of beasts, fowls, and fishes are rifled up, that they come in multitudes to wait upon any of our conceits; which certainly is as absurd a surfeit to the ears as is possible. For the force of a similitude not being to prove anything to a contrary disputer, but only to explain to a willing hearer, when that is done, the rest is a most tedious prattling, rather over-swaying the memory from the purpose whereto they were applied, than any whit informing the judgement, already either satisfied, or by similitudes not to be satisfied.[64]

This may indeed have been Sidney's opinion, but continued resentment of Oxford no doubt lent extra vehemence to its expression. Likewise, his scornful remarks about derivative and unconvincing love poets who rush into print would apply very aptly to Thomas Watson, whose *Hekatompathia* was dedicated to Oxford in the spring of 1582. A manuscript version had been presented to him a year or so earlier, and Watson obsequiously drew attention to Oxford's favourable perusal of it.[65] Though the entry in the Stationers'

Register referred to Watson's poems as 'manifesting the true frenzy of love', they are works of conspicuous pedantry. Each 'passion' is prefaced by a headnote summarizing its themes and drawing attention to its learned sources, and some are also 'puffed' with favourable comments by Watson's friends (cf. VII, XLVII, LXVII). In a Latin poem addressed to his book Watson expressed the hope that his verses might find their way to the desks of Sidney and Dyer:

Thereupon each will peruse you favourably with a serene countenance, and each will overlook your blemishes.[66]

However, Sidney probably viewed Watson's *Hekatompathia* with the same scorn as Lyly's *Euphues*, and it may have given an irritant, grit-in-oyster-like impetus to his own quite different sonnet sequence. There was that, at least, to be said for it. Just as Gascoigne's clod-hopping royal shows provoked Sidney's more fresh and fluent ones, and Gosson's puritanical diatribe provoked his richly humane *Defence*, Watson's 'passions', full of 'swelling phrases', sharpened Sidney's awareness of the need for urgency and naturalism in love poetry. This, however, was directed to a different audience.

While Sidney's most irresistible public face was displayed in the *Defence*, *Astrophil and Stella* revealed a darker, more private side. In place of the talented, well-travelled young man deeply interested in poetry as an adjunct to public life, *Astrophil and Stella* showed an introverted, withdrawn figure who thinks it 'As good to write, as for to lie and groan'.[67] He is unable to summon up any real interest in such topics as the likelihood of a Turkish advance, or the current standing of William of Orange in the Netherlands, or even his own father's achievements in Ireland, 'for still I think of you'.[68] Astrophil is at once self-absorbed and self-aware. He is conscious of the social effect of his introversion, yet unable to snap out of it. In one of many sonnets pervaded by *l'esprit de l'escalier*, he broods neurotically on the figure he cuts:

Because I oft, in dark abstracted guise,
Seem most alone in greatest company,
With dearth of words, or answers quite awry,
To them that would make speech of speech arise,
They deem, and of that doom the rumour flies,
That poison foul of bubbling pride doth lie
So in my swelling breast, that only I
Fawn on myself, and others do despise.
Yet pride, I think, doth not my soul possess ...[69]

We have already seen how the real-life Sidney could give deep offence by remaining 'in dead silence of purpose',[70] and any attempt to confine the silent, proud-seeming Astrophil to the world of fiction is defeated by a close parallel to this sonnet in a letter to Walsingham from Utrecht, 24 March 1585/6:

I understand I am called very ambitious and proud at home, but certainly if they knew my hea[rt] they would not altogether so judge me.[71]

If the cheerful and confident *Defence* was written for the benefit of the family Sidney was to marry into, the melancholy *Astrophil and Stella*, conversely, was written for the girl he did not marry, Penelope Devereux. The prose work radiates confidence in the future. The possibilities for English literature seemed boundless, and might be accompanied by military activism. If Sidney had lived to see the defeat of the Spanish Armada in 1588 and the advent of such writers as Marlowe, Nashe, Shakespeare and Jonson, he would have found his belief that English poetry was at its best 'even when the trumpet of Mars did sound loudest'[72] gloriously vindicated. *Astrophil and Stella*, on the other hand, plots the speaker's sterile journey into moral and emotional impasse.

Sidney must have known at the outset that this was where he was going. It has been suggested that he was attempting to construct a secondary world that offered him the 'mastery' he lacked in his external life.[73] This notion applies much better to the 'Old' *Arcadia* than to *Astrophil and Stella*. The idea that Sidney hoped to find compensation in the world of love for the 'defeat' he experienced in 'the viciously competitive world of the court'[74] underestimates his deliberate artistry. The careful design shows that Sidney knew well the direction in which his misguided lover was moving. Though the first-time reader may be surprised by Astrophil's repeated defeats, Sidney was not. Yet for Sidney personally, the composition of *Astrophil and Stella* may indeed have furnished some imaginative mastery of pain. It replaced the uncontrollable and largely unexpressible disappointments of his public life, in which he had been prepared for great things but fobbed off with small ones, with cathartic images of pain in a different sphere. Sidney, over and beyond Astrophil, could decide when and at what level of intensity to end his emotional self-laceration.

The extent to which, in *Astrophil and Stella*, 'love is not love' should not be exaggerated. Despite the claim that it shows 'metaphorizing of ambition as love',[75] there is no doubt that from the reader's point of view Sidney was exploring sexual rather than political frustration. While Thomas Watson's donnish lover made an easy transition from unconvincing love poems to a rather more convincing misogyny, Sidney's Astrophil is persuasively obsessive, self-deceived, over-excited, and tormented with lust which at moments finds expression in masturbatory fantasy (Song x). In considering the origins of *Astrophil and Stella* Sidney's sexuality cannot be wholly evaded, though it remains impossible to arrive at definite conclusions.

Outside his literary works there is little evidence of Sidney's susceptibility to women. According to his own self-projection as Astrophil, he was

> In nature apt to like, when I did see,
> Beauties, which were of many carats fine[76]

yet quite untroubled by passion until Stella came along. There may be something in this. Languet was worried by Sidney's lack of interest in marriage, and his disquiet at the 'unmanly' pursuits of the English Court[77] may suggest awareness of homo-erotic relationships there. At a distance of 400 years assessments of sexual orientation are deeply problematic, and the application of twentieth-century labels within such a different culture is apt to be extremely misleading.[78] Nevertheless, there is little doubt that Sidney's close friend Fulke Greville did approximate to what would now be called homosexual,[79] and that Greville was determined to suggest that his friendship with Sidney had priority over all other bonds. In 1615 he formed a grandiose scheme for a joint tomb for himself and Sidney in St Paul's, with a stone commemorating Sidney above, himself below.[80] The monument was never constructed. Even with Sidney's daughter safely dead, there were many people still alive who would have considered this memorial, which removed Sidney from his close family, unacceptable. Instead, Greville enshrined his friendship in his written *Dedication* (formerly known as *Life*). His own proclivities were less glamorously suggested by his sordid death in 1628, at the hands of a disgruntled servant. After clumsily stabbing Greville, who was half-undressed and 'coming from stool' at the time of the assault, the servant, Ralph Hayward, immediately ran to his own chamber and killed himself.[81] Before he knew that Hayward was dead, Greville asked that he should not be prosecuted. This could reflect magnanimity, but may more probably indicate that there were aspects of his relationship with Hayward which he did not wish to have exposed in court.

If Greville's attachment to Sidney had a homosexual element, that does not, of course, prove that it was reciprocated in equal terms. But Sidney's marked lack of enthusiasm for marriage, combined with the fact that his two closest friends, Dyer and Greville, were both among that 'tiny handful' of Elizabethan aristocrats who never married,[82] provokes the suspicion that male friendship was in some ways more congenial to him than heterosexual union. In the 'Two Pastoralls' included in Francis Davison's *A Poetical Rapsody* (1602) he suggested as much. Though they reached print rather late, Ringler endorses the authenticity of these poems. Their likely route of transmission identifies them as highly personal writings. Sidney is said to have died in the arms of his secretary, William Temple, who came into his service in 1585. Temple's next employer was William Davison, a long plea for whom forms the central poem in his son's compilation. The 'Two Pastoralls' were almost certainly among Sidney's papers at the time of his death, reaching the Davison family through Temple. Both celebrate his love for Dyer and Greville:

> ... My two and I be met,
> A happy blessed Trinity;
> As three most jointly set

In firmest band of unity.
Join hearts and hands, so let it be,
Make but one mind in bodies three.

Welcome my two to me, E.D. F.G. P.S.
The number best beloved,
Within my heart you be
In friendship unremoved ...[83]

In the first poem he gives this triple friendship the pre-eminence normally accorded to heterosexual unions:

Like lovers do their love
So joy I, in you seeing ...
And as the turtle-dove
To mate with whom he liveth,
Such comfort, fervent love
Of you, to my heart giveth.

The second poem, entitled 'Disprayse of a Courtly life', is more complex, portraying an unhappy Sidney-figure 'Now in servile Court remaining', who pines for the literary pleasures he once enjoyed with his two friends. He rejects the 'art of love' as irrelevant to true friendship, longing to return to the time when

under shade
Oaten reeds me music made,
Striving with my mates in song.[84]

He prays to Pan to help him:

Only for my two loves' sake, Sir Ed. D. and M.F.G.
In whose love I pleasure take,
Only two do me delight
With their ever-pleasing sight,
Of all men with thee retaining,
Grant me with those two remaining.[85]

In a period when male friendship was regarded as a lofty ideal, endorsed by Aristotle, Cicero and more recent writers such as Castiglione, Sidney's friendship poems should not be too crudely construed as declarations of homosexual attraction. They lack the technical intricacy and excited urgency of feeling of most of the far more numerous poems Sidney wrote within 'heterosexual' conventions. Yet if we are in search of his most deeply rooted attachments, we may find them here. In friendship with Greville, in particular, whom he had known as a 'good boy' (see above, p. 30) since the age of ten, he found a security and mutual understanding, analogous to what he enjoyed with his sister, far removed from the 'hell' of erotic passion[86] that he analysed in *Astrophil and Stella*.

A variety of motives prompted the composition of *Astrophil and Stella*. As he strove to defend English as a literary language Sidney became acutely aware of the shortcomings of native love poetry. Du Bellay and Estienne defended the French language with the strength of Ronsard and the Pléiade movement behind them, but Elizabethan writers had as yet produced no love lyrics with 'poetical sinews'. Alliteratively titled collections like *The Paradise of Dainty Devices* (1576) and *A Gorgeous Gallery of Gallant Inventions* (1578) were crammed with derivative and predictable love poems. A fairly typical specimen in *The Paradise* was 'The complaint of a lover wearing black and tawny', by Sidney's enemy Oxford, in bouncing poulter's measure:

> The more I followed on, the more she fled away,
> As Daphne did full long agone, Apollo's wishful prey;
> The more my plaints resound, the less she pities me,
> The more I sought the less I found, that mine she meant to be.[87]

Something had to be done to show that English could be handled more 'forcibly' than this. Sidney was probably already in the early stages of *Astrophil and Stella* when he wrote the *Defence*, but the completion of the treatise sharpened his sense of what was needed.

Whether Sidney was also deeply in love with Penelope Devereux, we have no way of knowing. Numerous details match up with what we know of actuality, or conform well with it. Yet all these may have been included in the interests of 'forcibleness'. For instance, the account in Sonnet 2 of the speaker falling in love 'Not at first sight' conforms with what we know about the non-fruition of the plan for Philip and Penelope to marry in 1576. Sonnet 33, which also seems to allude to this, has already been discussed (see above, p. 199). Stella, like Penelope Devereux, is musical, being at one point represented as singing Astrophil's songs (Sonnet 57; Songs iii and vi). Like Penelope Devereux, Stella is a fluent letter-writer (Song iv); like her, she is unhappily married to a man called Rich (Sonnets 24, 37); like her, she has a 'fair mother' (Song iv); like her, she has fair hair and dark eyes (Sonnets 7, 9, 20 and *passim*). Then again, Astrophil's crest, like Sidney's, is an arrow-head (Sonnet 65. 14); his father has tried to pacify Ireland (30. 9–10); he has a high reputation as a horseman and tilter (41, 49, 53); he has friends who want to discuss politics with him (30, 51); his Christian name may be Philip (83); and it is possible, if these sonnets were written after January 1583, that the addresses to himself as 'sir fool' and 'sir Phip' (53. 7, 83. 14) allude sarcastically to his recent acquisition of a knighthood.

Yet the fact that many details match up with things we know to be true of

Sidney and Penelope Devereux does not prove the authenticity of the inner emotions. There is no doubt that at his best Sidney is marvellously convincing. Some of the most persuasive sonnets are those in which Astrophil struggles to break free of his passion, such as 47:

> What, have I thus betrayed my liberty?
> Can those black beams such burning marks engrave
> In my free side? Or am I born a slave,
> Whose neck becomes such yoke of tyranny?
> Or want I sense to feel my misery?
> Or spirit, disdain of such disdain to have,
> Who for long faith, though daily help I crave,
> Mav get no alms, but scorn of beggary?
> Virtue, awake: beauty but beauty is;
> I may, I must, I can, I will, I do
> Leave following that, which it is gain to miss.
> Let her go. Soft, but here she comes. Go to,
> Unkind, I love you not – O me, that eye
> Doth make my heart give to my tongue the lie.

The present-tense immediacy of Stella's arrival – 'Soft, but here she comes' – gains extraordinary vividness from its containment within the sonnet's narrow room. But passages near the end of the sequence may cause us to re-interpret all that we have read before. The first sixty-three sonnets show Astrophil rejecting second-hand, pedantic poets like Lyly and Watson, and moving steadily towards a climax of excited anticipation, expressed in the quibble by which Astrophil maintains that Stella's 'No, no' is really 'Yes', for 'in one speech two negatives affirm' (63. 14). The First Song affirms his devotion to Stella alone. Sonnets 64–72 describe a rapprochement in which Stella, like Pamela in the 'Old' *Arcadia*, agrees to return his love on condition that he sustains a 'virtuous course'. Like Musidorus, Astrophil is unable to restrain himself. Song ii shows him stealing a kiss from Stella while she is asleep, and blaming himself 'for no more taking'. In the next ten sonnets he felicitates himself on his success, but 83, addressed to Stella's sparrow Philip, sounds a warning note. Like the lecherous lover, the lecherous bird kisses too greedily:

> Cannot such grace your silly self content,
> But you must needs with those lips billing be,
> And through those lips drink nectar from that tongue?
> Leave that, sir Phip, lest off your neck be wrung.
> (83. 11–14)

A fresh attempt to seduce Stella is dramatized in the Fourth Song, a night-time meeting, but ends in repulse. In Sonnet 86 Stella has changed her demeanour, and in the Fifth Song Astrophil, now hopeless, unleashes curses, using the threat of withdrawal of his poetic services to bully her into submission:

> Think now no more to hear of warm fine-odoured snow,
> Nor blushing lilies, nor pearls' ruby-hidden row,
> Nor of that golden sea, whose waves in curls are broken:
> But of thy soul, so fraught with such ungratefulness,
> As where thou soon might'st help, most faith doth most oppress;
> Ungrateful who is called, the worst of evils is spoken.
>
> (Song v. 37–42)

The crucial Eighth Song, told in an authoritative-sounding third person which merges in the final line into the first person, describes another encounter between the lovers, in spring, 'In a grove most rich of shade'. Both are unhappy, and mutually supportive:

> Him great harms had taught much care,
> Her fair neck a foul yoke bare,
> But her sight his cares did banish,
> In his sight her yoke did vanish.

Astrophil pleads urgently for fruition, and follows up his arguments with another attempted assault:

> There his hands in their speech fain
> Would have made tongue's language plain:
> But her hands his hands repelling
> Gave repulse all grace excelling.

Stella replies with an ambiguous speech in which in

> such wise she love denied
> As yet love she signified.

She acknowledges that she loves him, and derives all her joy in life from him. 'Tyrant honour' alone compels her to refuse him, and she forbids further approaches for fear of discovery:

> Therefore, dear, this no more move,
> Lest, though I leave not thy love,
> Which too deep in me is framed,
> I should blush when thou art named.

From this point on it is downhill almost all the way, following Astrophil's conclusion

> That therewith my song is broken.

It is noticeable that the relationship disintegrates faster on Astrophil's side than on Stella's. In Sonnet 87 Stella weeps for Astrophil's imminent departure, and he weeps because she weeps. Earlier we would have expected Astrophil alone to be desolated. Sonnets 88, 89 and 91 concern temptations to unfaithfulness. Though Astrophil protests that his attraction to other women testifies to his real devotion to Stella, this is not convincing; his account of the other girls' beauties is too long-drawn-out:

> If this dark place yet show, like candle light,
> Some beauty's piece, as amber-coloured head,
> Milk hands, rose cheeks, or lips more sweet, more red,
> Or seeing jets, black, but in blackness bright:
> They please, I do confess they please mine eyes.
> But why? Because of you they models be,
> Models such be wood-globes of glistering skies.
> Dear, therefore be not jealous over me ...
>
> (91. 5–12)

Stella's jealousy may be connected with her anger with Astrophil in Sonnet 93, which is succeeded by three sonnets of misery and self-hatred. In 97 another lady, 'Dian's peer', tries to console him. In 100 Stella is again weeping; in 101–2 she is ill. Though 103 and 104 reaffirm Astrophil's devotion, they do not remove the reader's suspicion that things are falling apart. A last encounter is enacted in the Eleventh Song, again a night-time dialogue, which Browning was to draw on in his menacingly dark 'Serenade at the Villa'. Once more, Astrophil has to reassure Stella of his fidelity:

> 'What if you new beauties see,
> Will they not stir new affection?'
> I will think they pictures be,
> Image-like of saints' perfection,
> Poorly counterfeiting thee.

Just as Astrophil seems on the point of getting some concession out of her they are interrupted, and he is compelled 'from louts to run away'. The mysterious Sonnet 105 chronicles a missed opportunity of seeing Stella, again by night:

> Cursed be the page from whom the bad torch fell,
> Cursed be the night which did your strife resist,
> Cursed be the coachman, which did drive so fast,
> With no worse curse than absence makes me taste.
>
> (105. 11–14)

Perhaps, as in the tragic myth of Hero and Leander, the wind has blown out the lamp which would have brought the lovers together. The Bright manuscript's reading of 'Unhappy light' rather than 'Unhappy sight' in the first line suggests that the addressee throughout is Astrophil's 'bad torch'.[88] Enclosed between two final sonnets of misery and solitude – 106 incorporating yet another reference to the 'store of fair ladies' who are trying to console him – is an extremely telling sonnet in which Astrophil begs Stella to release him from the servitude of writing verses for her:

> Sweet, for a while give respite to my heart,
> Which pants as though it still should leap to thee;
> And on my thoughts give thy lieutenancy
> To this great cause, which needs both use and art;
> And as a queen, who from her presence send
> Whom she employs, dismiss from thee my wit,
> Till it have wrought what thy own will attends.
> On servant's shame oft master's blame doth sit;
> O, let not fools in me thy works reprove,
> And scorning say, 'See, what it is to love!'
> (107. 5–14)

The proprietorial 'Sweet' suggests that, despite the lack of physical union, the lovers are now on extremely familiar terms. But Sidney/Astrophil wants to write no more love poems. He plans to exercise his 'wit' elsewhere, on a project that Penelope/Stella herself favours.

Perhaps all along, we suddenly suspect, Sidney may have been writing these explosively passionate love poems because Penelope Devereux, to whose family he had some long-standing obligations, had asked him to do so, even as his sister had 'desired' him to write the *Arcadia*. Penelope Devereux's later patronage of poets, translators and musicians shows her taste to have been exceptionally sophisticated.[89] The skills of the orator and the debater, which Sidney possessed in a high degree, are very close to those of the actor. It may be that the whole Astrophil–Stella love affair was a kind of literary charade, in which both real-life participants knew exactly what was going on. In the preface to the first printed edition, Nashe wrote of *Astrophil and Stella* as a 'theatre of pleasure':

> here you shall find a paper stage strewed with pearl, an artificial heaven to overshadow the fair frame, and crystal walls to encounter your curious eyes while the tragicomedy of love is performed by starlight.[90]

Nashe was a close and appreciative student of Sidney's writings, who may have understood the character of Sidney's sonnet sequence better than those post-Romantic readers who have referred confidently to Sidney as 'nourishing an adulterous passion'.[91] It is impossible to prove that Sidney did not nourish an adulterous passion for Penelope Devereux. Yet equally, Sonnet 107, especially coming after so many allusions to Astrophil's attraction to other women, may be read as giving the game away. The brilliant love poet Philip Sidney may have resembled the brilliant tilter Phalantus in the 'New' *Arcadia*. 'Taking love upon him like a fashion', Phalantus pays elaborate court to a woman he does not love:

> he with cheerful looks would speak sorrowful words, using the phrase of his affection in so high a style that Mercury would not have wooed Venus with more magnificent eloquence, but else neither in behaviour nor action accusing in himself any great trouble in mind whether he sped or no.[92]

This may have been how it was for Sidney. He enjoyed Penelope Devereux's society, he was sorry for her in her uncongenial marriage, and he felt guilty that he had failed to forestall it. But he had no real ambition to become her lover in the full sense. While making no lasting union with either of the Devereux sisters, he at least amused Penelope with a vivid portrayal of her as a woman whom he passionately adored.

If the writing of *Astrophil and Stella* was a kind of game, it was a risky one to play for a young man who wanted to be taken seriously by the older generation. Though the *Defence* strengthened his credentials as Walsingham's son-in-law, the sonnet sequence surely weakened them. It was a delicate balancing act. In the *Defence* Sidney criticized bad love poets for writing unconvincingly; yet if his own love sonnets were too convincing, and came to his father-in-law's eyes, they might not be taken in the right spirit. The solution may be outlined in Sonnet 34. 7–8:

> 'But will not wise men think thy words fond ware?'
> Then be they close, and so none shall displease.

Astrophil and Stella does not appear to have been circulated during Sidney's lifetime in the way that we know the 'Old' *Arcadia* was. Probably, apart from a few of the songs, it was effectively kept 'close', so that 'wise men' in Sidney's immediate circle knew little of it. Penelope Devereux was good at keeping secrets, as was shown a few years later in her coded correspondence with members of James VI's Court.[93] Physically, as well as thematically, *Astrophil and Stella* may have been confined to her and her immediate circle. Even many years later it was perceived as marginal to Sidney's literary achievements, for Fulke Greville, though he imitated many of its songs and sonnets in his own *Caelica*, did not even mention it in his *Dedication*.

The composition of *Astrophil and Stella* may have been an inappropriate preliminary to marriage to Frances Walsingham, but the disadvantage was not all on Sidney's side. Daughters of eminent statesmen were extremely attractive to fortune-hunters and aspirants to favour, and despite her extreme youth Frances Walsingham seems already to have been snapped up by one such. After the death of her sister Mary in 1580 she became her father's only heir. Walsingham could say, like old Capulet of Juliet,

> Earth hath swallowed all my hopes but she;
> She is the hopeful lady of my earth.[94]

Some time in 1581 a man called John Wickerson formed a 'rash contract with Mistress Frances', and wrote from the Marshalsea in about February 1582/3 to beg her father for release, after two years' imprisonment.[95] Some form of legal betrothal had been gone through, for Wickerson implored Walsingham to

> vouchsafe yet more at the length to grant your consent and goodwill for performance of their said contract in the holy state of matrimony.

As Wallace says, the document

> certainly seems to refer to Frances Walsingham. With whom else would Walsingham's dislike of Wickerson's contract of matrimony be so strong that he would imprison the would-be husband for two years?

Yet Wallace confines the episode to a footnote, and it is not even mentioned by other biographers. It must surely have been a factor contributing to Walsingham's willingness to enter on a fresh contract for his daughter which was financially disadvantageous. We have no way of knowing whether the Sidney family were aware of Frances's previous entanglement, still less whether she herself was a willing party to it. Nothing more is heard of John Wickerson. But on 18 February 1582/3 John Dee recorded:

> the Lady Walsingham came suddenly into my house very freely, and shortly after that she was gone came Sir Francis himself and Mr Dyer.[96]

The Walsinghams, whose house at Barn Elms was near Dee's at Mortlake, often paid him visits, consulting him about New World investments and other matters. On this occasion the worried parents may have come to discuss the perplexing affair of their daughter's marriage. The Wickerson problem may also explain Walsingham's curious failure to consult the Queen before entering on the contract with Sidney. On 19 March he wrote at length to Hatton expressing surprise at the Queen's indignation, yet it could easily have been foreseen:

> As I think myself infinitely bound unto you for your honourable and friendly defence of the intended match between my daughter and Mr Sidney, so do I find it strange

that Her Majesty should be offended withal. It is either to proceed of the matter or of the manner. For the matter, I hope when Her Majesty shall weigh the due circumstances of place, person and quality, there can grow no just cause of offence. If the manner be misliked for that Her Majesty is not made acquainted withal, I am no person of that state but that it may be thought a presumption for me to trouble Her Majesty with a private marriage between a free gentleman of equal calling with my daughter ... As I thought it always unfit for me to acquaint Her Majesty with a matter of so base a subject as this poor match, so did I never seek to have the matter concealed from Her Majesty, seeing no reason why there should grow any offence thereby. I pray you, Sir, therefore, if she enter into any further speech of the matter, let her understand that you learn generally that the match is held for concluded, and withal to let her know how just cause I shall have to find myself aggrieved if Her Majesty shall show her mislike thereof.[97]

Walsingham protests too much, and it is striking that in the heat of his self-righteous indignation he has forgotten that the match is no longer quite 'so base a subject' as it would have been a few weeks earlier, for on 13 January his future son-in-law had been knighted, and should now be referred to as 'Sir Philip'.

If the circumstances of Sidney's knighthood had been more gratifying Walsingham would probably have remembered about it. Disappointingly, though, the honour done to Sidney did not represent an acknowledgement by the Queen of his worth; it flowed from his old friend John Casimir, on whom she had bestowed the Garter four years earlier (see above, p. 158). Both he and the King of Denmark were formally installed at Windsor Castle, but *in absentia*.[98] The King of Denmark was represented by Peregrine Bertie, Lord Willoughby, whom Sidney was later to describe as 'my very friend, and indeed a valiant and frank gentleman'.[99] Willoughby had led a diplomatic mission to Denmark the previous summer. Casimir himself nominated Sidney as his proxy, with the consequence that he became a knight, though not one of the select band of Knights of the Garter. If anything, Casimir's choice of Sidney may have worsened his standing with Elizabeth. Greville reports Sidney's discerning comment on the Queen's failure to respond to William of Orange's appeals for his advancement:

princes love not that foreign powers should have extraordinary interest in their subjects, much less to be taught by them how they should place their own, as arguments either upbraiding ignorance or lack of large rewarding goodness in them.[100]

This observation gives the clue to Sidney's continued lack of advancement. In Elizabeth's eyes, foreign princes rated him too high, and she would prefer to honour him in her own good time, rather than being bounced into it by the hothead Casimir.

Yet Sidney did not cease to put his talents and resources at Elizabeth's disposal. At New Year 1582/3 he gave her

a jewel of gold like a castle, garnished with small diamonds on the one side, being a pot to set flowers in.[101]

No doubt the flowery fortress represented Elizabeth herself, her beauty and her strength. In the summer Sidney helped to entertain a flamboyant Polish visitor, the Palatine Prince Albert Alasco. Many attributes made Alasco memorable to his hosts, including his possession of

a white beard, of such length and breadth, as that lying in his bed, and parting the same with his hands, the same overspread all his breast and shoulders, himself greatly delighting therein, and reputing it an ornament.[102]

In June he was splendidly entertained in Oxford, where he was diverted with fireworks and plays at Christ Church and dinner at All Souls. Gager's comedy *Rivales* included scenes of rustic love-making and drunkenness; the Latin tragedy *Dido* was illustrated with a huge marchpane panel showing Dido feasting Aeneas.[103] Alasco was a conspicuous consumer, and crumbs of marzipan may have further adorned his magnificent beard. Among the disputations conducted for him was one to whose conclusion Sidney must have assented, denying the validity of astrology.[104] On returning from Oxford, Sidney, Sir William Russell and others accompanied Alasco on a visit to John Dee, arriving at Mortlake in the Queen's barge and heralded by the Queen's trumpeters.[105]

Alasco splashed his money about to such an extent that he had eventually to leave in a hurry to escape his English creditors.[106] He stayed just long enough to attend Sidney's wedding, which was at last solemnized on 21 September, place unknown (it may have been at St Olave's, Hart Street, just opposite Walsingham House). After this date Sidney seems to have written few original poems, though he continued to write prose. Perhaps he followed the example of his own Lalus, who when asked by Basilius to sing:

directly refused him, saying he should within few days be married to the fair Kala and since he had gotten his desire he would sing no more.[107]

11

1584–5

VISIONS AND REVISIONS

... And indeed there will be time ...
And time yet for a hundred indecisions
And for a thousand visions and revisions ...[1]

Hope deferred maketh the heart sick.[2]

When Sidney embarked on married life he seemed to have plenty of time in hand. Barn Elms in Surrey and Walsingham House in Seething Lane were new and congenial settings in which to pursue literary interests away from Court without having to make the long journey to Wiltshire. Though he wrote no more love poems, he was engaged on numerous long-term projects, chief among them being the radical revision and expansion of the *Arcadia*, on which he had already begun to work at the time of his marriage. A deepening commitment to the intellectual French brand of Protestantism fostered in Francis Walsingham's household was expressed in translations of his friend Du Plessis Mornay's treatise *De la vérité de la religion Chrestienne* (Antwerp, 1581) and of Salluste du Bartas's epic poem about the creation of the world, *La Semaine ou Création du monde* (Paris, 1578). Strangely, in neither case do any of the texts that we know to have existed appear to survive. Greville wrote to Walsingham of Sidney's translation, 'among divers other notable works', of 'Monsieur Du Plessis' book against Atheism':

so as both in respect of love between Plessis and him, besides other affinities in their courses, but especially Sir Philip's uncomparable judgement, I think fit there be made stay of that mercenary book, so that Sir Philip might have all those religious works which are worthily due to his life and death.[3]

The 'mercenary book' was Arthur Golding's translation of *De la vérité*, entered in the Stationers' Register within days of the news of Sidney's death, and

Engraved portrait of Sir Philip Sidney from Henry Holland, *Herōologica,* 1620 (Bodleian Library)

published early in 1587, which he claimed was completed at Sidney's request. However, it does not appear to retain any of Sidney's wording, being written with an avoidance of Latinisms which is not at all like Sidney, and Golding's close association with the Earl of Oxford (he was his uncle by marriage, and had been his tutor[4]) makes it probable that the project was, as Greville said, 'mercenary'. Sidney's translation of Du Bartas was known both to Moffet and Matthew Gwinne.[5] According to John Florio, Sidney's daughter, and perhaps also Lady Rich, had a copy of Sidney's translation of Du Bartas, for in his dedication of the second volume of Montaigne's *Essayes* to these two ladies he urged them to publish it:

> ... as that worthy did divinely even in French translating some part of that excellent Du Plessis, and (as I have seen) the first *Semaine* of that Arch-poet Du Bartas (which, good ladies, be so good to all, as all this age may see, and after-ages honour ...[6]

Copies of the translations from French may have been held by a small group of survivors from Sidney's circle. Yet for some reason no collection of the 'religious works' belonging to the last three years of Sidney's life was ever published, and apart from the forty-three Psalms that he translated they now appear to be lost.

Protestant French friends had taken a close interest in Sidney's marriage. In July 1583 an envoy of the King of Navarre, M. de Ségur, brought a letter to him from Du Plessis Mornay which concluded:

> I wish to know whether you are married or not. I suppose you are, for I have had no letters from you for three months, and I take it for granted that that could not be were you not busied in some very special fashion.[7]

In May Jean Lobbet wrote to Walsingham from Strasbourg:

I have been very glad to hear of the alliance to be between you and Mr Philip Sidney, who is to marry your daughter. I think I saw her in your house at Paris. I rejoice with them both, and it seems to me that the match is well made; I pray God to give it his blessing, which I am sure he will, as is promised in the 128th Psalm.[8]

Psalm CXXVIII promises the married man a long life of peace and prosperity:

Thy wife shall be as a fruitful vine by the sides of thy house: thy children like olive plants round about thy table ...
The Lord shall bless thee out of Zion: and thou shalt see the good of Jerusalem all the days of thy life.
Yea, thou shalt see thy children's children, and peace upon Israel.[9]

Lobbet's prayer was denied. Only three years and a day elapsed between Sidney's marriage and his fatal injury in the Netherlands. The good of 'Jerusalem', or England, was far from secure, with continual turbulence in Scotland, France and the Netherlands; and meanwhile the 'olive plants' round Sidney's table were slow to germinate. Alone among early biographers, Dr Moffet drew attention to this:

I shall not say what sorrow I have felt that such an illustrious man should have lacked children for all of two years – he whom all Englishmen had chosen and expected to father another Theseus or Hercules for us and our country. When I, in his presence, deplored this slight infertility in his wife, Philip, judging the matter fairly and weighing it according to its importance, answered that the inconvenience of sterility ought to be mitigated by a convenient patience, and ought to be accepted as in accord with the divine will, which alone brings anything to pass.[10]

We can only speculate about the reasons why Lady Sidney did not become pregnant until she had been married for over a year. If Moffet correctly, though from a smugly masculinist viewpoint, identified the problem as deriving from Frances's 'slight infertility', this may have been connected with her youth. She was born in about October 1567,[11] being barely sixteen at the time of her marriage. In a period when the average age at puberty was two or three years higher than it is in western Europe today she may as yet have been sub-fertile. It is even possible that consummation was postponed to await her full maturing, in which case Moffet's remark was tactless. Alternatively or additionally there may have been sexual difficulties which Sidney did not choose to discuss with Dr Moffet, deflecting further enquiry with his Calvinist response.

Though much of Sidney's time was now spent in the Walsingham household, there is no reason to think that his was a 'companionate' marriage. Despite his pleasure in the company of 'courtly nymphs' such as his sister and Penelope Devereux, he seems to have cared little for the society of his teenage bride.

Friendships with older men were what Sidney was best at, and the strength of the new bond lay in Francis Walsingham's unwavering respect for his talented 'son', not in any particularly close emotional attachment between the newlyweds. If Sidney ever discovered his wife's previous betrothal to John Wickerson, to which she may have actively consented, that must have tarnished the gilt on his gingerbread. To marry such a young girl, and still not be her first mate, would be exceedingly galling to someone so easily affronted as Sidney. Nor was young Frances a highly educated and spirited woman of letters like Penelope Devereux. It is clear that Sidney did not share his continuing literary pursuits with her. Frances had no copy of the 'New' *Arcadia* until after her husband's death, as we learn from Fulke Greville's letter to Walsingham in November 1586:

I have sent my lady your daughter at her request a correction of that old one ... which he left in trust with me ...[12]

It was to Greville, not to his wife, that he entrusted his literary work-in-progress when he left for the Netherlands, just as it was to Greville and Dyer, not to his wife, that he bequeathed all his books.[13] Once deprived of even that occasional part of his companionship that she had once enjoyed, Frances was clearly anxious to be excluded no longer from her husband's imaginative life. It would be interesting to know what she made of it. Despite her second, more splendid, marriage to the Earl of Essex there is a noticeable lack of dedications to Frances née Walsingham. For some reason, neither her parents nor her first husband seem to have fostered an interest in literature. The only printed works addressed to her are the English version of Thomas Watson's *Meliboeus* and Spenser's pastoral elegy *Astrophel*. Both poems are consolatory, suggesting that Sidney has attained heavenly fulfilment, leaving Frances free to enjoy her earthly union with Essex, and both look as much towards Essex as towards his new wife. In another book in 1590, *Italian Madrigals Englished*, Watson made much of Sidney's known friendship with his father-in-law 'Meliboeus', claiming that now he, too, is dead the two men have a welcome opportunity to continue in heaven the companionship begun in Paris and at Barn Elms:

When Meliboeus' soul, flying hence, departed,
Astrophil, whom not long before death darted,
Rising up fro the star with him late graced,
Down along the heavens he swiftly traced,
Where, meeting with his friend, they both embraced,
And both together joyfully were placed.
O thrice happy pair of friends, O Arcady's treasure,
Whose virtues drew them up to heavenly pleasure.[14]

In the penultimate lyric in the same volume, set to a cheerful melody by Luca

Marenzio which was originally associated with Amazons jousting, Watson made the point even clearer:

worthy Meliboeus, even in a moment,
With Astrophil was placed above the firmament.
O they live both in pleasure
Where joys excel all measure.[15]

External evidence confirms the notion that it was to the father, not the daughter, that Sidney was most closely attached. Nearly thirty letters survive written by Sidney to Francis Walsingham after his marriage, but in only one does he mention a letter to his wife. Only a year after his marriage Sidney, accompanied by Greville, tried to join Sir Francis Drake's officially sponsored expedition to the West Indies.[16] This would have taken him away from home for almost a year, so we must conclude that he did not value the society of his wife especially highly. Confirmation of this is provided by the postscript to a long letter Sidney wrote to his father-in-law from Utrecht on 24 March 1586, in which he was distinctly unenthusiastic about the suggestion that his wife might be sent over to join him:

[I] know n[ot] what to say to my wife's coming till you resolve better, for if you run a strange course I may take such a one here as will not be fit for any of the feminine gender.[17]

In context, it is clear that Sidney felt that his status was not being properly recognized in England, and in particular that he did not have a residence appropriate to his dignity, 'such a one' meaning 'such a house'. Presumably the threat was that he would take up residence in a battle-zone fortress crammed with soldiers and weaponry. His use of his wife as a bargaining counter suggests limited attachment. Evidently Walsingham wanted the young couple to be reunited; but Sidney, though he had not seen his wife and daughter for nearly six months, was equal to a continued separation.

Sidney's external life in 1584–5 was so *mouvementé*, and his inner, imaginative life so richly absorbing, that emotional bonds between himself and his bride had little chance to form. Given more time, perhaps they would have done so. There are instances in the period of husbands who became attached to their wives only after several years. Philip Howard, Earl of Arundel, neglected his Catholic wife Anne Dacre for almost a decade, leading a wild and extravagant life at Court, and while at home with her in Essex trying to seduce Gabriel Harvey's sister Mercy.[18] But after his conversion by Campion (see above, p. 215) he became devoted to Anne, and their two children were born in 1581 and 1586 despite the imprisonment which made their meetings difficult. For Sidney, there was no time. A succession of stops and starts, apparent new beginnings and sudden endings, during the intervals of which he wrote, studied and discussed intellectual and religious questions with his male friends, left Sidney with little space for marital domesticity, which in any case he may not have much relished. It is wholly appropriate to the stop-go rhythm of this phase of his life that the revised *Arcadia* should break off in mid-sentence, just as the disguised Pyrocles is battling to the death with the brutish Anaxius:

> But Zelmane [Pyrocles] putting it by with her right-hand sword, coming in with her left foot and hand would have given him a sharp visitation to his right side, but that he was fain to leap away – whereat ashamed, as having never done so much before in his life –[19]

The date on the only manuscript text[20] suggests that it was in 1584 that Sidney abandoned his romance.

Compared with the turbulence of political events the unsatisfying nature of Sidney's marriage and his wife's 'slight infertility' were matters of little moment. The balance of power in Europe was changing almost from week to week. Late in 1583 Walsingham had uncovered the 'Throckmorton Plot', which would if successful have unleashed an attack on England by the Duke of Guise's soldiers, and the displacement of Elizabeth by the Queen of Scots.[21] For the first time in her reign Elizabeth was compelled to take the threat of foreign invasion seriously. Confusing events at the Scottish Court, aptly described by Sidney as 'weltering',[22] led to Walsingham's dispatch to Scotland in August 1583, and his absence from his daughter's wedding. Despite his close relationship to Walsingham, Sidney's knowledge of the Throckmorton conspiracy seems to have been limited, for on 20 December 1583 he wrote soothingly about it to the Earl of Rutland:

> Her Majesty is well, but troubled with those suspicions which arise of some ill-minded subjects towards her. My Lord of Northumberland I hope will discharge himself well of these doubts conceived of him. He is yet kept in his house, but for aught I can learn no matter of moment laid unto him. The consideration of removing the Scottish Queen doth still continue, and I think my Lord of Shrewsbury doth shortly come up. The ambassadors of Spain and France be noted for great practisers, and truly my lord this is the sum of the most important news I can send you.[23]

Actually, Northumberland was to have played a key rôle in helping Guise's troops to land. Either Sidney did not know this or he was engaged in a double bluff, for Rutland himself was under some suspicion.[24] It was true enough that the Spanish ambassador, though not the French one, was discovered to be a 'great practiser'; Bernardino de Mendoza was expelled on 9 January 1583/4. The plots and counter-plots of this period made it vital for Sidney now to show the Queen clearly whose side he was on. His close alliance with

Walsingham strengthened his Protestant credentials, and it seems that he must at last have convinced the Queen that he was trustworthy enough to send abroad, for in the summer of 1584, seven years after his mission to the Emperor, he gained another important diplomatic appointment. It was this, almost certainly, that brought an end to his work on the *Arcadia*.

Two sudden deaths occasioned it. On 31 May Alençon, who had retreated to France after his hopelessly bloody and mismanaged campaign in the Netherlands, died of typhoid at St Omer. Like Sidney, he was twenty-nine. Personally it was no great loss to anyone except his mother, Catherine de' Medici, and his 'wife', Elizabeth I, who communicated touchingly with each other about their grief. The extinction of the Valois line was now at hand, since the monkish and minion-loving Henri III had no children. It was unlikely that the next heir, the Protestant Henri of Navarre, could ascend the throne without much bloodshed. England had lost a useful piece of diplomatic leverage in the shape of Elizabeth's flirtation, though since the collapse of Alençon's command in the Netherlands it had lost most of its value. A much graver loss came on 29 June, when William of Orange was shot at Delft by a man called Balthasar Gérard.[25] After his courageous recovery from a previous assassination attempt (see above, p. 224) his death came as an appalling shock. It was precisely to guard against such a vacancy that William had once hoped to have Sidney as his son-in-law.

Even before the news of William of Orange's death the Queen had been considering sending Sidney to France to convey her condolences for Alençon's death, though some of his friends thought he should not accept the appointment 'in this time of hard consideration of service'[26] – that is, a time when valiant service was apt to go unrewarded, and diplomats were often blamed for the messages they brought back. There was considerable irony in Sidney's being chosen to convey Elizabeth's personal grief at the death of a man whose defects of character he had carefully itemized five years before:

> he is the son of the Jezebel of our age ... as full of light ambition as is possible ... Monsieur being every way apt to use the occasion to hurt ... he, both by his own fancy and by his youthful governors embracing all ambitious hopes, having Alexander's image in his head, but perchance ill painted ...[27]

Now he was to visit that 'Jezebel' in an ambassadorial capacity, 'with an honourable train',[28] transmitting, in addition to condolences, some urgent questions about what the King of France planned to do to relieve the miseries of the leaderless Netherlands, and to check the swelling power of Spain.[29] The mission was an extremely important one, both because of Elizabeth's anxiety to convey her intense personal grief, and because much depended on the soundings about the Netherlands. The expedition was funded by the Queen to the tune of £3 6s. 8d. a day for 'diet', with an advance of £300,[30] which cannot have been anything like enough for the large train of horses and carriages that set out from London on 10 July. As it turned out, the party got no further than Gravesend. On 14 July Sir Edward Stafford, the resident English ambassador in Paris, wrote to Walsingham that the King 'had broken up his court', and was on the point of making a visit to Lyons with only four companions. The Queen Mother was left to explain this odd behaviour to Stafford. A large party of English noblemen in mourning dress would not be well received, for

> he [the French King] had left off their mourning three days ago ... all the princes and nobles are departed to their houses ... she desired me to stay Mr Sidney.[31]

Parisian high society, as so often in late summer, had fled to the country. This was extremely embarrassing, and clearly Stafford was somewhat enraged, guessing plausibly that the King's real reason for refusing to meet the English delegation was that he did not want to discuss the power vacuum in the Netherlands:

> If there be anything that hath made the King fly the tilt and be unwilling to hear Mr Sidney ... it is that he is advertised from Mauvissière that he hath to deal with him about the Low Countries.[32]

It tells us something about Stafford's image of Sidney that he saw his diplomatic meeting with Henri III as a 'tilt'. Sidney met Stafford's messenger at Gravesend, and immediately turned back, recalling the carriages that had been sent on ahead. The whole expedition lasted only eight days.[33] Though the Queen Mother continued to suggest that Sidney's delegation would be welcome to come over once the King had returned from Lyons, Elizabeth would have none of this: she

> answered that she had sent [Sidney] to do the King honour, 'but since he did not like to have him go over, she was for her part well content to stay him, and that for sending of him hereafter, she saw no cause thereof'.[34]

After all, she still had her resident ambassador, Stafford, to communicate with the French Court. If the King was prepared to abandon mourning for his brother after barely six weeks – she herself had wept every day for at least three[35] – and was not willing to receive ambassadors in proper style, she would risk no further humiliation.

For Sidney, all dressed up with nowhere to go, the episode was acutely disappointing. His second opportunity to represent his monarch and to display his remarkable verbal and social skills had been snatched from him at the very brink. What happened next is not clear, but it seems that he may have decided to take out some of his chagrin on Sir Edward Stafford, to whom he wrote immediately after his return to Court, on 21 July 1584:

Sir: The cause of my sending at this time, this bearer Mr Burnham will tell you. Only let me salute you in the kindest manner that one near friend can do another.

I would gladly know how you and your noble lady do, and what you do in this absence of the King.

We are here all solito. Methinks you should do well to begin betimes to demand something of Her Majesty as might be found fit for you; and let folks chafe as well when you ask, as when you do not. Her Majesty seems affected to deal in the Low Country matters, but I think nothing will come of it. We are half persuaded to enter into the journey of Sir Humphrey Gilbert very eagerly, whereunto your Mr Hakluyt hath served for a very good trumpet.

I can write no more, but that I pray for your long and happy life, and so commit you both to the giver of it.[36]

This reads like an affable, confiding letter, in which Sidney gives Stafford useful advice, confessing to him that he has lost hope of the Queen making any commitment to help the Netherlands, and is turning his own thoughts to the New World. Stafford, however, mistrusted it. He had heard from his mother, who was Mistress of the Queen's Wardrobe, and slept in the royal bedchamber, that Elizabeth was offended with him, presumably over his handling of the abortive mission, and believed that Sidney was urging him to plead directly to the Queen only in order to exacerbate her rage. Of Sidney and his letter he wrote to Burghley:

The gentleman I love very well, and if he had not been at a bad school, which may corrupt any good nature, I could trust him well, but all these things hanging together, I am more than half afraid that he is made a stale [snare] to take a bird withal, and that his counsel would make her [the Queen] rather worse than better.[37]

This is an unusually revealing assessment of Sidney. The 'bad school' in which he had been educated was that of his uncle Leicester. Stafford, married to Leicester's cast-off mistress Douglass Sheffield, saluted by Sidney as his 'noble lady', was hard-pressed to measure his personal liking for Sidney against his suspicion that he was Leicester's creature and tool. It is unpleasant to think that Sidney's attractively friendly letter was a trick to get Stafford into trouble, but such may have been the case. For someone who had just suffered a severe disappointment Sidney had sounded surprisingly breezy.

Whether Leicester put him up to it, we have no way of knowing. Immediately after he got back to London Sidney became once more deeply dependent on Leicester, for his cousin Robert Dudley died at Wanstead on 19 July, 'being of the age of three years and somewhat more'.[38] Though Leicester had made considerable provision for his wife Lettice, the little boy's death meant that the bulk of his estates, and perhaps his title, would now, after all, pass to his nephew. It was clear that little Robert had been their last chance; they would have no more children. This was an astonishing turn of events. If Sidney had hoped to work on the *Arcadia* again once his French mission was accomplished, new distractions prevented him. His recovery of position as Leicester's heir was rapidly followed, in about September, by the arrival in England of an eloquently persuasive libel against his uncle entitled *The Copy of a Letter written by a Master of Arts of Cambridge ... to his friend in London ... about the present state, and some proceedings of the Earl of Leicester and his friends in England*, soon known familiarly as *Leicester's Commonwealth*.[39] As Leicester's heir, he was obliged to reply to it in the strongest possible terms. From leisurely absorption in a complex and deeply reflective romance, directed ultimately towards an audience of intellectual English readers led by such friends as Greville, Dyer and Penelope Rich, he was drawn aside into a tirade against the unknown libeller of his uncle. It was the first and only piece he wrote for publication, and his impassioned flourishes of the pen were supported with dazzling flashes of sword and dagger:

> So again, in any place whereto thou wilt call me, provided that the place be such, as a servant of the Queen's may have free access unto, if I do not, having my life and liberty, prove this upon thee, I am content that this lie I have given thee return to my perpetual infamy ...[40]

While the *Arcadia* had broken off with Pyrocles using his sword to good purpose against an arrogant and bullying enemy, the *Defence of Leicester* closed with a real-life challenge, in which Sidney promised to fight with his uncle's libeller 'in any place of Europe'.[41]

Before Sidney's new and not altogether amiable rôle as his uncle's champion is considered further, something should be said of the vast imaginative world he left behind him, to which he was never able to return. The 'New' *Arcadia* is much more than a revision of the 'Old'. Though there are many passages in the first two books of 'revision' in the narrow sense, where sentences have been rearranged, images added, adjectives changed and comments expanded,[42] much of what is most memorable in it is wholly new. Not only is the 'New' version in every sense larger than the 'Old', it has a quite different imaginative climate, in which the problems and dilemmas faced by the characters are often insoluble; there is no 'right' course of action. It is a reflexion of its characteristically dark atmosphere that Shakespeare took the secondary plot of his bleakest tragedy, *King Lear*, from one of its episodes, the unhappy story of the 'Paphlagonian unkind king', told in the depth of a 'very cold' winter, which concerns the blinding of a father by his ungrateful son.[43]

From the outset, there is a sense of loss, struggle and separation. The romance opens with the two shepherds Strephon and Klaius on the coast of war-torn Laconia, engaged in ritual lament for the departure of the heavenly shepherdess Urania, whom they love without lust or rivalry, and who seems to represent an unattainable ideal of virtue:[44]

Hath not she thrown reason upon our desires and, as it were, given eyes unto Cupid? Hath in any, but in her, love-fellowship maintained friendship between rivals, and beauty taught the beholders chastity?[45]

Their reflexions are interrupted by the sight of a half-drowned young man washed up on the beach, whom they restore to life by holding upside down, 'making a great deal of salt water to come out of his mouth'.[46] This is Musidorus, who has been separated from Pyrocles in the course of a great sea battle, providing the first of many images of man's inhumanity to man:

amidst the precious things were a number of dead bodies which ... did not only testify both elements' violence, but that the chief violence was grown of human inhumanity, for their bodies were full of grisly wounds, and their blood had, as it were, filled the wrinkles of the sea's visage, which, it seemed, the sea would not wash away, that it might witness it is not always his fault when we condemn his cruelty.[47]

There is no longer an indulgent Chaucerian narrator to mediate between the princes and the reader's judgement: they are made to dazzle the reader directly with their glamour and courage, as in this first splendid vision of Pyrocles, clinging to the wreckage:

upon the mast they saw a young man ... who sate as on horseback, having nothing upon him but his shirt which, being wrought with blue silk and gold, had a kind of resemblance to the sea on which the sun then near his western home did shoot some of his beams. His hair, which the young men of Greece used to wear very long, was stirred up and down with the wind ... holding his head up full of unmoved majesty, he held a sword aloft with his fair arm which often he waved about his crown [top of his head] as though he would threaten the world in that extremity.[48]

At the beginning, as at the end, Pyrocles is a dauntless swordsman. The colours blue and gold connect him with Sidney, whose family crest was *or, a pheon azure*. His cavalier bravado, threatening 'the world' as he rocks about on the wide ocean, is comparable with Sidney's own when he threatened Leicester's unknown libeller. These rash gestures of defiance prefigure Sidney's end.

As the narrative unfolds, it is full of surprises. Books 1 and 2 have a labyrinthine structure of episodes, flashbacks and subsidiary narratives, yet incorporate most of the narrative of the equivalent books of the 'Old' version. Book 3 leaves it far behind, both emotionally and geographically, replacing sexual intrigue with dark images of imprisonment and pointless conflict. Some positive images seem like idealized versions of the world Sidney knew. His recollections of Accession Day Tilts and other court tournaments have already been mentioned (see above, pp. 145–6), as has his description of the Penshurst-like house, with its benign social order, presided over by the hospitable Kalander ('Good man'; see above, p. 75). Other passages reveal Sidney's appreciative observation of Venetian painting,[49] his interest in *imprese* and symbolic costume, and his keen eye for telling detail. The physical ambience of the female characters, in particular, is realized with some of the particularity of a Vermeer interior. Pamela in Book 2 is discovered by her sister late at night

> sitting in a chair, lying backward, with her head almost over the back of it, and looking upon a wax candle which burnt before her, in one hand holding a letter, in the other her handkerchief which had lately drunk up the tears of her eyes, leaving instead of them crimson circles like red flakes in the element when the weather is hottest ...[50]

Near Pamela's bed, we later learn, is a 'standish', or writing-stand, on which Musidorus leaves a self-pitying poem. Both girls, like Elizabethan women, wear bunches of knives at their girdles.[51] Like real-life great ladies, including Elizabeth and Mary Queen of Scots, Pamela beguiles the tedium of imprisonment with embroidery, 'working upon a purse certain roses and lilies', choosing her colours so carefully

> that it was not without marvel to see how a mind, which could cast a careless semblant upon the greatest conflicts of fortune, could command itself to take care for so small matters.[52]

In contrast with these 'small matters' are some large moral issues and character types which have their roots both in literature and in life.

The celebrated story of Argalus and Parthenia[53] incorporates childhood memories of Sidney's parents, elevated to a level of high tragedy. Argalus, a talented and courageous gentleman, falls in love with the beautiful and well-born Parthenia. A jealous rival, Demagoras, destroys her beauty by rubbing poison on her face. Though Argalus's love is undiminished, she flees from him.[54] Amazingly, her beauty is restored by a skilled physician employed by Queen Helen of Corinth – the nearest Sidney ever comes to the use of magic – and they are reunited and married.[55] This part of the story seems like a personal wish fulfilment fantasy; Sidney's mother, badly scarred in 1562, never enjoyed such a restoration. In Book 3 the devoted couple are used to illustrate the horrors of civil war. Argalus is called away to fight in Basilius's service; he is mortally wounded, and dies in Parthenia's lap in perhaps the most affecting scene Sidney ever wrote (loosely based on the death of Arcite in Chaucer's *Knight's Tale*):

> forcing up, the best he could, his feeble voice: 'My dear, my dear, my better half,' said he, 'I find I must now leave thee; and by that sweet hand and fair eyes of thine I

swear that death brings nothing with it to grieve me, but that I must leave thee ... But since so it pleaseth him whose wisdom and goodness guideth all, put thy confidence in him, and one day we shall blessedly meet again, never to depart' ...[56]

As this passage shows, the 'New' *Arcadia*, unlike the 'Old', is strongly charged with religious feeling. The virtuous characters are all but Christian, having a powerful faith in Divine Providence and life after death. It is all the more disconcerting therefore that Parthenia rejects her dying husband's appeal for patience, and takes her destiny into her own hands. The last part of the narrative derives, not from childhood experience, but from childhood reading, for it is based on the heroic story of Panthea and Abradates in Xenophon's *Cyropaedia*, in which Panthea stabs herself when left alone with the corpse of her husband, slain in battle.[57] Sidney transports her solitary act of self-slaughter into the public arena of chivalric combat. Disguised as 'The Knight of the Tomb' Parthenia encounters her husband's killer, Amphialus, knowing that she will inevitably be killed.[58] Despite what is in effect an act of suicide, Parthenia is buried beside her husband in 'a church', and marble effigies which sound distinctly Elizabethan are commissioned.[59]

In the extraordinarily potent and disturbing Book 3 of the 'New' *Arcadia* Sidney's writing is far more personal and searching than in the 'toyful book' he wrote three years earlier. Whiling away the leisure time of 'fair ladies' was no longer his aim. There were profound issues to explore, old scores to settle, and new visions to unfold. As John Carey has pointed out, he was forging a new and original kind of epic narrative:

In this part, with its persistent presentation of the horror and beauty of war and warriors, and the blood-dimmed tide of carnage, Sidney seems to have Homer's *Iliad* chiefly in mind: but, because the minds of the women are particularly closely studied ... it is a modern *Iliad*, involving a whole new level of sensibility.[60]

Heroic motifs are both Christianized and feminized, with the sorely tried patience of the princesses shown as more morally productive than the military action of the male characters. Pamela, in particular, is used as a mouthpiece for Du Plessis Mornay's account of the shared fundamentals of the Christian religion, spilling over from another of Sidney's current literary projects. These arguments offer a resounding challenge to religious bigotry or indifference. The Homeric theme of abduction and ensuing siege is strangely transformed, for the agent of abduction here is not a lustful man, like Paris, but a scheming woman, Cecropia, Basilius's sister-in-law. She takes her name from Cecrops, a mythical two-headed king of Athens; but her character and situation are unmistakably modelled on 'the Jezebel of the age', Catherine de' Medici. Just as Catherine had hoped to gain control of the English throne by marrying her weak-willed son Alençon to Queen Elizabeth, Cecropia is determined to gain control of Arcadia by marrying her son, the well-meaning but unfortunate Amphialus, to one or other of Basilius's daughters. To this end she has them abducted, together with the disguised Pyrocles, keeping them prisoner in a rocky fortress in the middle of a great lake.[61]

From this point on, Pyrocles is doubly imprisoned. The transvestite disguise which liberated him when he was fooling around in the Arcadian retreat now confines him totally, leaving him with no part to play, since Cecropia is not interested in him. Even in the last passage Sidney wrote, where Pyrocles fights manfully with three arrogant enemies, he is still dressed as a woman, using this disguise, rather unfairly, to humiliate the lordly Anaxius, 'punished by the weak sex, which thou most contemnest'.[62] Yet Musidorus, disguised in black as the 'Forsaken Knight', and fighting desperately with Amphialus, whom he wrongly believes to be in love with Pamela, achieves little more through his 'game of death'.[63] Sidney's vision of the pity of war is unsparing, as when Musidorus

strake Amphialus upon the belly so horrible a wound that his guts came out withal.[64]

The clumsy conflicts outside Cecropia's fortress resolve nothing, serving only to reveal the futility of this way of settling differences and the speciousness of military splendour:

for at the first, though it were terrible, yet terror was decked so bravely with rich furniture, gilt swords, shining armours, pleasant pencels [small pennons or streamers], that the eye with delight had scarce leisure to be afraid; but now all universally defiled with dust, blood, broken armours, mangled bodies, took away the mask and set forth horror in his own horrible manner.[65]

Ironically, given his own impending involvement in military conflict, Sidney seems, by the time he wrote Book 3, to have seen, with Milton,

the better fortitude
Of patience, and heroic martyrdom[66]

as a more rewarding form of moral struggle than physical combat. The implicit message inside the fortress is *vincit qui patitur*, he who suffers triumphs.

The dominant figure here is Pamela, whose unshakable courage and faith may reflect Sidney's own current convictions and ideals. Cecropia's temptation of Philoclea is relatively conventional, focusing on the liberty that marriage would offer her, the joy of progeny and the comforts of companionship;[67] her eloquent speeches are to no end, for Philoclea does not listen. But while Philoclea gives herself up to weeping and self-neglect, Pamela paces steadily up and down her chamber

till at length, as it were, awaking and strengthening herself, 'Well,' said she, 'yet this is best. And of this I am sure, that howsoever they wrong me, they cannot overmaster

God. No darkness blinds his eyes; no jail bars him out. To whom, then, else should I fly, but to him for succour?'[68]

The prayer which follows, addressed to the 'all-seeing light and eternal life of all things', was said by the author of *Eikon Basilike* (1648) to have been used by Charles I when he was imprisoned at Carisbrooke, and Milton in *Eikonoklastes* (1649) took the King to task for his citation of a 'vain, amatorious poem' in his private devotions. However, jottings in Milton's commonplace book suggest that he was himself an appreciative reader of the *Arcadia*.[69] After eavesdropping on Pamela's devotions, Cecropia knows that she must use different tactics with the older sister, deciding to assail the basis of her faith. The debate which ensues is tantamount to a confrontation between a godless, self-willed 'Machiavel' and a constant and courageous Protestant with Platonist leanings.[70] Cecropia tries to undermine Pamela's faith by invoking the old atheist saying, first given currency in English in the mouth of Chaucer's Criseyde,[71] that the gods were invented by men's fear. The world, she says, was created by chance, and if there are any gods they are indifferent to the lives of human individuals:

to think that those powers, if there be any such, above, are moved either by the eloquence of our prayers or in a chafe by the folly of our actions carries as much reason as if flies should think that men take great care which of them hums sweetest, and which of them flies nimblest.[72]

Pamela is stung into an eloquent rebuttal of the 'wicked woman', her aunt, based on an appeal to natural reason:

perfect order, perfect beauty, perfect constancy: if these be the children of chance, or fortune the efficient of these, let wisdom be counted the root of wickedness and eternity the fruit of her inconstancy.[73]

Man's reason reflects the rationality of his creator, infinite both in knowledge and power, to whom even 'the estate of flies (which you with so unsavoury scorn did jest at)' is well known. Sidney may have been thinking here of another of his current literary tasks, translating Du Bartas, who celebrated the creation of the insects in the Fifth Day:

these are also his wise workmanships,
Whose fame did never obscure work eclipse:
And sith, in these he shows us every hour
More wondrous proofs of his almighty power
Than in huge whales, or hideous elephants . . .[74]

Pamela's confident peroration is worthy of Sidney's aunt Lady Jane Grey, and may indeed partly derive from Foxe's accounts of her debates in the Tower (see above, p. 6):

Since, then, there is a God, and an all-knowing God so as he sees into the darkest of all natural secrets, which is the heart of man, and sees therein the deepest dissembled thoughts – nay, sees the thoughts before they be thought; since he is just to exercise his might, and mighty to perform his justice, assure thyself, most wicked woman, that hast so plaguily a corrupted mind as thou canst not keep thy sickness to thyself, but must most wickedly infect others, assure thyself, I say – for what I say depends of everlasting and unremovable causes – that the time will come when thou shalt know that power by feeling it, when thou shalt see his wisdom in the manifesting thy ugly shamefastness, and shalt only perceive him to have been a creator in thy destruction.[75]

Pamela's evident rightness – proved near the end of the revised fragment when Cecropia falls backwards to her death from the roof of her castle – serves only to exacerbate Cecropia's envious hatred of the princesses, which escalates into torture, first mental, 'sometimes with noises of horror, sometimes with sudden frightings in the night',[76] and then physical. Assisted by 'certain old women of wicked dispositions' Cecropia whips the princesses, taking care only to preserve their looks, and then makes each believe that the other is dead. Philoclea's lament, with its clear quotations from the Old Testament, underlines the proto-Christian nature of these female martyrs:

Pamela, my sister! My sister, Pamela! Woe is me for thee! I would I had died for thee![77]

echoing David's famous lament for Absalom:

O my son Absalom, my son, my son Absalom! Would God I had died for thee, O Absalom my son, my son![78]

As Philoclea continues, Sidney echoes Job's curses on the day of his birth:

And hast thou left me here, who have nothing good in me but that I did ever love thee, and ever will lament thee? Let this day be noted of all virtuous folks for most unfortunate. Let it never be mentioned but among curses.[79]

It was from lofty and poignant visions such as these that Sidney was violently wrenched back into the here and now. Clearly he hoped eventually to return to the *Arcadia*, and to find some resolution to the deadlock in which he had left his principal characters; but there was no time.[80] He was at last, after so many disappointments, called upon to play a part in the affairs of state, first in being appointed to lead the mission to France, and then in defending his uncle.

Leicester's Commonwealth is compulsive reading. Whoever the author was – and Sidney's riposte failed to flush him out – he was an extremely skilful writer. So gripping was it that Sir John Harington was discovered reading it in Leicester's presence, and pretended, blushing, that he was studying 'certain cantos of Ariost'.[81] True details, loaded insinuations, and false allegations are all so cleverly mixed up in it as to be impossible to disentangle. Despite its evident bias, all subsequent biographers of Leicester have to some extent drawn on the *Commonwealth*. As an all-out attack on one of Elizabeth's chief advisers it was also, implicitly, an attack on Elizabeth herself for her poor judgement in favouring this corrupt and self-serving individual. Its stress on the succession question was deliberately subversive. In the current atmosphere of plotting and feared invasion such a work could not be allowed to stand. Sidney, a practised writer and debater who was now once more Leicester's heir apparent, was the obvious person to take on the libeller. He may have set to work at high speed, with encouragement from the Queen and Council, perhaps in the first week of October 1584. Walsingham received a copy of the *Commonwealth* on 28 September, and planned to discuss it with the Queen on the 30th;[82] Sidney's treatise, evidently written in white heat, may have been the product of this meeting. Perhaps it was after deciding that Sidney's *Defence of Leicester* was not the answer that Elizabeth decided to issue her remarkably severe Proclamation against persons found distributing or possessing the *Commonwealth*, on 12 October 1584.[83]

Sidney's *Defence of the Earl of Leicester* is in several respects unusual. Alone among his writings, it survives in complete holograph.[84] Alone among his writings, it was intended for publication, as the final challenge shows:

> And from the date of this writing, imprinted and published, I will three months expect thine answer.[85]

Yet alone among surviving writings, it seems to have been a complete failure, for it was not in fact published, and there are no allusions to it among Sidney's circle of friends and correspondents. While the much slighter *Discourse on Irish Affairs*, seven years earlier, was warmly praised by Edward Waterhouse,[86] the more extended riposte to *Leicester's Commonwealth* met with a resounding silence. Probably those who read it saw immediately that Sidney was defending his uncle from far too narrow a base. While he makes some good general points about the implausibility of the portrait of Leicester –

> Dissimulation, hypocrisy, adultery, falsehood, treachery, poison, rebellion, treason, cowardice, atheism and what not, and all still so upon the superlative that it was no marvel though the good lawyer he speaks of made many a cross to keep him from such a father of lies ...[87]

– he devotes the greater part of the piece to a rebuttal of the libeller's claim that the Dudleys were 'no gentlemen'. This is not the most important issue in the *Commonwealth*, merely one of many arguments used to undermine Leicester's position and supposed aspirations. But Sidney, in the first flush of discovering that he himself might eventually become Earl of Leicester, was personally stung by it. The widespread Elizabethan interest in genealogy is evidenced in such passages as Spenser's *Faerie Queene* II. ix, in which Guyon eagerly cons a list of ancient British kings, or III.iii, in which the lovesick Britomart is cheered by a vision of her progeny. Spenser had also celebrated Leicester's ancestry in a Latin work called *Stemmata Dudleiana*, which Sidney may have known.[88]

But genealogy, however entertaining, was not what was called for in the present crisis, for the real point at issue was not Leicester's ancestry, but his integrity. Indeed, the genealogical approach was counter-productive, for it required the exhumation of some skeletons, such as that of John Dudley, Duke of Northumberland, which would have been better left in the family cupboard. As D. C. Peck observes, Sidney's

> point seems unfortunately to be that 'anybody who is anybody' has been executed for treason.[89]

Yet Sidney flaunts his connexion with this condemned traitor and undoubted aspirant to power:

> I am a Dudley in blood, that Duke's daughter's son, and do acknowledge, though in all truth I may justly affirm that I am by my father's side of ancient and always well-esteemed and well-matched gentry, yet I do acknowledge, I say, that my chiefest honour is to be a Dudley, and truly am glad to have cause to set forth the nobility of that blood whereof I am descended ...[90]

Actually, Sidney's account of his Dudley forebears makes it plain that they consistently bettered themselves through marriages with noble families, and that all their best connexions came through the female line. Just before Sidney wrote his treatise his brother Robert had continued the family tradition of capturing desirable heiresses by pursuing the newly orphaned and wealthy Barbara Gamage, of Coity Castle, Glamorgan. He married her on 23 September, to the chagrin of several rivals.[91] Sidney also papered over several cracks in the family tree, making much of the nobility of the family of Sutton, while ignoring the more important question of 'whether the Dudleys were lawfully related to that house at all'.[92]

Sidney may have thought genealogy a safer area for debate than his uncle's personal character, and in declaring to the libeller that

> thou therein liest in thy throat, which I will be ready to justify upon thee in any place of Europe ...[93]

he seemed to be gallantly drawing the enemy's fire to himself.

It is difficult to know how realistic Sidney's challenge was. Did he really think he might be summoned to fight with Robert Parsons, S.J., or Thomas

Morgan, or Charles Arundell, or Charles Paget, or any of the group of Catholic exiles suspected of having written the *Commonwealth*? Furthermore, did he believe that such a duel would be of the slightest use in clearing his uncle's name? The very large number of manuscript copies of the *Commonwealth*[94] shows the success with which it was distributed, despite repeated measures taken to suppress it. In the spring of 1585 an even more offensive French version, called *Discours de la vie abominable de my Lorde de Lecestre*, was published.[95] A sword fight by Sidney in Paris or Rouen was hardly likely to undo the harm done in the minds of those who read the pamphlet on either side of the Channel. The personal sub-text of Sidney's piece may have been his continued animosity towards the Earl of Oxford. He may have guessed that the likeliest originator of the *Commonwealth* was a crony of Oxford's, Charles Arundell,[96] who had also been a prime mover in Oxford's plots to have Sidney assassinated. Reverberations of the tennis-court quarrel can be heard in Sidney's passionate assertions of his aristocratic lineage. He was no puppy, but a Duke's grandson.

But if he really hoped to have it published, he was naive. The Queen, with her rooted objection to duelling, would never allow it, and may have suspected that the challenge was a ruse to get out of the country and beyond her control. After all, Sidney was still sore about the collapse of his French mission. Though the Queen and her advisers were determined to discover the libeller's identity and carry out reprisals, they immediately realized that Sidney's hotheaded challenge was no way to deal with this insidiously damaging piece of propaganda.

Perhaps Sidney had whipped himself up to too high a pitch of excitement when writing about Pyrocles' duel with Anaxius, being momentarily unable to distinguish between his fictional world and the slower-moving, more complex actualities of international politics. If he believed in the actuality and effectiveness of a duel with the libeller, he was ignoring the lessons of other passages in his own recent writing, which had shown the destructive futility of such encounters. However, Sidney's character was not consistent, and the common sense which characterized him at best was all too often interrupted by the 'psychotic-like attacks of rage' which Lawrence Stone has described as brought about by repressive Tudor methods of child-rearing.[97] Leicester's libeller, perhaps an associate of Oxford's, had got him on the raw, and he rushed impetuously into a show of solidarity with his Dudley relations without seeing that what was needed was a broad defence of Elizabeth's wise and peaceable government. He was too anxious to show himself Leicester's 'loyal and natural boy'.[98] By responding to the libel so narrowly he was implicitly reinforcing the claim that Leicester alone ran the country.

Despite the manifest failure of Sidney's defence of his uncle, Walsingham's support ensured that he continued to move steadily into the forefront of public affairs. In November 1584 he was again a Member of Parliament, and also a Knight of the Shire for Kent. Rather surprisingly, 'There is no evidence that he ever spoke in the House',[99] but he sat on several committees, including one concerned with drawing up savage measures against Jesuits and seminary priests. With the renewed sense of Protestant commitment that accompanied his immersion in the work of Du Plessis Mornay, and his ill-governed rage at the manifestly Catholic-based libel on his uncle,[100] he probably no longer felt much compunction about this. Some element of blackmail of families with Catholic associations may lie behind his request for a 'buck' from Lady Paget.[101]

Though it was not until July 1585 that he was officially appointed as Joint Master of the Ordnance,[102] from the summer of 1584 onwards his duties in the office became extremely onerous. The danger of foreign invasion provoked urgent measures for the fortification of Channel ports, and Sidney, under the direction of Walsingham, had particular responsibility for overseeing the strengthening of Dover Harbour.[103] This work gave him opportunities to make brief visits to Penshurst and other lands in Kent, including the Little Park at Otford, which his father had leased from the Crown since 1551. Otford, only twelve miles from London, was a useful place for stabling horses, and Sidney entrusted responsibilities there to his servant John Langford, who held the Keepership of Otford Park. Many years later Langford was to complain that Sidney's death had been his 'undoing'.[104] Frances Sidney probably accompanied her husband as far as Penshurst, and made herself known to the old family retainers who lived there.

The practicalities of talking to naval and military surveyors, such as Thomas Digges, and securing the necessary finances for building and armaments at Dover, left Sidney little time for domestic life and family affairs. He was also kept busy entertaining three banished Scottish peers, the Earls of Mar, Angus and Glamis, and negotiating, too trustingly, with the treacherous Master of Grey.[105] But by the spring of 1585 an olive plant was sprouting: Frances was pregnant. This provided some consolation for the death of his sister's three-year-old daughter Katherine, 'a child that promised much excellence', on 16 October 1584, which overshadowed the birth of her second son, Philip, the following day.[106] It has been plausibly suggested that the Countess's fourth labour was difficult and 'caused internal damage', for she had no more children, although she was only twenty-three.[107] It is not known whether Sidney attended the christening of his latest namesake and godson. If not, he had an opportunity to see the baby when he paid what was to be his last visit to Wilton in March 1585. Entertainment was provided on this occasion by a man with a harp and an instrument 'stringed with wire strings', perhaps an orpharion.

As Sidney moved into his fourth decade – his thirtieth birthday was on 30

November 1584 – he began to look more like a pillar of the establishment. If the 'Chesterfield' portrait-model, which belongs to this period, can be trusted, the change was reflected in his physical appearance.[108] His hair was longer, he sported a drooping moustache and a pearl ear-ring, and the slender youth of seven years earlier was starting to take on the thick-set look of a middle-aged Elizabethan statesman. However, he was still fit enough to appear regularly in the tiltyard. He took a leading part in the splendid and elaborate 1584 Accession Day Tilt at Westminster, which helped to rally devotion to the Queen in a time of national insecurity. Sir Henry Lee seems to have master-minded the occasion.[109] Sidney led off the response to Lee's challenge, running the whole six courses along the tilt,[110] and his companions included Fulke Greville, Edward Denny, Henry Brouncker and the Catholic Thomas Gerard. Three weeks later, on 6 December, Sidney was one of ten married men who engaged in a sword fight against ten bachelors, also at Westminster.[111] This time his opponent was Fulke Greville; his brother Robert, the Earl of Cumberland, Lord Willoughby and Sir Henry Lee were among fellow married men, and Henry Brouncker and Edward Denny were among the bachelors. Sidney's profile as a tilter was now so high that a learned Italian Protestant refugee, Scipio Gentile, in dedicating a translation of twenty-five Psalms into Latin hexameters to him in 1584 described his 'most magnificent devising of shows and his equestrian feats' as the most striking achievement of his mature manhood.[112]

Sidney's patronage in 1584–5 reflects the undiminished breadth of his interests. Timothy Bright dedicated a book on medicine to him, reminding him of the time they had spent together taking refuge from the terror in Walsingham's house in Paris in 1572.[113] Among other books dedicated to him were two major philosophical works by Giordano Bruno, one of them describing an Ash Wednesday supper at Fulke Greville's house at which Sidney was probably present;[114] David Powel's completion of Humfrey Lhuyd's history of Wales;[115] Christopher Clifford's interestingly autobiographical treatise on horsemanship;[116] Thomas Washington's lavishly illustrated translation of Nicholas de Nicolay's account of his travels in the Middle East;[117] Scipio Gentile's brother Alberico's treatise on the legal status of ambassadors;[118] and Simon Robson's curious essay on the 'triplicity of divinity, philosophy and poetry'.[119] We can assume that all these individuals, and many more besides, such as the musician who provided entertainment at Wilton, were rewarded by Sidney with his customary financial generosity. In the case of one writer, a learned logician called William Temple, we know that his patronage went further. Temple, a former Fellow of King's College, Cambridge, was schoolmaster at Lincoln Grammar School when he dedicated his edition of Ramus s *Dialecticae* to Sidney.[120] Both the text and its reminder of the celebrated martyr to Catholic savagery were welcome to Sidney, whose thank-you letter survives:

Good Mr Temple: I have received both your book and your letter, and think myself greatly beholding unto you for them. I greatly desire to know you better, I mean by sight; for else, your writings make you as well known as my knowledge ever can reach unto; and this assure yourself, Mr Temple, that while I live you shall have me ready to make known by my best power that I bear you goodwill, and greatly esteem those things I conceive in you. When you come to London or Court I pray you let me see you, meanwhile use me boldly: for I am beholding. God keep you well.

At Court this 23th of May 1584.[121]

It is interesting that Sidney felt able to write with such warmth to a man he had never met. Once they did meet, Temple lived up to expectation, for some time in 1585 he became Sidney's secretary. Probably his first piece of work in Sidney's employ was his Ramist 'logical analysis' of the *Defence of Poesy*.[122] It may have been intended to help Sidney to revise his treatise at some future date.[123] If the *Defence of the Earl of Leicester* showed Sidney at his arrogant worst, his letter to Temple showed him at his best: witty, affable and quick to appreciate the talents and achievements of others. Languet used to say that Sidney lacked the severity needed in a military commander.[124] It is true that he was lavish and generous to a fault, and had a marked ability to inspire devotion in friends and dependants. What counteracted this warmth was not a disciplined severity, but extreme impulsiveness. When he felt threatened or undervalued, as frequently happened, he was apt to behave in ways that no one expected.

In the summer of 1585 Sidney reached such a point of crisis. The honeymoon period with the Walsingham family was over. Though he had at last achieved his Mastership of the Ordnance, and was an expectant father, he was more than ever frustrated by lack of money, lack of status and above all lack of confidence in Elizabeth's foreign policy, of which Walsingham was a prime agent. Sidney foresaw that what the Queen was willing to do for the Netherlands would be too little and too late. While discussions and deliberations dragged on, with delays and indecision on the part of both Elizabeth and the representatives of the Dutch States, the Prince of Parma was steadily extending the boundaries of Spanish rule, and had captured the great city of Antwerp. In June 1585 Elizabeth was offered the sovereignty of the Netherlands, which she refused, conceding only that she would send over English troops, which must eventually be fully paid for by the Dutch, with the hand-over of three strategic ports to English rule as security against payment.[125] By the beginning of September this much was agreed, and it became clear that Leicester would go over as general of the English forces, which were supposed to be defensive only. This left open the question of appointments to governorships of the 'cautionary towns' of Flushing, Brill and Enckhuysen.

Though the Zeelanders themselves wanted Sidney for Flushing,[126] the Queen was deeply reluctant to appoint him. Her delay prompted desperate measures. Sidney had had more than he could take of his monarch's prevarication, and tried to make a getaway. In the first week of September, accompanied by Fulke Greville, he hurried to Plymouth to join Sir Francis Drake's fleet, then on the point of departure for the West Indies and America. His pretext was another meeting with the Portuguese pretender:

... the state hath intelligence that Don Antonio was at sea for England, and resolved to land at Plymouth. Sir Philip, turning the occasion into wisdom, puts himself into the employment of conducting up this king, and under that veil leaves the Court without suspicion, overshoots his father-in-law, then Secretary of State, in his own bow, comes to Plymouth, was feasted the first night by Sir Francis with a great deal of outward pomp and compliment.[127]

Greville goes on to describe a bed-time conversation with Sidney, who was puzzled by Drake's 'discountenance and depression', 'as if our coming were both beyond his expectation and desire'.[128] No doubt this was true. Drake, recently raised from buccaneer to Admiral, was well aware that the royal approval he had so lately won could all be lost again if he took with him a leading courtier who had no permission to leave. Though Sidney had long taken a keen interest in New World exploration, and had invested in it more lavishly than his means allowed, he had no experience whatsoever of naval warfare. The lyrical account in the 'New' *Arcadia* of how the princes learned about sailing shows both why Sidney believed he was qualified to take a naval command as Drake's equal, and why the well-seasoned Drake must have been appalled at the prospect:

... the two princes had leisure to see the practice of that which before they had learned by books: to consider the art of catching the wind prisoner, to no other end but to run away with it; to see how beauty and use can so well agree together that, of all the trinkets wherewith they [sailing vessels] are attired, there is not one but serves to some necessary purpose; and, O Lord, to see the admirable power and effects of love, whereby the seeming insensible loadstone, with a secret beauty holding the spirit of iron in it, can draw that hard-hearted thing unto it, and like a virtuous mistress, not only make it bow itself, but make it aspire to so high a love as of the heavenly poles, and thereby to bring forth the noblest deeds that the children of the earth can boast of ... so the princes delighting their conceits with confirming their knowledge, seeing wherein the sea-discipline differed from land-service ...[129]

In Drake's eyes, Sidney was a poet and dreamer, as well as a political embarrassment.

Within a few days, three letters arrived from Court. Drake was forbidden to receive Sidney into his fleet, which must have been an enormous relief to him. The Mayor of Plymouth was to ensure that the fleet did not set out if Sidney was aboard; and Sidney himself was to return immediately. Sidney's messenger, described by Greville as 'a peer of this realm', but unidentified, brought 'in the one hand grace, the other thunder'.[130] The 'thunder' was the Queen's anger at Sidney's attempt to escape from her control, though he managed on his return to persuade her that 'he never meant to go'.[131] The 'grace' was a promise of appointment to the governorship of Flushing.

Sidney's father-in-law, writing to Walter Davison, claimed that Sidney tried to join Drake's expedition purely out of disappointment at the possibility of not getting the Flushing post:

> Sir Philip Sidney hath taken a very hard resolution to accompany Sir Francis Drake in this voyage, moved hereunto for that he saw Her Majesty disposed to commit the charge of Flushing unto some other; which he reputed would fall out greatly to his disgrace, to see another preferred before him, both for birth and judgement inferior unto him. This resolution is greatly to the grief of Sir Philip's friends, but to none more than to myself. I know Her Majesty would easily have been induced to have placed him in Flushing, but he despaired hereof, and the disgrace that he doubted he should receive hath carried him into a desperate course ...[132]

Walsingham's account of Sidney's tendency to take offence and act impulsively is entirely convincing, but he underestimated the sincerity of his son-in-law's desire to cross the Atlantic. For many years now Sidney had longed passionately to see the New World, where he hoped to find the wealth, excitement and personal freedom which in England he could enjoy only in the realm of fiction. In the autumn of 1585 this glorious vision was closed to him once more. Instead of the Azores and Florida, he was bound for a small offshore island in the North Sea, and time was fast running out.

12

1586

LA CUISSE ROMPUE

Here again this restless soul of his – changing only the air, and not the chords, of her harmony – calls for music, especially that song which himself had entitled *La cuisse rompue* [the broken thigh]; partly (as I conceive by the name) to show that the glory of mortal flesh was shaken in him, and, by the music itself, to fashion and enfranchise his heavenly soul into that everlasting harmony of angels whereof these concords were a kind of terrestrial echo.[1]

How long, O Lord, shall I forgotten be?
What, ever?
How long wilt thou thy hidden face from me
Dissever?

How long shall I consult with careful sprite
In anguish?
How long shall I with foes' triumphant might
Thus languish?

Behold me, Lord! Let to thy hearing creep
My crying:
Nay, give me eyes, and light, lest that I sleep
In dying.[2]

In leaving England for the Netherlands Sidney was not abandoning literature or the life of the mind. He would have had no time for Auden's assertion that 'Poetry makes nothing happen',[3] for one of the strongest planks on which he rested his *Defence of Poesy* was the proposition that 'poetry is the companion of camps'. Soldiers, he claimed, enjoyed reading romances: 'I dare undertake, Orlando Furioso, or honest King Arthur, will never displease a soldier'; and Alexander the Great is said to have taken the poems of Homer with him when

Engraving of Prince Maurice of Nassau and Sidney surprising the town of Axel, from Willem Baudart, *Polemographia Auraico-Belgica*, 1622 (Bodleian Library)

he set out to conquer the world.[4] Sidney's letter of advice to Edward Denny,[5] then on the point of departure for Ireland with Lord Grey, shows that he viewed active military service as an occasion for new and intensified study, not for action divorced from contemplation. We do not know the contents of Sidney's travelling library. Judging by the length of the reading list he gave to Denny, it may have been very extensive. Nor can we be absolutely sure what literary tasks he had in hand. He cannot have been working on the *Arcadia*, for he left his working copy of that behind with Fulke Greville. The strong links between the revised Book 3 and Du Plessis Mornay's *De la vérité* suggest that he had been working on these concurrently, and this, too, he may have left behind with Greville. In a handsome collection of emblems and *imprese* dedicated to Leicester in the spring of 1586, from Leiden, Geffrey Whitney suggested that Sidney had left poetry behind him:

> More sweet than honey was the style that from his pen did flow,
> Wherewith, in youth, he used to banish idle fits,
> That now, his works of endless fame delight the worthy wits.[6]

Whitney, a member of Leicester's entourage, may have gathered that Sidney was no longer writing love poetry and romance, but was probably unaware of his continued work as a translator, and of the radical revision of the *Arcadia*.

For various reasons, it is likely that while he was in the Netherlands Sidney was working on his verse paraphrases of the Psalms. The revised Book 3 of the *Arcadia* indicates an increasing preoccupation with religion. As he approached what he foresaw would be a difficult and dangerous enterprise, requiring both patience and courage, he may well have turned to the Psalms for personal solace:

And this poesy must be used by whosoever will follow St James's counsel in singing Psalms when they are merry, and I know is used with fruit of comfort by some, when, in sorrowful pangs of their death-bringing sins, they find the consolation of the never-leaving goodness.[7]

Secondly, the birth of his daughter Elizabeth, some time in October 1585, meant that Sidney now saw himself as the future head of a household, with responsibility for the religious education of his children. The huge fifteenth-century family Psalter[8] was a beautiful family heirloom, but had lost its devotional function, becoming merely a handsome ledger in which to record births, deaths and marriages. Sidney probably hoped that ultimately his new Psalm versions would be sung in the parish church at Penshurst, or in his own family chapel. His renderings lack any strong flavour of individual personality, being directed towards corporate devotion. He may also have recalled his courageous friend François Perrot de Mésières, who in conditions of great difficulty had translated selected Psalms for the edification of his young daughter Esperance (see above, pp. 81–2). More recently, he had had two collections of Latin versions of the Psalms dedicated to him by Scipio Gentile, who also greeted the birth of Elizabeth with a prophetic Latin poem, *Nereus*.[9] Gentile's combined interest in psalmody and little Elizabeth helped to bring the two together in Sidney's mind. Thirdly, the Psalm versions themselves contain hints that the poet has put secular devotion behind him. The clearest suggestion comes in the opening of Psalm X:

Why standest thou so far,
O God, our only star?[10]

The 'star' image, unique to Sidney's rendering, may be a signal that, as Moffet floridly put it, he was

enraged at the eyes which had at one time preferred Stellas so very different from those given them by God.[11]

Finally, the Countess of Pembroke's poem addressed 'To the Angel Spirit' of her brother suggests that it was his wounding and death that brought an end to work on the Psalms. It seems that this was not an early work that he never got round to finishing, but a 'front-line' composition, left, like its author, maimed, sick and bleeding:

O had that soul which honour brought to rest
Too soon not left, and reft the world of all
What man could show, which we perfection call,
This half-maimed piece had sorted with the best.
Deep wounds enlarged, long festered in their gall,
Fresh bleeding smart: not eye-, but heart-tears fall.
Ah memory, what needs this new arrest?[12]

Mary Herbert brilliantly conveys her intimate relationship with her mortally wounded brother and his incomplete Psalter. She weeps, she bleeds, and the infection that cut off both life and writing is renewed in her own anguish. If the Psalms were what Sidney was working on just before he died, it would account for the obsessive devotion with which his sister laboured to complete the task. She would have been quite capable of completing his translations of Du Bartas or Du Plessis Mornay, and did indeed translate the latter's *Discours de la Vie et de la Mort* in 1590,[13] but the proximity of Sidney's versions of the Psalms to his own death gave them an especially powerful claim on her attention. It was a daunting assignment, for in rendering the first forty-two Psalms into the vernacular Sidney chose to overgo the Marot–Beza French model, in which almost every Psalm – in his case, every Psalm – was in a different verse form. Prolonged familiarity with the Marot–Beza versions may have made it possible to work on this project even in the difficult conditions of the command in the Netherlands, for the French Psalter seems to have been already in use in the Sidney family during his childhood.[14] But, as Ringler says, it appears 'that the metaphrase of the Psalms was not an early work of experimentation, but a later exhibition of virtuosity'.[15] The Countess continued her brother's method, bringing, in addition to technical virtuosity, a subtlety and insight to bear on the originals which has prompted several critics to prefer her renderings. It would not be surprising if hers were more polished, for she spent almost fourteen years completing what her brother had done in the spare moments of an exceptionally taxing ten months.[16]

Six weeks of hectic preparation for departure left Sidney little time to spend with his wife and newborn daughter. Given his interest in babies, he must have found this painful – though it has to be said that if he had succeeded in sailing with Drake he would not have seen his child for another nine months. The sexist Moffet found magnanimity in Sidney's pleasure at his daughter's birth:

he warmly greeted the little girl born of her, no less gratefully and lovingly than he would have if she had taken her sex, as well as her descent, from himself. What more delightful to Philip than that face? What could be granted more charming than that daughter? What had he ever heard with a better will than that he had been made a father, and that a little girl had opened the way for the son who would be his heir?[17]

Sidney may have been less disappointed with the sex of his child than Moffet imagined. As should by now be abundantly clear, from his earliest youth he had liked and admired women, and had a high view of their moral and intellectual capacities. This did not necessarily ensure a happy marriage, but he probably looked forward with pleasure to training his daughter up to be a cultivated Protestant aristocrat, like the fictional Pamela or his real-life sister Mary. Daughters were expensive, because of the need to provide them with dowries. But with the prospect of major inheritance from the Earls of Leicester and Warwick, he was confident that in the long term there would be plenty of money. In his will he was to assign £4,000 to Elizabeth for her 'portion' – £1,000 more than Mary Sidney had had when she married the Earl of Pembroke.

On 20 November Elizabeth Sidney was christened at St Olave's, Hart Street, just by Walsingham House, with the Queen herself attending as godmother.[18] But her father missed the splendid occasion, being already in Flushing. Levying soldiers and gathering together money, horses and munitions had been a major task. Two hundred men were conscripted from South Wales to man the garrison at Flushing,[19] and many friends and relations were called upon for horses. The Earl of Rutland, for instance, gave Sidney 'a fair horse' the day before he left, which may have been for his personal use.[20] Even after he was installed at Flushing Sidney continued to be 'a beggar to many of my good friends for horses'.[21] But by no means all the personnel were military or administrative. Leicester's very large train included not only lawyers, secretaries and chaplains but musicians, acrobats, players, and the jester and stunt-man Will Kempe. Sidney's more modest retinue contained at least one talented musician, the precocious Daniel Bachelar, aged about fourteen, who was to compose many instrumental pieces for Sir Francis Walsingham's household in the next few years.[22] Another of Sidney's pages, Henry Danvers, became a distinguished soldier and generous patron of learning in the Sidneian mould. In 1622 he gave Oxford University a plot of land for the construction of a physic garden, together with £5,000 for its enclosure and plantation; in 1626 he was created Earl of Danby.[23] Sidney's secretary was the learned William Temple, who in 1609 became Provost of Trinity College, Dublin.[24] There were some disappointing absentees. Another of Sidney's secretaries, a skilled linguist and foreign agent called Stephen le Sieur, was taken prisoner at Dunkirk in mid-October 1585, while trying to negotiate with the Prince of Parma for better terms for the newly conquered city of Antwerp.[25] Indignation on behalf of 'servant Stephen' was among Sidney's many troubles in the coming months. Even more upsettingly, Fulke Greville had been given command of a hundred horsemen by Leicester, but at the last minute the Queen refused to let him go.[26] Perhaps she did not trust Sidney and Greville together after their madcap

Plymouth escapade. The consequence was that, though Greville held Sidney's revised *Arcadia* manuscript against his return, the two friends never met again.

No doubt the absence of his close friend was depressing for Sidney when he set out, as soon as his letters patent were completed, on 9 November. But his melancholy, which was immediately remarked upon by Edward Burnham, the bailiff of Flushing,[27] had deeper roots. If Greville is to be believed, by the time he was appointed to the Flushing post Sidney had virtually lost interest in fighting the Spanish in the Netherlands. He correctly foresaw 'that it would be hard for us to become absolute masters of the field in Flanders'.[28] Like many other observers, both Dutch and English, he felt that Parma's advance was now unstoppable. Bolder action on a wider stage was what was now called for. He wanted England, instead, 'to carry war into the bowels of Spain',[29] using the rebel Dutch and other anti-Spanish states as allies in surprise attacks on the Spanish mainland. Even better, he would have liked to challenge the Spanish Empire by establishing more English colonies in the West Indies and in America.[30] His commitment to this is confirmed by a letter the Governor of the English colony at Roanoke, Virginia, Ralph Lane, wrote to him in August 1585:

> My most noble General ... finding by mine own view his [the King of Spain's] forces at land to be so mean, and his terror made too great amongst us in England, considering that the reputation thereof doth altogether grow from the mines of his treasure, and the same in places which we see here are so easy both to be taken, and kept by any small force sent by Her Majesty, I could not but write these ill-fashioned lines unto you, and to exhort you, my noble general, by occasion not to refuse the good opportunity of such a service to the Church of Christ, of great relief from many calamities that this treasure in Spaniards' hands doth inflict unto the members thereof, very honourable and profitable for Her Majesty and our country, and most commendable and fit for yourself to be the enterpriser of.[31]

For Ralph Lane, himself first Governor of Virginia, Sidney was already a 'General', future governor of large tracts of land in the New World. In the eyes of Elizabeth and Leicester, he was nothing so grand. Indeed, according to Greville Leicester began his Netherlands enterprise with a poor opinion of his nephew's capabilities:

> the Earl of Leicester ... told me ... that when he undertook the government of the Low Countries he carried his nephew over with him as one among the rest, not only despising his youth for a counsellor, but withal bearing a hand upon him as a forward young man.[32]

After so many false starts Sidney was at last being sent on active service, but it was not the kind of service he really wanted. Just when he had hoped to be in the New World with Greville and away from the control of his 'Dutch uncles', he was catapulted into a conflict he no longer believed to be worthwhile, without the support of his closest friend, and under the autocratic command of Leicester.

Yet it fell to the reluctant Sidney to initiate English assistance to the United Provinces. It was urgent for the new administrators to go over quickly, to convince the Dutch that Elizabeth really meant business. Sir Thomas Cecil was suffering from gout, and was not yet well enough to travel, and until the very last minute there was uncertainty about whether the Queen would release Leicester. On the point of embarkation Sidney sent the Queen a letter of exemplary loyalty, enclosing a 'cipher', or code:

Most gracious Sovereign: This rude piece of paper shall presume, because of your Majesty's commandment, most humbly to present such a cipher as little leisure could afford me. If there come any matter to my knowledge the importance whereof shall deserve to be so masked I will not fail (since your pleasure is my only boldness) to your own hands to recommend it. In the mean time I beseech your Majesty will vouchsafe legibly to read my heart in the course of my life, and though itself be but of a mean worth, yet to esteem it like a poor house well set. I most lowly kiss your hands, and pray to God your enemies may then only have peace when they are weary of knowing your force. At Gravesend this 10th of November.[33]

None of Sidney's coded reports, if he made any, survives. However, there are more letters from him during the last year of his life than for all the previous years put together. Much of the story of these stressful months can be told in his own words, including his account of his inauspicious arrival in Flushing.

Mid-November was not an ideal time for crossing the North Sea, and the weather was bad. It was too rough to land at Flushing itself, so Sidney, with his own small party, which included his brother Robert, landed at Rammekins on Thursday, 19 November. Having no horses, they had to walk four miles through mud to Flushing. The letter Sidney sent to Leicester was designed both to warn him of the difficulties he would encounter and to encourage him to embark as soon as possible:

Upon Thursday we came into this town, driven to land at Rammekins because the wind began to rise in such sort as our masters durst not anchor before the town, and from thence came with as dirty a walk as ever poor Governor entered his charge withal. I find the people very glad of me ... how great a jewel this is to the crown of England and the Queen's safety I need not write it to your Lordship, who knows it so well; yet I must needs say the better I know it the more I find the preciousness of it ... I shall but change and not increase the ensigns by any more than mine own company, for fear of breeding jealousies in this people, which is carried more by shows than substance, and therefore the way must be rather to increase the numbers of men in each company than the companies, and that may be done easily enough, with their good liking; but I mean to innovate as little as may be till your Lordship's coming, which is here longed for as Messias is of the Jews.[34]

The 'jewel in the crown' image shows that Sidney viewed Flushing as an English bridgehead on the Continent, a compensation for the loss of Calais in 1557 and the failed attempt to take Le Havre in 1562. But he was also well aware of the awkward and ill-defined powers of the new régime, and of the many problems he had walked into. He had no house of his own, but rented a house from M. Jacques Gelée, who went over to England in mid-December.[35] Soldiers were dispersed in lodgings throughout the town. Sidney found them 'indeed very sickly and miserable'. Almost two hundred were in hospital.[36] There were many 'abuses' among the resident Dutch and English captains which urgently required reform as soon as Leicester came over:

Good my Lord, haste away, if you do come, for all things considered, I had rather you came [not] at all than came not quickly, for only by your own presence those courses may be stopped whic[h] if they run on will be past remedy.[37]

There was grumbling anxiety about

Aldegonde, a man greatly suspected, but by no man charged. He lives restrained to his house, and for aught I can find deals with nothing, only desiring to have his case wholly referred to your Lordship ... I will leave hi[m] to his clearing or condemning when your Lordship sha[ll] hear him.[38]

Phillips Marnix, Sieur de St Aldegonde, Orangist patriot and author of the rousing 'Wilhelmus' song, was strongly suspected of having betrayed Antwerp to the Prince of Parma; he had been the city's External Burgomaster. During the present interregnum William of Orange's eighteen-year-old son, Prince Maurice, was becoming a power to be reckoned with:

They h[ave] newly made Count Maurice governor of Holla[nd] and Zeeland, which only grew by the delays of your Lordship's coming, but I cannot perceive a[ny] meaning of either diminishing or crossing your Lordship's authority, but rather that the Count means wholly to depend upon your Lordship's authority.

Despite Sidney's assurances, 'the rushed election of Count Maurice ... was ... ominous in its implied continuity of the House of Orange';[39] and though Sidney was 'the welcomer that he brought money'[40] it was already apparent that this was nothing like enough for the sick and demoralized troops stationed at Flushing, who had been unpaid for weeks, and some of whom were starving. They were dependent on the goodwill of the burghers for lodging and food:

With £3,000 charges, I could find means so to lodg[e] myself and soldiers in this town as would in an extremity command it, where now we are at their miserico[rd] [mercy] ... I have dealt earnestly with the States for the relief of Ostend, but yet can obtain nothing but delays.

To conclude, all will be lost if government be not presently used. Mr Davison is here very careful in Her Majesty's causes and in your Lordship's; he takes great pains therein, and goes to great charges for it. I am yet so new here that I cannot write so important matters as perhaps hereafter I shall, and therefore I will not any further triflingly trouble your Lordship, but humbly leave you to the blessed protection of the Almighty. At Flushing, this 22th of November 1585.

On the day he wrote this letter Sidney was sworn in as Governor at the States of Zeeland's house at Middelburg.[41] Two letters to Walsingham, of 23 and 27 November, relate to specific examples of the 'abuses' he found in Flushing. In both Sidney commends to Walsingham's protection individuals who have been 'miserably spoiled', probably by rapacious captains in pursuit of money and victuals. Sidney observed that

there needs must be sharp punishment used in such like cases, or else these men will take an evil taste of our government.[42]

His own 'credit' at Flushing depended on Walsingham's fair treatment of these men.

Sidney's suggestion that Leicester's arrival would soon set all to rights was unrealistic. Like Sidney, Leicester had a difficult crossing, compounded by his own lack of seamanship. He was determined to land at the Brill, and was only persuaded at the last minute by the Vice-Admiral, Stephen Burroughs, that the harbour there was too small for his whole fleet. The consequence was that part of the fleet sailed to Flushing, but the secondary fleet with horses and provisions, under a pilot who had not heard of the change of plan, went to the Brill.[43] It was some weeks before Leicester was able to take any decisive steps towards better management of the motley and demoralized troops, for welcoming ceremonies were followed immediately by Christmas and New Year festivities, first according to the continental, New Style, calendar, and ten days later by the English calendar, which together took up the better part of a month. Everywhere Leicester was greeted with celebratory peals of ordnance, bonfires, banquets, speeches, pageants and fireworks.[44] The first such banquet was at Flushing, where Sidney and Prince Maurice entertained him on 10 December. For the time being Sidney had to abandon his underfed and ill-prepared troops at Flushing in order to accompany his uncle on his progress. While the common soldiers were so poorly paid that many were near starvation, the Dutch and English grandees with their aristocratic companions feasted and caroused, sometimes becoming drunk and disorderly,[45] and often enjoying banquets at which food was used as much for propaganda as for consumption. At a feast in Delft, for instance, where Leicester stayed at the house in which William of Orange had been assassinated, there was a symbolic centrepiece:

a castle of crystal founded on a rock of pearl, about the which flowed silver streams in which lay fowls, fishes, and beasts of all kinds: some hurt, some slain, and some gasping for breath, on the top of the which was a fair virgin lady leaning and giving her hands over the castle to succour them.[46]

The 'fair virgin', of course, stood for Elizabeth, reaching across from England to help the poor Dutch beasts.

To his credit, Sidney made it clear that he was deeply concerned about the plight of the common soldiers. In a letter to Walsingham on 10 December he threatened to make a formal complaint to the Queen and Privy Council about corrupt victuallers who were grossly overcharging.[47] With his inadequate, sickly and underfed troops he felt quite unable to secure Flushing against enemy attack, yet for the time being he was compelled to abandon his post:

My Lord of Leicester will needs have me with him to help his settling, I leave the best order I can, having great good assistance of Mr Borlas.

Sidney later came to have doubts about the reliability of William Borlas, marshal of the garrison (see below, p. 289).

It was not until the progress reached Leiden, in the second week of January, that some proper negotiations began. On the 7th the deputies of the States conferred with Leicester, Davison and Sidney, and Leicester nominated Sidney as one of his deputies to continue discussions on subsequent days.[48] His remark to Greville that he had regarded Sidney as a 'forward young man', too young to act as his adviser, may have benefited from hindsight, for Sidney was deeply implicated in Leicester's unwise decision to accept the title of Governor-General. After a great muster of horsemen at the Hague on 10 January there was another conference at Leiden, at which Sidney made a speech, presumably in his fluent French. According to a Dutch report, he made a direct connexion between ancient history and the political exigencies of the present, for he said that

he had learnt from history that when the state of the Republic of Rome had been in utter peril or danger, as the Netherlands nowadays are, which we [the Dutch] fully acknowledge, it had been necessary to create a dictatorship, with absolute power and disposition over everything concerning the prosperity of the country, without any instruction, limitation or restriction.[49]

Sidney may privately have remembered the fourth book of his own 'Old' *Arcadia*, in which the loyal counsellor Philanax assumes control of the leaderless state. Whether most influenced by history or fiction, his nephew's enthusiasm or the excitement of all that feasting and adulation, two weeks later Leicester accepted the title of Governor-General. Though he tried valiantly to argue that real honour and power still belonged to the Queen –

... I being sent hither but as her minister and officer, they have, even for her sake, made me their governor and general absolute, with the whole commanding, not only of all their provinces, their towns, and men of war in all places, but likewise have given me power and authority to dispose of all their revenues, compositions, imposts, customs, and what else ... A very great show of trust and love in Her Majesty ...[50]

– Elizabeth was not fooled. In late February she sent over Sir Thomas Heneage to convey her extreme displeasure at what she saw as Leicester's betrayal of trust. She had always been firmly opposed to accepting sovereignty of the Netherlands, for that carried with it an open-ended financial commitment. Sidney continued to maintain that Leicester had done the right thing in accepting the post of Governor, as he wrote to Burghley on 18 March:

The news here I leave to Sir Th. Heneage, who hath with as much honesty, in my opinion, done as much hurt as any man this twelvemonth hath done with naughtiness; but I hope in God when Her Majesty finds the truth of things, her graciousness will not utterly overthrow a cause so behoveful and costly unto her, but that is beyond my office. I only cry for Flushing, and crave your favour ...[51]

Sidney had been an early beneficiary of Leicester's extended powers, for in late January he made him colonel of a Zeeland regiment, and there was even some talk of his being made 'Governor of all the Isles' of Zeeland, displacing Prince Maurice.[52] In exclaiming 'I only cry for Flushing' he was defining the limits of his territorial ambition.

By the end of March the Queen was in some fashion reconciled to Leicester, though she wrote to him sadly that

it is always thought a hard bargain when both parties are losers, and so doth fall out in the case between us two.[53]

But Sidney was not forgiven. The Queen seems to have suspected that he had egged his uncle on for his own ends, and she was still angry with him in July, as Walsingham reported:

Her Majesty doth give out that the Count of Hohenlohe's discontentment groweth in respect he was removed from the colonelship of the footmen serving in Zeeland, and the same bestowed upon Sir Philip Sidney ... she layeth the blame upon Sir Philip, as a thing by him ambitiously sought. I see Her Majesty very apt upon every light occasion to find fault with him.[54]

She had always feared that he was too ready to accept foreign honours and powers unsanctioned by herself, and his involvement in Leicester's breach of trust amply confirmed this. Her deep attachment to Leicester, which went back to childhood, ensured that she could never sustain her anger with him for very long; but this did not apply to Sidney.

It is not surprising that Elizabeth was strongly critical of Sidney. She may have read his heart all too 'legibly', as he bade her do in his valedictory letter.

The very charm and generosity that won unstinting respect from friends and loyalty from dependants made him dangerously uncontrollable. Behind his desire for greater powers for his uncle and himself lay an activist approach to the English intervention in the Netherlands that was directly contrary to her policy, for she insisted that the English forces were 'defensive only'. Leicester had no mandate for extensive reconquest of the towns recently captured by Parma, only for preventing further advances.[55] Throughout 1586, as Leicester uncomfortably realized, there was a strong possibility that she might decide to make a peace treaty with Spain. Yet within weeks of his arrival Sidney was impatient to take active measures against the 'enemy', believing that the propaganda advantage of some conspicuous military successes would remove the Queen's anger. According to the burgomasters of Flushing, who regretted only that their Governor was so rarely in residence, 'by day and night he studied means to enterprise something against the enemy'.[56] In February 1585/6 he formed a cunning plan to capture the town of Steenbergen, which Parma had taken in 1582. He wrote about it to Leicester from Bergen op Zoom on 2 February:

> I am only to beseech your Excellency ... that it will please you to send forces to the besieging of Steenbergen, with 200 of your footmen, besides them that these quarters [the garrison at Bergen op Zoom] may spare, and 300 of your horse with them hereabout: I will undertake upon my life either to win it, or to make the enemy raise his siege from Grave, or, which I most hope, both. And it shall be done in the sight of the world, which is most honourable and profitable.[57]

He asked also for Captain Tutty, Sir William Stanley and Sir William Russell to help to direct operations, 'and if God will, I will do you honour in it'. Leicester agreed, and on 27 February Sidney's scheme was put into effect. The Governor of Steenbergen, La Fergie, was fed with false information that the garrison at the nearby States-held Castle of Wou was about to defect.[58] At about midnight La Fergie led his troops to the Castle of Wou, when the garrison rushed out and killed him and five of his men. Meanwhile Sidney led a thousand soldiers towards Steenbergen, hoping to intercept the enemy force on their way to or from the castle, but unfortunately 'missed of them both ways'.[59] For two days and a night he kept his men outside the town, intending to seize it while the garrison was still unmanned,

> but could do no good, by reason that the moat about the town was frozen too hard for them to pass by their boats, but not hard enough to bear them, so they were enforced to depart without further success.[60]

These details about the defeat of Sidney's scheme by the slowly thawing ice come from a journal kept by a member of Leicester's train, probably the physician and archivist Dr John James. His account of the Steenbergen venture summarizes a verbal report to Leicester by one of the commanders, Captain Tutty.[61] Far from having completed a masterly coup 'in the sight of the world', Sidney had accomplished nothing. Nor did the attempt on Steenbergen have any effect as a diversionary tactic; Parma's siege of Grave continued, and at the end of May the city surrendered, for which Leicester was blamed.[62] As so often, Sidney was unlucky. While a successful manoeuvre early in Leicester's reign might indeed have created such enthusiasm in England that Elizabeth would have been compelled to give the campaign in general, and Sidney in particular, more wholehearted support, its failure served only to confirm her view that he was a dangerous hothead.

Naturally, Sidney was disheartened by the failure of his first serious military exploit, and still more so by news of the Queen's disfavour. Her entrenched hostility drove him to look more and more eagerly towards the rising sun in Scotland, the boy-king James VI. In May he wrote warmly to the Master of Grey with special greetings to 'your King, whom indeed I love',[63] and at some time in the summer he commissioned a civil lawyer, Dr John Hammond, to draw up a judgement on the lawfulness of executing Mary Queen of Scots.[64] Meanwhile, a long letter to Walsingham on 24 March shows him putting a brave face on things, yet clearly in a state of profound depression and anxiety. It is perhaps the most revealing letter he ever wrote, exposing the stresses and contradictions in his personality more vividly than anything in his fiction:

> Right honourable: I receive diverse letters from you, full of the discomfort which I see, and am sorry to see, that you daily meet with at home, and I think, such is the goodwill it pleaseth you to bear me, that my part of the trouble is something that troubles you; but I beseech you le[t] it not. I had before cast my count of dang[er], want and disgrace, and before God, Sir, it is true [that] in my heart the love of the cause doth so far overbalance them all that with God's grace they shall never make me weary of my resolution. If Her Majesty were the fountain I would fear, considering what I daily find, that we should wax dry; but she is but a means whom God useth, and I know not whether I am deceived, but I am faithfully persuaded that if she should withdraw herself other springs would rise to help this action. For methinks I see the great work indeed in hand, against the abusers of the world, wherein it is no greater fault to have confidence in man's power than it is too hastily to despair of God's work. I think a wise and constant man ought never to grieve while he doth play, as a man may say, his own part truly, though others be out; but if himself leave his hold because other marin[ers] will be idle, he will hardly forg[ive] himself his own fault. For me, I cannot promise of my own course ... because I know there is a higher power that must uphold me, or else I shall fall; but certainly I trust I shall not by other men's wants be drawn from myself.[65]

Sidney's current religious meditations pervade this passage. He sees the conflict in the Netherlands as a foreshadowing of Armageddon, and acknowledges ultimate dependence, not on military strength, but on God, as in Psalm XX:

Now in me knowledge says
That God from fall his own anointed stays;
From heavenly holy land
I know that he hears thee,
Yea, hears with powers and helps of helpful hand.

Let trust of some men be
In chariots armed, others in chivalry;
But let all our conceit
Upon God's holy name,
Who is our Lord, with due remembrance wait.[66]

He continues:

Therefore, good Sir, to whom for my particular I am more bound than to all men besides, be not troubled with my trouble, for I have seen the worst in my judgement beforehand, and worse than that cannot be. If the Queen pay not her soldiers she must lose her garrisons, there is no doubt thereof.

At this point he seems to realize that he is in the final act of a tragedy. We know from Book 3 of the 'New' *Arcadia* that he had indeed in a wider sense 'seen the worst beforehand', for his account of the long and unproductive siege of Cecropia's fortress, culminating in the bungled suicide of the well-meaning Amphialus,[67] is as dark a vision of stagnation and defeat as even the waterlogged Netherlands could offer. He continues self-righteously:

But no man living shall be able to say the fault is in me. What relief I can do them I will. I will spare no danger if occasion serve. I am sure no creature shall be able to lay injustice to my charge, and for further doubts, truly, I stand not upon them. I have written by Adams to the Council plainly thereof; let them determine. It hath been a costly beginning unto me this war, by reason I had nothing proportioned unto it; my servants unexperienced and myself every way unfurnished, and no helps; but hereafter, if the war continue, I shall pass much better through with it. For Bergen op Zoom, I delighted in it, I confess, because it was near the enemy, but especially, having a very fair house in it and an excellent air, I destinied it for my wife, but finding how you deal there, [a]nd that ill payment in my absence thence might bring forth some mischief, and considering how apt the Queen is to interpret everything to my disadvantage, I have resigned it to my Lord Willoughby, my very friend, and indeed a valiant and frank gentleman, and fit for that place.

In conjunction with the defensive tone, there is something unpleasant about Sidney's use of his young wife as a piece of emotional blackmail. If his services had been properly appreciated, Frances Sidney could have looked forward to being honourably installed in a fine residence; but as it is, the question of her coming to join him is postponed indefinitely (see above, p. 255). Though he had told Burghley a week earlier that he wanted only Flushing, he admits here to having nursed wider territorial ambitions. Whether Bergen's position, so 'near the enemy', would really have been suitable for Frances and her baby, is another matter.

As ever, Sidney was preoccupied with his own status, and once more he had given way to a nobleman of higher rank:

Therefore I pray you know that so much of my regality is fallen. I understand I am called very ambitious and proud at home, but certainly if they knew my hea[rt] they would not altogether so judge me. I wro[te] to you a letter by William my Lord of Leicester jesting player, enclosed in a letter to my wife, and I never had answer thereof; it contained something to my Lord of Leicester, and counsel that some way might be taken to stay my Lady there. I since divers times have writ to know whether y[ou] had received them, but you never answered me that point. I since find that the knave delivered the letters to my Lady of Leicester, but whether she sent them to you or not I know not, but earnestly desire to do, because I doubt there is [m]ore interpreted thereof.

Leicester's 'jesting player' was almost certainly Will Kempe, who was later to act the part of another inefficient postman, the clown Peter in Shakespeare's *Romeo and Juliet*.[68] The ghastly possibility that Sidney hoped to avert was that the Countess of Leicester might come over to join her husband in the Netherlands, bringing a huge retinue of ladies and carriages. If this had happened, as Sidney well realized, all hope of help and encouragement from Elizabeth would be lost. Perhaps, to do him justice, it was partly in order to discourage Leicester from having his wife come over that Sidney was rather off-putting about his own wife.

The letter ends with a summary of practicalities:

Mr Errington is with me at Flushing, and therefore I think myself at the more rest, having a man of his reputation; but I assure you, Sir, in good earnest I find Borlas another manner of man than he is taken ... I would to God Burn[ham could] obtain his suit ... Turner was good for nothing, and worst for the sound of the harquebuse. We shall have a sore war upon us this summer, wherein if appointment had been kept and these disgraces forborne, which have greatly weakened us, we had been victorious. I can say no more at this time, but pray for your long and happy life ... There was never so good a father had a more troublesome son.

Send Sir William Pelham, good Sir, and let him have Clerk's place, for we nee[d] no clerks, and it is most necessary to have such a one in the council.

Sidney's parting threat to take a house not 'fit for any of the feminine gender' has already been quoted (see above, p. 255); the affectionate apology to Walsingham as his loving 'father' was probably intended to mitigate it. The elderly Nicholas Errington, master of the artillery, was to act as deputy governor of Flushing in the interregnum after Sidney's death; he impoverished himself by feeding the soldiers at his own expense.[69] The 'Turner' whose cowardice Sidney despised seems to have been Richard Turner, water bailiff of Brill, distinguished for being the likely father of the dramatist Cyril Tourneur.[70] Neither Leicester nor Sidney was pleased with the service of the diminutive Bartholomew Clerk, a Cambridge humanist and lawyer who in 1570 had translated Castiglione's *Il Cortegiano* into Latin;[71] Sidney's dismissive pun on his name is typical of his readiness to quip even in the most stressful circumstances.

The most important point at the end of Sidney's letter was his prediction that 'We shall have a sore war upon us this summer.' For him, the summer was to be 'sore' in a special sense. On 5 May Sir Henry Sidney died suddenly at the Bishop's Palace at Worcester, aged fifty-six. The Queen refused to let Philip come home to sort out his personal affairs and comfort his mother,[72] and he had little leisure for mourning. His only surviving allusion to the loss is an urgent request to Walsingham to send over some 'serviceable horses which were my father's' for military use,[73] but he must have bottled up deeper feelings of guilt and sadness. It was with the object of providing him with some kind of domestic comfort that his wife Frances was, after all, sent over to join him, in late June. His anticipation of reunion with her, on 28 June, sounds cheerful:

> I am presently going toward Flushing, whence I hear that your daughter is very well and merry . . .[74]

and there is no doubt that conjugal relations were successfully resumed, for by September she was in the early stages of pregnancy.[75] In this alien setting, so far from the comforts of Barn Elms or Walsingham House, Sidney may have found his fondness for her deepening. The experiences of motherhood and a sea-crossing to a war zone forced her to grow up fast, and she found a new friend in Louise de Coligny, William of Orange's widow, who lived in the Prinsenhof at Flushing. Like many Elizabethan women, Frances Walsingham was little more than a child at the time of her marriage. As she matured she became more interesting and attractive to her husband, and given time they might have grown really close.

But the pleasures of married life had to be snatched in brief intervals, for the war was gathering momentum. It was urgent to achieve some successes to set against a dismal list of failures. Grave had fallen at the end of May, and on 19 June Venlo also fell, despite a daredevil raid on Parma's camp led by the fearless Roger Williams.[76] On 30 June Sidney, his brother Robert, and the hard-drinking Count Hohenlohe were engaged in harassing enemy troops from Breda,[77] and about the same time Sidney and Prince Maurice planned something more ambitious. Dutch sources give the eighteen-year-old Maurice chief credit for the surprise of Axel, English ones Sidney. There is no doubt that they were in it together, and that for once the plan worked; Axel was taken on 7 July. According to Stow, Sidney prepared his men for this daring 'camisado', or night raid,[78] by making a 'long oration' about a mile from the town in which he presented the conflict as a holy war:

he needed not to show against whom they fought, men of false religion, enemies to God and his church: against AntiChrist, and against a people whose unkindness both in nature and in life did so excel, that God would not leave them unpunished ... Again, the people whom they fought for were their neighbours, always friends, and well-willers to English men. And further, that no man should do any service worth the noting, but he himself would speak to the uttermost to prefer him to his wished purpose.[79]

Greville, too, mentions Sidney's rewards to his men:

... he revived that ancient and severe discipline of order and silence in their march, and after their entrance into the town placed a band of choice soldiers to make a stand in the market-place ... and, when the service was done, rewarded that obedience of discipline in every one liberally out of his own purse.[80]

Molyneux admiringly describes the follow-up to the capture of the town, in which Sidney caused dykes to be cut so that the whole surrounding country was flooded, 'the same having been the best and most fertile soil in those parts'.[81] Starvation was a normal tactic on both sides; no one much cared what happened to the 'boors', or native peasants.

Whether or not Sidney took the leading rôle in the capture of Axel, Greville's account of his generous rewards to his own soldiers is likely to be correct. In the last months of his life Sidney was spending money like water, and continually writing recommendations for individuals he considered deserving of more substantial help.[82] The very last letter he wrote before the skirmish near Zutphen was a testimonial for a Mr Richard Smith, a servant of the Queen's who 'now, being aged and weak', needed to be pensioned off.[83] His judgements were not always accepted. For instance, he wrote to Walsingham in defence of the Treasurer of the army, Richard Huddilston, whom he described as 'in all things whereby I could judge religious and honest', but Huddilston was later convicted of dishonesty.[84]

Only a week after his triumph at Axel, Sidney's willingness to think the best of people led him into near-disaster at the sea-port of Gravelines, which had been held by the Spanish since 1578. Parma's forces were aware that the capture of Leicester's nephew would be a major triumph, and set up a trap for him, described here by the unknown diarist:

certain of our men to the number of 40 were taken and slain by a treacherous practice of them of Gravelines, who had secretly covenanted with Sir Philip Sidney for the delivery of the castle and town, thinking to have entrapped himself, but failed of their purpose; for he for the more surety sent first only 27 men to the town, who were received in; and after, being expected to have come himself, he mistrusting their treachery sent yet 50 more; who being come near the town, were assailed by a 100 horse and 200 foot: yet escaped all (saving a 14 or 15) to their boats again.[85]

On 14 August Sidney wrote to Davison that

The long practice of Gravelines which was brought unto us is proved flat treason, I think even in them that dealt with us.[86]

It had been a close-run thing, and despite later attempts to salvage some honour from the affair the truth was that over forty men had been killed to no purpose, contributing to the growing list of defeats and blunders in the Leicestrian campaign, not all of which could be blamed on the Queen's refusal to fund it properly.

While Sidney was back at Flushing in mid-August he had another piece of bad news. His mother had died in London on 9 August. She may have been staying at Walsingham House, for her death was registered at St Olave's, Hart Street, before the body was taken away for burial beside her husband at Penshurst.[87] Her brief three months of widowhood, spent far away from her three sons, who were all in the Netherlands, must have been profoundly wretched. This time there was no question of Sidney going home for the funeral. According to modern medical opinion on 'accident proneness',

emotional stress is probably the most important factor. Cycles of accidents seem to occur in the months after stressful 'life events', regardless of the personality of the person involved.[88]

In July, at the time of the Gravelines fiasco, Sidney was exercising great caution in refusing to expose himself to risk. By the time he left off his thigh armour on the morning of 22 September he had apparently ceased to do so. It may have been his mother's death, and the total impossibility of taking any time off to grieve for her, that changed his attitude. If Moffet is right – and as the Countess of Pembroke's doctor, he may have been – the bad news of his mother's death was compounded by a rumour that his sister, too, was mortally ill.[89] Like many of the recently bereaved, he was overwhelmed by a sense of life's emptiness, as

a tale
Told by an idiot, full of sound and fury,
Signifying nothing . . .[90]

and it may not be coincidental that within six weeks of his mother's death he was seriously injured.

There were many other things to depress Sidney's spirits, and for the first time he was becoming openly critical of his uncle. In one of four letters written on 14 August, all reporting on the desperate condition of the Flushing garrison, he hinted this to Walsingham:

> I assure you, Sir, this night we were at a fair plunge to have lost all for want of it [pay]. We are now four months behind, a thing unsupportable in this place. To complain of my Lord of Leicester you know I may not, but this is the case, if once the soldiers fall to a thorough mutiny this town is lost in all likelihood. I did never think our nation had been so apt to go to the enemy as I find them.[91]

To underline his point he stressed the strategic importance of Flushing, claiming that without it 'all the King of Spain's force ... should be never able to invade England'. There was some truth in this, for Flushing would indeed have been an excellent point for Parma to reinforce Philip II's 'Invincible Armada' in the summer of 1588.

The 'sore war' continued through the summer of 1586, punctuated, for Leicester's immediate retinue, by frequent merrymakings. On 23 July, for instance, he had

> feasted all the ladies and gentlewomen and the noblemen of these countries with a great supper in an arbour made on purpose in the great garden at the Hague ...

at which there was 'music, dancing and fireworks'.[92] If he could not achieve much military success, at least he could win friends through the lavish hospitality he was so good at (see above, pp. 91–7). In the second half of August the campaign moved north into Gelderland, following the movements of Parma and his troops, and this, too, was marked with feasting. On 20 August Leicester arrived at Arnhem, his camp being set up at nearby Amerongen, and on the 24th

> being Bartholomewtide, his Excellency kept a solemn feast and prayer for the good success of the army against the enemy.[93]

Recollections of the massacre at Paris fourteen years earlier should have sharpened up the enthusiasm of the exhausted troops. But the strain of the last six months was beginning to tell. The fiery Count Hohenlohe, who not unnaturally resented Sidney's displacement of him as lieutenant of the Zeeland regiment, had also quarrelled with Leicester, with the veteran Sir John Norris, and with Sir William Pelham, Marshal of the camp; and on arrival at Amerongen a vehement quarrel broke out between Sir William Pelham and Sir John Norris about the quartering of their troops.[94]

On 2 September Leicester achieved one of his few successes, with a carefully organized siege of Doesburg. The town surrendered after ten hours of battery.

Sidney and his brother wanted to be among the first to enter the town, but Leicester forbade them, giving the hazardous privilege instead to the more experienced Norris.[95] Once inside the city, discipline broke down, and there was an orgy of rape and pillage, for which Sir William Stanley's men were chiefly blamed.

In mid-September Leicester moved to Deventer, where he summoned a meeting of the Council of State. From there, on 14 September, Sidney wrote a Latin letter to the humanist scholar Justus Lipsius, who in March had dedicated to him a treatise on the correct pronunciation of Latin.[96] Not surprisingly, Sidney declared himself 'almost overwhelmed by the floods of those affairs', yet he urged Lipsius to consider settling in England:

> The terms which I once obtained for you I shall get confirmed, so that even if I die they will not lapse. I know that you will be most welcome to our Queen and to many others ... may the Muses themselves attend you so that you may return, and not leave us who truly love you ... We struggle against many difficulties. I believe it is the will of God to temper things for his people so that we have neither triumph nor disaster.[97]

With part of himself, Sidney was preparing for the possibility of his own death; but with another part he was looking forward to a return to England and a renewal of the intellectual companionships he so much enjoyed.

It was not to be. On the very day after Sidney wrote to the philosopher Lipsius, Leicester left Deventer in a great hurry, hearing that Parma and his whole army were marching towards Zutphen, a town which had been held by the Spanish since 1583.[98] Sidney's regiment was left behind to guard Deventer, so when he fought the enemy near Zutphen on 22 September it was as an independent soldier.

The town of Zutphen, beside the River Issel, was notoriously well fortified. Leicester's immediate object was to capture as many as possible of its surrounding forts.[99] But on the evening of 21 September news came that a large convoy of provisions was expected to arrive at Zutphen the next morning. A hasty plan was made to intercept it, the leaders of the attack being Norris and Stanley. Sidney, in too much of a hurry, left off his thigh armour. Thomas Digges, who was there, described what happened:

> In the morning the 22 of September fell a great and thick mist, that you might hardly discern a man ten paces off, at the breaking up whereof the enemies appeared so near our companies, having planted all their muskets and harquebuses, being 2000, and their pikes being a thousand, very strongly on the high way, as our men, specially the noblemen and gentlemen, as the Earl of Essex, the Lord Willoughby, Sir Philip Sidney, Sir William Russell, Sir John Norris, and the rest, in number seven or eight score, who were in troop together in the face of the enemy before our footmen, received the whole volley of the enemy's shot.[100]

The early-morning mist meant that the troops were wrongly positioned, with the force of the enemy's attack falling on the mounted noblemen rather than on the foot soldiers. The size of the enemy force was far larger than expected, amounting, according to Stow, to 2,200 musketeers and 800 foot soldiers, against barely 200 horsemen and 300 or 400 foot. Sidney had his horse killed under him, but remounted and returned to the charge. Many of Parma's regiments were composed of Albanians, and an Albanian commander, George Crescier, was taken prisoner by Willoughby.[101] Willoughby himself pressed forward so deep into the enemy lines that he was in imminent danger of being captured, and it was while rescuing him from capture that Sidney received a musket shot in his left thigh, 'three fingers above the knee'.[102] A man called 'Udal', possibly Sidney's old servant John Uvedale, tried to lead Sidney's horse, which was restive and nervous after the musket-blast, back to the camp. But he insisted on riding away independently, wounded though he was, so that 'The foe shall miss the glory of my wound.'[103] Constant practice in the tiltyard had taught Sidney how to keep his seat firmly, and even with one leg badly injured he was able to guide his horse back to the camp. Then

> being brought to my lord lieutenant, his Excellency said, 'O Philip, I am sorry for thy hurt!', and Sir Philip answered, 'O my lord, this have I done to do you honour and Her Majesty service.' Sir William Russell coming to him kissed his hand, and said with tears, 'O noble Sir Philip, there was never man attained hurt more honourably than ye have done, nor any served like unto you.'[104]

Leicester wrote an account of Sidney's injury to Sir Thomas Heneage the following day:

> Albeit I must say it was too much loss for me, for this young man he was my greatest comfort, next Her Majesty, of all the world, and if I could buy his life with all I have to my shirt, I would give it. How God will dispose of him I know not, but fear I must needs greatly the worst; the blow in so dangerous a place, and so great; yet did I never hear of any man that did abide the dressing and setting his bones better than he did. And he was carried afterwards in my barge to Arnhem, and I hear this day he is still of good heart, and comforteth all about him as much as may be. God of his mercy grant me his life, which I cannot but doubt of greatly. I was abroad that time in the field giving some order to supply that business, which did endure almost two hours in continual fight, and meeting Philip coming upon his horseback, not a little to my grief. But I would you had stood by to hear his most loyal speeches to Her Majesty, his constant mind to the cause, his loving care over me, and his resolute determination for death, not one jot appalled for his blow, which is the most grievous that ever I saw with such a bullet; riding so a long mile and a half upon his horse ere he came to the camp; not ceasing to speak still of Her Majesty; being glad if his death might any way honour Her Majesty, for hers he was whilst he lived, and God's he was sure to be if he died; prayed all men to think that the cause was as well Her

Majesty's as the Countries' [i.e. the States General's], and not to be discouraged, for you have seen such success as may encourage us all, and this my hurt is the ordinance of God by the hap of the war. Well, I pray God, if it be his will, save me his life, even as well for Her Majesty's service' sake as for mine own comfort.[105]

This letter was evidently intended for consumption at Court, and though it was true that Sidney had managed to ride back to the camp despite his shattered leg, and that he submitted himself calmly to the surgeons, the loyal speeches may have been somewhat heightened by Leicester for propaganda purposes.

For the next twenty-five days Sidney lay at Arnhem in the house of a judge's widow, Mme Gruithuissens, having travelled there by barge along the River Issel. Despite his initial misgivings about the severity of the wound, Leicester was soon able to report hopefully on his nephew's progress. On 27 September he received an encouraging report from the surgeons; Sidney was sleeping quite well, and seemed to be recovering.[106] By 2 October the worst appeared to be over, as he wrote to Walsingham:

Good Mr Secretary, I trust now you shall have longer enjoying of your son, for all the worst days be passed, as both surgeons and physicians have informed me, and he amends as well as possible in this time, and himself finds it, for he sleeps and rests well, and hath a good stomach to eat, without fear, or any distemper at all. I thank God for it.[107]

On the 6th he wrote even more cheerfully:

... your son and mine is well amending as ever man hath done for so short a time. He feeleth no grief [pain] now but the long lying, which he must suffer. His wife is with him, and I tomorrow am going to him for a start. But for his hurt, that Thursday may run amongst any of our Thursdays, for there was never a more valiant service this 100 years by so few men against so many.[108]

The mythologizing of Zutphen was already under way. It is still going strong, as evidenced in a recent assertion that the encounter was a 'battle', not a 'skirmish', even though a 'skirmish' is what it is called in all eye-witness accounts.[109] Also, though it was a brave stand of the few against the many, it achieved nothing, for Zutphen was successfully revictualled a few days later. On 7 October Leicester visited Sidney, and saw for himself how he was; he came away in good enough spirits to give a feast for the Burgomasters and Magistrates of Deventer on the 14th.[110] But a manifest deterioration in Sidney's condition set in as soon as his uncle had left him. Greville must have sought eye-witness information about these agonizing days, for his chronology here seems to be correct, locating Sidney's decline immediately after Leicester's visit:

Now after the sixteenth day was past, and the very shoulder-bones of this delicate patient worn through his skin with constant and obedient posturing of his body to their art, he, judiciously observing the pangs his wound stang him with by fits, together with many other symptoms of decay, few or none of recovery, he began rather to submit his body to these artists [experts] than any further to believe in them. During which suspense he one morning, lifting up the clothes for change and ease of his body, smelt some extraordinary noisome savour about him, differing from oils and salves, as he conceived, and, either out of natural delicacy, or at least care not to offend others, grew a little troubled with it; which they that sat by perceiving, besought him to let them know what sudden indisposition he felt. Sir Philip ingenuously told it, and desired them as ingenuously to confess whether they felt any such noisome thing or no. They all protested against it, upon their credits, whence Sir Philip presently gave this severe doom upon himself, that it was inward mortification, and a welcome messenger of death.[111]

Leicester himself had admitted that Sidney was suffering pain from his 'long lying', which tallies with the excruciating bed-sores described by Greville. The truth was that the wounded leg was gangrenous and stinking, and further intervention did nothing but exacerbate the pain. According to Moffet, the 'stitched edges of the muscles [were] opened and pulled apart' by a doctor from Bergen;[112] but the bullet was never extracted, lying too deep in the thigh, and amputation, which might conceivably have saved his life, was apparently not attempted.[113] Some days earlier, a doctor generously sent to Sidney's aid by Count Hohenlohe, himself recovering from a musket shot in the throat received on 4 October, had reported ominously to his master that Sidney was 'not well'. The swashbuckling Hohenlohe riposted angrily:

Away, villain, never see my face again till thou bring better news of that man's recovery, for whose redemption many such as I were happily lost.[114]

The doctor, Adrian van der Spiegel, returned to Sidney's bedside, and was a beneficiary of his will.

In spite of pain, fever and the distracting presence of all those doctors and surgeons, Sidney's mind remained clear. Two pieces of prose writing survive from his death-bed. We know that there was once a third, for Edmund Molyneux records that a few days before his death

he wrote a large epistle to Belerius, a learned divine, in very pure and eloquent Latin (in like sort as many times he had done before to some great ones, upon occasions, and to others of learning and quality) the copy whereof was, not long after, for the excellency of the phrase, and pithiness of the matter, brought to Her Majesty's view.[115]

This letter ought to have achieved wide circulation, but unfortunately it cannot now be traced, nor can 'Belerius' be identified with certainty. It has been suggested that he was one Pierre Bellier, who had translated Philo Judaeus;

but an equally likely candidate is the Antwerp scholar-printer Jean Beller, who among many other works translated Thomas à Kempis's *Imitation of Christ*.[116]

Most probably Sidney's lost epistle had to do with the *prisca theologia* and Platonic arguments for the immortality of the soul. Like his own Arcadian heroes, he may have prepared for his expected death by setting out the philosophical arguments for belief in the survival of the individual mind, and celebrating this belief in song. This is what the Arcadian princes did. The night before his expected execution Pyrocles, in a speech inspired by Du Plessis Mornay's *De la vérité*, demonstrates the immortality of the soul, and Musidorus sings a sonnet against the fear of death:

Since nature's works be good, and death doth serve
As nature's work, why should we fear to die?
Since fear is vain, but when it may preserve,
Why should we fear that which we cannot fly?

Fear is more pain than is the pain it fears,
Disarming human minds of native might;
While each conceit an ugly figure bears,
Which were not ill, well viewed in reason's light.

Our owly eyes, which dimmed with passions be,
And scarce discern the dawn of coming day,
Let them be cleared, and now begin to see:
Our life is but a step in dusty way.
Then let us hold the bliss of peaceful mind;
Since this we feel, great loss we cannot find.[117]

Whether this was the song Sidney called 'La cuisse rompue', we have no way of knowing. He can only have given the song the nickname after his own thigh was broken. Alternatively, it may have been one of his own Psalm versions, such as the penitential Psalm VI:

... Lo, I am tired, while still I sigh and groan:
My moistened bed proofs of my sorrow showeth:
My bed, while I with black night mourn alone,
With my tears floweth.
Woe, like a moth, my face's beauty eats,
And age pulled on with pains all freshness fretteth:
The while a swarm of foes, with vexing feats
My life besetteth ...[118]

Or, again, it may have been a rather conventional lyric, with a setting by Byrd, which is attributed to Sidney in a manuscript belonging to a Fellow of All Souls called Robert Dow, who died in 1585:

O Lord, how vain are all our frail delights;
How mix'd with sour the sweet of our desire;
How subject oft to Fortune's subtle sleights;
How soon consum'd, like snow against the fire.
Sith in this life our pleasures all be vain,
O Lord, grant me that I may them disdain.

How fair in show where need doth force to wish;
How much they loathe, when heart hath them at will;
How things possess'd do seem not worth a rish [rush],
Where greedy minds for more do covet still.
Sith in this life etc.

What prince so great as doth not seem to want?
What man so rich, but still doth covet more?
To whom so large was ever Fortune's grant
As for to have a quiet mind in store?
Sith in this life etc.[119]

Whatever the song was that Sidney had sung to him, there can be little doubt of its singer. He was surely the talented page Daniel Bachelar, who was depicted in Thomas Lant's *Funeral Roll* as a little boy perched on a great horse caparisoned with cloth of gold.[120] Among the pieces he composed for Sidney's widow and father-in-law, such as 'The Lady Frances Sidneys Good Night', or 'The Widows Mite', may be musical reminiscences of the penitential lyric sung at Arnhem.

The two death-bed writings that survive point in opposite directions. In one, his will, Sidney prepared for death; in the other, his summons to Jan Wier, he clutched at a slender possibility of life. On 30 September, while still in relatively good health and spirits, Sidney made his will. Molyneux praised it as 'most bountiful and liberal ... if the same be performed according to his simple, sincere and good meaning'.[121] One of the lawyers in Leicester's retinue must have helped him to draw it up correctly. Neither he nor Sidney can be blamed for not realizing that there was nothing like enough money to satisfy his many creditors, and that a letter of attorney he had left with Walsingham, empowering him to raise money by selling lands, was invalidated by an entail.[122] Since Sidney had been unable to go home to sort out his father's affairs during the summer he was not in a position to know about this, nor about the many debts his father had left. It may also have been assumed that Leicester would salvage his nephew's honour by sharing some of the heavy financial burden that fell on Walsingham; in fact he refused to do so.

Read purely in terms of its intentions, the will is a splendid document, expressing the affability and munificence for which Sidney was well loved.[123] Frances was to have a life interest in half the estate, and his youngest brother

Thomas an annuity of £100. The chief heir, his brother Robert, was made responsible for paying his daughter Elizabeth her generous portion of £4,000. If Frances turned out to be with child with a boy, Robert would be displaced; if a girl, this second daughter would share with her sister a total portion of £5,000, 'the one to have as much as the other in every condition'. In the event, Frances miscarried in early December.[124] Sidney's rich uncles Leicester and Warwick required only tokens of esteem; to each he left £100. To his sister Mary he bequeathed 'my best jewel set with diamonds', and further jewels were left to three of his aunts, the Countesses of Huntingdon, Warwick and Leicester. His comrade-in-arms Sir William Russell, the Countess of Warwick's youngest brother, was to have 'my best gilted armour', and Dyer and Greville were to divide between them 'all my books'. Whether this denoted manuscripts and personal papers, as well as his extensive library, we do not know. His old travelling companion Edward Wotton was left 'one fee buck, to be taken yearly out of my park at Penshurst'. Sidney was generous to his servants of long standing. Griffin Maddox, who had been with him on the Grand Tour, was left an annuity of £40, and so were Harry White and Henry Lyndley. The illiterate Philip Jordayne and his wife, who were probably domestic attendants, got £30 a year. Stephen le Sieur, still a prisoner at Dunkirk, was to have £200 'to be paid unto him either to redeem him thence ... or after his coming out, for his better maintenance'. Other bequests related to Sidney's immediate circumstances. All the servants who had come to Flushing with him in October were to have £3 apiece, and Dr James, 'for his pains taken with me in this my hurt', was left £30. Frances Sidney was required to get diamond rings made for the Earls of Huntingdon and Pembroke, and the widowed Countess of Sussex. To his Walsingham parents-in-law he bequeathed £100 each, 'to bestow in jewels or other things as pleaseth them to wear for my remembrance'. There was little danger of their forgetting their remarkable son-in-law, however, for Walsingham was ruined by his expenditure on Sidney's behalf, and when he in turn died, in 1590, willed that he should be buried at night and without ceremony, 'in respect of the greatness of my debts and the mean estate I shall leave my wife and heir in'.[125]

Clearly Sidney had now come to love and trust his wife, for she was made 'sole executrix', and was given some independent responsibility:

> I pray mine executrix to be good and give so much money as to her discretion shall seem good to those mine old servants to whom by name particularly I have given nothing to, referring it to her as she shall think good.

In effect, though, it was the five joint supervisors, Leicester, Huntingdon, Warwick, Pembroke and Walsingham, who would oversee the execution of the will, and in practice it nearly all fell to Walsingham.

Some unfamiliar names crop up. For instance, we know nothing of Sidney's 'dear friend Mr William Hungate', to whom he left £20 for a ring, except that he went to Ostend with Robert Sidney in November 1585, was present at the skirmish near Zutphen, and witnessed the will.[126] The obscure Hungate is immediately followed by the Queen, who was to have a jewel worth £100. Nor is much known of Sidney's servants John Langford and John Uvedale, though the latter was to receive the substantial sum of £500 'immediately after my death'. This may have something to do with Uvedale's gallant attempt to lead Sidney's restive horse from the battlefield (see above, p. 295).

On 15 October the Earl of Leicester, himself unwell, came back to Arnhem to be with his dying nephew.[127] Two days later, on 17 October, Sidney composed a codicil to his will. Through it we can glimpse the people assembled in that fetid chamber in Mme Gruithuissens's house. Sidney is said to have died in the arms of his secretary, William Temple, who was left an annuity of £30.[128] For practical reasons, this may well be true, for Temple must have had to come very close to his feverish and emaciated master to take dictation of the final whispered bequests, and may have lain down beside him in order to do so. No fewer than eight medical men are remembered: 'Isert the bone-setter', 'Roger my apothecary', 'Mr Marten my surgeon'; four surgeons already named, Goodridge, Kelly, Adrian and John; and finally 'the doctor that came to me yesterday', Gisbert Enerwitz, to whom he bequeathed an additional fee of £20.[129] Leicester's devotion in coming to be with his nephew at the last was rewarded with 'the best hangings for one chamber; and the best piece of plate I have'. There were plenty of hangings to choose from, for when Sidney crossed to Flushing a whole boatload of tapestries had been brought across separately.[130] Leicester's stepson Essex received the symbolic gift of 'my best sword', and Willoughby was given the second-best one.

Despite Greville's stress on Sidney's summoning of numerous 'ministers ... who were all excellent men of divers nations',[131] only two clergymen are named in the will, each being left £20 in the codicil. 'Mr Gifford' was probably the Essex Puritan George Gifford, and 'Mr Fountain' the minister of the French church in London, Robert le Maçon, Sieur de la Fontaine.[132] De la Fontaine was a close associate of Du Plessis Mornay, and Sidney may have shared with him, as well as with the shadowy 'Belerius', his final reflexions on life after death. Soon after he made his bequests to the two ministers Sidney's strength failed him, for the last sentence of his will – like the last sentence of the *Arcadia* – is unfinished:

> Item, I give to my good friends Sir George Digby and Sir Henry Goodyear, either of them a ring of

To his last gasp, Sidney was giving things away.

The disproportion between doctors and clergymen in Sidney's will matches a contradiction in records of the manner of his death. Most accounts, such as Moffet's, Greville's and the treatise possibly by George Gifford, show him achieving a state of serene resignation. The speech that Greville claims Sidney made to his brother Robert is often quoted:

> Love my memory, cherish my friends: their faith to me may assure you they are honest; but above all govern your will and affections by the will and word of your Creator: in me beholding the end of this world with all her vanities.[133]

Yet Greville was not present, and may have reconstructed this beautiful valediction from Gifford's report that

> He did ... exhort his two brothers in an affectionated manner, giving them instruction in some points and namely to learn by him that all things here are vanity.[134]

Though there is little reason to doubt that Sidney did spend much time in religious discussion and devotion, struggling, like Pyrocles and Musidorus, to reconcile himself to his own physical extinction, he also had a natural longing to live. Of the early witnesses, only George Whetstone acknowledges this, attributing some convincingly robust sentiments to the dying Sidney:

> To tell you plain, to die I do not grieve,
> And yet of both, I rather wish to live;
> Which who gainsays, unwisely spends his breath:
> He fain would live, that most doth prate of death.[135]

Intellectually, Sidney was prepared for death, and he had never lacked physical courage. But accounts of his death concur in showing him as deeply remorseful for past vanities, which may or may not have included his delight in 'Lady Rich'. According to Gifford, he said that 'I have walked in a vain course':

> He did also sundry times complain that his mind was dull in prayer, that his thoughts did not ascend up so quick as he desired.[136]

Some days later, on being told

> that godly men in time of extreme afflictions did comfort and support themselves with the remembrance of their former life, in which they had glorified God: 'It is not so', said he, 'in me. I have no comfort that way. All things in my former life have been vain, vain, vain.'[137]

He longed desperately for 'time for amendment of life'. Despite all that he had suffered at the hands of the surgeons, he reached out after one last chance, as Molyneux recorded:

> The night before he departed, leaning upon a pillow in his bed, he wrote a line or two by way of letter to Wierus, a very expert and learned physician, to pray him to come unto him.[138]

The letter, which Molyneux quotes, survives in the Public Record Office; Sidney's wobbly hand reflects the pillow he leaned on and his debilitated state:

Mi weiere, veni, veni, de vita periclitor et te cupio. nec vivus nec mortuus ero ingratus. plura non possum sed obnixe oro ut festines. Vale. Arnemi.

Tuus Ph. Sidney

[My dear Wier, Come. Come. My life is in danger and I long to see you. Whether I live or die I shall not be ungrateful. I cannot write more but with what strength I have I beg you to hasten to me. Farewell. Arnhem. Your Philip Sidney][139]

Jan Wier, or Weier, aged seventy-one, was physician to the Duke of Cleves. He had written boldly against superstition and the persecution of supposed witches.[140] More to Sidney's present purpose, he had theories about how to treat fever and skin infections. The bearer of the letter, Dr Gisbert Enerwitz, was Wier's nephew. But in a long covering note Enerwitz said that he doubted whether Sidney would live, and the letter was never delivered.[141]

Next morning, 17 October, Sidney had strength only to dictate, not to write, the codicil to his will. According to Gifford, when too far gone to speak, he raised his hands

and set them together at his breast, and held them upwards, after the manner of those which make humble petition: and so his hands remained, and were so stiff that they would have so continued standing up, being once so set, but that we took them the one from the other.[142]

The unknown diarist tells the rest:

This afternoon about 2 o'clock, the most virtuous and honourable gentleman Sir Philip Sidney, Lord Governor of Flushing, being clean worn away with weakness (all strength of nature failing to continue longer life in him) departed in wonderful perfect memory even to the last gasp, and in so good and godly mind as they that were present stood astonished, in doubt whether they should receive greater comfort of the manner of his death, or grief for the loss of so rare a gentleman and so accomplished with all kind of virtue and true nobility, as few ages have ever brought forth his equal, and the very hope of our age seemeth to be utterly extinguished in him.[143]

EPILOGUE

In telling the story of Sidney's death I have omitted a famous anecdote. According to Fulke Greville, as Sidney was riding away from the skirmish at Zutphen,

> being thirsty with excess of bleeding, he called for drink, which was presently brought him; but as he was putting the bottle to his mouth he saw a poor soldier carried along, who had eaten his last at the same feast, ghastly casting up his eyes at the bottle; which Sir Philip perceiving, took it from his head before he drank, and delivered it to the poor man with these words: 'Thy necessity is yet greater than mine.'[1]

My object has been to get as close as possible to 'Sidney as he lived', with little reference to posthumous legend. Greville, writing at least thirty-five years after his death, sought to mould his friend to the form of an antique hero, and Plutarch had told a story of Alexander the Great in the desert giving a helmet full of water to his troops, keeping none for himself.[2] If Sidney really gave his water-bottle to a dying soldier, it is odd that none of the earliest accounts of his wounding, such as those of Leicester, Digges, Whetstone, Lant, Molyneux or Moffet, refers to it.

Yet Greville's story has a higher truth. Sidney was above all a *vir generosus,* a man 'in all ways generous', as Henri Estienne said,[3] whose magnificence often came near to prodigality.[4] From his gift of 12d. to a blind harper when he was only eleven until his very last breath, with which he tried to leave rings to the witnesses of his will, he spent a large part of his life rewarding merit. A few among the many others who received material benefits from him were his old nurse, Anne Mantell; the Protestant minister Théophile de Banos; the scholars Abraham Fraunce and Gabriel Harvey; the poet Edmund Spenser; the scrivener Richard Robinson; the Jesuit Edmund Campion; the jurist Henry

Page with elegies on Sidney and their musical setting by William Byrd from manuscript part-book (Christ Church, Oxford)

Finch;[5] the miniaturist Nicholas Hilliard;[6] the logician William Temple; and the young composer Daniel Bachelar. To the Queen he gave ingenious and expensive jewels and clothes; to male friends he gave books, firearms or dogs;[7] to innumerable servants and bearers of letters he gave both sums of money and the strength of his recommendation and influence. Probably every one of the sixty yeomen and gentlemen who followed in his funeral procession on 16 February 1587 had received particular and personal benefits at his hands.

He was aptly described in one of the many songs lamenting his death as 'he that did good to all men'.[8]

To his sister he presented his portrait and, most precious of all, his *Arcadia*, 'done only for you'. He may have asked for his literary works to be burnt,[9] but must have guessed that they would not be. Even in an age of magnificence, Sidney was superlatively generous with his money, his time and his talent. The nameless soldier to whom he gave his water-bottle may stand for us, the unknown beneficiaries of his literary genius.

NOTES

For abbreviations, see the Note on the Text, pp. xv–xviii.

PREFACE

1. *Hamlet* V. ii. 401–2.
2. Shelley, *Adonais, an elegy on the death of John Keats* (1821) 22.
3. Ben Jonson, 'Conversations with Drummond', in *Works* ed. C. H. Herford and P. Simpson (1925) i. 138–9.
4. *NA* 255.

CHAPTER 1

1. Pyrocles to Musidorus, *NA* 72–3.
2. *OA* 263.
3. W. S. Gilbert, *HMS Pinafore* (1878).
4. *NA* 238.
5. Ibid. 391.
6. C. S. Lewis, *Sixteenth Century Literature* (1954) 338.
7. For Mary I's love of children, cf. Warren W. Wooden, *Children's Literature of the English Renaissance* (Kentucky 1986) 55–72.
8. Feuillerat iii. 134.
9. William Higford, *Advice to his Grandson* (1658) 65.
10. Wallace 9. For further contemporary references to Mary Sidney's verbal skills, see Greville, *Prose Works* 179.
11. Cf. Beryl Rowland, *Birds with Human Souls: A Guide to Bird Symbolism* (Tennessee 1978) 119.
12. *NA* 240.
13. *Misc. Prose* 139.
14. Josephine Roberts ed., 'The Imaginary Epistles of Sir Philip Sidney and Lady Penelope Rich', *ELR* 15 (1985) 69.
15. Geffrey Fenton, *Tragicall Discourses* (1567).
16. Feuillerat iii. 122.
17. Elizabeth Clinton, Countess of Lincoln, *The Countess of Lincoln's Nursery* (Oxford 1622).
18. Webster, *The White Devil* III. ii. 336–8.

19. *HMC De L'Isle and Dudley* i. 240.
20. *Nobilis* 71.
21. Ibid. 70–71.
22. *Misc. Prose* 168.
23. Feuillerat iii. 104; Osborn 451.
24. T. P. Roche in Kay 191.
25. *OA* 66. 5.
26. Robert Naunton, *Fragmenta Regalia* (*circa* 1620) ed. E. Arber (1870) 30.
27. Claire Cross, *The Puritan Earl* (1966) 57.
28. D. M. Meads ed., *Diary of Lady Margaret Hoby 1599–1605* (1930).
29. Cross, *Puritan Earl* 56.
30. *HMC De L'Isle and Dudley* i. 259.
31. *Misc. Prose* 149.
32. *Complete Peerage* ii. 76.
33. Ibid. xii. 403.
34. Elizabeth Russell became a Maid of Honour, died young, and achieved sufficient fame from her monument in Westminster Abbey to be represented as one of Mrs Jarley's waxworks in Dickens's *Old Curiosity Shop* (1841) chapter XXVIII.
35. Osborn 371.
36. *AS* 82. 14.
37. *NA* 214.
38. Germaine Warkentin, 'The Meeting of the Muses', *Sir Philip Sidney and the Interpretation of Renaissance Culture* (1984) 17–33.
39. Stow, *Annales* (1592) 1191.
40. *Complete Peerage* vii. 552.
41. Feuillerat iii. 166–8.
42. There is an epitaph on her in BL MS Egerton 2642, fol. 214.
43. *AS* 11. 5–8. cf. also 'Lamon's Tale', *OP* 4. 180–84.
44. Translated from Feuillerat iii. 103.
45. Ibid. iii. 166–7.
46. *NA* 95.
47. Ibid. 96.
48. *Misc. Prose* 46–57.
49. Ringler xxii–iii.
50. *Nobilis* 74.
51. *OA* 3.
52. *NA* 214.
53. *OA* 245.
54. R. Mulcaster, *Positions* (1581) chapter 38.
55. *OA* 294–300.
56. *NA* 358–63.
57. *AS* 106. 9–11.
58. *OED*, 'charm'.

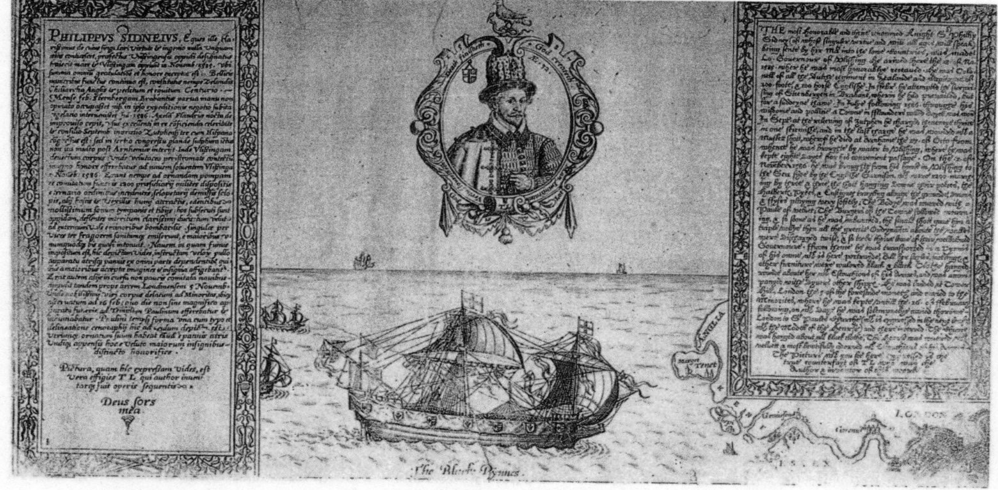

Theodore de Bry's thirty-two plates for Thomas Lant, 'Funeral Procession of Sir Philip Sidney' (Aldrich Collection, Christ Church, Oxford)

CHAPTER 2

1. *OA* 75.
2. *Nobilis* 90, 92; 77–8.
3. *FQ* II. vi. 44.
4. *NA* 464.
5. Pears 88–9.
6. Wallace 130.
7. Feuillerat iii. 124.
8. Greville, *Prose Works* 38–9.
9. Wallace 69.
10. *NA* 163.
11. *Nobilis* 71.
12. T. W. Baldwin, *Shakespear's Petty School* (1943) 67.
13. *Sidney* 289.
14. Wallace 117.
15. In 1573; cf. *HMC De L'Isle and Dudley* i. 264, 426–7.
16. *HMC Salisbury* i. 439.
17. Bodleian Ashmole Rolls 18. a.
18. John Stow, *A Survey of London*, ed. C. L. Kingsford (1908) i. 183–5, 74–5; ii. 143.
19. *HMC De L'Isle and Dudley* i. 242.
20. Wallace 409.
21. Rebholz 8–9.
22. Wallace 38.
23. Rebholz 9.
24. Wallace 50, 413.
25. *HMC De L'Isle and Dudley* i. 243.
26. Cf. *Victoria County History of Shropshire* iii (1979) 60, 241; *Camden Miscellany* ix. 44; P. W. Hasler, *The House of Commons 1558–1603* (1981) ii. 457.
27. Claudius Desainliens, alias Hollyband, *Campo di Fior, or else The Flowrie Field of Fowre Languages* (1583) 167–71.
28. Wallace 47.
29. Ibid. 47, 408.
30. *Nobilis* 72.
31. Ibid. 73.
32. Wallace 410.
33. *HMC Salisbury* i. 439.
34. Greville, *Prose Works* 5.
35. Cf. Wallace 42–3.
36. Ibid. 422.
37. Ibid. 408.
38. Jean Robertson, 'Sidney and Bandello', *The Library*, 5th series, xxi (1966) 326–8.
39. Nicholas Breton, 'Amoris

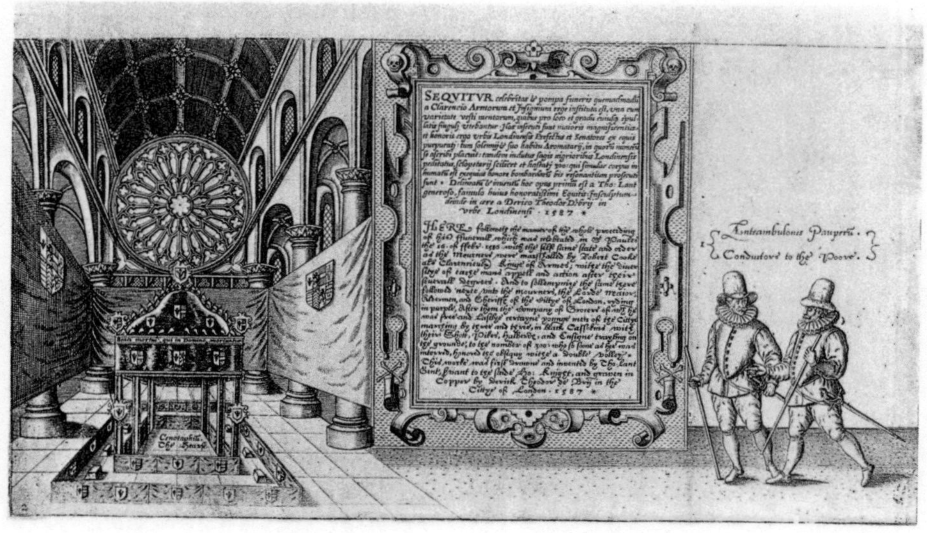

Lachrimae', *Brittons Bowre of Delights* (1591) sig. A1ᵛ.
40. Thomas Churchyard, *The Worthiness of Wales* (1587).
41. Wallace 48.
42. *OA* 129–30.
43. *NA* 288.
44. William Camden, *Britannia* (1610) 673.
45. *CSP Ireland 1509–1573* 286; Osborn 5.
46. Wallace 408.
47. Osborn 14.
48. *AS* 33. 12–13.
49. Michele Margetts, 'The Birth Date of Robert Devereux, 2nd Earl of Essex', *Notes & Queries* N.S. 35 (1988) 34–5.
50. Wallace 53–4.
51. Ibid. 57.
52. Ibid. 61.
53. *OA* 375.
54. John R. Elliott, 'Queen Elizabeth at Oxford: New Light on the Royal Plays of 1566', *ELR* 18 (1988) 218–29.
55. Wallace 63.
56. Nichols i. 211; cf. also John R. Elliott, art. cit.
57. John Rainolds, *Th'overthrow of Stage-Playes* (1599) 45.
58. James Calfhill, *An Answere to the treatise of the Crosse* (1565).
59. Cf. Elliott, art. cit. 225.
60. A. Golding trs., Philippe du Plessis Mornay, *A woorke concerning the trewnesse of the Christian religion* (1587) sigs.*3ᵛ–4ʳ.
61. *Misc. Prose* 97.
62. *HMC De L'Isle and Dudley* i. 244.
63. Osborn 15.
64. George Whetstone, *Sir Phillip Sidney, his honourable life, his valiant death, and true vertues* (?1587).
65. Feuillerat iii. 132.
66. Quoted in J. M. McConica ed., *History of the University of Oxford* iii (1986) 41.
67. *HMC De L'Isle and Dudley* i. 269.
68. Cf. Rosenberg 125–8.
69. John Aubrey, *Brief Lives*, ed. A. Clark (1898) i. 183.
70. Wallace 102.
71. Ibid. 101.
72. In a notebook belonging apparently to 1568, Camden included a Latin epigram 'Ad P. S. cum Horat.'; BL MS Cotton Appendix LXII, fol. 4ᵛ. I am indebted to Mr W. H. Kelliher for this reference.

73. Nathaniel Baxter, *Ourània* (1606) sigs. N1^v–N2^r.
74. *Nobilis* 76–7.
75. Ibid. 77–8.
76. Ibid.
77. *The Phoenix Nest* (1591) 8–10.
78. R. Carew, *Survey of Cornwall* (1602) fol. 102^v.
79. Osborn 23.
80. *OA* 71.
81. *NA* 286–7.
82. Ibid. 358.

CHAPTER 3

1. *AS* 21. 7–9.
2. *HMC Cecil* i. 404.
3. Philisides tells the story of his life, *OA* 334.
4. *Misc. Prose* 134.
5. Ibid. 139.
6. For a useful genealogy, cf. BL MS Stowe 652.
7. *Misc. Prose* 134.
8. Lawrence Stone, *The Crisis of the Aristocracy 1558–1641*, abridged ed. (1967) 196.
9. *HMC Cecil* i. 415–16.
10. Ibid. 404–5.
11. Wallace 25–34.
12. BL MS Lansdowne x. 193.
13. Sir John Summerson's opinion, quoted in Conyers Read, *Lord Burghley and Queen Elizabeth* (1960) 121–3.
14. Read, op. cit. 125.
15. Desmond Bland ed., *Gesta Grayorum [1594]* (1968) xxv.
16. Bland, ed. cit. 8.
17. C. T. Prouty, *George Gascoigne* (New York 1942) 25.
18. Wallace 89.
19. BL MS Lansdowne 104 fol. 193.
20. Collins i. 43–4.
21. Wallace 85.
22. Bodleian Ashmole MS 356.
23. *Nobilis* 75.
24. *OA* 5.
25. It has been claimed that the MS is in his hand, but Dr Andrew Watson has inspected it, and thinks it is not.
26. Cf. Rosenberg 36–7.
27. *HMC Rutland* i. 95.
28. Read, op. cit. 126.
29. *HMC Rutland* i. 94.
30. This is the opinion of Professor

S. W. May; but cf. also Ellen Moody, 'Six Elegiac Poems, possibly by Anne Cecil de Vere, Countess of Oxford', *ELR* 19 (1989) 152–70.

31. Although Alençon became Duke of Anjou after the death of Charles IX I refer to him throughout as 'Alençon' for the sake of clarity.

32. *Misc. Prose* 112.

33. Geffrey Whitney, *A choice of emblemes and other devises* (Leiden 1586) 196–7.

34. Wallace 114.

35. John Buxton and Bent Juel-Jensen, 'Sir Philip Sidney's First Passport Rediscovered', *The Library*, 5th series, xxv (1970) 42–6.

36. Wallace 105.

37. Osborn's assumption (24, 519) that Sidney was himself ill at Reading, and that this illness, unmentioned in the horoscope, indicates that it was cast earlier than the spring of 1571, is questionable. 'In time of sickness', the phrase in the Sidney accounts, probably refers to the epidemic that Sidney was being kept away from, rather than to his own sickness; and the large sum expended, £38 11s. 6d., suggests an extended stay at Reading. The relevant accounts cover the period May 1571 to June 1572, so whenever the stay at Reading was, it was later than spring 1571.

38. T. Coryat, *Coryat's Crudities* (1611) 171.

39. Wallace 115.

40. Osborn 42–3.

41. Sir J. Harington, *A New Discourse of a Stale Subject [1596]*, ed. E. S. Donno (1962) 108.

42. Cf. Keith Thomas, *Man and the Natural World* (1987) 154–7.

43. *OA* 259.

44. Bryskett, *A Discourse of Civill Life* (1606) 160–61, in Bryskett, *Works.*

45. T. Bright, *In Physicam Scribonii Animadversiones* (1584) *4r.

46. T. Bright, *An Abridgement of the Booke of Acts and Monuments* (1589) *5r.

47. *Misc. Prose* 48.

48. Ibid. 110.

CHAPTER 4

1. Sidney to his brother Robert, *circa* 1580; Feuillerat iii. 125.

2. Lodowick Bryskett, 'A pastoral Aeglogue upon the death of Sir Philip

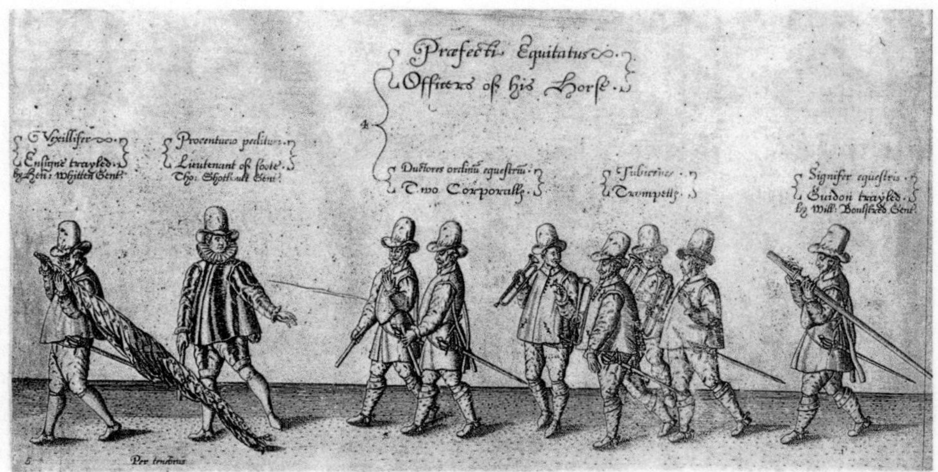

Sidney', recalling his travels with Sidney in 1572–5, from Bryskett, *Works* 292.
3. *OA* 66. 22–3.
4. Osborn 103–4.
5. Buxton 62.
6. Cf. letter to Languet of 21 April 1576, cited in C. S. Levy, 'A supplementary inventory of Sir Philip Sidney's correspondence', *Modern Philology* 67 (1969–70) 177–8.
7. *Misc. Prose* 97.
8. Feuillerat iii. 99.
9. Osborn 245.
10. *AS* 84. 4–5.
11. *OA* 71–2.
12. Osborn 302–3.
13. Fynes Moryson, *An Itinerary* (1617) III. I. 1.
14. J. J. Jusserand, 'Spenser's Twelve Private Morall Vertues as Aristotle hath Devised', *Modern Philology* 3 (1906) 373–83.
15. *Sidney* 287, 291.
16. Osborn 306–7.
17. Buxton 47.
18. Osborn 416–17; cf. also 424–5.
19. Ibid. 412–13.
20. Greville, *Prose Works* 5–6.
21. *HMC De L'Isle and Dudley* ii. 96.
22. Osborn 126.
23. Cf. K. Duncan-Jones, 'Sidney in Samothea yet again', *RES* xxxviii (1987) 226–7.
24. Osborn 141–7.
25. Ibid. 143.
26. I am indebted to the late John Buxton for this point.
27. *Misc. Prose* 140.
28. Pears 64.
29. Moryson, *An Itinerary* III. II. 1.
30. Aubrey, *Brief Lives*, ed. A. Clark (1898) ii. 249.
31. *NA* 142–3.
32. Pears 102, 148.
33. Ibid. 144, 149.
34. *Complete Peerage* ii. 1238.
35. Wallace 160–61.
36. Osborn 112.
37. Moryson, *An Itinerary* III. I. 2.
38. *NA* 12.
39. Feuillerat iii. 126.
40. *OA* 12.
41. Osborn 121.
42. K. Duncan-Jones, 'Sidney's Pictorial Imagination', unpublished B. Litt. thesis, University of Oxford (1964).
43. Osborn 138, 143.
44. Cf. W. L. Godshalk, 'A Sidney Autograph', *The Book Collector* 13 (1964) 65.

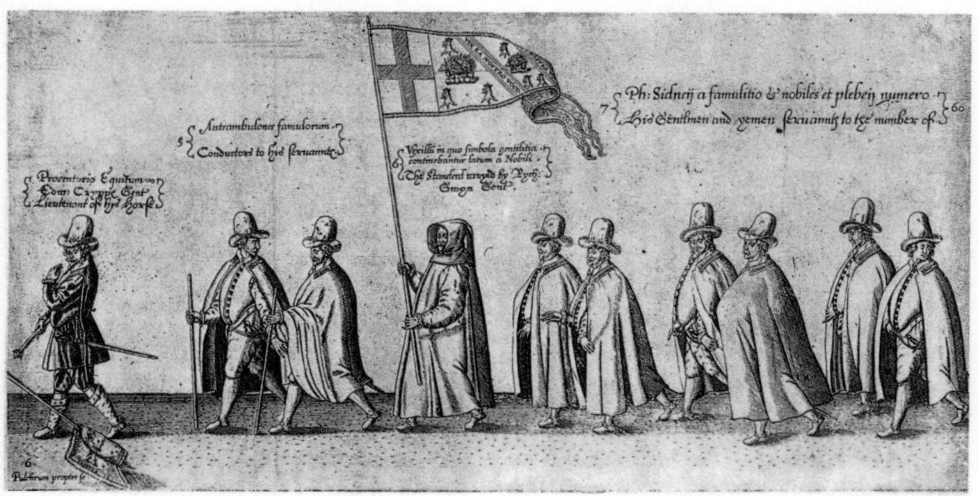

45. Osborn 121.
46. S. K. Heninger, 'The Typographical Layout of Spenser's *Shepheardes Calender*', in K. J. Höltgen *et al.* eds., *Word and Visual Imagination* (Erlangen 1988) 41.
47. Buxton 57.
48. Osborn 89.
49. Ibid. 428 and *passim*.
50. For an account of Bryskett's life and writings, see H. R. Plomer and T. P. Cross, *The Life and Correspondence of Lodowick Bryskett* (Chicago 1927).
51. Pietro Bizzari, *Varia opuscula* (Venice 1565).
52. Osborn 215.
53. Ibid. 108.
54. Pietro Bizzari, *Historia della guerra fatta in Ungheria dall'invitissimo Imperatore de Christiani, contra quello de Turchi* (Venice 1568).
55. Feuillerat iii. 127.
56. K. M. Lea ed., *Godfrey of Bulloigne* (1981) 27.
57. *OA* 31. 184; cf. Cesare Pavese, *Il Targa, dove si contengono le cento & cinquanta Favole* (Venice 1575) 28.
58. *Misc. Prose* 95.
59. Lucy Crump, *A Huguenot Family in the Sixteenth Century* (1926) 33.
60. Osborn 259.
61. Bryskett trs., *A Discourse of Civill Life* (1606) 17, in Bryskett, *Works*.
62. For a full account of Perrot's life and works, see Martha W. England, 'Sir Philip Sidney and François Perrot de Messieres: Their Verse Versions of the Psalms', *Bulletin of the New York Public Library* 75.1 (1971) 30–54, 101–10.
63. England, art. cit. 38.
64. Cf. F. J. Sypher ed., *A Woorke Concerning the Trewnesse of the Christian Religion* (New York 1976) xi–xv.
65. Osborn 294.
66. A translation is printed in Osborn 394–5.
67. Cf. Ringler 403.
68. Tennyson, 'Hendecasyllabics', 1863.
69. *OA* 33. 7–11.
70. *DNB*.
71. N. F. McClure ed., *The Letters of John Chamberlain* (1939) i. 179–80.
72. Sidney 212.
73. L. B. Osborn, *The Life, Letters and Writings of John Hoskyns* (1937) 155.
74. Pears 121.
75. Cf. Frances Yates, *John Florio* (1934) 220.
76. *Misc. Prose* 149.

77. Osborn 308.
78. Feuillerat iii. 125.
79. *HMC De L'Isle and Dudley* ii. 95.
80. Osborn 315–17.

CHAPTER 5

1. *OED* 9.a.
2. Sidney, *The Lady of May* (1578), *Misc. Prose* 29, on courtiers' pursuit of the Queen's favour.
3. Spenser, 'Mother Hubberds Tale', 895ff. from W. Oram *et al.* eds., *The Shorter Poems of Edmund Spenser* (Yale 1989) 364–5.
4. *OA* 35.
5. *CSP Ireland 1574–85*, 42.
6. Wallace 148, 152.
7. Grateful thanks to Mr Daniel Waissbein, who drew my attention to this document, and translated it from BL MS Add. 28, 263, fol. 2.
8. *CSP Spanish 1558–67* 133.
9. Ibid. 179.
10. *'tenido por Catholico'*, MS cit.
11. Wallace 83.
12. Kuin, *A Letter* 3.
13. *CSP Spanish 1558–67*, 459.
14. Kuin, *A Letter* 3; Marie Axton, *The Queen's Two Bodies* (1977) 63–4.
15. *OA* 321.
16. Osborn 389–90.
17. *Victoria County History: Warwickshire*, vol. vi, 137 and *passim*.
18. Kuin, *A Letter* 4–5.
19. Osborn 327.
20. Kuin, *A Letter* 78.
21. Greville, *Prose Works* 4–5.
22. *HMC De L'Isle and Dudley* i. 259.
23. *OA* 245.
24. *HMC De L'Isle and Dudley* i. 362.
25. Wallace 158.
26. See C. T. and R. Prouty, '*The Noble Art of Venerie* and Queen Elizabeth at Kenilworth', in J. McManaway, G. E. Dawson and F. E. Willoughby eds., *Joseph Quincy Adams Memorial Studies* (Washington 1948) 639–65.
27. *Arte of Venerie* (1575) 90.
28. Roy Strong, *The English Renaissance Miniature* (1983) 64.
29. *Arte of Venerie* (1575) 95.
30. Prouty, art. cit. 661.
31. De L'Isle MSS E93.
32. *NA* 53.

33. Ibid. 54.
34. Nichols i. 438.
35. Kuin, *A Letter* 46.
36. BL MS Harl. 6395, fol. 36^{v}; Kuin, *A Letter* 100.
37. Ringler 402.
38. George Gascoigne, *The Glasse of Governement etc.*, ed. J. W. Cunliffe (1910) 91 ff.
39. Ringler 65.
40. Osborn 347.
41. *Sidney* 11–12.
42. BL MS Royal 18A xlviii.
43. C. T. Prouty, *George Gascoigne* (1942) 93–7.
44. Bodleian MS Rawl. poet. 85, fol. 7^{r}.
45. E. K. Chambers, *Sir Henry Lee* (1936) 82 and *passim*; Sargent 20–23.
46. Sargent 24–6.
47. Ibid. 188; cf. Lamentations I. 12, 'Behold and see, if there be any sorrow like unto my sorrow.'
48. Sargent 35.
49. BL MS Add. 15214, fol. 12b.
50. *HMC De L'Isle and Dudley* ii. 201.
51. Sargent 5.
52. Tenison ed., *Baconiana* (1679).
53. *Three Letters* 31.
54. Peter Beal, 'Poems by Sir Philip Sidney: The Ottley Manuscript', *The Library*, 5th series, xxxiii (1978) 284–95.
55. CS 16. 11–14.
56. *OA* 9.61.
57. Geffrey Whitney, *A choice of emblemes and other devises* (Leiden 1586) 196–7.
58. *OA* 66. 40.
59. *Sidney* 247; Sargent 63.
60. Osborn 313–15 and *passim.*
61. Cf. Feuillerat iii. 77.
62. Osborn 421–2.
63. Ibid. 445.
64. Ibid. 427–9.
65. Carolus Clusius, *Rariorum stirpium per Hispanias observatorum* (Antwerp (Plantin) 1576).
66. Osborn 418.
67. Ibid. 445.
68. Ibid. 425.
69. Holinshed, *Second Volume of Chronicles, Ireland* (1587) 133b.
70. Ibid. 134a.
71. *DNB.*
72. Osborn 440.
73. *Sidney* 227.
74. Thomas Churchyard, *A general rehearsal of wars* (1579) sig. D2a.
75. *Sidney* 214.

76. Ibid. 250.
77. Wallace 167–8.
78. Anne Chambers, *Granuaile: The Life and Times of Grace O'Malley c. 1530–1603* (Dublin 1979) 86.
79. *NA* 248.
80. *OA* 204.
81. *HMC De L'Isle and Dudley* i. 434.
82. Ibid. ii. 48.
83. *Chronicles of Ireland* 143a.
84. Ibid. 143–4.
85. H. E. Rollins ed., *The Paradise of Dainty Devices* (1927) 87–8, 251–3.
86. Holinshed, *Chronicles* (1587) iii. 1552.

CHAPTER 6

1. Shelley, *Adonais* (1821) 45.
2. Ringler 345.
3. Cf. Cupbearer's receipt, dated 17 June 1577, with note 'while his picture was making', described in Thomas Thorpe, *Catalogue of a small but interesting collection of ancient MSS* (1840) III. 1107. Cf. H. R. Woudhuysen, 'A "Lost" Sidney Document', *Bodleian Library Record* 13 (1990) 353–9. Although Sir Roy Strong has recently discovered that the Longleat portrait once bore the date 1578, this may refer to the year of its completion. Alternatively, the Longleat exemplar may have been copied from a 1577 original.
4. Robert Sidney 174–5.
5. Osborn 203.
6. *AS* 2.5.
7. Cf. *HMC De L'Isle and Dudley* i. 249–50, 439; Wallace 188.
8. *HMC Rutland* i. 110, 111.
9. Ibid.
10. *HMC De L'Isle and Dudley* i. 270.
11. *Nobilis* 75.
12. Wallace 171.
13. *CSP Domestic 1547–80* 440, 443.
14. Grateful thanks to Dr Julian Roberts for pointing out that Dee's diary entry does not indicate that the meeting was at Mortlake.
15. Wallace 173.
16. P. French, *John Dee: The World of an Elizabethan Magus* (1972) 38–9.
17. Osborn 449.
18. French, op. cit. 182–3.

19. Sargent 40–45.
20. Cf. BL MS Eg. 2790, fols. 221–2.
21. Pears 119.
22. Marlowe, *Dr Faustus* I 52–61.
23. French, loc. cit.
24. Stern 150. Thanks to H. R. Woudhuysen for drawing my attention to this reference.
25. Rosenberg 323 ff.
26. Thomas Nashe, *Have With You to Saffron Walden* (1596) in Nashe, iii. 116, 76–7.
27. Cf. Rosenberg ibid.
28. Stern, loc. cit.
29. Ibid. 23.
30. P. Holland trs., *The Roman Historie* (1600) 46.
31. Stern 50–51.
32. Aubrey, *Brief Lives*, ed. A. Clark (1898) ii. 248–9.
33. Osborn 450.
34. *DNB*.
35. *CSP Dom. Addenda 1566–79* 516–17.
36. *DNB*.
37. *Nobilis* 82.
38. Cf. K. J. Höltgen, 'Why are there no wolves in England? Philip Camerarius and a German Version of Sidney's Table Talk', *Anglia* 99 (1981) 60–82.
39. Wallace 172–3.
40. Greville, *Prose Works* 20.
41. Osborn 454–5.
42. Feuillerat iii. 105–8.
43. Cf. K. J. Höltgen, art. cit.
44. Cf. A. P. McMahon, 'Sir Philip Sidney's Letter to the Camerarii', *Publications of the Modern Language Society of America* 62 (1947) 83–95.
45. R. Peterson trs., Della Casa, *Il Galateo* (1576) 12–13, 16–32.
46. Cf. *OA* 10. 16–18, a poem possibly quite close in time to this conversation, in which Geron's old dog Melampus is described as having once been a match for a wolf.
47. Osborn 464.
48. Wallace 174.
49. Simpson 67–8.
50. Fynes Moryson, *An Itinerary* (1617) I. I. II.
51. For a detailed and authoritative account of religion at the Imperial Court, cf. R. J. W. Evans, *The Making of the Habsburg Monarchy 1550–1700* (1979) 3–40.
52. Simpson 115–16.
53. Ibid. 115.
54. Ibid. 123.
55. Wallace 178; Buxton 88.
56. Wallace 179.

57. *Misc. Prose* 11.
58. BL MS Add. 139830, fols. 47–9.
59. Godfrey Anstruther, O.P., *Vaux of Harrowden* (1953) 131.
60. Feuillerat iii. 135.
61. Ibid. iii. 110–11.
62. Stern 234.
63. Cf. Evans, op. cit.
64. *The Tempest* I. ii. 75–7.
65. Feuillerat iii. 110.
66. Cf. T. DaCosta Kauffman, *The School of Prague: Painting at the Court of Rudolf II* (Chicago and London 1988) 66–70 and *passim*.
67. T. DaCosta Kauffman, 'The Allegories and Their Meaning' in P. Hulten *et al.*, *The Arcimboldo Effect* (1987) 89–108.
68. *OA* 8.
69. *AS* 29. 9–12.
70. *NA* 86.
71. *Misc. Prose* 92.
72. McMahon, art. cit. 84–5.
73. Feuillerat iii. 113.
74. Greville, *Prose Works* 25–6.
75. Rebholz 34.
76. Pears 108–9.
77. Osborn 482–90, 529–33.
78. Pears 117.
79. Wallace 181.
80. C. V. Wedgwood, *William the Silent* (1944) 155–6.
81. Greville, *Prose Works*, 13–14.
82. Wedgwood, op. cit. 173–4.
83. Ringler 209.
84. Wedgwood, op. cit. 138–9.
85. Cf. H. H. Rowen, *The Princes of Orange* (1988) 20–21.
86. Osborn 491n.
87. Wedgwood op. cit. 175.
88. Ringler 431.
89. Ibid. 152.
90. Collins i. 193.
91. Wallace 182–3.
92. Ibid. 184.
93. Woudhuysen 236n.
94. Wallace 185.
95. Simpson 115.
96. *NA* 102.
97. *Misc. Prose* 4–7, 175.
98. Collins i. 199.
99. *Misc. Prose* 3.
100. Cf. *DNB* entry for Thomas Butler, tenth Earl of Ormond (1532–1614).
101. Wallace 191–2.
102. BL MS Cotton Titus B XII, fols. 564–5.
103. *Misc. Prose* 8.
104. Ibid. 11.
105. Ibid. 4.

106. C. T. Prouty, *George Gascoigne* (1942) 278.
107. M. G. Brennan, *Literary Patronage in the English Renaissance: The Pembroke Family* (1988) 24.
108. *CSP Addenda 1566–79*, 522–3.
109. Feuillerat iii. 118–19.
110. *Complete Peerage* x.
111. Ringler 343–4.
112. *Misc. Prose* 78.

CHAPTER 7

1. *Sidney* 213.
2. Edmund Molyneux, *Historical Remembrance of the Sidneys*, in Holinshed, *The third volume of Chronicles*, 1588.
3. *Sidney* 242.
4. Cf. Pears 117, 137.
5. Ibid. 144–5, 146.
6. Buxton 91.
7. Ibid. 152.
8. J. A. van Dorsten, *Poets, Patrons and Professors: Sir Philip Sidney, Daniel Rogers, and the Leiden Humanists* (Leiden 1962) 52.
9. Pears 122, 131, 138; Wallace 197.
10. Van Dorsten, loc. cit.
11. Cf. Hannay 27 and *passim*.
12. Young 34–7.
13. *Sidney* 2–4.
14. *NA* 255.
15. Ibid. xv.
16. Ringler li.
17. *Sidney* 314.
18. *OA* 73.
19. Cf. *Nobilis* 74.
20. *OA* 66.
21. Sargent 69–9.
22. Nichols ii. 92–223.
23. *Misc. Prose* 21–32.
24. S. Sadie ed., *The New Grove Dictionary of Music and Musicians* (1980) vi. 401.
25. Rosenberg 302–3.
26. Ringler 361–2.
27. L. A. Montrose, 'Celebration and Insinuation; Sir Philip Sidney and the Motives of Elizabethan Courtiership', *Renaissance Drama* n.s. VII (1977) 3–35.
28. *Misc. Prose* 47.
29. *OA* 4.
30. Feuillerat iii. 122.
31. Ibid. iii. 123.
32. Ibid. iii. 120.

33. Roger Williams, *A Briefe discourse of Warre* (1590) 2; cf. also 17; Bryskett, *Works* A4ᵛ.
34. *DNB*; Peck, *LC* 207.
35. *Misc. Prose* 31.
36. *DNB*.
37. *Misc. Prose* 28.
38. *HMC De L'Isle and Dudley* i. 250.
39. Nichols ii. 77.
40. Ibid. 68, 78.
41. Collins i. 256.
42. Pears 148.
43. *CSP Foreign 1577–8* 820.
44. Wallace 199.
45. *CSP Foreign 1578–9* 149.
46. Pears 154.
47. Greville, *Prose Works* 21.
48. Bodleian MS Rawl. D. 345.
49. Ibid. fol. 17ʳ.
50. Stern 40–46.
51. BL MS Lansdowne 120, fols. 179–87.
52. Nashe iii. 92.
53. *OA* 22.
54. Cf. G. L. Barnett, 'Gabriel Harvey's *Castilio sive Aulicus* and *Aulica*: A Study of Their Place in the Literature of Courtesy', *Studies in Philology* 42 (1945) 146–53.
55. D. E. Baughan, 'Sidney and the Matchmakers', *MLR* XXXIII (1938) 515.
56. Wallace 196–7n.
57. Nichols ii. 249.
58. Ibid. ii. 81.
59. Ibid. ii. 260.
60. Wallace 204.
61. Camden, *Annals* (1635) 390.
62. Nichols ii.277.
63. Pears 157.
64. Ibid. 167.
65. For an account of the duties of the Royal Cupbearer, cf. BL MS Stowe 561. This was drawn up for Charles I, but incorporates traditions going back to the Court of Henry VIII.
66. Van Dorsten, op. cit. 66.
67. Camden, *Annals* 200.
68. *HMC Bath* v. 266.
69. Berry, *Stubbs* xlvii.
70. Cf. I. and P. Opie, *Oxford Dictionary of Nursery Rhymes* (1951) 177–81.
71. Berry, *Stubbs* 85.
72. Ibid. 24.
73. *DNB*.
74. Wallace 213.
75. Berry, *Stubbs* xlvii–xlix.
76. Pears 187.

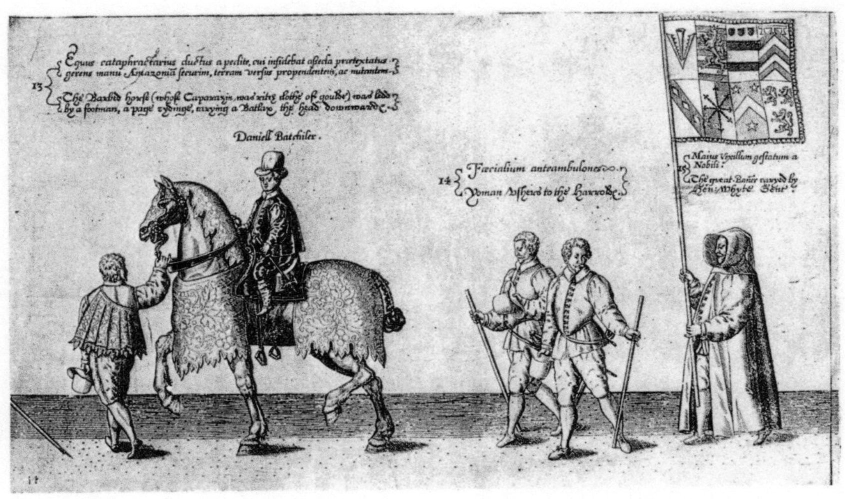

77. *Misc. Prose* 51.
78. Ibid. 50.
79. Ibid. 52.
80. Ibid. 56.
81. Ibid. 57.
82. Greville, *Prose Works* 38.
83. Contrast Wallace 216.
84. Feuillerat iii. 128.
85. If this is correct, the date I suggested in *Misc. Prose* 34, 'November or December 1579', is too late.
86. Greville, *Prose Works* 38.
87. Ibid. 39.
88. Ibid. 41.
89. Woudhuysen 259.
90. C. L. Kingsford, 'On some ancient deeds and seals belonging to Lord De L'Isle and Dudley', *Archaeologia* lxv (1913–14) 251–68.
91. Kingsford, art. cit. 253.
92. *Misc. Prose* 140.
93. May, 'Oxford and Essex', 12.
94. Pears 166.
95. D. C. Peck, 'Ralegh, Sidney, Oxford and the Catholics, 1579', *Notes & Queries* 223 (1978) 427–31.
96. May, 'Oxford and Essex', 11–12n.
97. From Bodleian MS Tanner 306, fol. 115^{b}, a single tipped-in sheet, apparently in the hand of Henry Spelman; cf. also fols. 117^{a-b}.
98. Woudhuysen 156.

CHAPTER 8

1. *OA* 3.
2. V. Woolf, 'The Countess of Pembroke's Arcadia', in *Collected Essays* (1966) i. 27.
3. *OA* 3.
4. Woudhuysen 310.
5. Nichols ii. 289–90.
6. Ringler 243–4.
7. Cf. Feuillerat iii. 337–41; *Sidney* 397.
8. Walter de la Mare ed., *Come Hither* (1923) item 286.
9. *Sidney* 290.
10. John Buxton, 'An Elizabethan reading-list', *The Times Literary Supplement* (24 March 1972) 343–4.
11. Despite the claim made in Osborn 536–7.
12. Buxton, art. cit.
13. Feuillerat iii. 134.
14. Aubrey, *Brief Lives* ed. A. Clark (1898) ii. 248.
15. *Fettiplace Receipt Book* 136–7.

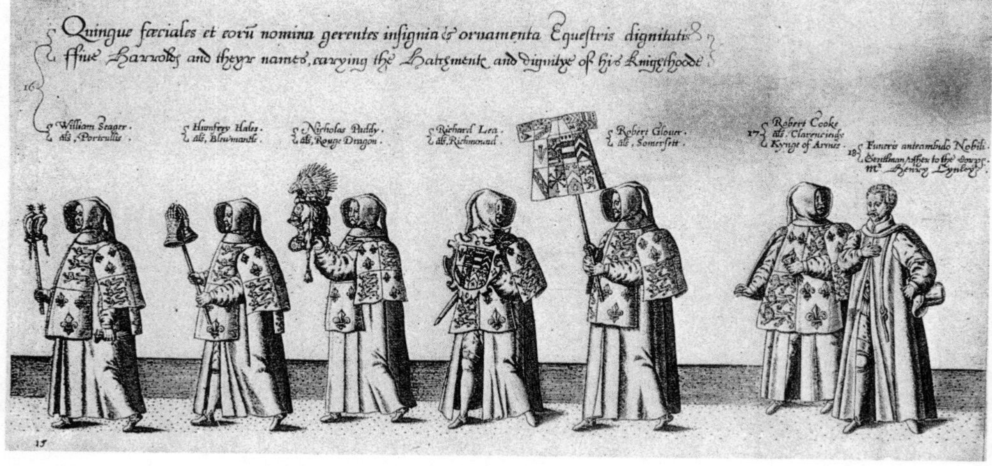

16. Stern 79n.
17. Buxton, art. cit.
18. Feuillerat iii. 137.
19. Buxton, art. cit.
20. D. C. Peck, 'Ralegh, Sidney, Oxford and the Catholics, 1579', *Notes & Queries* 223 (1978) 427–31.
21. *Sidney* 147.
22. Pears 181–2.
23. Hannay 196.
24. Feuillerat iii. 129.
25. *Misc. Prose* 111.
26. *Sidney* 311.
27. *Misc. Prose* 78.
28. *OA* 4.
29. Ibid. 283–4.
30. Ibid. 320.
31. Ibid. 5.
32. Ibid. 7–8.
33. M. S. Goldman, 'Sidney and Harington as Opponents of Superstition', *Journal of English and Germanic Philology* liv (1955) 526–48.
34. John Webster, *The Duchess of Malfi* III. ii. 78–9.
35. *OA* 9.
36. Theodore Spencer, 'The poetry of Sir Philip Sidney', *English Literary History* xii (1945) 267.
37. Wallace 237.
38. *OA* 244–5.
39. Ibid. 196. Frumenty was 'a dish made of hulled wheat boiled in milk and seasoned with cinnamon, sugar etc.' (*OED*); this rustic delicacy was to play a crucial part in Hardy's *The Mayor of Casterbridge* (1886).
40. Ibid. 272.
41. *Misc. Prose* 117.
42. Ben Jonson, 'An Elegie', in *Works*, ed. C. H. Herford and P. & E. Simpson (1947) viii. 119.
43. Lloyd E. Berry ed., *The English Works of Giles Fletcher the Elder* (Madison 1964) 76.
44. *HMC De L'Isle and Dudley* ii. 329, 171, 251–2, 440 and *passim*.
45. *Brief Lives* i. 312.
46. *Nobilis* 80.
47. *OA* 335.
48. *AS* 54. 14.
49. *OA* 4–5.
50. Ibid. 9.
51. Ibid. 108.
52. Ibid. 243.
53. Ibid. 292.
54. Alice Fox, *Virginia Woolf and the English Renaissance* (1990) 11.
55. *OA* 297–8.
56. Wallace 232.

57. *OA* 92. I have emended 'too' to 'so'.
58. Ibid. 117.
59. Ibid. 227.
60. Ibid. 205.
61. Ibid. 206.
62. Ibid. 376.
63. Ibid. 416.
64. Ibid. 283.
65. Ibid. 71–6.
66. Ibid. 76–9.
67. C. S. Lewis, *English Literature in the Sixteenth Century* (1954) 330.
68. *OA* 27.
69. Ibid. 37.
70. Ibid. 376.
71. Lewis, op. cit. 341.
72. Ibid. 225.
73. Ibid. 198.
74. Ibid. 283.
75. Ibid. 415–16.
76. *Misc. Prose* 102.
77. Stow, *Annales* (1592) 1176.
78. Stern 56–8.
79. Feuillerat iii. 128.
80. Collins, i. 273–6.
81. Simpson 166 ff.
82. Collins, loc. cit.
83. Ibid. i. 281.
84. *HMC De L'Isle and Dudley* i. 96; misdated by Collins, i. 246.
85. A. C. Judson, *The Life of Edmund Spenser* (1945) 91.
86. Ibid. 92.
87. Woudhuysen 158–9.
88. *Three Letters* 31.
89. Ibid. 54.
90. Cf. Ottley.
91. *Three Letters* 6–7.
92. *OA* 88–90.
93. *Misc. Prose* 120.
94. *OA* 3.
95. Woudhuysen 179.
96. Wallace 219.
97. Nichols ii. 301.
98. *NA* 405.
99. Nichols ii. 93.
100. *DNB*.

CHAPTER 9

1. W. Camden, *Remaines* (1605) 174.
2. I have reached this conclusion after correspondence with Dr Simon Adams. On 29 November 1580 Sidney wrote to

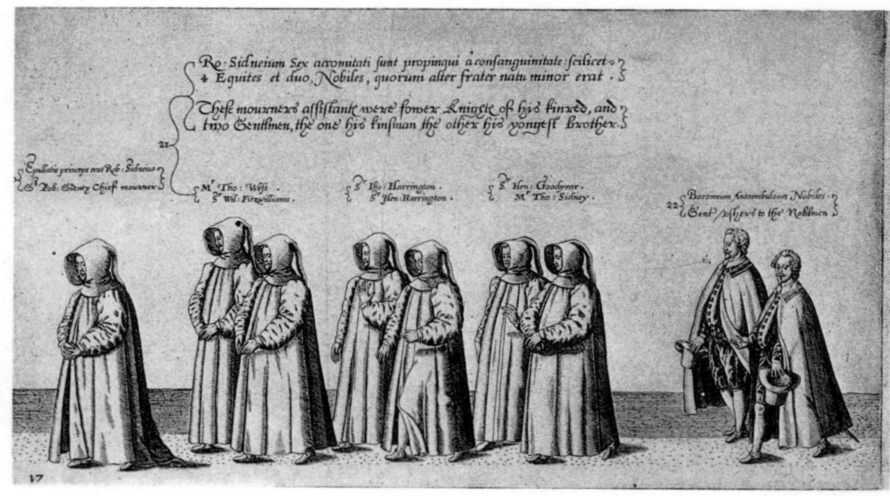

one Sebastian Pardini, in Paris, suffering from 'illness and melancholy', which may have been aggravated by the birth of his cousin; cf. *CSP Foreign 1581–2* 71.
3. Stow, *Annales* (1592) 1191.
4. G. Whetstone, *Sir Phillip Sidney, his honourable life, his valiant death, and true vertues* (?1587) sig. B3.
5. Cf. Young 49.
6. This is suggested by Woudhuysen 258.
7. Ringler 437–8.
8. Ibid.
9. Michele Margetts, 'Lady Penelope Rich: Hilliard's lost miniatures and a surviving portrait', *The Burlington Magazine* CXXX (October 1988) 758–61.
10. Margetts, art. cit.
11. Nichols ii. 389.
12. Wallace 262; P. W. Hasler, *The House of Commons 1558–1603* iii (1981) 383.
13. Feuillerat iii. 135.
14. Rebholz 203.
15. Collins i. 293–4.
16. Feuillerat iii. 128–9, 134.
17. Wallace 246.
18. *Sidney* 165–6.
19. Ringler 472.
20. From R. Browning, *Jocoseria* (1883).
21. *OA* 260–63.
22. Pears 102.
23. *OA* 73.
24. Ibid. 260–61.
25. Wallace 261–2.
26. Woudhuysen 311.
27. Ibid. 312–16; Young 148–9.
28. 'Callophisus challenge', printed by Charlewood; cf. *STC* Films Reel 738.
29. *DNB*.
30. Young 48.
31. Ibid. 93–5.
32. *Malone Society Collections* II. i (1908) 181–7.
33. *Complete Peerage* xii. 798.
34. *NA* 256.
35. *Misc. Prose* 29.
36. BL MS Lansdowne 99, fol. 259.
37. *NA* 92–104.
38. Stow, *Annales* (1592) 1179.
39. Woudhuysen 318ff.
40. Cf. *Sidney* 402.
41. Ibid. 314.
42. *Misc. Prose* 21.
43. *Sidney* 299.
44. *Misc. Prose* 53.
45. Young 146–7.
46. *OA* 3.
47. *Sidney* 299–300.
48. Ibid. 310–11.

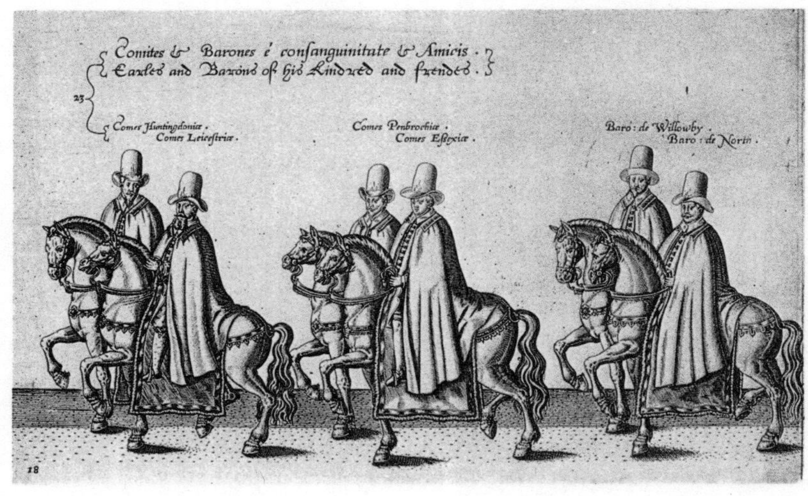

49. *AS* ii. 15.
50. Ibid. 83. 14.
51. H. S. Donow, *A Concordance to the Poems of Sir Philip Sidney* (Ithaca and London 1975).
52. *CS* 31. 14.
53. *Sidney* 304.
54. Gerard Legh, *The Accedens of Armory* (1562) fol. 11.
55. Cf. Young 71 for a portrait of Windsor's brother with a unicorn device and silver unicorns on his armour.
56. *Sidney* 301–2.
57. *OA* 108, 439.
58. *Sidney* 314.
59. Legh, *The Accedens of Armory* fols. 6, 12ᵛ.
60. Ringler 474.
61. *Sidney* 169.
62. Woudhuysen 346.
63. Ibid. 318–26.
64. Josephine Roberts ed., 'The Imaginary Epistles of Sir Philip Sidney and Lady Penelope Rich', *ELR* 15 (1985) 681.
65. *Sidney* 404.
66. *NA* 253–4.
67. Anon. *Campian Englished* (1632) 184; Simpson 299–304.
68. BL MS Lansdowne 33 fols. 145–9.
69. Simpson 310.
70. Ibid. 322.
71. Ibid. 338.
72. Cf. for instance Wallace 285–6.
73. Wallace 267.
74. *DNB.*
75. Simpson 363–77.
76. Ibid. 379.
77. Ibid. 394–7.
78. Ibid. 405.
79. Ibid. 447–57.
80. The Duke of Norfolk ed., *The Lives of Philip Howard ... and of Anne Dacres his Wife* (1857) 19.
81. K. T. Rowe, 'Romantic Love and Parental Authority in Sidney's *Arcadia*', *University of Michigan Contributions in Modern Philology* 1–12 (1947–9) 18–19.
82. Cf. *OA* xvii.
83. George Peele, *The Battle of Alcazar*, ed. John Yoklavich, in *The Dramatic Works of George Peele*, ii (Yale 1961).
84. Ibid. 249–50.
85. Wallace 268.
86. Collins i. 294.
87. *CSP Dom. 1581–90* 21, 22.
88. Wallace 268.
89. Feuillerat iii. 135–6.
90. Ibid. 133.

91. *CSP Dom. 1581–90* 26.
92. Feuillerat iii. 136–7.
93. Pears 177.
94. Ringler 444–5.
95. BL MS Lansdowne 885, fol. 86[v].
96. Penry Williams, 'The Crown and the Counties', C. Haig ed., *The Reign of Elizabeth I* (1984) 133.
97. *Sidney* 167.
98. Ringler 473.
99. The Drummond/Dymoke MS, University of Edinburgh MS De.5.96.
100. Feuillerat iii. 138.
101. Wallace 271.
102. Bodleian MS Ashmole 845, fol. 165[r].
103. See E. Malcolm Parkinson, 'Sidney's Portrayal of Mounted Combat with Lances', *Spenser Studies* V (1985) 245.
104. Feuillerat iii. 139.
105. Ibid. 140.
106. For an account of this tilt, cf. Woudhuysen 346–9; Young 203.
107. Feuillerat iii. 140–41.
108. Longleat, Dudley Papers, III. 56.
109. Sargent 200–201.

CHAPTER 10

1. *AS* 54. 1–8.
2. From 'Philophilippos', *The Life and Death of Sir Philip Sidney*, prefaced to the tenth edition of *The Countess of Pembroke's Arcadia*, 1655, sig. b1[v].
3. Leicester Bradner ed., *The Poems of Queen Elizabeth I* (Providence 1964) 5; the second 'am' in line 5 has been adopted from the text in BL MS Stowe 962, fol. 231[v].
4. Wallace 278.
5. It is surprising that Sidney is not known to have written any elegy or memorial epigram for his old friend. Perhaps there was no time; or perhaps he was too much preoccupied with larger literary projects to write occasional verses.
6. Wallace 278. For an account of Alençon's reception in the Netherlands, see Nichols ii. 343–87.
7. C. V. Wedgwood, *William the Silent* (1944) 229.
8. Ibid. 234–5.
9. *CSP Foreign 1581–2* 624–5.
10. Wallace 288–9.
11. Sargent 76; PRO SP12/159, fol. 126.

12. Wallace 280–81.
13. Collins i. 96.
14. Feuillerat iii. 142–3.
15. Wallace 290.
16. A full text of the letter is given in H. F. Hore ed., 'Sir Henry Sidney's Memoir of his Government of Ireland. 1583', *Ulster Journal of Archaeology* iii (1855) 33–52, 336–53; v (1857) 299–323; viii (1860) 179–95. All the following quotations are taken from this text. Extracts are also to be found in *Carew MSS 1575–88*.
17. *HMC De L'Isle and Dudley* i. 272–3.
18. Longleat, Dudley Papers III. 56, fol. 11.
19. Ringler 443.
20. Sylvia Freedman, *Poor Penelope* (1983) 70–72.
21. BL MS Lansdowne 72, fols. 10–11, on which the following account is based.
22. Greville, *Prose Works* 21.
23. BL MS Royal 18A LXVI, fol. 5v.
24. Issued nine days later without the dedications and under the title of *The pathwaie to Martiall Discipline*; *STC* 23414. Perhaps the earlier issue was got together in haste as a New Year's gift to Sidney.
25. Feuillerat iii. 145.
26. Greville, *Prose Works* 21.
27. Wallace 285.
28. *CSP Col. Add. 1574–1674* 22–3.
29. Roger Howell, *Sir Philip Sidney: The Shepherd Knight* (Boston 1968) 120.
30. *Sidney* 242.
31. Ibid. 236.
32. *AS* 10. 14.
33. *Sidney* 219.
34. Ringler 542–6.
35. Cf. T. P. Roche, '*Astrophil and Stella*: A Radical Reading', in Kay 184–226.
36. W. B. Yeats, 'Adam's Curse', from *In the Seven Woods* (1904).
37. For an excellent account, see G. Shepherd ed., *Sidney: An Apology for Poetry* (1965) 19–91.
38. *Sidney* 212.
39. *Three Letters* 54.
40. *OA* 80–81, 89–90.
41. For texts of Gosson's pamphlets and a full account of the controversy, see A. F. Kinney ed., *Markets of Bawdrie: The Dramatic Criticism of Stephen Gosson* (Salzburg 1974).
42. See *Misc. Prose* 198, 200, 204, 207.
43. *AS* 18. 9.
44. Cf. Castiglione, *The Book of the Courtyer*, trs. T. Hoby (1561), ed. W. Ralegh (1900) 59.

45. *Sidney* 241.
46. P. J. S. Dufey ed., *Oeuvres Complètes de Michel L'Hospital* (Paris 1824) i. 286–7; Lucy Crump, *A Huguenot Family in the Sixteenth Century* (1926) 128.
47. *Sidney* 212.
48. Ibid. 214.
49. Ibid. 231.
50. Ibid. 246.
51. Ibid. 227.
52. Ibid. 231; and see above, p. 38.
53. Ibid. 247.
54. Ibid. 241.
55. Ibid. 241–2.
56. Ibid. 242–3.
57. Cf. Conyers Read, *Mr Secretary Walsingham and the Policy of Queen Elizabeth* (1925) iii. 433–4.
58. Spenser, *Shorter Poems*, ed. W. Oram *et al.* (Yale 1989) 12.
59. Greville, *Prose Works* 18–19.
60. *Sidney* 216.
61. Ibid. 226–7.
62. Ibid. 243.
63. Ibid. 235.
64. Ibid. 247.
65. S. K. Heninger ed., *The Hekatompathia by Thomas Watson* (1964) x–xii; BL MS Harley 3277.
66. Heninger, ed. cit. xv.
67. *AS* 40. 1.
68. Ibid. 30. 14.
69. Ibid. 27. 1–9; cf. also 23.
70. Wallace 191.
71. *Sidney* 296.
72. Ibid. 241.
73. Arthur F. Marotti, '"Love is not Love": Elizabethan Sonnet Sequences and the Social Order', *English Literary History* 49 (1982) 396–42.
74. Ibid. 405.
75. Ibid. 400.
76. *AS* 16. 1–2.
77. Pears 167.
78. See Alan Bray, *Homosexuality in Renaissance England* (1982).
79. Cf. Lawrence Stone, *The Crisis of the Aristocracy 1558–1641* (1965) 654.
80. Rebholz 316–17.
81. Ibid. 314–15.
82. Stone, loc. cit.
83. Ringler 260–61.
84. Ibid. 262–4.
85. Since Dyer was not knighted until 1596, the 'Sir' cannot be Sidney's. However, the curious marginal addition of the initials may be authorial, with Dyer's status updated by Davison.
86. *AS* 1. 14.
87. May, 'Oxford and Essex' 26.

88. BL MS Add. 15232, fol. 36^{v}.
89. 'Lady Rich' 184–9; Freedman, *Poor Penelope* 96–103.
90. Nashe iii. 329.
91. Robert Sidney 62.
92. *NA* 91, 92–3.
93. 'Lady Rich' 188–9.
94. *Romeo and Juliet* I. ii. 13–14.
95. PRO SP12/158.85, fol. 210; Wallace 295n.
96. John Dee, *Private Diary*, ed. J. Halliwell, Camden Society 19 (1842) 18.
97. BL MS Add. 15891, fol. 101^{b}; Wallace 293.
98. There is a copy of the Queen's commission for this ceremony in Bodleian MS Ashmole 1110, fols. 56^{v}–7.
99. Feuillerat iii. 167.
100. Greville, *Prose Works* 17.
101. Nichols ii. 397.
102. Ibid. ii. 398.
103. D. H. Horne, *Life and Minor Works of George Peele* (Yale 1952) 57–62.
104. Nichols ii. 408.
105. Dee, *Diary*, ed. cit. 18.
106. Nichols ii. 410.
107. *OA* 159.

CHAPTER 11

1. T. S. Eliot, 'The Love Song of J. Alfred Prufrock' (1917).
2. Proverbs 13. 12.
3. Wallace 326.
4. B. M. Ward, *The Seventeenth Earl of Oxford* (1928) 10–11.
5. *Nobilis* 74, 116.
6. John Florio trs., *The Essayes of Michaell de Montaigne* (1603), sig. R2^{v}.
7. Wallace 297.
8. *CSP Foreign 1583 & Addenda* 354–5.
9. Psalm CXXVIII. 3, 5–6.
10. *Nobilis* 85.
11. Conyers Read, *Mr Secretary Walsingham and the Policy of Queen Elizabeth* (1925) iii. 423.
12. SP12.195, fol. 33; Ringler 530.
13. *Misc. Prose* 149.
14. T. Watson, *Italian Madrigals Englished* (1590) XXIII.
15. Ibid. XXVII; cf. Winifred Maynard, *Elizabethan Lyric Poetry and its Music* (Oxford 1986) 44.
16. Wallace 331–3.

17. Feuillerat iii. 168.
18. *DNB*; Stern 36–8.
19. *NA* 465.
20. CUL MS Kk.I.5.(2).
21. Wallace 297.
22. *AS* 30. 11.
23. Feuillerat iii. 144.
24. Wallace 297; Read, op. cit. ii. 387–8.
25. C. V. Wedgwood, *William the Silent* (1944) 248–50.
26. *CSP Foreign 1583–4* 579.
27. *Misc. Prose* 48–52.
28. *CSP Foreign 1583–4* 611.
29. Ibid. 603; there is a copy of Sidney's instructions, dated 8 July 1584, in BL MS Cotton Galba E VI fols. 252r–4v.
30. PRO E 403/2559, fol. 217r. Many thanks to Professor S. W. May for drawing my attention to this document.
31. *CSP Foreign 1583–4* 611–12.
32. Ibid.
33. Cf. Bodleian MS Tanner 78, fol. 90r.
34. *CSP Foreign 1583–4* 644–6.
35. Ibid. 579.
36. Feuillerat iii. 145. Richard Hakluyt was Stafford's chaplain.
37. *CSP Foreign 1594–5* 19–20.
38. Stow, *Annales* (1592) 1191.
39. Peck *LC* 5.
40. *Misc. Prose* 140–41.
41. Ibid.
42. For an analysis of parallel passages, see Feuillerat iv. 397–403. R. W. Zandvoort, *Sidney's Arcadia: A Comparison between the Two Versions* (Amsterdam 1929, repr. Philadelphia 1969).
43. *NA* 179–86.
44. Cf. K. Duncan-Jones, 'Sidney's Urania', *RES* xvii (1966) 123–32.
45. *NA* 5.
46. Ibid. 6.
47. Ibid. 7.
48. Ibid. 7–8.
49. Cf. K. Duncan-Jones, 'Sidney and Titian', in J. Carey ed., *English Renaissance Studies: Essays presented to Dame Helen Gardner* (1980) 1–11, but for 'Vienna' read 'Prague'.
50. *NA* 150.
51. Ibid. 317.
52. Ibid. 354–5.
53. Adapted by Francis Quarles in an extremely popular narrative poem (1629); edited by David Freeman, *Argalus and Parthenia*, Renaissance English Texts Society (1986), and further adapted in many chap-book versions.

54. *NA* 28–32.
55. Ibid. 43–7.
56. Ibid. 378.
57. Xenophon, *Cyropaedia* VII. iii. 14.
58. *NA* 395–8.
59. Ibid. 399.
60. Kay 252.
61. *NA* 316–17.
62. Ibid. 465.
63. Ibid. 406.
64. Ibid. 411.
65. Ibid. 344–5.
66. Milton, *Paradise Lost* IX. 31–2.
67. *NA* 330–33. This passage influenced Shakespeare's *Sonnets* 1–17.
68. *NA* 335.
69. Ruth Mohl ed., Milton's *Commonplace Book*, in *Complete Prose Works of John Milton*, i (Yale 1953) 371–2, 463–4.
70. For a learned discussion of Sidney's use of his sources, see D. P. Walker, *The Ancient Theology: Studies in Christian Platonism from the Fifteenth to the Eighteenth Century* (1972) 132–62.
71. Chaucer, *Troilus and Criseyde* IV. 1408.
72. *NA* 359.
73. Ibid. 360.
74. Susan Snyder ed., *The Divine Weeks and Works of Du Bartas, translated by Joshua Sylvester* (1979) i. 256.
75. *NA* 362–3.
76. Ibid. 419.
77. Ibid. 426.
78. 2. Samuel 18. 33.
79. Cf. Job 3. 1–10.
80. I do not agree with the suggestion of T. P. Roche, 'Ending the *New Arcadia*: Virgil and Ariosto', *Sidney Newsletter* 10 (1989) 3–12, that the final passage shows that Sidney 'is telling us that he cannot overgo Ariosto, cannot complete the epic quest'; and I find no warrant in the text for Roche's suggestion that Pyrocles is aiming his sword at Anaxius's genitals; the phrase used is 'his right side'.
81. Peck, *LC* 8.
82. Ibid. 285–6.
83. Ibid. 279–81.
84. Pierpont Morgan Library, New York, MS MA 1475.
85. *Misc. Prose* 141.
86. Ibid. 4.
87. Ibid. 131; the word 'adultery' has been added later, showing that Sidney nearly forgot to include this serious charge, from which Leicester could not be easily cleared.
88. *Three Letters* 26.

89. Peck, *LC* 264.
90. *Misc. Prose* 134.
91. Wallace 310–13.
92. Peck, *LC* 251.
93. *Misc. Prose* 140.
94. Cf. Peck, *LC* 222–7.
95. Ibid. 228–48.
96. Ibid. 31–2.
97. Lawrence Stone, *The Family, Sex and Marriage in England 1500–1800* (1977) 100–101.
98. *King Lear* II. i. 84.
99. P. W. Hasler, *The House of Commons 1558–1603* (1981) iii. 384.
100. *Misc. Prose* 130.
101. Wallace 304–5.
102. *CSP Dom. 1581–90* 220–21.
103. Wallace 306–7; *CSP Dom. 1581–90* 189, 220, 225, 263.
104. K. Duncan-Jones, '"Thy deayth my undoing": John Langford's copy of the 1605 *Arcadia*', *Bodleian Library Record* 13 (1990) 360–64.
105. Wallace 320–22.
106. Ibid. 305.
107. Hannay 55.
108. Cf. A. C. Judson, *Sidney's Appearance* (Indiana 1935) 39–42; Roy Strong, *National Portrait Gallery Tudor and Jacobean Portraits* (1969) i. 292.
109. Young 160.
110. Cf. 'tilting cheque' reproduced in Young 48–9.
111. Bodleian MS Ashmole 845, fol. 16r.
112. Scipio Gentile, *Scipii Gentilis in xxv. Davidis Psalmos epicae paraphrases* (1584) sig. *4v.
113. T. Bright, *In physicam G. A. Scribonii* (Cambridge 1584).
114. Giordano Bruno, *La cena de le ceneri* (1584): *Spaccio de la besta trionfante* (1584).
115. H. Lhuyd, *The historie of Cambria* (1584).
116. Christopher Clifford, *The schoole of horsmanship* (1585). On fol. 38 Clifford records that he was recommended to Prince Casimir's service by Sidney, and travelled to the Continent with Fulke Greville.
117. Nicholas de Nicolay, *The navigations into Turkie* (1585).
118. Alberico Gentile, *De legationibus libri tres* (1585).
119. Simon Robson, *The choise of change: containing the triplicitie of divinitie, philosophie, and poetrie* (1585).
120. Ramus, *Dialecticae* (Cambridge 1584).
121. Feuillerat iii. 145; Bodleian MS Tanner 79, fols. 229–30. The letter is

endorsed 'To my assured good friend Mr William Temple'.
122. John Webster ed. and trs., *William Temple's Analysis of Sir Philip Sidney's Apology for Poetry* (New York 1984).
123. Webster, ed. cit. 186.
124. Pears 177.
125. Alan Kendall, *Robert Dudley, Earl of Leicester* (1980) 204–7.
126. *CSP Foreign 1585–6* 6–7.
127. Greville, *Prose Works* 43.
128. Ibid. 44.
129. *NA* 165.
130. Greville, *Prose Works* 45.
131. Wallace 332.
132. *CSP Foreign 1585–6* 23–4. Sidney's rival for the Flushing post seems to have been Thomas Cecil, Burghley's talentless eldest son, who was instead appointed Governor of the Brill.

CHAPTER 12

1. Greville, *Prose Works* 82.
2. The beginning of Sidney's translation of Psalm XIII, from Ringler 285.
3. W. H. Auden, 'In Memory of W. B. Yeats' (1939).
4. *Sidney* 237–8.
5. Ibid. 287–90; see above, p. 172.
6. Geffrey Whitney, *A choice of emblemes and other devises* (Leiden 1586) 196–7.
7. *Sidney* 217.
8. Trinity College, Cambridge, MS R.17.2.
9. Scipio Gentile, *Paraphrasis aliquot Psalmorum Davidi* (1581); *S. Gentilis in xxv. Davidis Psalmos epicae paraphrases* (1584); *Nereus, sive de natali Elizabethae P. Sydnaei filiae* (1585). For accounts of the writings of Scipio and Alberico Gentile see J. W. Binns, *Intellectual Culture in Elizabethan and Jacobean England: The Latin Writings of the Age* (1990).
10. Ringler 281.
11. *Nobilis* 61.
12. Ringler 267. For some additional evidence that Sidney was translating the Psalms in 1586, and in particular that Psalms XXXVIII–XLII may have been translated in the very last weeks of his life, see Richard Todd, 'Humanist Prosodic Theory, Dutch Synods, and the Poetics of the Sidney–Pembroke Psalter',

Huntington Library Quarterly 52(2) (1989) 273–93.

13. Mary Herbert, Countess of Pembroke, *A Discourse of Life and Death. Written in French by Ph. Mornay. Antonius. A tragedie written also in French by R. Garnier* (1590).
14. Hannay 85.
15. Ringler 501.
16. Ibid. 500–501; Hannay 84–105.
17. *Nobilis* 85.
18. Wallace 333.
19. S. L. Adams, 'The Gentry of North Wales and the Earl of Leicester's Expedition to the Netherlands', *Welsh History Review* 7.2 (1974) 132.
20. *HMC Rutland* i. 181.
21. Feuillerat iii. 156; Wallace 341.
22. S. Sadie ed., *The New Grove Dictionary of Music and Musicians* (1980) i. 880; Warwick Edwards, 'The Walsingham Consort Books', *Music and Letters* lv (1974) 209–12.
23. *DNB.*
24. Ibid.
25. *Misc. Prose* 219.
26. Rebholz 73–4.
27. *CSP Foreign 1585–6* 212.
28. Greville, *Prose Works* 53.
29. Ibid. 54.
30. Ibid. 65–9.
31. Wallace 319.
32. Greville, *Prose Works* 18.
33. Feuillerat iii. 147.
34. Ibid. 147–8.
35. Poort, 'Successor' 28; Feuillerat iii. 155.
36. Wallace 345.
37. Feuillerat iii. 148.
38. Ibid. 148–9.
39. *Leicester's Triumph* 33.
40. Wallace 342.
41. Poort, 'Successor' 28.
42. Feuillerat iii. 150.
43. *Leicester's Triumph* 31–2.
44. Amply described in *Leicester's Triumph* 31ff.
45. Ibid. 36.
46. Ibid. 41.
47. Feuillerat iii. 153.
48. Poort, 'Successor' 29.
49. Ibid.
50. *Leycester Correspondence* 85.
51. Feuillerat iii. 165.
52. Wallace 355; *CSP Foreign 1585–6* 324.
53. *Leicester's Triumph* 59.
54. *Leycester Correspondence* 345.

55. For a detailed account of Parma's conquests, see Geoffrey Parker, *The Dutch Revolt* (1977) 199–224.
56. *CSP Foreign 1586–7* 217.
57. Feuillerat iii. 158–9.
58. *CSP Foreign 1585–6* 484.
59. BL MS Add. 48014, fol. 153[v].
60. Ibid.; cf. also *CSP Foreign 1585–6* 556; Lant, *Roll*, plate 1.
61. This interesting document was first cited and described by Felix Barker, '"So Rare a Gentleman": Sir Philip Sidney and the Forgotten War of 1586', *History Today* (November 1986) 40–46.
62. *CSP Foreign 1585–6* 694–5.
63. Feuillerat iii. 174–5.
64. BL MS Add. 48027, fol. 380ff.; cf. also Woudhuysen 73.
65. Feuillerat iii. 166–8.
66. Ringler 296.
67. *NA* 441–2.
68. Cf. Brian Gibbons ed., *Romeo and Juliet* (New Arden Shakespeare, 1980) 14.
69. *CSP Foreign 1586–7* 28; *CSP Dom. 1581–90* 517, 521.
70. Cf. A. Nicoll ed., *The Works of Cyril Tourneur* (1930) 3–4.
71. Cf. *Leycester Correspondence* 33, 75.
72. Wallace 365.
73. Feuillerat iii. 176.
74. Ibid. iii. 177.
75. The suggestion of Alan Kendall, *Robert Dudley, Earl of Leicester* (1980) 216, that Frances Sidney was 'six months' pregnant' at the time of her husband's death is not very complimentary to her, since the pair had been reunited for less than three months by the time he was wounded.
76. Wallace 367; BL MS Add. 48014, fol. 158[r].
77. Wallace 369.
78. Cf. *OA* 69.
79. Stow, *Annales* (1592) 1245.
80. Greville, *Prose Works* 72.
81. *Sidney* 312.
82. Cf. Feuillerat iii. 155–6, 157, 164, 166, 170, 174, 175, 177, 178, 179–80.
83. Ibid. 182–3.
84. Ibid. iii. 175; C.G. Cruikshank, *Elizabeth's Army* (1966) 148–9.
85. BL MS Add. 48014, fol.159[r].
86. Feuillerat iii. 177–8.
87. Wallace 363.

88. Dr Tony Smith ed., *The Complete Family Health Encyclopedia* (1990) 60.
89. *Nobilis* 86, 132.
90. *Macbeth* V. v. 26–8.
91. Feuillerat iii. 180.
92. BL MS Add. 48104, fol. 160[r]; Stow, *Annales* 1245.
93. BL MS Add. 48104, fol. 160[r].
94. Ibid.
95. *CSP Foreign 1586–7* 150–52.
96. Justus Lipsius, *De recta pronunciatione Latinae linguae dialogus* (Leiden 1586).
97. *Sidney* 296–7.
98. Stow, *Annales* 1250.
99. Ibid. 1251.
100. T.D., *A Briefe Reporte of the Militarie Service done in the Low Countries, by the Erle of Leicester* (1587) sig. D1[r].
101. Stow, *Annales* 1252.
102. *Nobilis* 90.
103. George Whetstone, *Sir Phillip Sidney, his honourable life, his valiant death, and true vertues* (?1587) sig. C1[r].
104. Stow, *Annales* 1253.
105. Wallace 381.
106. *Leycester Correspondence* 414–15.
107. Ibid. 422.
108. Ibid. 429–30.
109. Roger Kuin, 'The Courtier and the Text', *ELR* 19 (1989) 250. Leicester himself called it a 'skirmish'; cf. Wallace 381.
110. BL MS Add. 48104, fol. 163[r].
111. Greville, *Prose Works* 79–80.
112. *Nobilis* 90.
113. According to a Spanish report of 6 November 1586, Sidney's leg was cut off (cf. *CSP Spanish 1580–6*, 650); and Whetstone compared Sidney's fortitude to that of Caius Marius, who 'smiled while his thigh was a cutting off', *Sir Phillip Sidney*, sig. C2[r]. But this may not be intended as an exact analogy.
114. Greville, *Prose Works* 78–9.
115. *Sidney* 313.
116. Mona Wilson, *Sir Philip Sidney* (1950) 272.
117. *OA* 371–4, 479–80.
118. Ringler 276; I owe this suggestion to Professor John Gouws.
119. Christ Church, Oxford, MS 984, no. 117; this poem was accepted as authentic by Professor Ringler, 'The Text of *The Poems of Sidney* Twenty-five Years After', in M. J. B. Allen, D. Baker-Smith and A. F. Kinney eds., *Sir Philip Sidney's Achievements* (New York 1990) 137, 141.

120. Lant, *Roll*, plate 14.
121. *Sidney* 314.
122. *Misc. Prose* 143–4.
123. There is a text in *Misc. Prose* 147–52.
124. *Leycester Correspondence* 480–81.
125. *Misc. Prose* 145.
126. *CSP Foreign 1585–6* 184; Whetstone, *Sir Phillip Sidney*, sig. B4[v].
127. BL MS Add. 48014, fol. 163[r].
128. *DNB*, 'William Temple'.
129. Cf. G. F. Beltz, 'Memorials of the last achievement, illness and death of Sir Philip Sidney', *Archaeologia* xxvii (1840) 31–3.
130. *CSP Foreign 1585–6* 219.
131. Greville, *Prose Works* 81.
132. *Misc. Prose* 222.
133. Greville, *Prose Works* 83.
134. *Misc. Prose* 171.
135. Whetstone, *Sir Phillip Sidney*, sigs. C2[r–v].
136. *Misc. Prose* 167.
137. Ibid. 171.
138. *Sidney* 313.
139. PRO SP 84/10, no. 13; Feuillerat iii. 183; *Sidney* 297.
140. Jan Wier, *De praestigiis daemonum et incantationibus ac veneficiis* (Bâle 1564).
141. Beltz, art. cit., 33.
142. *Misc. Prose* 172.
143. BL MS Add. 48014, fol.163[r].

EPILOGUE

1. Greville, *Prose Works* 77.
2. Plutarch, *Alexander* XLII. 3–6.
3. Henri Estienne, *He Kaine Diatheke. Novum Testamentum* (Geneva 1576) sig.*2.
4. Sidney is rightly included as the final example by Richard Helgerson in his excellent book *Elizabethan Prodigals* (1977).
5. Cf. Bodleian MS Rawl. C. 43, a book on common law dedicated to Sidney.
6. Hilliard records a conversation with Sidney about how to represent the size of a sitter in his 'Art of Limning', Walpole Society i (1911–12) 27, describing him as 'a great lover of all vertu and cunning'.
7. For instance, in 1577 Sidney gave a New Year's gift to Walsingham of 'a fair case of dags' (pistols); cf. Woudhuysen 234. In 1578 Sidney sent some dogs as a wedding present to the Count of Hanau; cf. Pears 145.
8. William Byrd, *Psalmes, Sonets, & songs of sadnes and pietie* (1588) xxxiv.
9. *Nobilis* 91; George Whetstone, *Sir Phillip Sidney, his honourable life, his valiant death, and true vertues* (?1587) sig. B2[v].

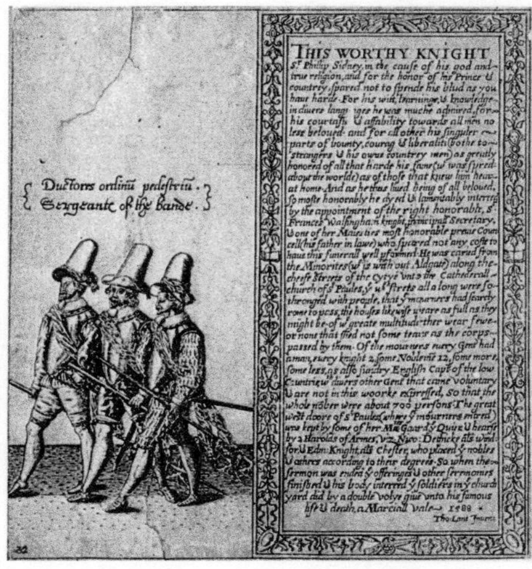

FAMILY TREE OF THE SIDNEYS

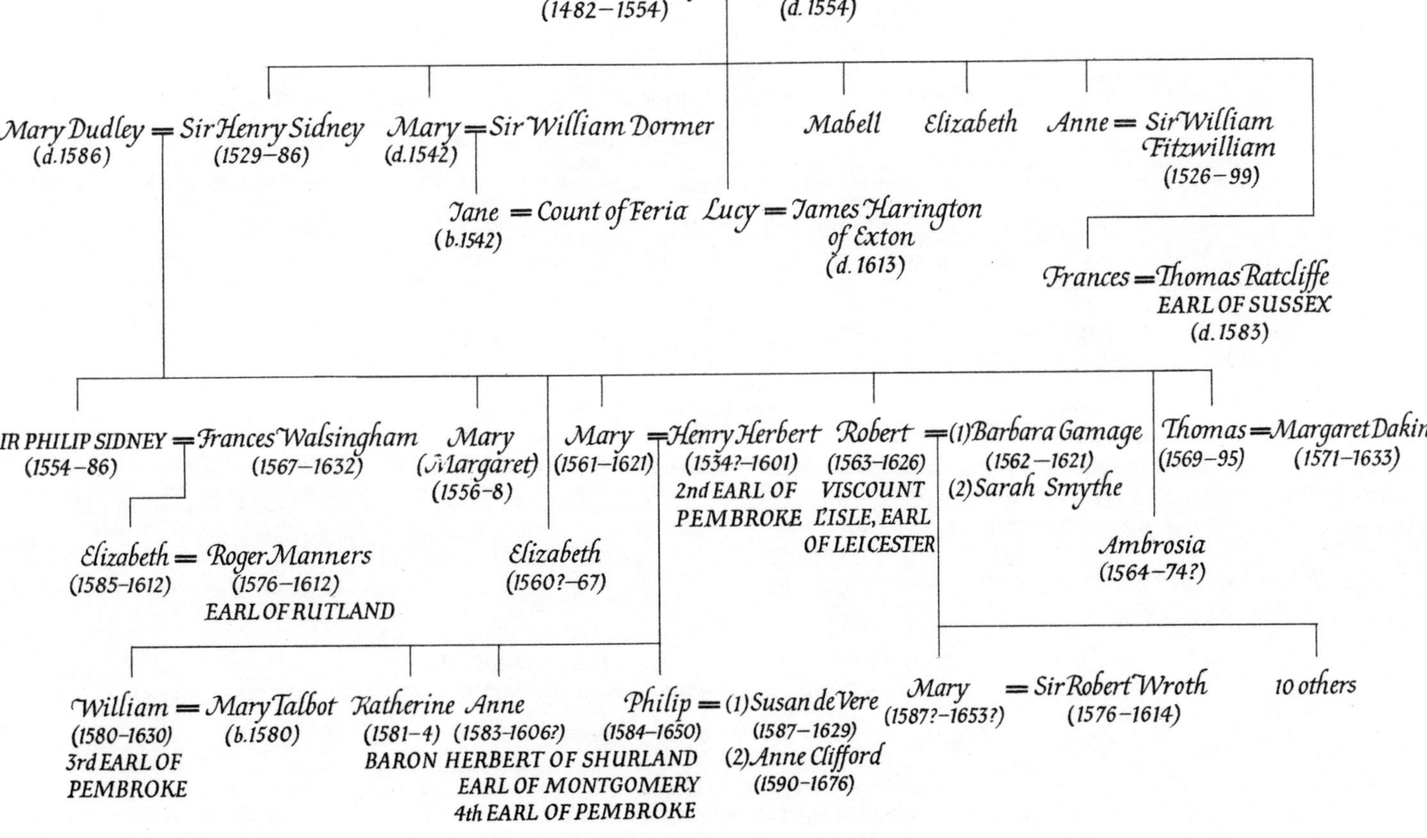

FAMILY TREE OF THE DUDLEYS

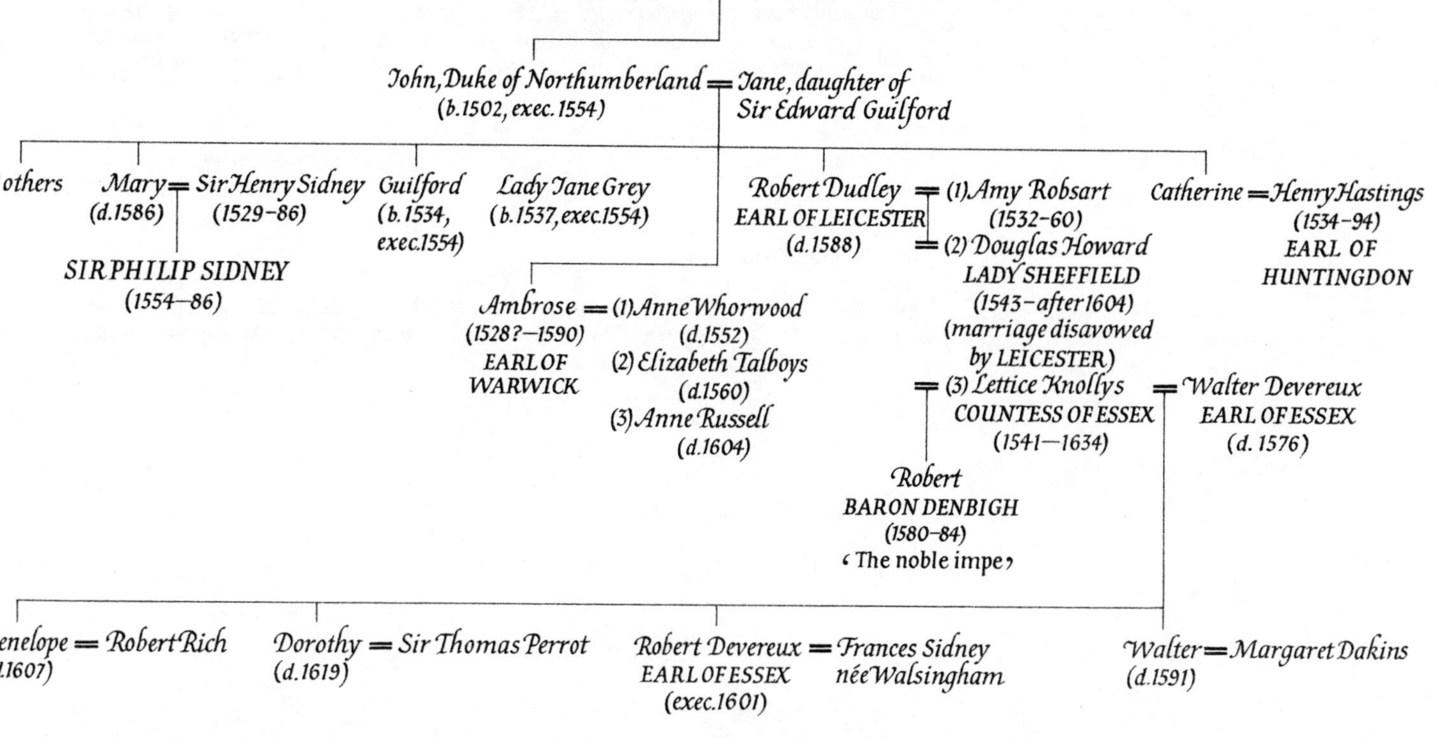

Note: *Frances Sidney appears twice, as wife of Philip Sidney, then as wife of Robert Devereux; so does Margaret Dakins, as wife of Walter Devereux, then of Thomas Sidney.*

Index